# ECHOING GOD'S WORD
## Formation for Catechists and Homilists in a Catechumenal Church

# ECHOING GOD'S WORD

## Formation for Catechists and Homilists in a Catechumenal Church

James B. Dunning

**The North American Forum on the Catechumenate**

# ACKNOWLEDGMENTS

All biblical quotations are taken from *The New Revised Standard Version*, © 1989, Division of Christian Education of the National Council of Churches of Christ in the United States of America. Published by Oxford University Press, Inc.

All references to the *Rite of Christian Initiation of Adults* (RCIA) are based on the text and the paragraph numbers of the 1988 edition, © 1985, United States Catholic Conference.

Copyright © 1993, James B. Dunning. All rights reserved.

Published by The North American Forum on the Catechumenate, 5510 Columbia Pike, Suite 310, Arlington VA 22204. For further information regarding Forum, call 703-671-0330. To order this book, call 1-800-933-1800 or FAX 1-800-933-7094.

This book was edited by Victoria M. Tufano with the assistance of Peter Mazar, Sarah Huck, Theresa Pincich and Jerry Reedy. It was designed by Jill Smith and typeset by Mark Hollopeter. The cover art is by Ronald Li. The text is set in Futura and Goudy. *Echoing God's Word* has been printed and bound by Bookcrafters.

Printed in the United States of America

Printed on recycled paper

Library of Congress Cataloging-in-Publication Data
Dunning, James B.
    Echoing God's word: formation for catechists and homilists in a catechumenal church / James B. Dunning.
        p.      cm.
    Includes bibliographical references.
    ISBN 0-929650-63-8 (pbk.)
    1. Catechetics—Catholic Church. 2. Catechists. 3. Evangelistic work. 4. Catholic Church. *Ordo initiationis Christianae adultorum*. 5. Bible—Homiletical use.
    I. Title.
    BX1968.D86 1992                                                    92-32924
    268'.82—dc20                                                          CIP

# C O N T E N T S

# FOREWORD

## Michael Warren

I have been waiting for this book for a long time, but I realized the fact only after agreeing to read the manuscript with an eye to writing this foreword. We all read books in certain contexts made up of the interests, convictions, questions and insights that have been guiding us. For me, the immediate context of *Echoing God's Word* was the reading of two other splendid books, one by a physicist on a religious search, the other by an ethicist seeking to reground ethics in saintly practice. Both books got me ready for Jim Dunning's passionate and joyful excursus into a unified pastoral ministry.

The first book, Chet Raymo's *Honey from Stone: A Naturalist's Search for God* (Penguin, 1987), is a long meditation done in sparkling prose by a physicist and geologist who, near the age of 50, rethinks the Roman Catholic tradition he had abandoned as he took academic degrees in science. He notes early in his essay, "Nothing of what I had been taught in my religious education seemed quite capacious to encompass what I learned in science." If I could put words into Raymo's mouth to describe the catechesis of his Massachusetts youth, "The God they taught me was much too small."

Jim Dunning's book unveils a vision of a unified pastoral ministry that will not permit God to be spoken of in abstract terms cut off from the deeper treasures of the tradition. What Raymo searched for—and then found in the writing of various Christian mystics—was a theology that opened onto worship and everyday living. In his own words,

> The questions I now asked were these: What is the relevance of traditional religion in the world described by contemporary science? Is scientific knowledge a satisfactory ground for the religious experience? Can the language of traditional religion constitute *an approximately modern language of praise?* (p. xi, emphasis added).

In *Echoing God's Word,* Dunning is aiming at similar questions, at least in his concern to fashion a faith that meets the dilemmas of discipleship in our time and that leads to deeply sacramental forms of worship.

Answering yes to his own questions, Raymo dares construct his book around the canonical hours of praise, tying each to an exhilarating and wide-ranging discussion of astronomy, astrophysics, physics and geology, all unified in one small geographical area, the Dingle Peninsula of County Kerry, Ireland. Dunning's own far-ranging discussion of worship's connection with word and pastoral ministry is also unified by its focus on a single, specific context: the local church.

Having read Raymo and Dunning at about the same time, I found myself fantasizing the two of them in deep discussion over a glass of stout in some Kerry pub in the land of Dunning's ancestors and of Raymo's adoption. They belong together, for what Raymo does in his scientific reflections, Dunning does in his reflections on pastoral ministry. Each masterfully brings together elements of reality meant to be conjoined but too often kept apart, separated, compartmentalized. Both exercise a kind of mystical vision that sees the connection among matters long thought by the superficial to be disparate. To paraphrase Rabbi Abraham Heschel, they both "keep God and humans in one thought at all times."

For Dunning, catechesis cannot be understood without the living witness of a believable community. Worship is the coming to fruition of the practice of discipleship. Armed with a huge conceptual dust mop, he wades into the cobwebs spun by ecclesial functionaries little in touch with the radical call of the gospel. The brash sweeps of his mop may raise some eyebrows, at least until one sees that he has disturbed only the obstructing webs and in the process has reclaimed a room now ready to be made habitable. That room is the local church. Dunning is well aware that no book can make that room habitable; only living people can. His book was written to remind us.

Another feature of Dunning's work—actually his work beyond this book and including his organizational and pastoral leadership of the past 25 years—is to bring various pastoral groups into a much needed dialogue. Here he brings liturgists and catechists together, reminding both that they are in a ministry of justice and peace. Such a dialogue is long overdue.

Jim Dunning also brings liturgists and catechists/religious educators together to encourage them to look over and then jump over the fences they have allowed to separate them. In a similar way, he brings together catechists and religious educators and shows them their large points of connection and their somewhat small points of disagreement. He brings, above all, clergy and laity together with an appropriate stress on the lay role of leading the dialogue while insisting on having equal partnership in it. "The word of God on the lips of all; the works of God in the hands of all" might be an alternative subtitle for this book. If I could extend my pub fantasy above, Jim rises from the table again and again, moves to someone's side and quietly announces, "There's someone here I'd like you to meet."

The other book that Dunning's manuscript fell in among on my desk is Edith Wyschogrod's *Saints and Postmodernism* (University of Chicago Press, 1990). Though *Saints* is a closely argued, "difficult" book, it has about it a clarity that resembles the clarity of Dunning's clear and vibrant prose. And like Dunning, Wyschogrod is trying to reground thought in the material conditions of practice. In a hundred ways she shows how theory has tended to replace ethical practice with thought. This thought privileges not the human being in the near-animality of desperate need but the person thinking the thoughts. Underlying *Echoing God's Word*, I find the same kind of concern with the splitting off of reflection from action. Dunning's goal of a credible community of believers centers on those who walk the walk and do the deeds of justice. In the very first words of his introduction, he dislocates us to the struggling poor in South Africa. Such persons remain the important shadow persons in this book. Dunning obviously understands Wyschogrod's contention that moral agency is founded on an ability to respond to the corporeal needs of the wretched. As she puts it, "The saintly response to the other entails putting her/his own body and material goods at the disposal of the Other [meaning the wretched]" (p. xxii).

Both Wyschogrod and Dunning also prize not theoretical as much as narratological approaches to goodness. The enactment of a living discipleship, including the struggle over how it is to be worked out, is the most legible text of good news. Such a living discipleship is also the necessary condition for the celebration of the eucharist. Dunning implies throughout this remarkable and refreshing book that the echoing of God's word is not to be on the lips only but preeminently in the ears and eyes and in the hands and feet.

My hope is that this book will set off a chain reaction that will produce other books that break down, or at least lower, the obstacles to pastoral collaboration among various specialties. Such collaboration born of a unified, coherent vision of the church will be one more source of hope for the future.

Jamaica, New York
28 May 1992

# INTRODUCTION

*Catechesis: The process of "echoing" the gospel . . .*[1]
• Richard McBrien

I write to you during and following a sabbatical year in 1991–1992. I began the year by meeting for some months with catechumenate groups and small Christian communities as they gathered around the word of God in Kenya, Zambia and South Africa. During my first week in South Africa, Peter Hortop, OP, took me to Phola Park, a shanty town of some 100,000 black people outside Johannesburg. Under apartheid, all blacks were segregated into townships, which included some middle-class homes. Within Phola Park is the Mandisa squatter camp where about 35,000 people have put up shacks made of plywood, cardboard or corrugated metal, held together by wire or rocks. Some are built on the property of more permanent homes for a small rental fee (there was one in back of Peter's church). Others are built illegally on open space. These periodically are bulldozed by the police (as in the opening scenes of the movie "Cry Freedom") or torched by rival groups, sometimes with the support of police thugs. There are only 80 chemical toilets for these 35,000 people.

When Peter and I drove into Phola Park, a crowd of people immediately surrounded our car. They told Peter that a police van had just driven into the camp, and they implored him to find out what the police were doing. We drove quickly down the bumpy, sewage-clogged alleys, but we arrived too late. The police had just beaten a man, torn down his shack and killed his dog before making a quick exit. Welcome to South Africa!

I was scheduled to lead a workshop on Christian initiation the following week with people from all over South Africa. After the visit to Phola Park, I wondered what I could bring to people living the dying of Jesus in ways that I shall never know. I had no reason to worry. Precisely because these people live Jesus' death in their horrific oppression, they have, through their faith and solidarity with each other, a taste of resurrection. They took over the workshop. At our celebration of a Vigil of the Resurrection, they proclaimed the story of creation in seven tribal languages. They included Desmond Tutu and Nelson Mandela in the litany of the saints. They composed original music. They poured water over each other to renew their baptism. And after communion they spontaneously sang *"Nikosi Sikeli-Africka"* ("God Bless Africa"), the hymn that is the national anthem of Zambia, Tanzania and Zimbabwe but which might have landed them in jail until recently if they had sung it in South Africa. These people made the connection between the covenant with the God of the exodus from slavery to freedom and from death to life—which we celebrate at the altar—and the struggle for justice in places like Phola Park.

Ultimately, that is the purpose of this book—to connect our initiation into the covenant with God to the call of Jesus to extend that covenant in our families, neighborhoods and civic communities to the hungry, the thirsty, the stranger, the naked, the sick and the prisoners of Matthew 25. The ultimate goal of initiation is "apostolic witness" (*Rite of Christian Initiation of Adults*, #75.4) and discovering the inexorable link between gospel, eucharist and the works of charity and justice (#244).

Some claim that people like those in Phola Park do not need theologians or scriptural exegetes to help them interpret the scriptures. Because they know oppression, as the people by whom and for whom the scriptures were first written did,[2] and because their tribal culture is communal, as were those of the people in biblical times, they intuitively hear a message of hope and liberation for a community. In a largely middle-class, individualistic North American culture, we may need the help of interpreters who make God's word accessible and echo it in ways that release its liberating and social message.[3]

To get there, chapter one surveys the good news and bad news about the implementation of the order of Christian initiation of adults. Chapters two and three offer an overall vision and "map" of evangelization and catechesis. Chapter four explores how the order of initiation enfleshes that vision specifically for the catechumenate period in #75— through ministries of word, community, worship and witness. Chapters five and six focus on how to hear and echo God's word in the liturgy of the word and a method of "conversing" with scripture. I treat only the catechumenate period, although the principles apply to the entire journey of initiation and conversion. I hope that this method of hearing God's word becomes second nature for all homilists and catechists doing evangelization/catechesis. Chapters seven through ten offer reflections on the gospels as grist for the second step in that method.

Allow me to offer a few comments on what is here and what is not here. First, with great hesitation I have limited my reflections on the liturgy of the word to the gospels (to the relief of the copy editors of this book). I stress, as do others, that catechesis for the catechumenate period based on the liturgy of the word (and at times the liturgy of the eucharist) includes not just the gospel but also the other readings and how they relate to each other in the liturgical season[4] (which is different from the way they are presented in the Bible), the prayers and psalm, the liturgical season and the liturgical year, the gestures, the silences and the panoply of images and symbols that are part of the entire liturgy. I plead lack of time and lack of competence to deal with all that. I simply offer reflections on the gospels as one piece of the catechetical pie that might be of assistance when homilists and catechists focus on the gospel (which is often the case) in its biblical context. Whenever I refer to a gospel text, I note when the text occurs during the liturgical year. All these references, some brief, some more extensive, are listed in the appendix so that you can check them for a given Sunday or feast.

Second, this book is aimed especially at catechists and homilists who are ministers in the Christian initiation of adults. The focus is on a vision and a method for inviting catechumens into the conversation between our lives and God's word. Chapters one through five center on a vision of initiation and catechesis. Chapter six offers a method for catechists and homilists to prepare themselves for that conversation, and chapters seven through eleven center on what might be part of that method: reflections on the four gospels and an approach to conversing with our Catholic postbiblical tradition. This method would be used weekly at a preparation session for homilists and catechists so that both ministries might collaborate more closely; too often catechists have no idea what the homilist will be preaching about. With this preparation, catechists might continue more effectively in catechesis (after sending forth the catechumens) what the preacher has begun in the homily. However, the goal is not simply a pragmatic preparation for dealing with catechumens; the method first invites ministers to converse with life and with God's word. It is a method for preparing homilies that the United

States bishops encourage for all homilists. It promises the same kind of faith sharing, ongoing conversion and spiritual journey experienced by catechumens.[5] Such sessions can become integral to the ministers' own experience of God's Spirit and word in community.

Because the dimensions of this catechetical vision and method are true for all evangelization/catechesis, other catechists also might adapt this book to their own needs. In fact, the method offered in chapter six was partially developed in a parish where all the catechists (not just those in the ministry of initiation) met weekly to converse with God's word and to prepare for their groups of children or adults. Ultimately, all catechists and homilists minister within and for the church as an initiating community in which all members are catechized to echo with each other God's word.

I offer these reflections as a contribution to the dialogue among other catechetical theorists (many cited in the text and footnotes) and those of us whose primary experience is what we are learning about catechesis in Christian initiation. At times there have been tensions among some theorists in catechesis and religious education, as well as among liturgical theologians. These reflections may resolve some of those tensions; at least they may advance the conversation.

Third, I had intended to write a second volume, a workbook that would have applied the method and content of this book to many Sundays and feasts. Philip McBrien has saved me that effort. In some ways, in *How to Teach with the Lectionary* and the accompanying leader's guide, he has written the book that I would have written. In chapter six of this book I offer an overview of his method for catechist formation with the lectionary. I am enormously grateful to him for his insights and research. His own volumes enable a true conversation between the word of the scriptures and the word of our lives in ways that do not impose his method as the only way to interpret the lectionary readings. He invites us to converse with him and find ways that are best for us and our communities. If you only read my book, I fear that you might have the motivation but not the skills and practical "how tos" to do the hard work of struggling with the meanings of the lectionary readings and their powerful call to covenant and conversion. Therefore, I strongly recommend

Phil's books as companions to *Echoing God's Word.* (See the announcement regarding Philip McBrien's books on the last page of this book.)

I refer you to other resources in the select bibliography and the footnotes. Phil's leader's guide also includes a helpful annotated bibliography of resources for interpreting the lectionary. I want to recommend especially *The Cultural World of Jesus Sunday by Sunday* by John Pilch. These are one-page commentaries on the gospels of the lectionary, mailed quarterly.[6]

Fourth, I am not a scripture scholar. In fact, my seminary training occurred prior to Vatican II—four years of Catholic biblical (and doctrinal) fundamentalism. I find the best of biblical scholarship to be the most exciting development in our church, far more radical (back to our roots—in Latin, *radices*) than all the controversies in moral theology. Therefore, with much humility and great hesitation, I offer you a taste of biblical scholarship on the gospels. I do so because some criticize the institutes on Christian initiation that we at the North American Forum on the Catechumenate offer because we have not included that scholarship in our biblical reflections; perhaps we have contributed to North American fundamentalism and privatism. More positively, I offer this biblical scholarship, too, because what I find to be the most exciting and powerful reflection on the word of God does not show up in many popular commentaries. Some offer more fluff than substance and focus on what I shall later call a psychological hearing of scripture leading to privatism rather than a pastoral/theological hearing leading to church mission. At the other extreme, some of the more scholarly commentaries fall into what I later call historicism—historical criticism of texts with few pastoral "so whats." In that regard, I find the literary critics more helpful. These present the scriptures as stories with a plot, usually of conflict, that calls for decision, for taking sides in the midst of the conflict, in biblical times and our times. I offer this book as one small contribution that offers a vision of why and how we ground evangelization/catechesis in the word of God and that makes some of the best scholarly conversation with that word more accessible so that it echoes, reverberates and literally resounds in our times. The method proposed still calls for preparation and hard work, but I have tried to save you some of the work by reading through many pages of heavy tomes to lift out a few biblical gems that might be helpful pastorally.

Fifth, because I do rely upon the research of others, there are many notes at the end of each chapter. Don't let them frighten you. They range from the popular language of "Peanuts" to the convoluted language of systematic theologian Karl Rahner. Some can hear Charlie Brown, others Karl. I include all these conversation partners to respect their original contributions, but also to broaden the conversation. If their names are familiar to you and if what they say speaks to you, bring them into the conversation. If not, move on to the next conversation partner. Many of the notes are included because I needed support from biblical scholars when I adopted a controversial position. Other footnotes are not references to other authors but my extended comments, which some readers may find helpful and provocative. Please read them.

Sixth, in my echoing of the word of God, I have taken a stance toward the scriptures that interprets everything through the lens of God's *covenant/union* in Christ through the Spirit with all people, especially the outcast and outsider. There are other points of view. I chose this one as obviously central because we call our scriptures "testaments"—stories of the covenants. I do so also because that point of view extends to and offers acceptance to many potential catechumens whom we are not reaching—those most hurting and most oppressed. And I do so for all of us—including the entire church community (#4, 9)—who minister with those catechumens, that our faith might be formed by God's stance of covenant/inclusion in times when our church in some quarters seems to be increasingly exclusive.

Some complain that we put too much energy into the initiation of a few catechumens. However, if we situate these rites and sacraments of initiation where we have always situated eucharist—in the community on Sundays and feasts when it gathers to hear the word—then well-prepared homilies that are faithful to the astounding love, mercy and acceptance of the God of the covenant and that invite not only catechumens but the entire community to re-sound that word in their lives and hearts might become a transforming experience for the whole parish.

Seventh, since I propose that we "converse" with God's word, I propose that you converse with me, with yourself and with other catechists and homilists. In the text, I offer "conversation starters" that invite you to dialogue with material just read. I also offer invitations to "take a stand," to name your own stance toward an issue or question before we explore it together. If learners retain little of what they read, more of what they say and almost all of what they do, these conversations and the action following from them are critical.

Eighth, a few remarks regarding style. Many people tell me that I write the way I talk. That irritates some who expect footnotes to be accompanied by scholarly syntax. I am not an academic theologian. I try to be a pastoral theologian, and as such I try to use language that will converse with people in pastoral ministry. Also, although I am three generations away from my roots in the Irish sod, people tell me that my humor is thoroughly the satire of the Irish. I get in more trouble at workshops with my attempts at humor than I do with my supposed attempts at prophecy. A guideline: When in doubt, don't take me seriously.

Ninth, I have tried to use inclusive language about humans and God. When others do not, I have usually added inclusive language within brackets unless the intent of the text is clearly noninclusive. In some cases, certain language in the scriptures is retained as it is given in the text of the New Revised Standard Version of the Bible. This is done at the request of the copyright holders.

Like the ritual text on adult initiation, when I use the word "candidate," I am referring both to unbaptized catechumens and baptized candidates for full communion with the Catholic church. When not referring to the official English title of the document, *Rite of Christian Initiation of Adults,* I use terms such as the "order of initiation." I do so not primarily because of accuracy (the Latin title is *ordo*) but for pastoral reasons. People associate most acronyms with programs (CCD, CFM, CYO) or organizations (NCEA, FDLC, IBM). Most programs are optional. Note how some speak of the "RCIA program" or claim it is optional. But the order of initiation is a sacrament of the church (would anyone call eucharist a program?). And like all other sacraments, it is not optional. It has been the official rite of initiation since the translation was approved in 1974. I certainly am not suggesting an even worse *faux pas*—calling it OCIA!

Tenth, you will find in these pages frequent critiques of church folk, particularly church leaders, when we succumb to perks of power as James and John did (Mark 10:35–45), especially when we exclude from our communities the poor and powerless. At times this male cleric has succumbed to those demons, and I lament in others what I most lament in myself. So I hope that this critique comes off not as anger nor as strident bashing of the always frail and fallible institutional church. It is a lament from one within the institution. I hope it speaks with the grief out of which the prophets critiqued the kings of Israel.

> The prophet does not scold or reprimand. The prophet brings to public expression the dread of endings, the collapse of our self-madeness, the barriers and pecking orders that secure us at each other's expense, and the fearful practice of eating off the table of a hungry brother or sister. . . . I believe that the proper idiom for the prophet in cutting through the royal numbness and denial is the *language of grief.* . . . That crying in pathos is the ultimate form of criticism, for it announces the sure end of the whole royal arrangement.[7]

Some thank yous. The cliché runs that Andrew Greeley has never had an unpublished thought. Well, I have never had an unplagiarized thought. In this book I echo not only God's word but also the words of all those whose insights have taken flesh in me. Therefore, I thank especially the staff, team members and steering committee of the North American Forum on the Catechumenate and all those who participate in our institutes. God's Spirit in them forms my spirit. Thanks to my domestic family and ecclesial family in the archdiocese of Seattle, who in my formative years echoed God's word for me. The vision, stories and examples in this book would have been more narrow, more North American and European were it not for the people of Africa and Asia, who, during my recent sabbatical, opened my eyes to what Rahner calls "world/church" and to the many peoples and cultures with whom God unites us in covenant. My gratitude to them for "blowing my mind" open.

For several years our Forum staff met annually with a scripture scholar to reflect on the gospels of the current lectionary year. That is, in part, why I focused only on the gospels in this volume. The insights of these scholars course throughout this book. Therefore, thanks to Donald Senior, Leonard Doohan and especially to Eugene LaVerdiere, who also reviewed chapters seven through ten on scripture. In fairness to Gene, I must note that at times I have chosen scriptural interpretations that differ from his. Thanks, too, to Mary Boys for reviewing and critiqueing chapter three, and to Thomas Groome for reading and critiqueing chapter four. My gratitude to Vicky Tufano, the editor of this book, for her suggestions and particularly for her patience and tolerance of my sometimes unorthodox writing style. Not many would allow both "street talk" and "Rahner talk" in the same paragraph.

Finally, I dedicate this book to Christiane Brusselmans and to all who echo God's word in her spirit because she made that word incarnate for them. In 1976, Christiane ordered this priest to "come follow her" into the ministry of initiation and conversion. In 1978, she invited 32 Africans, Europeans and North Americans to follow her to a former Cistercian abbey in Senanque, France, where we talked, celebrated and sang our way into this journey of initiation. In 1981, she gathered some 200 people in Estes Park, Colorado, no longer to follow her but to take "baby steps" on our own way. The North American Forum on the Catechumenate was born. Indirectly, then, she has gathered over 50,000 people who have been part of Forum institutes as of Lent 1992.

Few knew the darkness of depression that plagued this ebullient woman for many years. It brought her to a tragic suicide on the train tracks near her home in Korbeek-Lo, Belgium. I still have nightmares imagining that scene, and I wake screaming, "No! Christiane, don't do it!" Yet I firmly believe that in her illness her way of dying was her faith-filled Yes! "Yes, I believe in a God who brings light into darkness and life from a death even as tragic as this!" She said as much in her good-bye note. In her memory we dedicate ourselves to helping our sisters and brothers say "Yes!" and "Amen!" to the God who calls all people through death to "life—life in all its fullness" (John 10:10).

At the end of the workshop in Johannesburg they gave me a new name—*Indabaye Nkosi* ("God's Story"). That was what Christiane was for so many of us. I dedicate this book to her and to those who "echo the word" of that story.

## Endnotes

[1] Richard McBrien, *Catholicism*, Volume II (Minneapolis: Winston Press, 1980), xxiii.

[2] One of the few commentaries on the lectionary readings that I find helpful comes from a country that knows this oppression: "Commentaries on the Readings" and

"Eucharistic Celebrations," *Pastoral Service* (monthly publication sent by mail). Pastoral Center, CICM Missionaries, PO Box 1323, 1099 Manila, Philippines.

[3] I found that in Africa there is a resistance to biblical scholarship because of the fear of excluding the people who cannot read or write, yet who intuit the biblical message of good news for the poor because they live like the poor people of biblical times. I believe, however, that these people, too, would benefit from some of that scholarship, which reveals a God clearly on the side of the poor.

[4] Richard Fragomeni distinguishes between lectionary-based catechesis and lectionary catechesis. He claims that the former is "a catechesis based on the lectionary readings, as an agenda for Bible study." It will use all the scriptural aids proposed in this book. I disassociate myself from such "catechesis." The purpose of catechesis is never just Bible study but the echoing of God's word to summon conversion. I use the resources of this book not to critique Bible texts primarily but to let Bible texts critique our lives. Fragomeni says that lectionary catechesis "honors and interprets the lectionary as lectionary: a unique ecclesial proclamation of the covenant, offering a new canon of inspired texts for Christian interpretation . . . a normative liturgical reading of tradition" ("Catechesis and Life," *Modern Liturgy* 19:3, 46). I encourage him and others to pursue this provocative approach. At this stage of development, however, I find lectionary-based catechesis (better, catechesis based on the liturgy of the word) more helpful.

[5] "Fulfilled in Your Hearing" (Washington DC: United States Catholic Conference [USCC], 1982), 36–37.

[6] Available from Initiatives Publications, PO Box 218332, Columbus OH 43221; 1-800-745-8018.

[7] Walter Brueggemann, *The Prophetic Imagination* (Philadelphia: Fortress Press, 1978), 50, 51. I admit that in expressing this hope, it may sound as if I am making a self-made claim to prophecy. I would rather keep perspective by recalling the theory of one wag who reasons: "Prophets are not accepted in their own country (cf. Luke 4:24). I am not accepted. *Therefore,* I am a prophet." Some "prophets" are unaccepted because they are false prophets!

CHAPTER ONE

# New Wineskins,
# Old Churchskins

*The ecumenical council has not really been put into practice in the church either according to its letter or according to its spirit. In general, we are living through a "wintry season," as I have often said. . . . It is part of Christian hope that we don't interpret these wintry times as a prelude to ultimate death. Each one of us should instead see these times as a personal challenge to work so that the inner core of faith becomes alive. . . . If that were sufficiently present in a lively way, then many clerical, bureaucratic and canonical measures would seem totally superfluous.*[1]

• Karl Rahner

HOPE IS A VIRTUE, according to G. K. Chesterton, only when things look hopeless. If you have reasons for optimism, it is not hope but logic.

> **Conversation Starter:** What are some concrete signs of Rahner's "wintry times"? In "wintertime," for what do you hope? What and who sustains your hope?

Let us be clear: Our new rites of adult initiation are about a revolution. They are, as one bishop has called them, "explosive."[2] These rites are radical (if radical means not just "far out" but a return to our roots—in Latin, *radices*). They carry us back to our roots in a church of martyrs[3] under siege in the Roman Empire. Their hopes were sustained by each other and by that "inner core of faith" in Jesus, who is martyr-witness to God's power to bring life out of death.

In that church of martyrs, to become a Christian often meant to choose both Christ and the lions; "the Hound of Heaven may be gentle, but the news he brings us has teeth"[4]—in the early church, lions' teeth! In that church, conversion meant changing loyalties (from the emperor to Christ), not changing churches (from Baptist to Catholic). In that church, "evangelization of individuals had nothing in common with modern approaches to a gospel of personal salvation which elicits no concern for justice and which gladly joins in contemporary versions of emperor worship."[5] In that church, conversion meant not just "choosing Christ as my personal savior" but choosing and entering a community where Christ saves, where he is recognized in the breaking of the bread and in the brokenness of lives united in Jesus' body and blood. In that church of martyrs, people journeyed with Christ and found Christ where he said he would be: in their shared brokenness, in the hungry, the thirsty, the stranger, the naked, the sick and the prisoner (Matthew 25). In that church, conversion meant personal surrender to God revealed in a crucified Jesus and present in a risen Christ who, through the Spirit in the community, called Christians to make his journey through death to life.

In our church in North America, conversion often means not gateway to martyrdom but to marriage (most catechumens are engaged to or married to a Catholic), not siege but security and "fire insurance," not choosing Christ but choosing catechism, not dying and rising but data and reasons, not death but doctrines.[6]

> **Conversation Starter:** In your experience, what do most catechumens seek? Why do they come? At the beginning, how do they understand conversion?

Aidan Kavanagh, in a summons to a baptismal spirituality nourished by our early tradition, contends that our long history of infant baptism reduces us to general illiteracy and liturgical minimalism and blinds us to biblical images of adult conversion such as

> standing in great peril, being swallowed whole by some horror from the deep, being eaten by lions, being betrayed by colleagues, being reviled by the jeers of the unclean, and to great baptismal figures such as Jonah, Esther, Moses, Israel escaping Pharaoh through the Red Sea, Daniel, the three young men in the fiery furnace, John the Baptist, and finally Jesus the Christ.[7]

Our church in these rites calls us back to these roots: to conversion to God, in Christ, through the Spirit, in a community that knows that death is the only gateway to life; to conversion in a culture where we are assaulted not by Roman centurions and lions but by instant gratification by credit card; to conversion in a land bombarded by television images of "another world" and "one life to live" and the "life-styles of the rich and famous" and "a current affair,"[8] where prime-time TV titillated us with some 20,000 sexual episodes in 1990 and where the search for meaning shrinks to "what inquiring minds want to know"; to conversion in which the cultural demons jeer the first being last and the last being first, fidelity until death, love of enemies, outrageously generous wages to latecomers to the vineyard and rejoicing over the return of scandalously reprobate prodigal sons and daughters. For people confronted by these cultural "lions," the rites demand a revolutionary shift from our recent history of inquiry classes and catechisms (can anyone fend off lions with theologies and books?) or of private instructions leading to entry into passive, unaware congregations (can anyone face these lions alone?). The rites of Christian initiation catapult us back to our early history: conversion to Christ, through the Spirit, in a welcoming, committed, faith-filled community that "renews their own conversion" and "provides an example that will help the catechumens to obey the Holy Spirit more generously" (*Rite of Christian Initiation of Adults*, 4).[9] As Ralph Keifer wrote in the early 1970s: "This is a revolution quite without precedent, because the Catholic church has never at any time in its history done such violence to its ritual practice as to make its rites so wholly incongruous with its concrete reality."[10]

Ten years ago, I wrote a book on the order of Christian initiation of adults,[11] *New Wine, New Wineskins*.[12] In Greek, new (*neos*) wine denotes new in time, and new (*kainos*) wineskins means new in quality.[13] Both symbolize a new era, so the title implies that in these rites we drink new wine in a new era at that banquet promised by Isaiah where all peoples, especially all outcasts and outsiders, will come to the mountain and share "the richest food and the finest wine" (Isaiah 25:6). We celebrate in these rites Jesus' astounding good news about God's covenant love for all people. And in these rites we drink the wine that is "the cup of my blood, the blood of the new and everlasting covenant." When we share this meal and drink this cup, we become the broken body and the shed blood of the Lord given for the life of the world.

Once again, we are back to our roots. Through the rediscovery, renewal and reform of the adult rites of initiation, new Christians and old drink Jesus' new wine, celebrate his good news and give witness to God's covenant-promise of healing, forgiveness and freedom for all people. This is more than class and catechism. This is good news that summons conversion. This is radical. For a tired old church, this means something old made new.

But new wine can burst old wineskins (Mark 2:22). Ten years ago, I warned that these new rites might burst our old "churchskins." I quoted another classic phrase from Ralph Keifer, who claimed that this vision of initiation was so far from present pastoral practice that it was "either suicide or prophecy of a very high order."[14] If prophecy means not the prediction of the future but the faithful proclaiming of God's word in the present that inaugurates a new future, then in some parishes these rites have indeed been prophetic.

## New Wineskins

This robust new wine has fermented well in some fresh new wineskins. We North Americans sometimes are so self-critical that we fail to see how far we have come. Let a foreigner open our eyes. German theologian Balthasar Fischer, godfather of these rites and chairperson of the commission that constructed them, says, "The new beginnings of the rite in the United States . . . are the most remarkable achievements so far in the Catholic world. What has happened only very slowly in Europe, especially in Germany, my home country, has occurred quickly here."[15] I agree. In 1990–1991, I surveyed the catechumenate in Australia and New Zealand, in parts of Africa and Asia and at a meeting with representatives from nine European countries. In recent years I also have been blessed by meetings with people from every state in the United States and every province of Canada. I find Christian initiation most alive and well in North America. (I would extend Fischer's accolades to Canada.)

In fairness to Europe, we have been spared the devastating world wars and massive secularization that are immense obstacles to faith and Christian conversion; but in our land, where most people claim belief in God, we encounter more subtle forms of the secularism through new imperial forces commanding loyalty to the idolatrous gods of power, greed and private interest.

In Africa, in those burgeoning new churches, there are many new wineskins akin to the catechumenate but without the name, such as small Christian communities, communal mission and spirituality. Such new wineskins can be found in Latin America as well. But in terms of formal implementation of the new rites, the waters of initiation flow nowhere more powerfully than in those parishes in North America that center Christian life in who we are and who we are to become through the sacraments of initiation.

> **Conversation Starter:** When and why did your community begin the catechumenate?

Many of those parishes began this journey of initiation not because of a command from on high but as an offshoot of building community at the grassroots. During the late 1970s, when the United States bishops surveyed parishes that they identified as the best in the land, they found that 61 percent of these parishes were implementing the catechumenate. There were obvious links in those parishes between the new wineskins of community, mission and initiation as a welcome into a Spirit-charged community. In other words, although some nonpastors such as Andrew Greeley [16] berate the current order of Christian initiation as an archaic curiosity contrived by oppressive and out-of-touch liturgists and foisted on us from past times, many pastoral ministers[17] saw its implications for genuine conversion for the whole community, not just for the catechumens. Ray Kemp, a pastor in Washington, D.C., observes,

> Without question, the restoration of the catechumenate has restored our parish and has been the prime force in helping us realize that we exist to initiate adults into the saving death-resurrection of Christ. . . . The beginnings of cross-fertilization between parishioners of 60 years wondering whether or not their parish would survive, and the young and old who wanted "God in my life" came with the introduction of the rite to our parish.[18]

During the 1980s, even before the United States bishops mandated implementation of the rites (in 1988), I heard literally thousands of catechumenate ministers testify to the power of this ministry to renew their own faith and conversion.[19] I must admit that they witnessed to a greater impact on their own personal faith than on the faith of the wider community, although the latter is the hope of the rites. It has been a joy and a privilege, however, to hear catechists and sponsors tell of their own conversions in and through their journey with catechumens. It is a delight to hear priests, young and old, report that the highlight of their week is their time with the catechumenate community. They claim that it is a time when they are most about the gospel.

> **Conversation Starter:** What has changed for the better for your catechumens, for the catechumenate community, for your parish as a result of implementing the order of Christian initiation?

Perhaps it was good that the catechumenate was a movement before it was a mandate. This sacrament demands more changes than any other. In fact, it demands changes that make the other sacraments possible. We tried to change eucharist, for example, by changing language and furniture. Of course, it didn't work. We change eucharist by changing churches—from church understood only as institution (in which Christ is seen as present only at the consecration, only in the bread and wine and only through the power of the priest) to church understood as community[20] (in which Christ is known to be present in the word, throughout the meal, in all the ministries and in the entire assembly).[21]

Initiation is precisely about changing to a vision of church as a community empowered not just to receive sacraments but also to be a sacrament and to do the sacraments: "The initiation of catechumens is a gradual process that takes place within the community of the faithful" (#4), and "The people of God, as represented by the local church, should understand and show by their concern that the initiation of adults is the responsibility of all the baptized" (#9). What if we could say that every sacrament—eucharist, reconciliation, marriage, anointing of the sick and so on—takes place within the community and is the responsibility of all the baptized! That change might give life to all the sacraments. It calls the entire community beyond mere vocal and sung responses at liturgy to the genuine "full, conscious and active participation" envisioned by Vatican II.[22] It is this vision—explicit or implicit—that brings many parish ministers to begin these rites of initiation without a mandate.

That is why I have said to many pastoral ministers, especially priests, "If this vision of initiation fits your vision of church, try it. You'll like it. If it does not, if you begin catechumenate only because of a mandate, if this is just one more burden on an already crowded calendar, it might be better not to do it."[23] Without such a vision, they will pour the new wine of adult initiation not into new wineskins of a Spirit-filled community but into the old churchskins of tired structures and institutions epitomized by inquiry classes and lectures. They will initiate new members not into a community but into a book and a priest. They will invite catechumens not into a lifelong journey that varies for each person (#5),[24] but into a terminal program of classes with a few perfunctory, mechanical liturgies thrown in, and call it a catechumenate. They will lose the new wine by pouring it into old churchskins.

## Old Churchskins

The early church's new wine burst the skins of many old institutions. Many people found it impossible to be taken by, grasped by, graced by, gifted by, accepted by the preaching and way of Jesus. With outlandish compassion and healing, Jesus and those who preached his message proclaimed that God accepted sinners, prostitutes, outcasts, foreigners, people left out by the economic and religious systems and laws, "weirdos, misfits, miscreants, who tumbled into heaven—witnesses to God's all-inclusive grace."[25] It caused many to grumble, "This fellow welcomes sinners and eats with them" (Luke 15:2).

Yes, there is law. But first there is covenant. First there is God's astounding, free choice and election[26] of slaves, sinners, weirdos and misfits. First there is God's turning to us in unconditional love.

> It was not because you were more numerous than any other people that the LORD set his heart on you and chose you—for you were the fewest of all peoples. It was because the LORD loved you and kept the oath that he swore to your ancestors, that the LORD has brought you out with a mighty hand, and redeemed you from the house of slavery, from the hand of Pharaoh king of Egypt. . . . Therefore, observe diligently the commandments—the statutes, and the ordinances—that I am commanding you today. (Deuteronomy 7:7–8, 11)

First we gasp in awe and wonder that God has grasped slaves and sinners. "They were all amazed and glorified God, saying, 'We have never seen anything like this!'" (Mark 2:12) Then there is law, which does not save but which responds to salvation as gift. Indeed, Paul can lay down the law,[27] but the first word is always Spirit and grace: "A person is justified not by the works of the law. . . . The only thing I want to learn from you is this: Did you receive the Spirit by doing the works of the law or by believing what you heard? Are you so foolish? Having started with the Spirit, are you now ending with the flesh?" (Galatians 2:16, 3:2–3)

The journey of conversion in the precatechumenate begins with a time of evangelization during which, "faithfully and constantly, the living God is proclaimed and Jesus Christ whom he has sent for the salvation of all. . . . From evangelization . . . come the faith and initial conversion that cause a person to feel called away from sin and drawn into the mystery of God's love" (#36, 37). *Away from sin and into the mystery of God's love:* That is the new wine.

First, covenant. First, good news. First, God's astounding love for sinners and misfits. First, initial faith (relationship with God in love). First, the basics: covenant, gospel, love, faith. First, conversion to God, in the risen Christ, through the Spirit, in a community journeying into death and life. Then, doctrine and law. That order again bursts the institutional churchskins. It again causes apoplexy for those who still grumble if we eat with outcasts and sinners:

- A diocese decrees that people cannot be accepted even as catechumens until their marriage cases are completed.

- Several bishops require catechumenate coordinators to prove how every doctrine will be covered if catechesis is based on the liturgical year and the lectionary.

- A diocesan pastoral council votes to ask its bishop to petition the National Conference of Bishops to do away with homilies based on the lectionary and to return to a syllabus of doctrinal topics.

- A cardinal-archbishop asks for assurance that all catechumens will practice an orthodox morality.

- A priest designs a true/false test for catechumens. Samples: "The Logos assumed Jesus of Nazareth." (T or F). "The human freedom of Jesus belongs to the Logos." (T or F). "When Jesus decides to cleanse the Temple, it is the Logos who decides this." (T or F). Jesus would have flunked that exam!

- An archbishop decrees that a parish cannot construct an immersion pool because "that's just for Africans."

- A parish boasts that it initiates a "class" averaging 75 people each year, all of whom begin in September and are "ready" by Easter (even when Lent comes early).

- A priest reports that his pastor now lectures his version of orthodoxy for nine months instead of three months, and he calls this a catechumenate.

- New members disappear after Easter because the church that they experienced in the catechumenate—a small group sharing and celebrating faith—no longer exists for them. They are lost in the lonely crowd.

> **Conversation Starter:** Are any of these "old church-skins" clothing initiation in your parish?

Why should we be surprised at these old churchskins, which contain and restrain the catechumenate? If these rites are official sacraments of the church, by definition they are acts of the church as institution. Unlike other movements for renewal, such as Marriage Encounter, Cursillo and the Charismatic Renewal, the sacraments of initiation are wedded for better or worse to the parish. For better, these rites happen where they might celebrate the faith and baptism of the vast number of Catholics. For better, a sacrament is not a passing fad. It is the heart and center of the ongoing life of the community until Jesus comes again. For better, initiation is situated and structured into the ongoing life of the church. For worse, these rites will encounter all the lethargy, institutional malaise and even the ecclesial "imperial powers and lions" that mightily resist change and reform.[28] Larry Cuban says of all institutional reforms, "It should come as no surprise that many reforms seldom go beyond getting adopted as policy. Most get implemented in word rather than in deed. . . . Seldom are the deepest structures . . . altered, even at those historical moments when reforms see those alterations as the goal."[29]

Because the parish is indeed a church institution, there will always be legitimate institutional concerns about passing on the tradition. In the church, these concerns began early. For example, in the pastoral epistles, the author clearly wants to get things in order and set the tradition straight. That disturbs one modern reader of Titus: "I was disappointed. Paul's[30] bare-bones directive is threefold: appoint elders who are above reproach; rein in the congregation and make everyone behave; and rout the heretics. . . . The emphasis of the letter is on upright behavior. . . . I have nothing against upright behavior; I can understand the need for it. But is it really the heart of Christ's message?"[31] No, it is not. This same epistle finds that it is not: "When the goodness and loving kindness of God our Savior appeared, he saved us, not because of any works of righteousness that we had done but according to his mercy, through the water of rebirth and renewal by the Holy Spirit" (Titus 3:4–5). Once again, first the kindness, love, mercy and Spirit of God. Then doctrine, law, behavior and tradition.

Too often, however, doctrine and law prevail without a living faith. The tension is between institutions and tradition as the dead faith of living people and Tradition as the living faith of dead people (in Jaroslav Pelikan's wonderful phrase[32]). With these rites of initiation, there is the special tension between the prophecy that challenges dead faith in the institution and the mandate by that same institution to do these rites. Institutions usually do not mandate prophecy. Institutions do not demand revolutions. Institutions do not command actions that summon conversion and radical change at the very core of the institution.

Much research about the faith of people (including the leaders) in our church institution indicates that many equate faith with doctrine (*fides qua*—the content of faith *which* we believe, the expressions of faith given us by a previous generation) not with a personal relationship with God in community (*fides quo*—faith as union with God *by which* we believe).[33] For example, according to a study by George Gallup, Jr., and Jim Castelli, Catholics scored the lowest of all denominations in agreeing with the statement "God loves you a great deal" and in believing that they have a personal relationship with God.[34] One study of priests found that two-thirds were underdeveloped in their ability to articulate a personal faith; and another found that 38 percent of all priests and 55 percent of those aged 56 to 65 say, "Faith means essentially belief in the doctrines of the Catholic church."[35] People sometimes hand on only what they have received; and that can be the dead faith of living people, faith as "religious stuff" without a covenant relationship with God whom they have made their own.

When radical change threatens the very core of the institution, ecclesial powers will struggle to keep control. Such a radical change began not with these new rites of initiation but with changes made by the bishops in Vatican II's *Constitution on the Church*. When the bishops arrived at the Council, they received a document that put the hierarchy first, then the rest of the church. The bishops reversed the order, beginning the document with a chapter on the mystery of God's presence, which led into a chapter on the presence of God in the entire people of God. This chapter then was followed by chapter three on the presence of God in the leaders of that people, the hierarchy.

The Spirit of God is cast on all God's people, some of whom are ordained to minister within that people: first, baptism for mission to the world, then ordination of some of the baptized to enable and empower that mission. That is a radical shift from the theology of ministry of the 1950s, which had seen the lay apostolate only as being delegated by bishops. The sacraments of initiation incorporated that shift. More than any other rites, they translated the vision of the church as a community into practice. They enfleshed it in rites that celebrate God's universal presence in the community of all the baptized and the universal call of that entire community to mission.

Since Vatican II, we have experienced the tensions between institutional leaders voting for documents or mandating sacraments with a new vision of church and the way those same leaders live the realities of that vision. Institutions and ecclesial powers sometimes turn loose their own lions to control and maintain the status quo in many areas of church life, including the sacraments. As Vincent Donovan laments, "So much energy is expended in tension and controversy determining just who has the power and authority to *dispense* the sacraments, as if they were medicine to be doled out by a licensed physician." The institutional issues range from power to say the words of consecration, to baptize, to preside, to anoint, to preach and proclaim the word of God, to bless and to serve Mass, all "swirling around an altar or sanctuary or baptismal font . . . [none of which] has anything to do with *refounding* the church."[36] After a study of four parish catechumenates, James Morgan concluded,

> In its organizational structures, the RCIA appears to have fitted nicely into the existing hierarchical arrangement of the institutional church. It also seems that the catechumenate, far from being the most radical rite that would subvert

the pastoral practice of the church and how it views the meaning of member-ship, functions in a conserving manner and identifies with the established patterns of how the church behaves organizationally.[37]

Therefore, what organization consultant Joel Barker says of "para-digm shifts" will be true of this ecclesial shift from institutional mainte-nance to conversion in community.[38] A paradigm is a set of parameters, rules and regulations, often made unconsciously, that establishes bound-aries for our thinking and doing. It leads us to address issues and problems within the boundaries and according to the norms it sets. Our old paradigm of "convert instruction" led us to assert, "We've always done it that way. We've always taught with lectures, inquiry classes and cate-chisms. The priest always did it." Of course it isn't so, but *we* have never seen anything different.

Paradigms become the filters that allow friendly data to enter our consciousness, but they sift out data that does not fit our presuppositions. Sometimes we can't even *see* data that doesn't fit. If we have a personal and emotional commitment to a particular paradigm, we do not want to see anything else. The great disease of all institutions is "paradigm paralysis," described by Barker as the "terminal disease of certainty." Those involved and invested most in the present model will be the most paralyzed and will fight hardest against change.

The data coming in suggests that our present paradigm of church as institution isn't working. The paradox is that because initiation is an official sacrament of the institution, the leaders charged with changing the paradigms from the old churchskin of institution to the new wineskin of community in the process of Christian initiation are precisely those most committed to the old paradigm.

What Richard Reichert says about all catechesis captures what happens with many catechumenates. He summarizes what we have said by naming two sources: first, an ecclesiological schizophrenia between an institutional model of church committed to maintenance through doctrine and law, and a model of church as a community committed to conversion and mission; and second, the error of catechists who thought they could provide in catechetical sessions what only the entire commu-nity could provide: the life of conversion, worship and mission. Cate-chists should lament about that, but they should have no guilt about not doing the impossible.[39]

**Conversation Starter:** Who most resists "paradigm shifts" and perpetuates "paradigm paralysis" in your parish? How do you respond to and minister with them? How do they respond to or minister with you?

## It's Just Not Working

Discussing children's religious education in general and the initiation of children in particular, Maureen Kelly and Robert Duggan contend, "Our starting point is an admission of failure. We want to shout, 'The emperor has no clothes!' to all who have grown complacent with or chosen to ignore what is happening with our children's religious education across the country. We want to force an admission that *it's just not working*."[40] Kelly and Duggan root their vision of the initiation of children in the journey of adult initiation and conversion.

**Conversation Starter:** In your parish, is religious education "working" for children? Why or why not?

If ministry with our children is not working, it is because the institutional model of church is not working. We lack the adult community of faith within which children and adults come to faith (#4). With much sadness, a father told me that his 11-year-old son recently participated with a friend at the friend's Methodist Sunday service. His mother suggested that he might invite his Methodist friend to Mass the next week. The Catholic boy hung his head and said, "No thanks." "Why?" "Boring!" The parents are very much involved in their parish, but they are saying that they need to change parishes for the sake of their children.

Robert Fuller, formerly the national director of RENEW, agrees:

> In spite of our blood, sweat and tears, our parishes are not working. . . . Almost every sociological study done on American Catholics shows that we are a reflection of American society. Catholics differ very little from Americans in general in attitudes toward the poor, justice issues, the competitive values of society, even abortion.[41]

The situation is so bleak that one sociologist speaks of "the church of the wholly downward spiral."[42]

Ralph Keifer complains,

> The conception of church as local communion in faith, as vehicle of the experience of the Risen Lord, as eschatological sign, exists only in official text and clerical rhetoric, not something perceived by the great majority of churchgoers. Our operative model is still that of the established church, a bastion of conservation, convention and respectability. . . . Our present catechetics continually puts us in the position of telling people, "Yes, Virginia, there is a church."[43]

Margaret O'Brien Steinfels speaks of the "quiet crisis of plausibility" between church words and church realities.[44]

After many years in Africa, a missionary reports on what he sees in that church in the United States:

> An aging church population. The absence of the young in any meaningful numbers. A tired and besieged church; a threatened Catholic school system; a church lacking in sufficient ministers and personnel to reach into the future; a growing number of priests "leading lives of quiet desperation."

Despite a flurry of good-willed activity on the diocesan level, he sees a feeble church at the parish level: "a church that shows no reasonable hope of reaching deeply into the twenty-first century in its present form."[45] Another commentator sees hope, but he also sees the present decade as a time of crisis: "I do suspect that the 1990s are a crucial period that could either see the beginnings of an exciting regeneration of Catholicism in our country or its decline into a reactionary remnant that resembles a Roman equivalent of the '700 Club.'"[46]

Our culture's assault on Christian faith and values is massive. In this culture, if there is to be any depth of faith, it usually will not happen in huge parishes with anonymous crowds. Growth in faith normally happens in small groups that allow personal relationships. If faith is a relationship with God, it is nurtured by sharing with other people who are also in that relationship. These people convince us that we do not stand alone, that it is not crazy to believe in poverty of spirit, purity of heart, thirst for justice and the making of peace. If we cannot depend on families and neighborhoods to communicate these values, we need to offer them in the parish. We need a change of churches, in Robert Fuller's words, "a new way of being church, structuring the parish into a community of smaller communities."[47]

In another sense, too, parishes aren't working. After Vatican II, many parishes multiplied the number of programs that they offered—all with ministries performed by the parish staff—without seeing mission to the world as "the responsibility of all the baptized" (#9). Despite all the programs, one study claims that only eight percent (another says 13 percent) of all parishioners participate in anything—from serving on the pastoral council to mowing the grass—in addition to Sunday Mass. Patrick Brennan comments,

> Only the most naive among us would not admit that the parish, in its status quo form . . . is not as effective in passing on and celebrating faith as it once was. . . . Though Vatican II vocabulary resounds through our parishes, and though many parishes have experienced an explosion of lay ministries, often the paradigm for parish remains basically the same as it was for our grand-parents: child-centered school and CCD programs and organizations.[48]

One pastor likens the programmatic parish to a "black hole" that sucks the staff into oblivion. Another pastor writes, "We are gradually recognizing that customary approaches to communion and mission are simply not working." He notes that some tackle the problem by multiplying staffs and programs. They think, "We must be doing something right because we're always tired!" Others, however, "have taken a courageous new direction, opting for an approach favoring the *restructuring* of the parish itself."[49]

Other cultures, those with a more communal sense, need not restructure because people's consciousness is already "structured" for community. John LeMay, pastor of St. Teresa Parish in Eastleigh (on the outskirts of Nairobi), told me that "small Christian communities are simply our way of being church." People need not attend community meetings to be members of that small church any more than people need to attend Mass to be Catholic. But when anything significant happens in their lives—crises, marriages, births, illnesses, deaths—the small Christian community is the place for formation, care and ministry.

In a 1975 talk to the United States bishops, Albert H. Ottenweller, who was then a pastor in Toledo and who later became bishop of Toledo, insisted that parishes are not working and that ministers in parishes are working too hard because we still have a vision of church as institution (with just the professionals doing ministry). According to him, we poured all the demands of Vatican II and since Vatican II through a funnel onto the heads of those already saturated professionals.[50] Ottenweller argued that the vision of the Council never would see the light of day until we become a church of small communities that enable and empower all the people of God to serve each other. That holds true not just because we now have fewer priests but because that is the biblical vision of church. That is how the church began—in house churches.[51] That is the vision of church expressed in the *Constitution on the Church* and in the texts of the sacraments of initiation. In church seen as community, these rites call the faith-full to empower new members to witness to faith.

**Conversation Starter:**   What has your parish done to restructure into small Christian communities?

If the church is not working, then the catechumenate won't work. Aidan Kavanagh, an American godfather of these rites, comments with some sadness: "I give it less than a 50 percent chance of success. . . . My gloom is due to the state of the church in North America at the present time. I find it confused, lacking in morale, apostolic direction and discipline."[52] Anne Marie Winters, in a doctoral dissertation completed in 1991, assesses that "apostolic direction" by contrasting statements on catechesis by the United States bishops with the same bishops' implementation of the sacraments of initiation—contrasting what they say with what they do. She concludes:

> Most of the bishops did not seem to question *what* was happening in the conversion process itself. They were more concerned about *how* that process should look when it was done. While the topography of the rite was being studied, it seemed that its inner dynamism was being seriously neglected. The bishops seem to be more interested in the pragmatic aspects of the rite. . . . It might be better to place the focus where it belongs: on the faith life of the community and the Holy Spirit by which that faith life is activated.[53]

We are back to the basics, to Rahner's "inner core of faith" and conversion in and through the Spirit in the community.

M. Francis Mannion complains that some gratuitously extend the implementation of these rites to an agenda for renewal and change of the entire church.[54] Yes and no. No, in the sense that there is more to church life than the sacraments of initiation. No, because there are other hopeful efforts at reform and renewal.

But yes in the sense that initiation raises the most basic issues for all the baptized: What is "the faith life of the community and the Holy Spirit by which that faith life is activated"? What are evangelization, catechesis, conversion, faith, mission? How do we celebrate them for new members with old members? What happens to the entire community when it sees "that the initiation of adults is the responsibility of all the baptized"? What happens when the community is "prepared for the pursuit of its apostolic vocation to give help to those who are searching for Christ" (#9)?

Yes, if Aidan Kavanagh is correct: "It may well be that only in initiating such people will we be able to rediscover our own ecclesial selves."[55] Yes, if liturgist-musician Tom Conry has it right:

> The importance of the RCIA . . . is simply this. It is the last, best hope that the promise and vision of Vatican II will ever come to pass. I believe that if we allow the RCIA to work in our parishes . . . then the church will be irreversibly renewed. . . . So the moment lies largely in our hands. We musicians and liturgists [and catechists, other pastoral ministers and especially the church community] have it in our power to turn the lathe that may shape the new church. Or not.[56]

Will it work? Will these rites succeed? To ask such questions is to fall into the trap of the North American obsession with success. Jesus' cross and death are hardly a great success. Yet if these are radical rites that send us back to our roots, we are back to Jesus' opening salvo in Mark's gospel: "The time is fulfilled, and the kingdom of God has come near; repent and believe in the good news" (Mark 1:15). Those words summon conversion. They may not be any more successful for us than they were the first time around. Ours, however, is not to be successful. Like Jesus the Christ, ours is to be faithful. "It is part of Christian hope that we don't interpret these wintry times as a prelude to ultimate death" (Karl Rahner once again). Godfrey Diekmann, a pioneer American liturgist who is now in his 80s and who might have every reason to be discouraged, insists, "I for one refuse to be part of the faintheartedness, the pessimism, the fear, that seems currently to have infected so many."[57] A United States archbishop, in contrasting the difference between the church today and 25 years ago at the end of Vatican II, says about hope: "I would have to say that somehow the enthusiasm has spun itself out. All of the optimism and enthusiasm that characterized the termination of the Council seem now to have dissipated. . . . If it was naive then, now it can be the mature hope that has come from experience and a certain amount of disillusionment." One wag puts it more graphically: "Like Noah, when storms outside threaten to destroy us, we can endure the stench inside of the ark and the church."

I have often said, "We may fail, but at least we fail trying the right thing." We do the right thing (with this "rite thing") if we move into the inner dynamics of the good news that summons faith and conversion. We need to ground our pragmatic concerns of timing, scheduling and doctrinal content in our faith life as a community that activates the faith life of others through the Spirit.

I also have often said, "Thou shalt not do to others what thou hast not done to thyself." Better, "Let God do *to* thee what God wants to do *through* thee." In other words, we need to taste the new wine ourselves and to shed those old churchskins. We need more than the topography of the rites, more than bureaucratic, pragmatic institutional concerns. We need more than the plethora of how-to-do-it texts now flooding the market (even those based on the liturgical year) with their preconceived designs and content. We need formation and transformation, not just information. We need to take the journey ourselves.[58] As ministers, we need both the *what* (such as the vision of church, faith, conversion, liturgical catechesis in these rites) and also some *hows* (some practical ways for pastoral ministers and catechumens to do that liturgical catechesis). We need methods, especially for catechists and homilists, that bring the word of God to echo in and through our lives in the community and that situate doctrine and law within the good news. This book is an effort to let that word resound. Therefore, we turn in the next chapter to an overview of catechesis, which is the ministry of re-sounding, of echoing God's word.

> **Conversation Starter:**   What have you done individually, as a catechumenate team and as a parish to take the conversion journey envisioned by the rites of initiation? What were the results of your efforts?

## Endnotes

[1] Karl Rahner, *Faith in a Wintry Season* (New York: Crossroad Publishing Co., 1990), 39, 200. This was written in 1984, a few months before he died.

[2] Maurice Dingman, "The Role of the Bishop in Christian Initiation," in *Becoming a Catholic Christian* (New York: Wm. H. Sadlier, Inc., 1978), 145.

[3] In Greek, *martyrion* means "witness." The early Christians gave witness to the crucified Lord most powerfully by their own physical death. But they and we give witness in many kinds of dying — in our physical and spiritual poverty, hunger, thirst, etc. In dying we lose control. Dying demands conversion for Americans fed on a diet of win/lose, cutthroat competition, upward mobility, superpower and "never losing control."

[4] Aidan Kavanagh, "Critical Issues in the Growth of the RCIA in North America," *Catechumenate* 10 (March 1988): 15.

[5] Ralph Keifer, "Christian Initiation: The State of the Question," in *Made Not Born* (Notre Dame: University of Notre Dame Press, 1978), 144.

[6] This is not true in Latin America. There, once again, we have a church of martyrs; and catechists are often the first villagers assassinated. Michael Warren claims that although in the United States the catechist "is the most predictable and safest of persons," in Latin America "we have the catechist as subversive, the catechist as dangerous person" because a *delegado de la palabra* (delegate of the word) preaches an upsetting word that "calls for the replacing of everyday injustice and unjust systems with ways in keeping with the kingdom of God." *Faith, Culture and the Worshiping Community* (New York: Paulist Press, 1989), 70.

[7] Kavanagh, "Critical Issues," 19. Kavanagh adds that the images of Susanna and the dirty old men who spied on her in her bath (Daniel 13:1–62), which appear on the walls of the early baptistries, conjure up only secular ideologies of sexism and oppression, not of catechumens facing opprobrium from the world for the purity and simplicity of their new lives.

[8] George Gerbner comments on the power of TV: "We have moved away from the historic experience of humankind. Children used to grow up in a home where parents told most of the stories. Today television tells most of the stories to most of the people most of the time." ("The Challenge of Television," unpublished paper, 1982, p. 8) Michael Warren adds, "Every tradition embodies many stories, and the stories that make up that tradition must be told and known if persons are to be part of that tradition. When the stories die, the tradition is dead." *Faith, Culture,* 181.

[9] All paragraph numbers refer to the *Rite of Christian Initiation of Adults* unless otherwise noted.

[10] Keifer, "Christian Initiation," 149.

[11] The acronym RCIA *(Rite of Christian Initiation of Adults)* is inaccurate. The Latin text has *ordo,* which speaks more clearly about an order of rites with many celebrations.

[12] James Dunning, *New Wine, New Wineskins* (New York: Wm. H. Sadlier, Inc., 1981).

[13] J. Massyngbaerde Ford, *My Enemy Is My Guest* (Maryknoll NY: Orbis Books, 1984), 74.

[14] Keifer, "Christian Initiation," 402.

[15] Balthasar Fischer, "The Rite of Christian Initiation of Adults: Rediscovery and New Beginnings," *Worship* 64 (March 1990): 104–5.

[16] Andrew Greeley, *The Catholic Why Book* (Chicago: Thomas More Press, 1983), 150.

[17] Balthasar Fischer contends that the same is true of the commission that gave us this document: "More and more we discovered that what the early Christians established in regard to the catechumenate was fundamentally a timeless pattern. Likewise we were pleased to find that the highly critical pastors and experienced missionaries on the commission shared the same views of the restored catechumenate as the professors in the group. If the professors had been too idealistic, they would certainly have been brought back to reality by the missionary pastors." "The Rite of Christian Initiation of Adults," 102.

[18] Ray Kemp, "The Rite of Christian Initiation of Adults at Ten Years," *Worship* 56 (July 1982): 310, 311.

[19] Strictly speaking, this rite has been mandated since 1974 when the first English translation was approved for the United States in accord with the decree in 1972 by the Vatican Congregation for Divine Worship that this rite will "replace the rite of baptism of adults now in the Roman Ritual." That first English translation had as its subtitle "Provisional Text." It should have said "provisional translation." The text never has been provisional. The new translation approved by the United States bishops in 1986 was mandated for implementation by September 1, 1988.

[20] Cf. *Constitution on the Sacred Liturgy, #7.*

[21] Vincent Donovan comments: "Everything that builds up the community of Christ is baptismal . . . ; everything that makes the members of that community vitally interrelated to one another so that the fate of one lies in the hands of the others . . . ; everything that enables the members of that community to discern the body of Christ in the community, so that, when they gather for eucharist, it is indeed the Lord's Supper they are making—all this is baptismal ministry." *The Church in the Midst of Creation* (Maryknoll NY: Orbis Books, 1989), 73–74.

[22] *Constitution on the Sacred Liturgy, #14.*

[23] I say this with some caution. Although some people insist that some parishes should not do the catechumenate because there is no community into which to initiate, others contend that *if* such parishes can at least offer the catechumens a small catechumenal community, they should begin and hope that catechumens might bring new life to a community just as new babies enliven a family. Also, even though some might begin the catechumenate primarily because of a mandate, there is hope that "the law might educate" to a deeper vision and practice, just as civil-rights legislation has educated our larger society.

[24] Although this book focuses on catechesis during the catechumenate period, it assumes an ongoing inquiry group for the precatechumenate that candidates can enter at any time during the year and in which they remain for a time adapted to their needs and readiness for the rite of acceptance into the order of catechumens. It assumes a similar flexibility for the catechumenate period, although the United States bishops have established one year as the norm for the unbaptized (*National Statutes for the Catechumenate, #6*). Finally, it assumes that the parish offers sessions to neophytes for at least a year after initiation (*Statutes, #24*) and that conversion continues for a lifetime. For suggestions regarding the structure of an ongoing process, see Karen Hinman, "An Ongoing Precatechumenate," *Catechumenate* 8 (March 1986): 4–11; Marguerite Main, "An Ongoing Precatechumenate Process," in *Come Follow Me*, ed. Joseph P. Sinwell (New York: Paulist Press, 1990), 3–9; and Thomas H. Morris, *The RCIA: Transforming the Church* (New York: Paulist Press, 1989), 22–27, 69.

[25] Nathan D. Mitchell, "A Parish of Prodigals," *Church* 7 (Summer 1991): 49.

[26] The word "election" in our culture might proclaim elitism. When catechizing for the rite of election, we need to present it in its biblical context—God's choice of slaves and sinners. The elect are those who know that they are not elite. It is the rite of election, not a rite of perfection.

[27] Cf. Galatians 5:16–26.

[28] "Enliveners of community may have been replaced in many modern churches by an entirely different kind of person, who functions as a bureaucratic functionary, a manager of doctrinal inputs." Warren, *Faith, Culture,* 52.

[29] Larry Cuban, "Reforming, Again, Again and Again," *Educational Researcher* 191:3–13.

[30] Although Paul most likely is not the author of the pastoral letters (1 Timothy, 2 Timothy and Titus), it is not uncommon for people to refer to him as the author.

[31] Josephine Humphreys, "The Epistle of Paul to Titus," in *Incarnation,* ed. Alfred Cor (New York: Viking Penguin, Inc., 1990), 248–49.

[32] Jaroslav Pelikan, *The Vindication of Tradition* (New Haven: Yale University Press, 1984), 65.

[33] "Though the response to God's revelation and love will vary according to one's background and circumstances, the act of faith involves 'total adherence . . . under the influence of grace to God revealing himself' (*General Catechetical Directory,* #36). This is the faith *by which* one believes. Total adherence includes not only the mind but also the will and emotions; it is the response of the whole person, including belief in the 'content of revelation and of the Christian message' (*General Catechetical Directory,* #36). The latter is the faith *which* one believes." *Sharing the Light of Faith: National Catechetical Directory for Catholics of the United States* (Washington DC: USCC, 1979), #56.

[34] George Gallup, Jr., and Jim Castelli, *The American Catholic People: Their Beliefs, Practices and Values* (Garden City NY: Doubleday, 1987), 193.

[35] Dean Hoge et al., "Changing Age Distribution and Theological Attitudes of Catholic Priests, 1970–1985" (Washington DC: Catholic University, 1987).

[36] Donovan, *The Church in the Midst,* 67.

[37] James Morgan, "The Shape of the Catechumenate," *The Living Light* 27 (Spring 1991): 201.

[38] Joel Barker, *Discovering the Future: The Business of Paradigms* (St. Paul: ILI Press, 1985).

[39] Richard Reichert, "Catechists Confront Ecclesiological Schizophrenia," *The Living Light* 27 (Winter 1991): 166–74.

[40] Robert D. Duggan and Maureen A. Kelly, *The Christian Initiation of Children* (New York: Paulist Press, 1990), 2. In a very critical review of this book, Thomas Groome

complains that "the authors seem to dismiss the efforts of countless generous people who have given their time and talents in parish and school catechesis" ("Book Reviews," *The Living Light* 28 [Fall 1991]). I applaud those efforts but contend that they will lead to increasing frustration if they are not situated in the ongoing conversion of the adult/family communities in a church that is increasingly counter-cultural. Groome agrees that we must "call on the entire Catholic community to become involved in passing on to our children an ancient heritage of faith . . . " (Duggan and Kelly, *Christian Initiation*, 17). Contra Groome, these authors also insist that "it is not the intention of this book to make religious education the scapegoat for our present failures" (p. 2).

[41] Robert Fuller, "Amen!" *Church* 7 (Summer 1991): 64.

[42] William McCready, cited in the *National Catholic Reporter* (29 July 1988), 5. In a critique that extends to the contemporary universal church, Michael Crosby writes from the vantage point both of scripture and the dynamics of 12-step fellowships about a "dysfunctional church" afflicted by a "deadly disease" of addiction to the preservation of power through a male, celibate, clerical model of church in which many of us are codependent; "unless drastic action is taken, [it] will prove deadly at least in the First World." *The Dysfunctional Church* (Notre Dame: Ave Maria Press, 1991), 7.

[43] Keifer, "Christian Initiation," 141, 142.

[44] Margaret O'Brien Steinfels, "The Church and Its Public Life," *America* (10 June 1989): 552.

[45] Donovan, *The Church in the Midst*, ix, x.

[46] Michael Leach, "The Last Catholics in America," *America* 165 (30 November 1991): 412.

[47] Fuller, "Amen!" 64. For efforts to re-envision and restructure parishes, see Arthur Baranowski, *Creating Small Faith Communities, Pastoring the Pastors* and *Praying Alone and Together* (Cincinnati: St. Anthony Messenger Press, 1988); Patrick Brennan, *The Evangelizing Parish* (Allen TX: Tabor Publishing, 1987) and *Re-Imagining the Parish* (New York: Crossroad Publishing Co., 1990); James Hopewell, *Congregation: Stories and Structures* (Philadelphia: Fortress Press, 1987); Thomas Kleissler et al., *Small Christian Communities* and *Resources for Small Christian Communities* (New York: Paulist Press, 1991); Bernard Lee and Michael Cowan, *Dangerous Memories* (Kansas City: Sheed and Ward, 1986); Bernard Lee, ed., *Alternative Futures for Worship, Volume 3, The Eucharist* (Collegeville: The Liturgical Press, 1987); James Hug, ed., *Tracing the Spirit* (New York: Paulist Press, 1983).

[48] Brennan, *Re-Imagining*, ix.

[49] Richard Ling, "Small Ecclesial Communities: A Constitutive Element of Catholic Christian Life," newsletter of the National Alliance of Parishes Restructuring into Communities, Spring 1991, 7. Arthur Baranowski is one pastor committed to restructuring parishes into small Christian communities; he has initiated the National Alliance of Parishes Restructuring into Communities; see his *Creating Small Faith Communities*.

[50] Clearly, that funnel kept on pouring. The United States bishops' study of the morale of priests in 1988 indicated that morale is low simply because priests are tired and feel caught between the demands of the Council and the hierarchy on one side and the people on the other; cf. Committee of Priestly Life and Ministry of the NCCB, "Reflections on the Morale of Priests," *Origins* 18 (January 1989): 497, 499–505.

[51] "Parish" comes from two Greek words, *"par oikos,"* meaning "beyond the house." "Diocese" comes from *"dia oikos"* and means "cutting across the houses." Both words presume the existence of smaller communities of faithful.

[52] Kavanagh, "Critical Issues," 20–21.

[53] Anne Marie Winters, *The Sacraments of Initiation in the United States since the Second Vatican Council*, unpublished doctoral dissertation (New York: Fordham University, 1991), 250–51, 257.

[54] M. Francis Mannion, "RCIA Enthusiasts May Spoil Its Success," *The Progress* (January 30, 1992).

[55] Kavanagh, "Critical Issues," 21.

[56] Tom Conry, "The Last, Best Hope," *Pastoral Music* 13 (February/March 1989): 51.

[57] Quoted in *The Monk's Tale* by Kathleen Hughes (Collegeville: The Liturgical Press, 1991).

[58] Hundreds of catechumenate ministers testify that there is no better way to enter the dynamics of these rites than through the "Beginnings and Beyond Institutes" offered by the North American Forum on the Catechumenate. For information contact Forum, 5510 Columbia Pike, Suite 310, Arlington VA 22204.

# CHAPTER TWO

## A Vision of Catechesis

*Though I know of no one who would deny that catechesis is educational, its framework is not that of education but rather that of pastoral ministry. . . . Catechesis is distinct while at the same time closely related to all other ministries: to the ministry of healing, to ministries of counsel and education, and to ministries of play and worship. Some may say that catechesis is by my own admission too tightly "churchy." I say instead that its relationship to other ministries makes catechesis wholistic and open to a wide range of human needs that surface in this world of ours, many of them quite unchurchy.[1]*

• Michael Warren

OBVIOUSLY, "CATECHUMENATE" and "catechesis" share the same etymological roots. Both come from the Greek *katechein: kata*, meaning "down," and *echein*, "to sound." Catechesis is literally a "sounding down," a "re-sounding," a "re-echoing down to another." This re-sounding is not just in our ears but in our life in the Spirit. In the fourth century, during the "golden age" of the catechumenate, St. Cyril of Jerusalem addressed the following words to the newly initiated:

> Look with what great worthiness Jesus salutes you joyfully. You were called a catechumen, meaning, "hearing with the ears"—hearing hope, but not understanding, hearing mysteries, yet not understanding, hearing scriptures, yet not understanding the depth. No longer do you hear with the ears but in an internal way, for the indwelling Spirit builds your mind into a house of God. (*Procatechesis*)

Some people protest that "catechesis" is one more piece of jargon that complicates religious conversation. I like its root meaning in the Greek, and when people ask what it means, we have a teachable moment.[2] The term is also free of some of the baggage of schooling that some attach to the term "religious education," baggage that good religious educators also disclaim. Others complain that "catechesis" is too limited, churchy and unecumenical to meet all the challenges of church mission in the modern world. Thomas Groome suggests that the term "catechesis," which originally meant oral instruction, is too weak to carry all the weight of initiation into a community given to it by the "new catechetics."[3] Gabriel Moran sees "religious education" as a broader term, although he affirms the validity of the word "catechesis," especially when it is connected with liturgy and specifically the catechumenate.[4] For that reason, I use the term "catechesis," although I admit that I give it a wider meaning than it had in early church history.

> **Conversation Starter:**   In your parish, in practice, do catechumens and others use school words such as "program," "instructions" and "class" to describe what they are experiencing? Does that language truly reflect what you are offering (such as a nine-month program) and what they experience (classroom lectures, for instance)?

This chapter, after looking at the recent history of catechesis, will explore three dimensions of my vision of catechesis: first, catechesis as ministry of the word; second, the relationship between catechesis and evangelization; and third, catechesis as socialization.

## The Recent History of Catechesis

Developments in catechesis in the twentieth century gather around three issues: method, message (content) and milieu (inculturation)—the three Ms.

*Method*   In this century, religious educators became increasingly dissatisfied with the question-and-answer method of the catechisms. This method often centered on the rote learning of information about God, not on transformation into God's life. Religious educators turned to the behavioral sciences, especially psychology, for catechetical methods attentive to the ways that humans learn. They learned the power of stories, images and symbols that go beyond the cognitive and arise from life experience, and they discovered the value of learning by doing. These methods invited learners into personal and communal formation, transformation and conversion to God, not just to knowledge about God.

The "Munich method" was one of the first efforts using this type of experiential catechesis. In post-Christian Europe, when to be a believer was more clearly countercultural than it had been for centuries, cate-chetical theorists also found that methods that were almost exclusively cognitive could not communicate the living tradition of the community. They rediscovered the early catechumenate with its process of journey-ing in community, which originated at a time when Christianity was also countercultural.

*Message*   During the 1930s, the catechetical movement began to focus on the content of the Christian message and entered the "kerygmatic phase" centered on the "kerygma" or good news of God's presence and promise to us in Jesus. That movement called for religious educators to center on the center, that is, on the core Christian message about God's love for us through Jesus in the Spirit. Until then, much theologizing and catechizing had been abstract theorizing (such as the number of natures, persons, processions, missions and the circumincession in the Trinity) or hypocritical and sometimes humorous moralizing (for example, does an olive in the martini break the law of fasting?).

The seminal book of the movement was *The Good News and Our Own Preaching of the Faith* by Josef Jungmann who, as a liturgist, symbolized in his own person the moorings of catechesis in scripture and liturgy. That book, published in 1936, rankled devotees of catechisms, who had it removed from print and blocked its English translation until 1962. In the United States, the *On Our Way* series by Sister Maria de la Cruz was one of the first efforts to take up this approach.

*Milieu*   The third phase, still in progress, focuses on *milieu*—the cul-tural and political environment in which the church lives its mission to enflesh God's word in the world. Central to this phase are the interna-tional study weeks on catechesis that were held from 1960 (Eichstatt, Germany) until 1968 (Medellín, Colombia). All but one took place in poor nations, where issues of freedom and justice were clearly seen as gos-pel issues (especially at Medellín). The oft-quoted thesis of *Justice in the World* from the 1971 synod of bishops affirms that vision: "Action on behalf of justice and participation in the transformation of the world appear to us as a constitutive dimension of the preaching of the gospel."[5]

This issue of cultural and political milieu dominates contemporary reflections in modern catechetics. For the first time in history we are called to be what Karl Rahner calls "world/church"—a truly catholic (universal) church that not only celebrates the good news in all languages and cultures but also confronts all political systems with the call of prophets and Jesus to "let justice roll down like waters, and righteousness like an everflowing stream" (Amos 5:24) and "to bring good news to the poor, release to captives, freedom to the oppressed" (Luke 4:16–21).

These developments resulted in the publication of official charter documents for the ministry of catechesis: the *General Catechetical Directory* called for by Vatican II (1971); the United States directory, *Sharing the Light of Faith* (1979); the synod of bishops on *Evangelization in the Modern World* (1974), followed by Paul VI's apostolic exhortation *Evangelii Nuntiandi* (1975); and the synod on *Catechesis in Our Time* (1977), followed by John Paul II's exhortation *Catechesi Tradendae* (1979).

## Catechesis as Ministry of the Word

The quotation from Michael Warren that begins this chapter shifts catechesis from being under the umbrella of education to the umbrella of ministry—the ministry of the word. This approach situates catechesis more clearly within the church's mission and vocation to proclaim the good news. It also captures the biblical and liturgical roots of catechesis, especially of the adult initiation process that celebrates the Sunday liturgy of the word as the prime time for formal catechesis.[6] For that reason, much of what is said of catechesis and catechists also is true of homilies and homilists.

The Word is far more expansive than words. "In the beginning was the Word, and the Word was with God, and the Word was God. He was in the beginning with God. All things came into being through him, and without him not one thing came into being" (John 1:1–3). Unlike our sometimes feeble and empty words, God's word is *dabar*—in Hebrew, "word-deed": a sacramental word with power to effect what it signifies.

> For as the rain and the snow come down from the heaven,
>    and do not return there until they have watered the earth,
> making it bring forth and sprout,
>    giving seed for the sower and bread to the eater,

so shall my word be that goes from my mouth;
  it shall not return to me empty,
but it shall accomplish that which I purpose.
  *(Isaiah 55:10–11)*

"God speaks by acting; [God] acts in speaking."[7] "Let there be light." "Let the waters bring forth swarms of living creatures." (Genesis 1). God's word-deed speaks and acts especially in those created in God's image and likeness, humans who in healing and caring, liberating and reconciling, loving and peacemaking are little words of the Word. God does not speak empty words. God is so fully present in those words that they become images into whom God pours real presence. Therefore, when humans become *dabar*, when our words say who we really are as images of a healing, caring, liberating, reconciling, loving and peacemaking God, we are revelations of God's word. We become God's word by reading the signs of the times and acting as God would act, in faith, in obedience (from the Latin *obedire*, "to hear"), hearing the word and giving not just our minds but our whole selves to doing God's word-deeds.[8]

But we don't. In our tradition, Israel stammered words through the prophets, but even then the people often did not read the signs of the times. They lost sight of the image of God as covenant. "Long ago God spoke to our ancestors in many and various ways by the prophets, but in these last days [God] has spoken to us by a Son" (Hebrews 1:1–2). "He is the image of the invisible God" (Colossians 1:15). In him, "the Word became flesh and lived among us" (John 1:14). God's *dabar* acted as never before or since, healing, liberating, loving; so that Jesus became, in Karl Rahner's terms, not just the Word but the poetry of God our Father. Jesus' faith, however, his obedience to the signs of the times, brought him to be "obedient to the point of death — even death on a cross" (Philippians 2:8).

In that death, humans finally heard the Word. "We declare to you what was from the beginning, what we have heard, what we have seen with our own eyes, what we have looked at and touched with our hands, concerning the word of life" (1 John 1:1). Believers who heard that word and read the signs of Jesus' time finally saw what had always been true — that humans had forever been words of God, *dabarim*, images of God who speak and act to reveal God's presence and promise. God's Spirit, forever present to human history, is finally received by believers through the resurrection of Jesus and the mighty winds and fires of Pentecost. Therefore, all who are baptized in Christ Jesus "have been buried with him by baptism into his death, so that, just as Christ was raised from the dead by the glory of the Father, so [they] too might walk in newness of life" (Romans 6:4). "In those days I will pour out my Spirit, and they will prophesy" (Acts 2:18 and Joel 2:28). They become words of the Word. They speak/act in the Spirit of God. That is always good news.

That is the vision of catechesis as ministry of the word. Every person and community can be *dabar*. The church, when people are faithful to that vision, is simply those who know who we are. When that happens, church becomes word. This expands catechesis far beyond mere verbal proclamation. Catechesis becomes all the ways that Christians, who know that they are the word of God, allow God to reveal God's own presence and promise through healing, liberating, loving. That expands the ministry of the word to all who are church.

> **Conversation Starter:** Name three persons in your life who, without training or degrees in religious education, have been *dabar* and ministers of God's word to you.

## Evangelization, Catechesis and Religious Education

> **Take a Stand:** What is your reaction and the reaction of people you know to the word "evangelization"? Finish these sentences:
>
> 1. Evangelization means, involves, includes _____ .
> 2. Catechesis means, involves, includes _____ .
> 3. Religious education means, involves, includes _____ .

Much of the thrust behind the modern revival of catechesis stems from a renewed interest in evangelization, especially in secularized nations and in mission lands. In fact, one of the key insights of catechists in secularized Europe is that these countries, too, are mission countries. In France, Pierre-Andre Liege insists, "The first task in the church's mission . . . is evangelization . . . in all places where the gospel has not yet been announced, a matter to be decided on sociological grounds as well as on geographical ones."[9] In India, D. S. Amalorpavadass writes that baptized Christians need evangelization. "In catechesis, we do proclaim the word, but the form of proclamation that most of our people need . . . is not catechesis but evangelization: a creative, dynamic, global and interpellating word, for the first result we expect is faith and conversion."[10] He adds that until there is initial conversion to the person of Jesus Christ, we do not begin formal catechesis. In our land, Patrick Brennan asserts, "It is a mistake to presume [that] baptized Christians have had primary conversion experiences, or have had the foundational experience of consciously choosing Jesus Christ as Truth for and Lord of life."[11] Too often with nominal Christians, we celebrate infant baptism and follow it with some years of religious education and information, so that by the eighth grade, these children "know it all" and endure confirmation as their "rite of exit."

In a sense, Vatican II rediscovered the need for basic evangelization. Avery Dulles notes that Vatican I used the term "gospel" (*evangelium*) only once and never used the terms "evangelize" or "evangelization." Vatican II mentioned "gospel" 157 times, "evangelize" 18 times and "evangelization" 31 times.[12]

*Evangelization and Catechesis*    What are the relationships and distinctions between evangelization and catechesis? To try to clarify this language is to enter dangerous territory. On the one hand, "evangelization" conjures for many people images of Sunday morning hard-sell TV evangelists. Because "evangelization" occurs in so many church documents, we probably need to keep the word; but we need to translate it in terms of its Greek roots, *evangelion*, "good news." Evangelization is proclaiming the good news of Jesus Christ.

On the other hand, in *Evangelii Nuntiandi*, Paul VI uses "evangelization" in the broadest sense—as all the ways that the church proclaims the good news, including formal catechesis as one moment in evangelization.[13] Other authors, including those cited previously, see evangelization more narrowly as a time preceding catechesis. Evangelization is the first step, and its goal is initial conversion. "Only after conversion can catechesis proper be undertaken, since true catechesis is undertaken in

an ambience of faith and allegiance to the person of Jesus."[14] Liege calls
the ministry that summons conversion and initial faith-response a
ministry of a *primordial word:* missionary preaching, *kerygma,* evangelization. After that comes *subsequent preaching:* catechesis. "The primordial
function of the ministry of the word in the church will be to stir up the
faith of conversion, basis of all life of faith, without ever being able to
suppose it completely acquired. . . . In its doctrinal function, the ministry of preaching must always have missionary energy so as to sustain and
deepen conversion."[15] Liege relates evangelization to *initial* conversion
and catechesis to *deepening* communion and conversion. The two are in
constant dialogue. "It is like an extension of conversion to communion
and back again. Conversion develops into communion but on condition
that communion is ceaselessly animated by fuller conversion."[16]

The *Rite of Christian Initiation of Adults* sees evangelization in the
precatechumenate period in this more limited sense of initial conversion
and awakening faith (#36 and #37), and it implies that catechesis in the
catechumenate period deepens conversion and a maturing faith (#75
and #76). In this book, we shall use the terms in that sense, because we
are dealing with the rites of initiation.

> **Conversation Starter:** Some identify catechesis not
> with deepening conversion but with learning church teach-
> ings. Did you? Has your understanding changed? If so, how?

This definition of evangelization has enormous implications for
who belongs in a catechumenate. Part II, chapters four and five, of the
order of initiation deals with the completion of initiation for baptized but
uncatechized adults. This fact contradicts Aidan Kavanagh's claim that
"the RCIA is *not* directed to the already baptized . . . and the already baptized are presumed to be its agents."[17] Kavanagh's chief complaint, with
which I agree, seems to be that religious educators are using a "catechumenal model" for everyone from first communicants to those preparing
for marriage, with "renewal rites" for an initiation that supposedly has
already taken place. Forced, frivolous models we can do without. But
catechists and liturgists cited agree that the mere pouring of water hardly
makes a Christian or achieves evangelization, catechesis and initiation
into a community. Ralph Keifer wrote, "The great distinction in those

who wish to belong in our church is not that of baptized and nonbaptized, but between those who have some practice in faith (whether they are baptized or not) and those who have none (whether baptized or not).[18] John Paul II speaks of uncatechized adults as "quasi-catechumens" as does the Vatican document on adult catechesis, *Catechesi Tradendae*.[19] This document also affirms, with the Synod of 1977, that "the model of all catechesis is the catechumenate" (#66). In light of that, part II of the Roman order of initiation refers primarily to baptized but uncatechized Catholics in secularized Europe, although the North American experience usually is that of baptized, uncatechized Protestants. Regarding the baptized and uncatechized, Balthasar Fischer insists, "The RCIA, part II, is made for all of them . . . you cannot rebaptize those who are baptized, of course. But they should follow the whole thing. The rites should be used. There is the question of the wording in the rites."[20] The words are "unevangelized" and "uncatechized," not "uninstructed." If we have a vision of evangelization and catechesis as always leading to conversion, then good numbers of the baptized but uncatechized, both Catholic and Protestant, belong in a catechumenate and follow the guidelines of part II.[21] With Kavanagh, I hope that we have enough baptized "faithful" (evangelized and catechized) to be agents of initiation both for the unbaptized and baptized "unfaithful."

> **Conversation Starter:** Do you find big differences between unbaptized catechumens and baptized candidates for full communion in the Roman Catholic Church? If so, what are they and why are they?

This vision of catechesis as ongoing conversion and communion also implies that a person never completes that journey. Kavanagh correctly insists that initiation is about the beginnings of conversion and catechesis. Parish adult education is about conversion and communion (catechesis), not just about information. The faithful do not belong in a catechumenate, but they are never "faith-full." What we offer the baptized is aimed at deepening faith and echoing the word, not at awarding theological degrees or certificates. Even a survey of church history should lead to the question "How does the Spirit call *us* to deeper faith, even through the foibles and fidelity of our ancestors?"

In the ministry of the word through evangelization and catechesis, we keep focus on the unique journey and life of each person before us (cf. #5) and the signs of the times in which that person lives. This is difficult in a "class" of 30! If we listen to that life and those times, we shall know when to evangelize (awaken to the beginnings of faith) or catechize (nurture to a maturing faith) or when to do both, because the living reality of faith is both conversion and communion.

In the ministry of the word through evangelization and catechesis, we also keep focus on the ongoing conversion of the whole church, which keeps that church faithful in all its ministries. D. S. Amalorpavadass reminds us, "Without the ministry of the word, everything degenerates: liturgy into magic and ritualism, the law into legalism and juridicism, institutions into institutionalism, and pastors into administrative bosses. A constant prophetic effort is called for to set right this deviation and degeneration."[22]

**Catechesis and Religious Education**   To distinguish between catechesis and religious education (or adult religious education) is to enter even more dangerous territory. Some resist the word "education" because it conjures for too many people the baggage of a school model. In chapter three, we shall see that Mary Boys broadens the term far beyond the school model and insists that its goal is always conversion. *Catechesi Tradendae* sees catechesis as a time that succeeds evangelization but that still "consists in an initial deepening of the faith received at baptism, in an elementary, complete and systematic way, with a view to helping individuals all life long grow to the full maturity of Christ" (#32). This document says that catechesis differs from "formal religious education, which goes beyond the basic elements of faith in more systematic and specialized courses" (#32). I would prefer to call catechesis every ministry aimed at fostering the mature faith of adults, and I would insist that normally all such efforts seek to deepen conversion.

I say "normally" because I understand the concern of Gabriel Moran that religious education (or religious studies) on a college campus, for example, might explore the meanings of a religious tradition both without inviting a faith commitment and with the aim of uniting with other traditions in service to the world. We shall explore those concerns in chapter three. I also agree with Thomas Waters and Joseph Leddy that, at times, not only initiated Christians but catechumens, too, may need the freedom to stand back from faith and, in freedom, objectively critique the tradition. "In this sense, the doctrines, beliefs, myths, language, rituals, traditions and social organization of a belief system are studied, explored, and experienced for the sake of perfecting those characteristics of the person which make him or her specifically human." Waters and Leddy add that catechesis "assumes a freedom *in* faith," and that religious education "assumes a freedom *from* faith." Although these authors say that "it is our belief that catechesis not only *includes* religious education but depends upon it," they also say the two are "*distinct*, though closely related, endeavors."[23] I would say, rather, that catechesis (and the use of scriptural scholarship in homilies, for example) includes the use of critical intelligence to avoid both fundamentalism and idolatries but always for the sake of a conversion that is more free, more mature, more reflective, more committed. This more analytical critique usually would happen not in the homily but in the catechetical session following dismissal.

A final note for this section: My sense is that we have catechists who are skilled at nurturing and interpreting faith, but not enough evangelizers who are able to listen, to invite and to proclaim the good news with passion. Perhaps catechists and homilists also need evangelization before we dare to offer words and the word to others. Bernanos has the curate of Torcy say to a fellow priest: "Teaching, my little man, is no joke! . . . The word of God! It is a red-hot iron. And you who teach want to take it up with tongs for fear of burning yourself; why don't you grasp it with both hands?"[24]

> **Conversation Starter:**   Recall a time in your life when God's word challenged and struck you like a "red-hot iron."

## Catechesis as Socialization

The "new catechetics" presented previously moves away from an education-schooling model to a socialization model adapted from the worlds of sociology and anthropology. Thomas Groome warns that to cut off catechesis from the discipline of education "fails to name and thus severs

the Christian educational enterprise from its commonality with education and religious education. If this happens, then from what discipline
does one draw to empower the activity?"[25] Groome fears that if separated
from education, catechists will look only to theology and scripture
studies for their formation and not to educational skills. Mary Boys adds
that advocates of the new catechetics show discomfort with educational
language lest catechesis "appear too linked with schooling models and,
therefore, betray an excessively cognitive end. . . . These arguments
provide at least a partial explanation for the fact that catechetical theory
in general has given little sustained attention to matters of curriculum
and teaching."[26] I do resist the language of education because of people's
understanding of education as schooling. In later chapters, I shall give
attention to curriculum and teaching.

In the name of catechesis, John Westerhoff responds that catechesis as
socialization demands that catechists turn to many sources for nourishment. He describes socialization as all those formal and informal influ-
ences through which people acquire their understandings and ways of
living by *interacting with a community*. It includes education but much more.

> [Education] is an aspect of socialization involving all deliberate, systematic and
> sustained efforts to transmit or evolve knowledge, attitudes, values, behaviors
> or sensibilities. The history of religious education, therefore, needs to include
> the family, public schools, community ethos, religious literature and church
> life. Schooling, on the other hand, is only one specific and very limited form of
> education. The schooling-educational paradigm has made this small part into
> the whole.[27]

Mark Searle contends that children "learn to speak, to think, to
love, to cure, to feel, to play, to politik and to work without the
interference of a teacher."[28] I would nuance those remarks by saying that
teachers with finely honed skills in the discipline of education are a gift to
those on a journey of conversion. The journey, however, is into dying and
rising in a Spirit-touched community. That requires all the resources of
that community.

***From a Teaching Model to an Initiation Model***   We discussed the need
for a paradigm shift for initiation in chapter one. Figures 1 and 2 describe
two authors' views of such a shift from a teaching/schooling model

(paradigm) to an initiation/catechesis model.[29] The differences in these models are much like those between the model of an inquiry class and the model of the catechumenate. A teaching/schooling model might have been effective when culture, community and family were more active in initiation and catechesis. In other words, all that we did in the past through teaching/schooling was not wrong. It is simply not working today in a more pluralistic world.

**Figure 1**

| Comparison of Teaching and Initiation Models | | |
| --- | --- | --- |
| **MODELS** | **TEACHING** | **INITIATION** |
| **Goal** | Know the faith | Person in community |
| **Method** | Textbook | Experiential (#75) |
| **Relationship** | Teacher/school | Newcomer/community |
| **Outcome** | Knowledgeable Catholics | Member/missionary |

The people most resistant to changing paradigms are those most involved in the old models. For example, the Swiss, who discovered the quartz watch, were so wedded to the spring-driven model that they let the Japanese overtake the market with quartz watches while the Swiss watch industry hit bottom. Teachers, especially college teachers and those taught by universities and seminaries are most resistant to an initiation/catechesis model for the catechumenate. The initiation/catechesis model will incorporate methods, resources and goals of the teaching model, such as religious knowledge; but it goes far beyond those methods, resources and goals. Many who prefer the term "religious education" to "catechesis" expand their definition of religious education far beyond a teaching/schooling model.

**Figure 2**

| A Summary of the Different Emphases of Catechesis and Religious Educations | | |
|---|---|---|
| **FOCUS** | **CATECHESIS** | **RELIGIOUS STUDIES** |
| **Goal** | Growth in commitment | Growth in understanding |
| **Reaches Fulfillment in** | Worship and action for justice | Mastery in an intellectual sense |
| **Presumes** | Conversation: that participants stand within the circle of faith | Some commitment to disciplined inquiry |
| **Examines religious questions from** | A position of commitment | A more objective position than that taken in catechesis |
| **Is a part of** | Church pastoral ministry | Education |
| **Is a "cousin" of** | Celebration | Study |
| **Style** | A way of "walking along" with people | A way of studying |
| **Choice** | Involves a conscious choice to meet specifically for the enrichment of "faith" life | May not involve such a choice |
| **Need for freedom** | Can only occur in an ambience of freedom | May take place in a zone of obligatory attendance |

**Conversation Starter:**   Using figures 1 and 2, name concrete characteristics of your catechumenate that identify it as a teaching model or an initiation model and as catechesis or religious studies.

Michael Warren summarizes what he considers to be a healthy dialogue between catechesis and education:

I myself judge that in the United States many have overstated the possibilities of education as the cure-all for multiple ills. . . . The better approach is to hold fast to our understanding of the ministry of meanings as part of *pastoral ministry* and then consciously to cross over into the field of education with its specialized concepts and language. Working from this end, we may well enrich education; working from the other end . . . I am not sure we have enriched education, though I am inclined to see that we have very much confused pastoral ministry.[30]

Indeed, catechesis will turn to scripture and theology for content. However, catechesis as socialization introduces catechumens into the present life of the community. As ministers of a living word of God present to every society and culture in the signs of the times, catechists and homilists will turn to all the sources in a community that put the meaning of past religious tradition into dialogue with insights into events of the present and glimpses of the future. The gospel sometimes will affirm contemporary understandings and sometimes challenge them. Contemporary insights will at times challenge past understandings of the gospel. This dialogue will open up a new future, one more faithful to the gospel and to our times.

To enable this dialogue, we shall need to know more than Bernard Lonergan from the world of theology or Malcolm Knowles from the world of adult education. Jacques Audinet said at the International Catechetical Congress in Medellín:

This perspective runs a risk of upsetting a little our concept of education, of programs, and also of the very structure of what we call catechesis. Indeed we will discover again the Bible, the liturgy, the dogmatic language. But we will not pay attention to their content in itself alone but to the way in which what they express is related to the experience and the image which this group has of itself. In this way catechesis becomes the place where the Christian group creates the experience of faith and invents a new language to express it.[31]

That is what the focus on the political/cultural milieu adds to Joseph Jungmann's call to return to the good news of the biblical message. We exegete lives, primarily, not texts. We interpret contemporary personal and communal lives in light of present and past events. The word does not become God's word for us until it becomes more than text. It becomes God's word when it is enfleshed in our own journeys of conversion.

Jacques Audinet speaks of a new language. That addresses another criticism directed at catechesis as socialization. Some fear an oppressive socialization that is really indoctrination into a limited understanding of our religious tradition, one that is closed to new language and expressions of faith and that is concerned primarily with institutional membership, survival and control. Mary Boys notes, "What seems to be missing in catechetical theory—and here is a clue to education as a political activity—is any sense of critical ecclesiology. Contemporary catechetics seems to account only for the process of being socialized into the believing community."[32] That kind of socialization could mean old churchskins.

I agree that the church as institution can rob both catechesis and the catechumenate of their power for personal and ecclesial change. In terms of catechetical theory based on a model of socialization, however, the critique seems misguided. Within the field of sociology is a discipline called the sociology of knowledge. That discipline speaks of the "social construction of reality" in the sense that all culture and language are human products.[33] That includes religious language and institutions. Christians believe in the Spirit's presence in the process of developing religious language and culture; but Catholic Christians do not believe that the scriptural language of an agrarian, peasant culture in Palestine is the only way to speak of our experience of God in Christ. Neither is the philosophical, urban language of Greece and Rome of the first six centuries. Nor are monarchical structures of authority from a medieval culture the only way to construct church institutions.

The sociologists of knowledge also note that later generations interiorize the products of their ancestors' culture and begin to believe that things have "always been this way." In this way, a society *maintains* its values, traditions, meanings. Sociological theorists insist, however, that things were not "always this way." They remind us that at times we are called to *transform* culture and to be as creative as our ancestors. Regarding church forms and structures, the creative Spirit of God and the creative spirits of humans can move us to speak, sing, dance and organize our community life in God in new ways. Socialization theory should not oppress but liberate. It frees us for a critical ecclesiology, theology and every other "ology." Part of our religious crisis today is that language from the first, fifth and sixteenth centuries, and structures from the Roman Empire and medieval fiefdoms don't "tell it like it is" for people who have heard the language of Thomas Jefferson, Elie Wiesel,

Mahalia Jackson, Mohandas Gandhi, Dorothy Day, Cesar Chávez, Flannery O'Connor, Walker Percy, Steven Spielberg or Bruce Springsteen.

Socialization theory also should free catechumens from indoctrination. "The socialization theme in catechesis arises not from a desire to impose understanding on persons in ways they cannot resist, but out of fidelity to its communal nature and out of recognition that faith is not 'transmitted' in teacher-student interactions but within a community concerned with living Jesus' way."[34] We are not about indoctrination into an institution; we are about invitation and initiation into a community that does not simply mouth doctrines from the past but re-sounds (catechizes) God's word anew for the present and future.

> **Conversation Starter:**   Tell of a time in your life when you felt that you were indoctrinated. Who and what helped free you of that indoctrination?

I conclude this chapter with words from a pioneer in catechesis, Johannes Hofinger. At the end of his life, in looking back at the three phases of the twentieth-century renewal of catechetics, he said,

> The specific contribution of the three phases of catechetical renewal can be compared with the different phases we find in the construction of a building. The pioneers did the hard and dirty groundwork [giving us new *method*]. The kerygmatic renewal built up a noble construction on that basis [a return to the biblical *message* of good news], but it still needed a crowning roof. The promoters of the human approach [by exploring the political and cultural *milieu*] provided us with a fine roof but, unfortunately, instead of placing the roof upon the walls, they constructed the roof on the ground beside the edifice; and now it needs a fourth phase for elevating this valuable roof to its proper place upon the walls. . . . The fourth phase will be the result not primarily of scientific research but rather of a new spirit which has its proper source in a deep religious renewal. What we need now in the field of catechesis are not walls and a new roof, but the roof on its right place.[35]

In the next chapter, I shall reassert the unabashed commitment of catechesis for Christian initiation not just to education in religious knowledge but also to personal faith and conversion through hearing God's revealing word proclaimed and lived in a community of faith. Initiation is first and foremost about Hofinger's "new spirit" and the "deep religious renewal," which are the foundation of the house of catechesis.

## Endnotes

[1] Michael Warren, ed., "Catechesis: An Enriching Category for Religious Education," *Sourcebook for Modern Catechetics* (Winona MN: St. Mary's Press, 1983), 385.

[2] In general, I prefer to use the language of the order of initiation unless it proves pastorally impossible. Language that has roots in a different culture can invite us into a different world, beyond the ordinary. Despite its liabilities, the Latin liturgy did open up such a world. Sociologists call this liminality—language and images at the edge of our culture that invite us beyond the edge.

[3] Thomas Groome, *Christian Religious Education* (San Francisco: Harper & Row, 1980), 26–27.

[4] Michael Warren, "Catechetics in Context . . . Later Reflections," in *Sourcebook*, 291.

[5] We nonetheless get the "spiritual bends" moving from that statement to other declarations by our church: "Christ, to be sure, gave his church no proper mission in the political, economic, or social order. The purpose which he set before it is a religious one" (*Constitution on the Church in the Modern World*, #42). That text refers to an earlier statement of Pius XII: "The church can never lose sight of the strictly religious, supernatural goal. The meaning of all its activities, down to the last canon of its code, can only cooperate directly or indirectly in this goal," AAS 38 (1965), 212. Lucien Richard comments that "in many of the Vatican II documents the church does not seem to have overcome an ongoing dualism between body/soul, temporal/eternal, profane/sacred and church/world." "On Evangelization, Culture and Spirituality," *The Catholic World* 234:1, 400, 64.

[6] We explore the vision of catechesis in #75 of the order of initiation in chapter four of this book. I use the term "formal catechesis" for the systematic reflection on our tradition, especially in the Sunday liturgy, as envisioned in #75.1 and #75.3.

[7] Pierre-Andre Liege, "The Ministry of the Word: From Kerygma to Catechesis," in *Sourcebook*, ed. Michael Warren, 315.

[8] "'The obedience of faith' (Romans 16:26; cf. 1:5; 2 Corinthians 10:5–6) must be given to God who reveals an obedience by which we entrust our whole self freely to God" (*Constitution on Divine Revelation*, #5).

[9] Liege, "The Ministry of the Word," 331.

[10] D. S. Amalorpavadass, "Catechesis as a Pastoral Task of the Church," in *Sourcebook*, ed. Michael Warren, 354–55.

[11] Patrick Brennan, "Catholic Evangelization in the United States," in *Catholic Evangelization Today*, ed. Kenneth Boyack (New York: Paulist Press, 1987).

[12] Avery Dulles, "John Paul II and the New Evangelization," *America* 166 (1 February 1992): 52.

[13] For example, "Evangelizing means bringing the good news into all the strata of humanity, and through its influence transforming humanity from within and making it new" (*Evangelii Nuntiandi*, #18). John Paul II adds, "Within the whole process of evangelization, the aim of catechesis is to be the teaching and maturation stage, that is to say, the period in which the Christian, having accepted by faith the person of Jesus Christ as the one Lord and having given him complete adherence by sincere conversion of heart, endeavors to know better this Jesus to whom he has entrusted himself [herself]," *Catechesi Tradendae*, #20.

[14] Michael Warren, "Evangelization: A Catechetical Concern," in *Sourcebook*, 330.

[15] Liege, "The Ministry of the Word," 322–23.

[16] Liege, "The Ministry of the Word," 321.

[17] Aidan Kavanagh, "Critical Issues in the Growth of the RCIA in North America," *Catechumenate* 10 (March 1988): 13.

[18] Ralph Keifer, in *Liturgy 70*, 8 (November 1977): 8, 9.

[19] *Catechesi Tradendae*, #44; "Adult Catechesis in the Christian Community" (Washington DC: USCC, 1990), #18.

[20] "Interview with Balthasar Fischer," *The Chicago Catechumenate* 6 (December 1983): 7–14. That is why the United States bishops approved adapted liturgies for the baptized/uncatechized seeking full communion in the Catholic church (#400–472).

[21] The North American Forum on the Catechumenate has developed a process for inactive Catholics who made a deliberate choice to separate themselves from the church. The dynamics of their evangelization/catechesis (with liturgies) is much like that of the catechumenate, but their stories are significantly different. They deserve a

separate ministry that Forum has called "Re-Membering Church"; for information, write to 5510 Columbia Pike, #310, Arlington VA 22204.

[22] Amalorpavadass, "Catechesis," 340–41.

[23] Thomas Waters and Joseph Leddy, "Religious Education: Focusing the Light of Faith," *The Living Light* 27 (Summer 1991): 304–5 (emphasis added).

[24] Cited by Liege, "Ministry of the Word," in *Sourcebook*, ed. Michael Warren, p. 319.

[25] Groome, *Christian Religious Education*, 27.

[26] Mary Boys, *Educating in Faith* (San Francisco: Harper & Row, 1989), 101. Boys herself prefers the term religious education to catechesis, but her model of education goes far beyond schooling.

[27] John Westerhoff, *Will Our Children Have Faith?* (New York: Seabury Press, 1976), 17.

[28] Mark Searle, "The Pedagogical Function of the Liturgy," *Worship* 55 (July 1981): 343.

[29] Figure 1 is adapted from an unpublished presentation by Barbara O'Dea; figure 2 is a development of an Australian schema by Michael Warren, *The Living Light*, 1987; cf. remarks on "paradigm shifts" in chapter one. Both are used with permission.

[30] Warren, "Catechesis: An Enriching Category," 386 (emphasis added).

[31] Jacques Audinet, "Catechetical Renewal in the Present Situation" in *The Medellín Paper*, ed. J. Hofinger and T. Sheridan (Manila: East Asian Pastoral Institute, 1969), 66–67.

[32] Boys, *Educating in Faith*, 102.

[33] Cf. Peter Berger and Thomas Luckman, *The Social Construction of Reality* (Garden City: Doubleday, 1966); and Peter Berger, *The Sacred Canopy: Elements of a Sociological Theory of Religion* (Garden City: Doubleday, 1969).

[34] Warren, "Catechesis: An Enriching Category," 385.

[35] Johannes Hofinger, "Looking Backward and Forward: Journey of Catechesis," *The Living Light* 20 (Summer 1984): 356, 357.

CHAPTER THREE

# A Map of Catechesis

*All theory, as Michael Polanyi reminds us, "is a kind of map extended over space and time."[1] Thus, I am using the metaphor of map to present a particular way of thinking about a fascinating and complex endeavor, educating religiously.[2]*

• Mary Boys

IN HER BOOK *Educating in Faith*, Mary Boys surveys various approaches to education in the faith by looking at four classic expressions in the field (evangelism, Christian education, religious education, Catholic education/catechesis) with their contemporary modifications. She concludes her study by presenting new movements in the field and outlining her own approach. For each of these expressions of how education in faith occurs, she constructs a "map," defined as "a graphic symbolization of one's milieu" and "a means of conceptualizing the territory."[3]

In drawing that map, Boys asks foundational questions that, with some modifications, are helpful in drawing together the strands of our own survey of catechesis. To clarify the vision of catechesis that I am presenting, and to distinguish it from other disciplines, this chapter shall pose Boys's foundational questions to catechesis in the journey of initiation.

My map of catechesis differs from that of Boys, who prefers the language of religious education. She notes that some catechists resist the language of education and thus neglect some skills that that language makes possible, for example, the skills of teaching, adult learning and curriculum building. I shall try to integrate those skills in my response to her foundational questions.

At the same time, she suggests that the common vision of catechesis is so broad that it seems to include all of pastoral ministry. I agree. My understanding of catechesis is the broad vision of our national catechetical directory;[4] it is also the vision of #75 of the order of Christian initiation with its four dimensions of message, community, worship and witness. We shall explore that vision in chapter four. I identify *formal catechesis* in the catechumenate period largely with the

Christian message, especially as it is proclaimed at worship in the liturgy of the word. We ministers in adult initiation use the term "catechesis" because it is wedded to the term "catechumenate," but our approach is broader than the classic, historical expression of catechesis. This chapter presents the understanding of catechesis generally offered by myself and my fellow team members at institutes offered by the North American Forum on the Catechumenate.

To complete the map of this vision of catechesis, I would make explicit at least two questions that Boys leaves implicit: What is the relationship of catechesis/religious education to evangelization? What is their relationship to life in community, to worship, to mission? I have asked the first question in chapter two and shall ask the second question in chapter four. I am grateful to Mary Boys for her questions, which help to fill in the rest of the map.

## Foundational Questions

Boys identifies two sets of foundational questions under the headings: What does it mean to be religious? What does it mean to educate in faith?

The religious questions are:
1. How is God revealed?
2. What does it mean to be converted?
3. What is faith? Belief? How are faith and belief related?
4. What is the role of theology?
5. What is the relation of religion to culture?

The educational questions are:
1. To what purposes does one educate another (or oneself)?
2. What does it mean to know? To learn?
3. What is the role of the social sciences in religious education?
4. How shall we think of curriculum and teaching?
5. In what way is education a political activity?

Responses to these questions each could take a separate tome. I shall hit the highlights.

> **Conversation Starter:**   As you survey my map of cate-
> chesis, please mark a plus (+) next to the paragraphs with

which you agree and that affirm what you are doing in catechesis, and a minus (−) next to the paragraphs with which you disagree or that challenge you. At the end of the chapter, we shall review these pluses and minuses.

## What Does It Mean to Be Religious?

*1. How Is God Revealed?* Most catechists and catechetical materials show the influence of what George Lindbeck calls the "experiential-expressive" vision of Karl Rahner and Bernard Lonergan.[5] In that vision, God is present and is revealing God's self to all humans as a core *experience* at the preconscious level. Key personal and communal events, especially crises (such as the exodus and Jesus' dying and rising) bring that revelation to self-conscious reflection and expression. William Luipen puts it in more poetic language:

> A child is born and the believer exclaims "God!"
> In health or illness that believer shouts "God!"
> He sexually unites with another person
>     and in his ecstacy the believer calls "God!"
> She is dying and her lips whisper "God!"
> At the rising and the setting of the sun,
>     in the pale light of the moon and the stars,
>     before the roaring of the sea,
>     at the undulating of the wheat stalks,
>     the threat of a storm and the menace of a flood,
>     at the welling up of a spring and the germinating of the seed,
>     the believer exclaims "God!"
> [Conquering in] battle or [suffering] defeat,
>     [living] in poverty or in prosperity,
>     [enduring] injustice or [finding] justice,
>     the religious [person] calls "God!"
> When they are reduced to slavery in Egypt,
>     rise against their oppressors
>     and when they overcome the terrible risk
>     of their revolt against their masters,
>     believers exclaim "God!" . . .
> And when they must go into exile, they complain "God!"
> When they can again return from . . . exile, they joyfully shout "God!"[6]

**Conversation Starter:** Tell of an event in your life or in the life of your family or community that brought you to exclaim "God!"

For Christians, the scriptures are the normative expressions of revelation that interpret all other experiences and expressions. With that understanding, D. S. Amalorpavadass writes,

> The whole of life and all of human history — past, present and future — can be and are *a milieu and sign of revelation*. They have to be interpreted by God's word, and the discovery is from within one's life, group, community, milieu and the world. We have therefore to be attentive to everything and to be in expectation of seeing God and discovering God's designs.[7]

The word of God from the past does not bring to a close God's word in the present and future. That word present in the life of Israel and in Jesus reveals that God always reveals God's self in the lives and events of persons and communities when they are seen in the light of Jesus and Israel. That word calls us to hoist antennae to the presence of God in our own lives and times.

This understanding of revelation moves us from handing on the truths of the faith in a teaching/schooling model to the personalist and biblical vision of Vatican II's *Constitution on Divine Revelation*, which sees revelation not as truths in propositions but as the very self-revelation of God. "The invisible God (cf. Colossians 1:15; 1 Timothy 1:17) out of the abundance of . . . love speaks to [people] as friends (cf. Exodus 33:11; John 15:14–15) and lives among them (cf. Baruch 3:38), so that [God] may invite and take them into fellowship with [the divine]" (#2).

That document also wedded scripture and tradition into one continuous expression of revelation, although it called for a new appreciation of scripture: These writings are expressions of revelation; they do not contain revelation. It is dangerous to identify the medium with the message, to confuse the doctrine, precept, ritual or religious practice with the experience. The mission of catechesis, therefore, is to introduce people to God and not just to texts and doctrines about God. We shall note in chapter four, however, the power of biblical and liturgical images not only to express our experience of God but also to form and shape it.

No expression, no image of our religious heritage *is* God, nor does any capture, exhaust or define the mystery of God. This is not because nothing can be known of God. There is so much, too much to know, that "we see now in a mirror, dimly" (1 Corinthians 13:12). True, Jesus in his humanity is *the* image of God,[8] and his radiance lights up that mirror; but "the world itself could not contain the books that would be written" about him (John 21:25). Therefore, like biblical communities and Christian communities of every time, the Spirit moves us to find words, music, dance, rituals, paintings, sculptures, stained-glass windows, communities and so much else that can invite us to taste a hint of the God who is always revealing in images, signs and symbols.

> **Conversation Starter:** Describe one of your family in one paragraph. What have you learned about capturing, defining or exhausting the mystery of any person or of God?

*2. What Does It Mean to Be Converted?* Those who see revelation as truths and propositions about God often see conversion as learning how Catholic truths differ from Baptist, Lutheran or other denominational truths. Conversion to them means changing churches. Biblical conversion calls people to change gods.

> Return to the LORD, your God,
>     for [God] is gracious and merciful,
> slow to anger, and abounding in steadfast love,
>     and relents from punishing.
> (Joel 2:13)

Key images of conversion in the Hebrew Scriptures are *exodus* from slavery to freedom[9] and *journey* from exile to homecoming.[10] Images in the Christian Scriptures are birth and new creation,[11] and dying and rising.[12] God *is* our freedom, our home, our life and our resurrection.

Although the Catholic Christian experience of conversion sometimes identifies key moments, we do not identify a single "born again" experience when we are "baptized in the Spirit."[13] We have a liturgical year, in part, because we see our lives as an ongoing conversion journey in which we are called to be born again and again, and to die again and again to sin, and to live anew in Christ Jesus.[14] The liturgy invites us into that journey yearly, a journey that is not cyclic (spinning continually in the same circle) but spiral (moving more deeply into God). "Circularity, yes, but not simple repetition. With each turn of the spiral we move upward even as we swing back over our past, for the resurrection of Jesus sprang us out of our two-dimensional prison into a universe with a divinely stamped future."[15] All Christians are sacramentally baptized in the Spirit who makes that journey possible.

Another favorite image of conversion for catechumenate ministers is the journey of any 12-step fellowship. Alcoholics Anonymous insists that alcoholics never are recovered. They always are recovering. Christians never are converted but always are being converted.[16]

Catechists' vision of conversion, especially those ministering in the catechumenate, has been most influenced, as we already have noted, by Bernard Lonergan.[17] He sees conversion as a radical change at every level of the person; a change that affects our grasp of life's meaning (intellectual conversion) and our values (moral conversion); a change that goes beyond ourselves into love of God—an "other-worldly falling in love" (religious conversion).[18] To Lonergan's list of changes, others have added: a change in our ability to express feelings (affective conversion), a change from relating to Christ as historical figure to Christ as Risen Lord (Christic conversion), a change from relating to church as institution to church as community (ecclesial conversion) and a movement from focusing on personal salvation to participating in Christian mission in the world (gospel conversion). Gospel conversion is the "bottom-line" conversion—personal transformation happens within community transformation for the goal of world transformation.

Others have been especially attentive to the social dimensions of conversion.[19] The order of initiation itself speaks of "progressive change of outlook and conduct . . . manifest by means of its social consequences" (#75.2). In particular, the scrutinies name and exorcise not only personal sin but also social sin seen as "the very organization of some level of society systematically [functioning] to the detriment of groups or individuals in the society."[20] For example, that will include the "isms" of racism, sexism, privatism, materialism and consumerism that we did not create but in which we participate. We name that social sin in both church and society.[21]

Let Nathan Mitchell conclude our reflections on conversion:

> If you hope to become part of God's reign, you must let yourself be overtaken, knocked breathless, by a Presence, a Reality you can neither invent nor control. In a word, you have to open your life to the holy violence of

conversion—a tumultuous experience that is liable to leave you feeling drenched and exhausted, as though the sea had seized, swallowed and spat you back alive on shore. Newborn and salted, you sense that nothing looks the same, nothing can ever be the same—for in conversion's crucible a new and terrible beauty is born.[22]

> **Conversation Starter:** Identify changes in your life that you see as Christian conversion. If there was conversion and change, there must have been movement *from* something *to* something (for example, from fear to hope). Name all the "froms" and "tos" of your conversions.

**3. What Is Faith? Belief? How Are Faith and Belief Related?**  The *General Catechetical Directory* distinguishes between "faith" (our relationship with God) and "the faith" (the content of beliefs that express that relationship). Faith as relationship is "the total adherence given by [people] under the influence of grace to God revealing himself" (#36). When, in the gospel of Matthew, the Roman centurion tells Jesus only to say the word and his servant will be healed, Jesus exclaims, "I have not found such faith in Israel." Matthew is telling the members of his community who knew doctrine and law that faith is more than doctrine and law. Faith is more than "the faith," more than beliefs, more than statements about God. In revelation, God does not simply give truths about who God is. God gives God's very self in Jesus. Revelation and faith are relational and personal—selves giving selves.

Faith is more than "intellectual assent to truths on the authority of God revealing," as Vatican I declared. Faith is the surrender in trust of the whole person as a response to God's gift and presence in Christ Jesus. Faith is "the constant confidence that God has given us our life as sheer gift. It is the courage to remain standing in that place, not to be scared by anxiety, fear or lack of trust in that old creation based on justification by works."[23] Faith is the orientation of our whole being, our basic stance, attitude, response and answer to God that gives birth to words, doctrines, theologies or beliefs that express faith. Faith is response to the good news of God's presence and promise in Christ still present to us in the Spirit.

Faith is personal, but that does not mean faith is private. In the Catholic tradition, Jesus is not, ultimately, my personal savior. The Spirit is mediated in and through the community, which is Christ's body. The idea of Jesus as "personal Lord and savior" comes from the fundamentalist tradition, and it certainly is one dimension of faith. But we are saved corporately "in Christ." St. Paul proclaims that 164 times. We enter a relationship with God, in and through the Spirit of the risen Christ, with and through all those who also live in God.

The Catholic intellectual tradition affirms the importance of the clear articulation of our faith (relationship) into *beliefs*. "Beliefs come from believing (faith); and believing is generated in experience."[24] In the words of the national catechetical directory, *Sharing the Light of Faith*, "As the community of believers grows in understanding, its faith is expressed in creeds, dogmas, and moral principles and teachings" (#59). Beliefs are expressions of faith that significant segments of the Christian community find useful. They take many forms: charter documents (the scriptures); official teachings based on scripture and ongoing, Spirit-led experience (doctrines); official teachings so important that to reject them is heresy (dogmas); or official celebrations (liturgy).

Those beliefs and creeds, however, never should become sterile intellectualizing. *Credo* in Latin means "I give my heart to" or "I hereby commit myself." "Belief" in English has roots in the old English word *lief*, expressing preference, and to the German *belieben*—to consider lovely, to like, to wish for, to choose.[25] Beliefs change minds because they change hearts. The original creeds were formulated for the rite of baptism and so were tied to worship. During the second and third centuries they became a standard to guarantee sound doctrine, and in the fourth century, they became theological statements used as a formal test of orthodoxy.[26] "The old creeds were creeds for catechumens, the new creed was a creed for bishops,"[27] i.e., the creeds of the early ecumenical councils.

We need to return to creeds and expressions of beliefs that more readily bring us to surrender ourselves in worship; that includes the ancient creeds. In that regard, the narrative language of the Apostles' Creed is more prayerful than the philosophical language of the Nicene Creed, which is used for Sunday worship. That also includes creeds in contemporary language that touch the minds and hearts of our times. For example, a creed of the Second National Meeting of United Church of Christ Women proclaims:

O God, because you are the source of all life and love and being,
We call you Creator. . . .

Because we know the history of your presence
among your covenanted people and honor their tradition,
We call you Lord. . . .

Because our Savior, Jesus Christ, your obedient child,
knew you intimately and spoke of you so,
We call you Father. . . .

Because you are present in each act of birth
and because you shelter, nurture and care for us,
We call you Mother. . . .

Because you hold us up
and give us strength and courage
when we are weak and in need,
We call you Sustainer. . . .

Because we have known you in our pain and suffering,
We call you Comforter. . . .

Because beyond pain lies your promise of all things made new,
We call you Hope. . . .

Because you are the means of liberation
and the way to freedom,
We call you Deliverer. . . .

Because you have chosen to come among us
and share our common lot,
making the hard choices, suffering and dying;
because you rose victorious, bringing new life,
We call you Redeemer. . . .

Confident that you will hear,
we call upon you with all the names
that make you real to us,
the names which create an image in our minds and hearts,
an image which our souls can understand and touch.
And yet we know that you are more than all of these.
Blessing and power, glory and honor be unto you, our God.
Amen.

We need such contemporary expressions of faith because many of
our dogmas are framed in the culture-bound language of the first six

centuries or in the language of the sixteenth-century Council of Trent.[28] As William Cantwell Smith says, "One's faith is given by God, one's beliefs by one's century."[29] We need language from our century both to clarify and to pray our faith.

> **Conversation Starter:** Individually or in a small group, go through the Apostles' Creed line by line and tell of your experience of God as creator, of Jesus as dying and rising in your life and in the lives of other people, and of the Holy Spirit in your life and in the life of the church.

We also need to express our faith in more than words, more than beliefs. In a very helpful analysis of the content of faith, James Michael Lee names eight overlapping kinds of content: product, process, cognitive, affective, verbal, nonverbal, unconscious and life-style.[30] If faith is the surrender of our whole person, then we need to express our faith in a panoply of ways that touch our whole person, especially when we gather in community. Good liturgy taps into all those contents much better than a good theology class does.

**4. What Is the Role of Theology?** In Anselm's classic phrase, theology is "faith seeking understanding." "Theology is not a case of thinking one's way to faith but of being driven by faith to more deeply understand."[31] Theology is given birth by faith and beliefs by theology. Theology is a process; beliefs are one of its several products.

In the broadest sense, any expression of faith presents a theology (from the Greek *theos* and *legein*, meaning "to speak of God"). El Greco speaks of God in painting. It has been said that in music, Johann Sebastian Bach speaks of a God so unfathomable that he leads us on such an urgent chase that there is almost no time to space the notes, a chase after something that will escape him if he does not hurry. In this broad sense, everyone with faith theologizes.

> Nowhere can we discover and isolate "pure faith." Real faith, living faith, if you will, exists always and only in a cognitive, (more or less) reflective, (more or less) scientific state. . . . Theology comes into play at that very moment when the person of faith becomes intellectually conscious of his or her faith.[32]

When some complain, therefore, about theology contaminating faith, they probably mean that they prefer a different theology.

In the strict sense, however, theology is the systematic reflection and interpretation of faith, usually with the aid of philosophical categories and, today, with insights from the behavioral sciences. The new catechetics relied heavily on theological reflection, especially in Europe prior to Vatican II and increasingly in the Southern Hemisphere subsequent to the Council. Theology continues the healthy Catholic respect for an intellectual tradition and offers methods to interpret and enliven that tradition.

The best of that intellectual heritage of systematic theology frees homilists and catechists from teaching people complicated theology. Good theologians, such as Karl Rahner and Bernard Lonergan, send us to human experience, to our personal and communal stories to discover God. Good theologians send us to wonder and awe, to prayer and worship because they know that all knowledge falls short of mystery. Such a theologian's theologian was Thomas Aquinas who, at the end, fell mute and proclaimed that all his writings were straw. He wrote, "We reach the highest point of our knowledge about God when we know that we know not God."[33]

Later in this book, we shall examine the concerns of those who fear that formal catechesis is flabby on knowledge and "soft on doctrine" if its source is primarily the liturgy of the word. When questioned, their concern usually is that those being catechized should be exposed to Catholic practices and devotions and to morality, by which they often mean not official doctrine or dogma but the theological commentaries on doctrine that fill most catechisms. For most people, however, that is not the best language.

Pioneer catechist F. X. Drinkwater identified four kinds of language: scientific difficult (Thomas Aquinas), scientific simple (the catechism), poetic difficult (Gerard Manley Hopkins) and poetic simple (the "language of the heart" such as the Gettysburg Address and the parables of Jesus—both simple in language and profound in meaning). If we teach as Jesus did, we shall tell stories—the stories of scripture and our stories in homilies/catechesis—full of images and simple poetry interspersed with a few doctrinal one-liners that summarize the meaning of the stories.

But hearts can be both fickle and faithful. We need to think with our cortex and not just with our emotions to distinguish true gods from false, and so we do need, at times, the reflection of systematic theology to critique and interpret the stories and the language of the heart. Theology that frees us to understand God apart from biblical language and worldviews also can free us from apparent obstacles to faith. We need not think of God "up there" or of God massacring all of Israel's foes. We need not present an image of God as a shepherd to people in Chicago or Detroit or Atlanta who never have seen a sheep.

Furthermore, we do our world no service by abandoning careful, reflective thinking about a mystery-laden, ever-expanding universe and what that means about our vision of creation or by neglecting moral reflection on issues involving life-support machines or genetic engineering.[34]

But even a systematic theologian, Karl Rahner, who can churn out the most convoluted language, calls for Drinkwater's simple poetry. Rahner contrasts "primordial words" with the "utility words" of ordinary speech. Primordial words are like "seashells in which can be heard the sound of the ocean of infinity, no matter how small they are in themselves." Words such as "blossom, night, star and day, root and source, wind and laughter, rose, blood, and earth . . . kiss, lightning, breath, stillness" have this power. Such words do not merely speak *about* their objects; rather they speak *them*.[35]

We celebrate Jesus' stories at liturgy, which teaches not in the abstractions of theological commentaries or catechisms but "nondiscursively, richly, ambiguously, elementally"[36] in images and symbols. With most people most of the time, we shall turn not to systematic theologians and catechisms but to El Greco and Johann Sebastian Bach, Flannery O'Connor and Leonard Bernstein and, yes, even to "Peanuts," if we teach as Jesus did.

> **Conversation Starter:**  Read through one of the gospels and look for the images and "primordial" words in the parables and even in the discourses of Jesus. What is one of your favorite stories or parables of Jesus? In one line (doctrine), what does that reveal about Jesus' God?

**5. *What Is the Relation of Religion to Culture?*[37]** We have noted the challenge to express faith in contemporary language and culture. Long ago, St. Augustine said, "God speaks to people in the way people speak to themselves." In our times, what John Paul II said of Africa is true of every culture: "Christ, in the members of his body, is himself African. . . . The church is to be fully African and fully Christian."[38] Because faith does not exist without expression, we must turn to the culture for a language with which to voice our faith. That language is "not just its vocabulary but its thought patterns, cultural idioms, customs and symbols"[39]—what sociologist Clifford Geertz calls a "web of significance."[40] The process of finding that language is called *inculturation*—the adaptation and appropriation of a local culture in ways that do not compromise basic faith in Christ.[41]

Although he was later frustrated by Vatican restraints, one patron saint of inculturation is Matteo Ricci, who attempted to make the church "fully Chinese and fully Christian." A contemporary said of him, "Now he can speak our language fluently, write our script, and act according to our rules of conduct. He is an extremely impressive man—a person of inner refinement, outwardly most straightforward. . . . Amongst people of my acquaintance, no one is comparable to him."[42]

Some prefer the term *incarnation* and insist that we need to discover how God is already incarnate, already enfleshed in a given culture. An anonymous author writes, "Our first task in approaching another people, another culture, another religion is to take off our shoes, for the place we are approaching is holy. Else we may find ourselves treading on another's dream; and, more serious still, we may forget that God was there before our arrival."

Inculturation marked the discussion at the international catechetical study weeks, especially at Medellín (1968), and it was the keyword at the 1985 synod of bishops. The United States bishops wrote, "Within the fundamental unity of the faith, there is room for a plurality of cultural differences, forms of expression, and theological views."[43] That is more easily said than done in this land, which has always been less a melting pot than a stew pot where immigrants in former times and new immigrants and refugees in our times want to keep their own unique taste in the stew. To use John Paul's image, how are catechesis and liturgy in one parish to be fully African American, fully Hispanic, fully Vietnamese and fully Christian?[44] Especially in countries such as the United States, Canada and Australia, which are increasingly becoming stew pots, the challenges to being multicultural (which is much more than being multilingual) are immense. Mark Francis suggests that "the *conscious* goal of helping people from a variety of cultural groups to simultaneously celebrate their faith in the liturgy is a pastoral task without precedent in the history of Christianity."[45]

> **Conversation Starter:** Is your parish/community initiating people from different cultures? What are the tensions and possibilities?

Mary Boys's question "What is the relation of religion to culture?" refers, however, to the political relationship between church and culture in terms of H. Richard Niebuhr's classic *Christ and Culture* and his two polarities of Christ within culture (culture friendly) and Christ against culture (countercultural).[46] Are we cozy with American culture or are we countercultural? We are both. We see the light and shadow sides of our culture and all things human, like psychologist Ernst Becker's humans who are "angels who crap"[47] and Chilean poet Pablo Neruda's "confused impurity of the human condition . . . smelling of lilies and urine"[48] and Viktor Frankl's humans who built the gas chambers of the Third Reich but also went into those chambers with the Lord's Prayer or the *Shema Israel* on their lips.[49] We are friends of the cultural "angels" and enemies of the cultural "demons."

Anthony Padovano makes the striking claims that the future not only of the church in the United States but that of the entire Roman Catholic Church resides in the willingness to listen to angels (messengers) from this land of "life, liberty and the pursuit of happiness." Among these messengers he includes the collegial principle of maximum participation by members of the community, commitments to "liberty and justice for all," the ability to live with pluralism and the openness to dialogue and dissent with the assumption that human reason and freedom are suitable instruments in the search for the good and the true. He concludes, "Americans have something unique and irreplaceable to offer the Catholic church in the areas we have surveyed."[50]

Padovano speaks from the religious left. From the religious center right, George Weigel contends that "Catholic social teaching, in the United States and in Rome, should more fully integrate the experience of the American Founding . . . into its reflection on the quest for human freedom." Our church also has much to learn from a democratic religious tradition with roots in such figures as the first archbishop of Baltimore, John Carroll, with "his optimism about the American experiment; his ecumenism and his commitment to the constitutional separation of church and state; his active role in civic life; his passion for Catholic education; his nonsycophantic loyalty to the Holy See."[51]

Specifically regarding catechesis, those freedom-loving cultural angels should influence the way we minister with adults. Methods of catechesis should respect the dignity of each person's life and history; respect the histories and stories of all communities and cultures; encourage freedom and responsibility to raise questions; invite exploration of the meaning of faith, not just through lectures by "experts" but also in groups in which all have experience to share; and assume that people can move beyond fundamentalism or childhood faith to mature, adult faith.

James DeBoy submits that the most neglected letter in the acronym RCIA is the A. He defines an adult as "a self-directing person who makes informed decisions and accepts the consequences of them."[52] Although the church is not a democracy, might we learn from our culture to use democratic methods that treat people as adults, acknowledging that adults sometimes question, disagree, cause tensions and even leave, but that out of such birth pains come insight, maturity, responsibility, ownership, decisions and actions? Yes, there may be tensions when we treat people as adults in their search for answers that mean something to them. As Thomas Walters notes, "The apparent question is 'How can the community recognize people's right to their own answers and still be faithful to the Catholic tradition?' The more accurate question is 'How can the community *not* do this and still be faithful to the Catholic tradition?'"[53]

**Conversation Starter:** What is your experience of American democratic angels in your church and catechumenate?

Paul VI says that there is also a countercultural thrust in inculturation. He insists that "the split between the gospel and culture is without a doubt the drama of our time" and that what really matters for the church now "is to evangelize human cultures . . . in a vital way, in depth, and right to their very roots . . . [thereby] affecting the standards by which people make judgments, their prevailing values, their interests and thought patterns, the things that move them to action and their models of human living."[54] He implies that there are evil structures, social sin, that need exorcism.

How might catechesis be countercultural, transforming of culture, exorcising the *demons?* We take up that discussion more at length in the next chapter when we see how the catechumenate thrived in the early church when Christianity was countercultural and how it was restored in baptized Europe and in unbaptized Africa, where the gospel is often against culture. In our land, catechesis and gospel are countercultural wherever the demonic "isms" make their home in us: consumerism, privatism, secularism, racism, militarism, sexism, fatalism, hedonism, "me-ism," elitism, authoritarianism.[55] Ralph Keifer claims that those American demons infect Catholics just as much as everyone else:

> We are as American as the pollution of Lake Erie, as beaches littered with flip tops, as houses not 40 years old and in shambles, as health care that sucks away the lifeblood of the destitute. We are as American as the quick solution, the throw-away art, the despising of all that is not obvious, instantly perceptible and of immediate pragmatic relevance. We are as American as the tolerance of all ugliness except human misery, which can be hidden away in nursing homes and ghettos and buried under rhetoric.[56]

Confronting those demons, we take up the challenge of Paul VI: "What matters is to evangelize human culture and cultures."[57]

Many Catholics can resound with the clarion call to conversion by Jim Wallis from the evangelical tradition:

> The Kingdom indeed represents a radical reversal for us. Aggrandizement, ambition and aggression are normal to us and our society. Money is the measure of respect, and power is the way to success. Competition is the character of most of our relationships, and violence is regularly sanctioned by our culture as the final means to solve our deepest conflicts. . . . To put it mildly, the Sermon on the Mount . . . stands our values on their heads.[58]

**Conversation Starter:** What is your experience of American "demons" and "isms" in church and society?

These demons inhabit both civic and ecclesial houses and structures. Demonology renders both a critical sociology and a critical ecclesiology. Jesus seemed more preoccupied with the latter: "The gospel writers do not portray Jesus as excessively concerned with Greco-Roman paganism. Rather, it is the unbelief of his disciples that concerns him. . . . A church or nation may give lip service to faith in Jesus, while actually resting its hope and action on consumer goods or nuclear weapons."[59] I have already noted that in a visit to Central America, Michael Warren discovered that countercultural catechesis means that village catechists are sometimes the first ones murdered. He claims that in our country, catechists are predictable and safe.[60] Perhaps we are not cozy enough with our cultural angels and too cozy with the demons.

Walter Brueggemann chides our fear and embarrassment about using the psalms of lament in liturgy and prayer. "Israel's first speech, which may be replicated by the preacher, is a speech of profound need and hostility. The lament psalms offer Israel's characteristic way of opening a new world by way of daring protest."[61] Bartimaeus, the marginalized blind man, comes to a new life of discipleship precisely in his lament from his helplessness and pain, and follows Jesus down the road (Mark 10:46–53—30th Sunday in Ordinary Time, Year B). That "first speech" is pain or hurt addressed to someone who matters intensely, who continues to matter even in absence:

> How long, O Lord? Will your forget me forever?
>   How long will you hide your face from me?
> . . . . . . . . . . . . . . . . . . . . . . . . . . . . . . . . .
> How long shall my enemy be exalted over me?
> (Psalm 13:1, 2)

At our Forum workshops on Re-Membering Church, we are finding that none of the official liturgies of reconciliation allow people to voice their lament toward God in the church. Some people need to confess sins to the community, but others need to hear the community confess its sins and acknowledge and exorcise the ecclesial demons that exclude those with whom Jesus ate at table. The heart of the psalms of lament is the cry, "Where were you, God, when . . . ?" At Forum, we are developing liturgies of reconciliation and lament that allow people to cry, "Where were you, church, when . . . ?" These liturgies call the church to grieve and to voice sorrow for the absence of those who have been alienated, just as Cardinal Joseph Bernardin of Chicago began his first televised lenten retreat by voicing his sorrow and asking forgiveness for the pain that the institutional church had caused the people of Chicago.

I close this treatment of culture by noting a fascinating study by John Pilch that contrasts both the demons and the angels of the North American culture with those of the Mediterranean culture of the Bible. He names five pairs of eyeglasses through which both cultures can see and value: human activity, human relationships, time orientation, nature and human nature. In many cases, that which is most valued by North Americans is least valued by biblical culture. For example, regarding relationships, middle-class North Americans first value the individual, then the group, then hierarchies; but Mediterranean peasants value first the group, then hierarchies, then the individual. Pilch suggests that Jesus first values the group, then the individual and last the hierarchies.

Regarding human activity, Pilch notes middle-class North American men, who place *doing* first, value work and job, "nose to the grindstone," competition, achievement, control of feelings and upward mobility; they ask "What do you do?" and base their self-esteem on how the world views their accomplishments. Mediterranean male peasants, who place *being* first, value making friends and enjoying life, "sweet idleness," collaboration, expression of inner feelings and resignation to one's fate; they ask "How are you?" and base their self-esteem on how the world views them as persons.

Pilch suggests that Jesus, who places *being-in-becoming* first, values developing all of human potential, beginning new tasks before completing previous tasks, enthusiasm, variety, expression of the full range of emotions, being all things to all people; he asks "What's next?" and bases self-esteem on how many stages of development we have successfully maneuvered.[62]

Pilch's warning: Do not read and interpret the Mediterranean world of the scriptures through the biases of a North American set of eyeglasses.

## What Does It Mean to Educate in Faith?

*1. To What Purposes Does One Catechize Another (or Oneself)?*   The goal of catechesis is conversion. But in surveying intellectual conversion (accepting truths) versus personal conversion (surrender to God), or one-time, "born-again" conversion versus lifetime, continual conversion, we have seen that conversion is not so simple. In a Catholic Christian catechumenate, everything we do is aimed at an evangelization that gives birth to initial conversion and at a catechesis that nurtures ongoing communion and conversion. If information does not invite the catechumen to personal and communal ongoing transformation, it does not belong in the catechumenate. That much is simple.

> **Conversation Starter:**  How would you connect information about church history (for example, the Protestant Reformation) or information about church practice (for example, the rosary or the stations of the cross) to conversion?

Some religious educators see "religious education" as a broader term than "catechesis" because religious education embraces courses of religious study (for example, about Christianity or Islam or Buddhism) that require freedom from the invitation to conversion. Gabriel Moran pleads for an expansive discipline of religious education that crosses the barriers of church and world religions so that "the whole religious community educates the whole religious community to make free and intelligent decisions vis-à-vis the whole world."[63] That brings religious education into the public forum with a language that crosses boundaries, that is free of the jargon of a particular group and that unites diverse groups in transforming the world into a place of justice.

If, however, people move from studying about Catholicism to exploring the possibility of becoming a Catholic, then we unabashedly catechize in a way that invites them to conversion (although we insist on their freedom to say no). We call them to a conversion to God in Christ Jesus in a Spirit-charged community that launches people to work for justice in a better world with their Hindu or Jewish brothers and sisters. We catechize into a Christian community that calls them to a radical conversion into a people in which "there is no longer Jew or Greek, there is no longer slave or free, there is no longer male and female" (Galatians 3:28). With that conversion, they are freed for Moran's "whole religious community to make free and intelligent decisions vis-à-vis the world." In other words, genuine conversion and transformation in our own tradition should free us to unite with other traditions for the transformation of the world.

In catechumenate ministry, we have a saying that summarizes the entire journey of conversion: "Inquirers come from the world community to journey with a catechumenal community, within a larger church community, so that they may return to the world community to live the reign of God." In that context, we quote George Albert Coe, a kindred spirit of Moran, regarding a religious education freed to serve the world: "Shall the primary purpose of Christian education be to hand on a religion or to create a new world?"[64]

Coe and Moran fear that too much Bible distracts from the task of creating a new world. I would agree that bad Bible teaching distracts. But good Bible teaching transforms us with the Spirit of the prophets who call us "to do justice, and to love kindness, and to walk humbly with your God" (Micah 6:8). Good Bible teaching transforms us into Jesus' body broken and blood shed not for the church but for the life of the world. That is conversion, the goal of catechesis, plain and simple. A 70-year-old pastor contends, "The entire life of the parish is about conversion. If something ain't about that, drop it." That's plain, but not so simple.

> **Conversation Starter:** What are the "new worlds" that, according to George Coe, Christian education/catechesis might create? Tell a story of how your Christian education and conversion has changed life in one of those "worlds."

**2. What Does It Mean to Know? To Learn?** If, as we have seen, faith means not just that we know texts and truths about God but that we know God, then knowledge is more than ideas or information. It is what the Hebrews meant by knowing: to know personally and intimately. The closest image of such knowing is the "knowledge" of sexual intercourse. "Intercourse" recalls the exchange explored when we looked at revelation and faith—selves giving selves, God giving self and humans giving selves in return. Just as "word" (*dabar*) for Hebrews means word-deed, so "knowing" (*yada*) means knowledge-action, orthodoxy-orthopraxis (right teaching and right practice). That is how we want to know Christ Jesus and those who are in Christ. In Hebrew, knowing arises from the *lev*— from the heart, the very center of the person.[65]

> To 'know' in the biblical sense is to be touched and changed in one's very being, in one's identity and agency, in who one is and how one lives; knowing is akin to loving, and as such engages the whole person.[66]

In modern terms, James Michael Lee distinguishes *knowledge* (apprehension of the facts, such as biblical events), *understanding* (the "why" of the facts, for example, recognizing which principles apply in making a moral decision) and *wisdom* (the relating of all things to God, for example, the awareness of God's presence in a sacramental world).[67]

In concert with Lee, Thomas Groome prefers the term "wisdom" to "knowledge" as the goal of catechesis; we are in the ministry of "wisdom education" in the tradition of the Wisdom literature (cf. Wisdom 7:22 – 8:1) and the tradition of Matthew, who identifies the Wisdom of God with Jesus (Matthew 23:34, 39 and 11:28 – 30). Groome suggests, first, that people become wise by acting wisely; second, that catechizing for wisdom will encourage imaginative questions that prompt people to see and decide for themselves; third, that wisdom is learned from wise people, both past and present, whose stories and lives we share; fourth, that when people share their reflections on life, they become sources of wisdom for each other; and fifth, that when we share our heritage, we keep "practical wisdom" in mind—for example, when teaching the exodus, we explore how God wants all people to be free and how we are to be in solidarity with the enslaved, the addicted, the outcasts and the outsiders who cry for freedom now.[68]

**Conversation Starter:**   Tell of a wise person in your life.

In light of Groome, Mary Boys envisions religious education as "making accessible the traditions of the religious community and making manifest the intrinsic connection between traditions and transformations."[69] We have just examined how catechesis is forever about transformations. The moorings of catechesis in the Bible and the liturgy reveal its strong roots in the tradition. However, that tradition is not just the Bible and theology or the rites of liturgy. In the presentations of the creed and of the Lord's Prayer in the order of initiation, we hand over (in Latin, *tradere*) the living tradition of faith enfleshed in the community. In these rites, the community hands over its life, its word-deeds, its knowledge-action and its orthodoxy-orthopraxis; and it invites catechumens into that life, that knowledge, that tradition. We make that tradition accessible by sponsoring apprentice Christians into a life, not just into words or rites.

The best access to the tradition for most people is not systematic theology but the language of simple poetry and word-deed. A scripture scholar observes, "If I had anything to do with training a preacher, I would be tempted to spend less time on performance and more time on massive doses of reading in literature, especially poetry, and in the Bible itself."[70]

Walter Burghardt, an extraordinary homilist now in his 70s, bombards us with images that enliven homilies and catechesis:

> Heavy metal and MTV; the computer, car phones and crack; stretch limos or a Volvo with a baby seat; country, pop and rock; "We shall overcome" and "Power to the people"; Michael Jackson and Jesse Jackson; . . . Rambo and Dirty Harry's "Make my day"; a comic-strip Peanuts and a former president's jelly beans; yuppie or Alzheimer's; Walkman and the boob tube; . . . sushi or Mexican beer; Super Bowl or Big Mac; . . . a wasted *Challenger* or a Mars-bound *Discovery*; Wall Street and Häagen-Dazs; the "Army: Be all that you can be" or the Community for Creative Nonviolence; . . . Bill Cosby or "The Young and the Restless"; . . . AIDS and the compassionate Christ; 55 and still counting.[71]

To choose the language of image, story and symbol as the best expression of our own faith is to say that they best deepen someone else's faith. They remain closer to our primary experiences of fear and hope, despair and promise, hurt and healing than the language of systematic theology, which is a few steps removed. When we imagine ourselves into stories, we can imagine ourselves into faith—into the relationship with God experienced by the persons and the communities in the stories.[72] And we can imagine ourselves into lack of faith. So we can see ourselves as a church throwing parties when the lost are found (cf. Luke 15:6, 9, 23), for example, or we can see ourselves as a church grumbling that Jesus eats with sinners (cf. Luke 15:1–3).

William Lynch writes, "The Christian faith should never think of itself as a conceptual bundle of ideas which begs imaginative support from literature and art. . . . This faith is (itself) also a life of the imagination—historical, concrete, and ironic."[73] George Bernard Shaw's Joan of Arc knew that:

> **Joan:**   I hear voices. They come from God.
> **Robert:**   They come from your imagination.
> **Joan:**   Of course. That is how the messages of God come to us.[74]

Joseph Cunneen adds, "I am calling attention to the power of imagination which affects our lives even when, perhaps especially when, we are least aware of it. My claim is that our lives will largely reflect the kind of stories we listen to and tell each other."[75]

By situating formal catechesis in the liturgy of the word with stories of scripture and homily and images and symbols of robust ritual, we offer an environment that most powerfully invites both catechumens and the baptized to faith. Andrew Greeley's research certifies what G. K. Chesterton intuited: "The crucial issue for Catholics is the fact that liturgy drums into our nervous systems 'an imagination that views creatures as metaphors of God, hints of what God is like.' The main thing is not the prose but the poetry of the faith."[76]

> **Conversation Starter:**   What are some of the biblical and cultural images that you shared in a recent catechetical session?

Because the discussion in this book will lead, I hope, to ways to make our scriptural and doctrinal tradition accessible, I want to say a word about "know-how." Mary Boys calls us to make not only *knowledge* (in which she includes reason, contemplation and empathy) accessible but also *know-how.*[77] Do we catechize/homilize in ways that allow people to know just what we know? Or do we use methods and strategies that give adults of maturing faith access to the tradition so that they have the skills and know-how to find and act on its meaning independent of us? Catechetical sessions easily allow such flexible methods, but what about the liturgy of the word, especially the homily, which seems so monological and didactic?

I have had a conversion concerning the preaching of scripture. In the past, I would do the hard work of listening to the signs of our times, to the questions and issues in my community. Then I would study the scriptures to search for issues with which biblical communities struggled. Might past connect to present? If it did, I made the connections with contemporary stories and images; but I did not preach the scripture study or sometimes even much of the scripture text. In Boys's terms, I kept "access" to the tradition to myself, and I "made manifest the connection" between the tradition and our call to conversion today.[78]

In recent years, however, I have been preaching more of the scripture research—what message the authors of the scriptures proclaimed for their communities and why. I do so to give our community members access, to enable and empower them to take up the scriptures on their own and, with the help of scripture scholarship, to discover its energizing power, which they can then connect with their own lives and times. At the end of the Year A course of readings, for example, the community should be sufficiently literate about Matthew that they can bring the word alive in transforming our world as Matthew sought to transform his.

It is hard to preach that way. We have all heard homilies that testified to ponderous studies of texts but contained few "so whats?" for life. It is hard to make the historical tradition accessible—to talk about what the texts *did* mean—and to connect what that means for life today in ways that keep the focus on God's ongoing revelation, not on the texts. But that has forever been the ministry of catechists and homilists. In chapter five and succeeding chapters, we shall look at methods of preparing homilies with groups of Christians so that what the homilist preaches emerges not out of monologue but out of conversation.[79]

In chapter two, I suggested that we include within catechesis the skills of critical thinking and analysis, especially in community, which discern whether our beliefs, ethics and liturgies are hallucinations or hints of the Holy One. Homilists and catechists who commit themselves to that kind of catechesis will *themselves* need both knowledge and know-how not just regarding catechizing the scriptures but throughout their ministries. Mary Boys says that a person who would be a catechist needs knowledge and skills as listener, convener, explorer, lecturer, analyst, inquirer, mediator, facilitator, advocate and evaluator. . . . To provide access means to erect bridges, to make metaphors, to build highways, to provide introductions and commentaries, to translate foreign terms, to remove barriers, to make maps, to demolish blockages, to demonstrate effects, to energize and sustain participation, and to be hospitable.

There is one more skill a catechist needs; for those of us accustomed to the power built into our roles as preacher and teacher, it may be the most critical skill: "sufficient ego strength to 'get out of the way,' not to impose his or her own needs for recognition."[80]

**3. What Is the Role of the Social Sciences in Catechesis?** We already have noted the place of sociology in a socialization model for initiation and catechesis and in naming our cultural angels and demons. And cultural anthropology serves us in the immense tasks of inculturation. If, however, philosophy used to be the bride of theology, and if that marriage has been strained, the "other woman" is doubtless psychology.

My own doctoral dissertation was an interdisciplinary study of the humanistic psychologists, such as Abraham Maslow, and the theology of Karl Rahner. Developmental psychologists also piqued my attention and that of many catechists. These included Erik Erikson and his stage development theory, Jean Piaget on cognitive development and Lawrence Kohlberg's writings on moral development, all of which contributed to theories of faith development, such as those of James Fowler.

Catechists who found "journey" an apt metaphor for conversion migrated toward guides who offered psychological markers, stages and maps for the journey. Catechists who recognized the importance of the religious imagination and the language of image and symbol tapped the insights of psychologists who explore the power of images to help people change. Those who explore the journey within, into the depths of the unconscious, moved toward the psychoanalytic school—Sigmund Freud, Alfred Adler and Carl Jung (the last the more friendly companion for religious types).

The impact of psychological theories upon catechesis is immense. The potential for damage, however, is also immense. Rather than survey the positive impact, I list three areas for possible damage control.

First, psychological theories that focus on the psyche, on foraging around in our past for the sources of present problems, and on "getting in touch with our feelings" can play right into a privatistic, even fatalistic view of life: We can't change anything because we're determined and trapped by our toilet training. We don't change behavior because we're wallowing in our feelings.

Psychology gives us a jargon in which everything is psychologized. The result is what some have called the "triumph of the therapeutic" in North America. In Australia, I came upon a wonderful radio talk show hostess, Caroline Jones, who had been a catechumen. In this very secularized land, she interviews people who grapple in nonreligious language with religious questions in their "Search for Meaning" (the program's title). The show's producer, David Millikan, commented after a trip to North America to observe talk shows:

> In Australia, we are, to a large extent, free of the psychologizing of belief. It is here that the difference between Australians and what I heard in North America is very clear. . . . I long to hear the words of people who do not know the language of recent psychology. That ease of expression seems to bring with it a loss of innocence.[81]

He speaks also of the politicization of belief by politicians who quote the God of religious evangelicals (a phenomenon rare "down under"). He concludes that North Americans say more than they know about God.

What Americans say in the language of therapeutic psychology or pentecostal evangelism often reveals a religious privatism in which we look to Jesus as our personal savior from all our neuroses. Listen for psychobabble and Bible-babble on Donahue, Oprah, Sally or Geraldo with its resident psychologists on stage and infallible "experts" on scripture in the audience.[82] But also check out a catechumenate session. Often you will hear "Put yourself in the scripture story" (the return of the prodigal son, for example). "Who are you—the child returning, the parent embracing or the elder brother sulking? How are you *feeling*? How is what is going on *within* you like what was going on within the characters in the story?" In a culture of psychobabble, catechumens can fall into and expect a psychological, emotive, often individualistic and fundamentalist hearing of scripture. Chapter five will discuss this issue further.

Second, a preoccupation with self in a narcissistic culture interprets and evaluates everything through the lens of individualistic self-fulfillment. John Pilch argues,

> American culture is one of the most highly individualistic cultures that has ever existed on the face of this planet. . . . The American television family (Roseanne, the Simpsons, the Cosby Show) gravitates around the individualism of each member. Even the United States bishops defined the American family as "a community of individual persons joined by human love and living a community life that provides for the greatest expression of individualism" (*Human Life in Our Day*, 1968).[83]

Individuals often come to catechumenates as they come to everything else—to fulfill self and to find out who they are. They search for identity, not for meaning or vocation, even though they may speak of spirituality and the life of the Spirit. That is "the privatization and individuation of spirituality; it is the opposition of the spiritual life to the social/political life. . . . In a narcissistic spirituality, the divine is located within the personal history and geography of the individual."[84] Bernard Lee suggests that this psychological approach reinforces individualism in some parish programs (including some catechumenates).

> An earlier fascination with Jungian typologies (the Myers-Briggs) is now largely relocated in the Enneagram. Both of these are useful interpretative schemes, but neither calls us to engage, for example, in issues of social justice or ecology. Self-help strategies and support groups have had significant influence on U.S. Catholic spirituality. There is no question about the goodness and helpfulness of these activities. But they do not provide a structure for the public social life [of small Christian communities].[85]

The paradox is that the originators of these psychological theories often did not mean them to be exclusively self-focused. Erik Erikson suggests that we resolve the crisis of identity when we go beyond ourselves through intimacy with another and through vocation to others in "public social life." Viktor Frankl insists that we fulfill self in self-transcendence—going beyond self through the gift of love to another who gives our self back to us as gift.[86] He insists that seeking self is precisely the way not to find self. Jesus, too, said something about losing self to find self (Mark 8:35).

Sociologist Tex Sample claims that those who seek themselves already are frustrated and know, at least intuitively, that they fail in their quest. The "me generation," which he places on the "cultural left," emerged from the failed dreams of the 1960s alienated by society's core institutions, including the church. Without those institutions, he contends, the self is imprisoned.

> To be alienated from core institutions, then, to see oneself as different from, to define oneself over against, is to lose relationships that are not only external but internal. The result is to lose the emotional charges of these relationships and to suffer a social and personal gulf between the self and the institutionalized framework of the wider society.[87]

When that alienation happens, we lose our capacity to feel and to find self through others. Therefore, the church as institution will not assault people for privatism; it will offer them fellow travelers to support them on their journey of finding self in community.[88]

Even groups as groups can gather primarily for self-fulfillment. We live in a culture of self-help groups, some of which are turned inward on themselves and not outward toward service, vocation and justice/liberation in the wider community.[89] (I call them "navel observatories.") That culture can conflict with church communities that are defined by self-giving, self-transcendence and self-sacrifice—call it mission.

Third, naming stages of development perhaps is helpful if we see them as models, lenses, ways of looking at ourselves with greater insight. In our competitive culture, these stages can become destructive if we make them norms by which we judge each other. If we accept these stages uncritically, we begin to look at them as ladders by which we climb toward perfection. Such a model contradicts the biblical understanding of how we become our true selves. In the desert, the Hebrew people learn that they are imperfect, former slaves who never must think that they have made themselves wealthy by their own power and strength (cf. Deuteronomy 8:11–20). In the desert, Jesus learns that he is a suffering servant, not a wonder worker nor the ruler of all the kingdoms of the world. In our "deserts," we find not perfection, "but God proves his love for us in that while we still were sinners Christ died for us" (Romans 5:8). At the end of the catechumenate period, we celebrate not a rite of perfection but of election—God's unconditional, free election and choice of people who know that only the ungifted can be gifted, only the powerless empowered, only the wounded healed, only the empty filled and only the imperfect perfected.

Catechists often say "holiness means wholeness." Catechesis that echoes Jesus' good news of liberty to captives, sight to the blind and freedom to the oppressed can heal the spiritually captive, blind and oppressed at levels untouched on the psychiatrist's couch. Our sacraments of reconciliation and healing also can celebrate spiritual health. Union with the Spirit often brings health and healing to the human psyche and spirit. But if it does not, the last word is not the psychologist's diagnosis. The last word is God's word of acceptance. Most of us know some very fractured, wounded people who are gripping testimony to God's acceptance of our brokenness.[90] We continue to recognize Jesus in the breaking of the bread of all those who are his broken body.

> **Conversation Starter:**  In your experience of the catechumenate, have you observed too much focus on feelings, therapy and inner psychological trips? Too much focus on self-fulfillment and not on mission? Too much focus on psychological development and perfection of the healthy and not on God's love and election of the unhealthy?

**4. How Shall We Think of Curriculum and Teaching?**  When looking earlier at the process of catechesis as socialization, we cited multiple institutions that initiate new members into the life of the community. Lawrence Cremin writes about an "ecology" of education that happens through many resources, each with its own curriculum: families, schools, museums, factories, camps, churches, television, film, day-care centers, newspapers and self-help groups.[91]

In her courses in religious education, Mary Boys asks participants to design a curriculum for adults inquiring into Catholicism. I have taken their list of suggestions and grouped them under the four dimensions of catechesis in the period of the catechumenate: message, community, worship and witness.[92]

*1. Proclaiming the Message*

Take learners through some evangelizing event such as a parish mission, a Cursillo, a preached retreat, Marriage Encounter, a Life in the Spirit seminar.

Lavish the learners with stories. The core stories, of course, are from the scriptures, especially the gospels: the parables of Jesus, the stories of healing, the passion story. One should find a variety of ways to hand them on: learners telling them in their own words; acting them out; experiencing them imaginatively, as in Ignatian contemplation; seeing classic paintings or seeing stained-glass windows; exploring the findings of scripture scholars. (I would add that the primary place that the stories are passed on is the liturgy of the word.)

Analyze a systematic theologian (Augustine, Thomas Aquinas or Karl Rahner, for example) as a way to integrate the different elements of the faith. Or study a popular work such as *The Dutch Catechism* or Richard McBrien's *Catholicism*.

Explore the expressions of Catholic imagination: Gregorian chant, medieval cathedrals, Dante's poetry, Michelangelo's paintings and sculptures, for example.

Study a major event in the tradition (Vatican II or the Council of Nicea for example) with an eye to seeing how the church finds its way to its teaching. See the historical circumstances and doctrinal debates that occurred before, during and after. Perhaps bring the event alive by re-creating the debates.

Invite the local bishop for a catechetical session. Follow up on the concerns of the National Conference of Catholic Bishops.

Do case studies on moral questions. Discuss first, then explore biblical, systematic and magisterial contributions to these questions. Explore what "prudence" is in these concrete cases.

Engage in an exercise in dreaming. Try to visualize how one's city might look if the reign of God were actualized.

*2. Developing Community*

Explore the lives of the saints; take on a patron saint.

Chart out the local story. Have members of the local community tell their own stories of conversion and faith. Have an elderly member tell the story of the parish.

Help the catechumens discover our commonalities with other Christians by studying their church buildings and their self-descriptions, by attending a service or by speaking with their priests or ministers.

Pray. Learn forms of prayer, such as the Jesus Prayer or the rosary. Find a spiritual director. Read one of the classics of Western spirituality, such as *The Cloud of Unknowing* or the writings of Teresa of Avila.

Learn the international face of Catholicism. Become a sister parish with a parish in Africa or Asia. Explore Eastern prayer forms or the Latin American *comunidades de base*.

Study a tradition of spirituality as it is concretely embodied, such as a visit to a monastery or a Catholic hospital.

Tap the rich life experience of the local community to see the variety of ways that Christian life is concretely lived: the experience of the elderly, the parents of a large family, the health professional, a local politician.

Find sponsors with whom learners can share, from whom they can seek guidance, whom they can befriend and whom they can imitate.

### 3. Celebrating Liturgy

Lavish the learners with rituals, official and unofficial: eucharists, liturgies of the word, vespers, penance services. Make full use of sacramentals, whether ashes, anointings, lighted candles or pilgrimages. Let the catechumens experience the rituals first; only afterward reflect on the cluster of meanings.

### 4. Witness to Faith

Have the catechumens do some work of charity, preferably on an ongoing basis. Invite them to volunteer in a soup kitchen or a nursing home.

Encourage the catechumenate to do some work of social justice: Help in community organizing, join in a peace march, write their representative in congress.

Accompany a minister through the rounds of his or her work, such as a eucharistic minister visiting shut-ins, a deacon in the process of preparing a homily.

Engage in an exercise in reading the signs of the times. Take a newspaper and focus on a current story, investigate it, discuss it with an eye to what resources faith has to bring to it. Give witness in that area.[93]

Obviously, this is a curriculum of possibilities. From this list, we develop an appropriate curriculum for each catechumen. The list assures catechists that curricula do not end at the classroom door. In a catechumenate, most of what appears on this list happens outside classrooms, and even the more cognitive dimensions would better take place in a home or more comfortable environment than at school desks. Note the weight this list gives to items under "proclaiming the message." In a catechumenate, much of that will happen in "celebrating worship" during the liturgy of the word, followed by significant time given to breaking open that word.

Spiritually and theologically, the vision of the catechist's role is that of a minister of the word who is called to evangelize/catechize with good news and to initiate new members into the community through socialization. In terms of educational methods, the catechist ministers from a vision that respects how adults learn. Malcolm Knowles is the father of the term "andragogy"—from the Greek *aner* (with the stem *andr-*), which means "man" (Greek has no term for "adult woman") and *agogus*, meaning "leading"; hence "the art and science of helping adults learn." Figures 3a and 3b present a schema that indicates how Knowles distinguishes teacher-directed learning from self-directed learning (andragogy).[94]

A caution: Knowles writes about the discipline of adult education, not about adult religious education, and certainly not about adult initiation focused on the liturgy of the Word. But the wonderful, robust images and symbols of the liturgy plus the dialogical methods of both homilist and catechist should catechize adults in ways that express and deepen their experience as adults, perhaps more so than Knowles can do in a classroom.

**Conversation Starter:**   Using figures 3a and 3b, evaluate your catechumenate in terms of teacher-directed learning and self-directed learning.

**Figure 3a**

| ASSUMPTIONS | | |
|---|---|---|
| **ABOUT** | **TEACHER-DIRECTED LEARNING** | **SELF-DIRECTED LEARNING** |
| **Concept of learner** | Dependent personality | Increasingly self-directed personality |
| **Role of learner's experience** | To be built on more than used | A rich source for learning |
| **Readiness to learn** | Varies with levels of maturation | Develops from life tasks and problems |
| **Orientation to learning** | Subject-centered | Task- or problem-centered |
| **Motivation** | External rewards and punishments | Internal incentives Curiosity |
| **Time Perspective** | Postponed application | Immediacy of application |

**5. In What Way Is Education a Political Activity?**   This dimension of catechesis has been explored already in this book: in our survey of catechesis and the increased awareness of its cultural/political dimension; in our vision of a socialization that does not indoctrinate but liberates for a critique of all societal and ecclesial structures and language; in our vision of social conversion that seeks to transform society into the place of God's justice and freedom; in our scrutinizing of cultural angels, which we celebrate, and demons, which we exorcise.

In addition, let us affirm with Michael Warren:

> If there has been any quantum leap in modern catechetics, it has not been one from content to person, but rather one to a recognition of the relation of catechesis to political realities and to a realization that the beloved community has to attend to systemic evil found in social and political structures.[95]

**Figure 3b**

| PROCESS ELEMENTS | | |
|---|---|---|
| **ELEMENTS** | **TEACHER-DIRECTED LEARNING** | **SELF-DIRECTED LEARNING** |
| **Climate** | Formal authority-oriented Competitive Judgmental | Informal Mutually respectful Consensual Collaborative Supportive |
| **Planning** | Primarily by teacher | By participative decision making |
| **Diagnosis of needs** | Primarily by teacher | By mutual assessment |
| **Setting goals** | Primarily by teacher | By mutual negotiation |
| **Designing a learning plan** | Content units, course syllabus, logical sequence | Learning projects Learning contracts Sequenced in terms of readiness Problem units |
| **Learning activities** | Transmittal techniques Assigned readings | Inquiry projects Independent study Experimental techniques |
| **Evaluation** | Primarily by teacher | By mutual assessment of self-collected evidence |

For some, the word "political" raises red flags and conjures images of the machinations of popes and bishops in civil affairs or of churches and clergy blurring the separation between church and state in our times—from ayatollahs in Iran to priests in Nicaragua. Sometimes the encroachment into religion comes from the side of the state. In 1992, George Bush informed religious broadcasters, "In the Persian Gulf we fought for good versus evil—it was that clear to me—right versus wrong, dignity against oppression. . . . I want to thank you for helping America, *as Christ ordained*, to be a light to the world."[96]

"Politics" comes from the Greek *polites*—citizen. In its broadest meaning, politics is the life of the citizenry, the life of the people. In that sense, the gospel calls all of us to political activity on behalf of our nation and world, our church, on behalf of all peoples. This is especially true if we hear the scriptures as political documents about the Jews enslaved in Egypt and exiled in Babylon and oppressed in the Roman Empire.[97]

However, even in that sense, there is hardly a "quantum leap" in practice. There may be leaps in documents. There are leaps in some Latin American base communities, many of whom gather the oppressed (as Jesus gathered the oppressed) who can hear God's promise of liberty and freedom precisely because they know their oppression (as did the people who first heard Jesus). Much of North America is not that. Like Matthew's community, we are not physically impoverished; we are spiritually impoverished, but often we don't know it (cf. Matthew 5:3). I recently visited five economically impoverished nations in Africa and three in Asia. I met with many small Christian communities, but unlike the Latin American base communities, these communities usually were unable to make the leap to political activity. Instead, some studied documents from their bishops about the paralyzing effects of political and economic oppression. That is the reason these oppressed people cannot make the leap—they are paralyzed and terrified.

In our country, we do a disservice, perhaps, by limiting our political activity to massive issues such as national welfare and health-care systems or global hunger. They demand attention, but we also need to raise the consciousness of catechumens about local efforts, such as care and compassion at food banks and hospices for persons with AIDS, systemic change in care for the environment, provisions for housing, efforts to free neighborhoods from the purveyors of drugs and the reverence for life as a "seamless garment."[98] I find that many of these issues, especially care for the ecology, can unite people of different political persuasions.

It is for such action in the name of Jesus Christ that we enable and empower catechumens, not first for liturgical or catechetical ministries, not even for sponsoring new catechumens. Once again, to paraphrase George Albert Coe: Our ultimate purpose is not to hand on a religion or to turn this year's catechumen into next year's sponsor but to create a new world. Our hope is that of sociologist John Coleman: "The tradition of biblical religion seems the most potent symbolic resource we possess to address the sense of drift in American identity and purpose."[99] George Weigel insists that our principal contribution as a church to the new world that Coe envisions is this biblical tradition and "the core tenets of Catholic social ethics—personalism, the common good, subsidiarity, solidarity"[100]—when we apply our heritage to international issues of peace and the environment, national issues of the economy, and to such local and neighborhood issues as housing and crime.

In concluding our reflections, let Nathan Mitchell's words summon us to a "political activity" that unites our world to God's reign:

> There is little in Jesus' message or ministry to suggest he was interested in reforming religious practices or initiating new ones. Instead, Jesus seems to have been completely preoccupied by the paradox of God's presence—the *arrival* of God's forgiveness which, simultaneously, signals God's *disappearance* into people, into the liberating practice of justice and mercy. . . . Christian worship . . . rehearses the *end* of religion, announces the arrival of that "new and more cheerful order of things" which Jesus called "reign of God."[101]

**Conversation Starter:** Tell stories of how catechumens and neophytes have taken up "political activity," especially in their neighborhoods and civic community.

I offer you this map of catechesis. It is my map. It charts only some of the terrain that I have traveled with many fine companions. It may at times leave what has been the more limited terrain of catechesis and cross over into turf occupied, for example, by those with an expansive and more ecumenical vision of religious education. I trust that they will not see this as encroachment of boundaries but as an invitation to "cultural exchange." We have much to learn from each other.

Maps are unfinished. On the day on which I write these lines, astronomers report that they have discovered a new planet 30,000 light years away, outside our solar system. That will send the space cartographers back to their drawing boards. Perhaps if we minister with the radical vision of a church that evangelizes, catechizes and initiates toward the ongoing conversion of all who call ourselves church, we shall discover something new outside our system—on God's territory, which confounds all of our maps.

> **Conversation Starter:** Review your pluses and minuses with your catechumenate team.

## Endnotes

[1] Michael Polanyi, *Personal Knowledge* (New York: Harper & Row, 1964), 4.

[2] Mary Boys, *Educating in Faith* (San Francisco: Harper & Row, 1989), ix.

[3] Boys, *Educating in Faith*, viii, ix.

[4] *Sharing the Light of Faith: National Catechetical Directory for Catholics of the United States* (Washington DC: USCC, 1979), cf. #213.

[5] Bernard Lonergan offers six theses articulating his position in *Method in Theology* (New York: Herder and Herder, 1972), 101–24. George Lindbeck critiques this approach in *The Nature of Doctrine* (Philadelphia: The Westminster Press, 1984), 30–45.

[6] William Luipen, *What Can You Say About God?*, trans. Henry Koren (New York: Paulist Press, 1971), 4–5.

[7] D. S. Amalorpavadass, "Catechesis as a Pastoral Task," in *Sourcebook for Modern Catechetics*, ed. Michael Warren (Winona MN: St. Mary's Press, 1983), 354–55.

[8] Cf. Colossians 1:15.

[9] Cf. Deuteronomy 7:7–11.

[10] Cf. Isaiah 40–55.

[11] Cf. John 3:1–21.

[12] Cf. Romans 6:1–12.

[13] A recent study, however, concludes that unlike the private "born again" experience of Pentecostal churches, the early church expected a true *experience* of the gifts

of the Spirit with initiation into the community. The experience was ecclesial and sacramental. "It should be obvious from our study that the New Testament church and the major streams of the church's tradition for the first four centuries considered Christian initiation itself to be the 'baptism in the Holy Spirit,' with all that meant of conferring the fullness of the Spirit, including charisms." With Paul I would focus on the gift of charity and not on speaking in tongues. Kilian McDonnell and George Montague, *Christian Initiation and Baptism in the Holy Spirit* (Collegeville: The Liturgical Press, 1991), 337.

[14] Cf. Mark Searle, "The Journey of Conversion," *Worship* 54 (January 1980): 35–55.

[15] John Breslin, "Introduction," in *The Substance of Things Hoped For,* ed. John Breslin (New York: Doubleday, 1988), xii–xiii.

[16] Cf. James B. Dunning, "Dynamics of Evangelization in the Catechumenate" in *Catholic Evangelization Today,* ed. Kenneth Boyack (New York: Paulist Press, 1987), 111–20.

[17] Lonergan, *Method,* 130–31.

[18] Lonergan, *Method,* 240.

[19] Cf. James B. Dunning, "The Social Dimensions of Conversion" in *Conversion in the Catechumenate,* ed. Robert Duggan (New York: Paulist Press, 1984), 23–42.

[20] Richard McBrien, *Catholicism* (Minneapolis: Winston Press, 1980), 983.

[21] Some complain, however, that in their present form, the scrutinies are very weak. In the homily and in the litany, we need to name more clearly the personal and social sin from which we need exorcism. For further reflections on conversion in adult initiation, see Robert Duggan, ed., *Conversion in the Catechumenate* (New York: Paulist Press, 1984); James B. Dunning, *New Wine, New Wineskins* (New York: Wm. H. Sadlier, Inc., 1981), 20–26; and James B. Dunning, "Conversion: Being Born Again and Again and Again," *Catholic Update,* April 1988.

[22] Nathan Mitchell, "The Kingdom Journey of Justice," *Modern Liturgy* 18 (October 1991): 8.

[23] This is Robin Scroggs's description of Pauline faith in Robin Scroggs, *Paul for a New Day* (Philadelphia: Fortress Press, 1977), 26.

[24] Richard R. Niebuhr, *Experiential Religion* (New York: Harper & Row, 1972), 69.

[25] Cf. William Cantwell Smith, *Faith and Belief* (Princeton: Princeton University Press, 1979), 76.

[26] Cf. Berard Marthaler, *The Creed* (Mystic CT: Twenty-third Publications, 1987), 2–16.

[27] C. H. Turner, quoted in J. N. D. Kelly, *Early Christian Creeds* (Essex, U.K.: Longman, 1972), 205.

[28] That language can be confusing. For example, the Greeks with a philosophical understanding of person decreed that Christ is a divine person but not a human person. To moderns with a psychological understanding of person (as personality), that probably communicates heresy, because it implies that Christ is not fully human.

[29] Cited by Charles Hefling, *Why Doctrines?* (Cambridge MA: Cowley Publications, 1984), 23.

[30] James Michael Lee, *The Content of Religious Instruction* (Birmingham: Religious Education Press, 1985).

[31] Brennan Hill, "Fundamentals of Religious Education: Theology," PACE 17, 114.

[32] McBrien, *Catholicism*, 25–26.

[33] *De Potentia*, 7, 5, ad. 14.

[34] Such reflection often is more appropriate for catechesis after initiation, but some catechumens may want to explore these questions with the tools of systematic theology. This is best done not in the homily but in the catechetical session after dismissal.

[35] Karl Rahner "Priest and Poet," *Theological Investigations* 3 (Baltimore: Helicon, 1967), 296, 298–99.

[36] Aidan Kavanagh, "Teaching through the Liturgy," *Notre Dame Journal of Education* 5 (Spring 1974): 41.

[37] Cf. John Paul II, *Catechesi Tradendae*, #53.

[38] Cited by Archbishop James Lyke in the foreword of *Faith and Culture* (Washington DC: USCC, 1987), 1. In the introduction to the same book, Armantina Pelaez adds, "Every person is a story of God; so too is every race, culture, and ethnic group," p. 3.

[39] *Sharing the Light of Faith*, #194.

[40] Clifford Geertz, "Thick Description: Toward an Interpretive Theory of Culture," in *Interpretation of Cultures* (New York: Basic Books, 1973), 5.

[41] For a fine presentation of issues of inculturation, see Robert Schreiter, *Constructing Local Theologies* (Maryknoll NY: Orbis Books, 1986).

[42] J. D. Spence, *The Memory Palace of Matteo Ricci* (New York: Viking Penguin Inc., 1984), 255.

[43] "To Teach as Jesus Did," 1972.

[44] Cf. "What We Have Seen and Heard: A Pastoral Letter on Evangelization from the Black Bishops of the United States" (Cincinnati: St. Anthony Messenger Press, 1984); and the pastoral letter of the United States bishops, "The Hispanic Presence: Challenge and Commitment," 1983. For the difficulties of inculturation in our country, cf. Allan Deck, "The Crisis of Hispanic Ministry: Multiculturalism as an Ideology," *America* 163 (July 21, 1990): 33–36.

[45] Mark Francis, *Liturgy in a Multicultural Community* (Collegeville: The Liturgical Press, 1991), 49.

[46] H. Richard Niebuhr, *Christ and Culture* (New York: Harper & Row, 1951).

[47] Ernest Becker, *The Denial of Death* (New York: Free Press, 1973).

[48] Pablo Neruda, *The Heights of Macchu Picchu* (New York: Farrar, Straus & Giroux Inc., 1966).

[49] Viktor Frankl, *Man's Search for Meaning* (New York: Washington Square Press, 1963).

[50] Anthony Padovano, "American History and Catholic Ecclesiology," *New Catholic World* 230 (May/June 1987): 116.

[51] George Weigel, *Freedom and Its Discontents* (Washington DC: Ethics and Public Policy Center, 1992), 47, 132.

[52] James DeBoy, *Getting Started in Adult Religious Education* (New York: Paulist Press, 1979), 22.

[53] Thomas Walters, "Catechesis and the Community of Faith," *PACE* 17:132.

[54] *Evangelii Nuntiandi*, #20.

[55] For a masterful approach to naming the demonic in our times, see Walter Wink, *Unmasking the Powers* (Philadelphia: Fortress Press, 1986).

[56] Ralph Keifer, "Christian Initiation: The State of the Question," *Worship* 48 (September 1974): 392–404.

[57] *Evangelii Nuntiandi*, 19.

[58] Jim Wallis, *The Call to Conversion* (New York: Harper & Row, 1981), 12.

[59] Kathleen Fischer and Thomas Hart, *Christian Foundations* (New York: Paulist Press, 1986), 104; Jesus does seem outraged by economic and political injustice in the empire.

[60] Michael Warren, *Faith, Culture and the Worshiping Community* (New York: Paulist Press, 1989), 69–70; cf. chapter one in this book, note 4.

[61] Walter Brueggemann, *Finally Comes the Poet* (Minneapolis: Fortress Press, 1989), 52–53.

[62] John Pilch, *Introducing the Cultural Context of the New Testament: Hear the Word Vol. 2* (New York: Paulist Press, 1991), 98, 123–25.

[63] Gabriel Moran, *Religious Body* (New York: Seabury Press, 1974), 150.

[64] George Albert Coe, *What Is Christian Education?* (New York: Charles Scribner's Sons, 1929), 29.

[65] "Purity of heart" for Matthew (5:8), therefore, means not sexual chastity but having our center centered, our whole life focused on and responding to God. A better translation would be "single-hearted."

[66] Thomas Groome, "Wisdom in Christian Faith," *Catechist's Connection* 7:69, 1.

[67] James Michael Lee, "Forward to the Basics," *Catechist* 20 (April/May 1987): 50–51. Lee adds that to stimulate religious wisdom, catechists should turn especially to "extrarational" cognitive content found in symbols, myths and dreams.

[68] Groome, "Wisdom," 2.

[69] Boys, *Educating in Faith*, 214. Michael Warren submits that some limit religious education to the study of "religious questions, including Christian ones, not so much

from the point of religious commitment, which is the perspective of catechesis, but from that of intellectual inquiry" (*Faith, Culture*, 127). In this definition, Boys clearly sees conversion and transformation as the goal of religious education.

[70] Donald Senior, "Scripture and Homiletics: What the Bible Can Teach the Preacher," *Worship* 65 (September 1991): 386–98.

[71] Walter Burghardt, "Preaching as Art and Craft," *The New Dictionary of Sacramental Worship* (Collegeville: The Liturgical Press, 1990), 973.

[72] John Coulson, our premier Newman scholar, claims, "The real assent we make to the primary forms of religious faith (expressed in metaphor, symbol and story) is of the same kind as the imaginative assent we make to the primary forms of literature." If we make a real assent in faith, we must use our imagination. John Coulson, *Religion and Imagination: In Aid of a Grammar of Assent* (New York: Oxford Press, 1980), 11.

[73] William Lynch, *Christ and Apollo* (New York: Sheed and Ward, 1960).

[74] George Bernard Shaw, *Saint Joan*. Cited by Justin J. Kelly, "Absence Into Presence: A Theology of Imagination," Warren Lecture Series in Catholic Studies, no. 16. Available from the Warren Center, University of Tulsa.

[75] Joseph Cunneen, "The Catholic Imagination: Fiction and Film," Warren Lecture Series in Catholic Studies, March 10, 1991, p. 3; available from the Warren Center, University of Tulsa. Cunneen complains, "The stories most North Americans hear most often are those minidramas that are TV commercials, which in one minute succeed in projecting their consistent theme that happiness can be achieved and tragedy averted through the use or consumption of specific goods or services."

[76] "The Secret We Keep to Ourselves," editorial in *America* 164 (May 4, 1991): 484. For the importance of imagination in communicating the Christian heritage, cf.: in theology, Julian Hartt, *Theological Method and Imagination* (New York: Seabury Press, 1977); in Christian life, Kathleen Fischer, *The Inner Rainbow* (New York: Paulist Press, 1983); in ministry, Urban Holmes, *Ministry and Imagination* (New York: Seabury Press, 1981); in ethics, Philip Keane, *Christian Ethics and Imagination* (New York: Paulist Press, 1984); in religious sociology, Andrew Greeley, *The Religious Imagination* (New York: Wm. H. Sadlier, Inc., 1981).

[77] Boys, *Educating in Faith*, 207–10.

[78] Boys, *Educating in Faith*, 208–9.

[79] Having noted the dangers of scholarly theorizing, I therefore disagree with Mary Collins, who states that homilies/catechesis should not take up "issues of historical-critical method, even while the catechist-narrator should be critically informed." Mary Collins, "Becoming a Priestly People," *Catechumenate* 13 (May 1991): 4. For further reflections on my approach to preaching, see my "Diary" column in *Catechumenate* 12 (July 1990): 40–41.

[80] Boys, *Educating in Faith*, 209.

[81] David Milliken in Caroline Jones, *The Search for Meaning* (Crows Nest, New South Wales: ABC Enterprises, 1989), 3.

[82] *Time* comments on the talk shows: "Stories of individual pain and grief are now hot-button issues. Conversation is replaced by political cant and psychological bromides. No personal story is too outlandish for nationwide consumption, no private emotion safe from public exploitation," "Running Off at the Mouth," *Time* 138: 15, 79.

[83] John Pilch, "The Year of Mark: Mediterranean Groups and American Individuals," *Modern Liturgy* 18 (April 1991): 35. Pilch adds, "Such individualism is totally lacking in the Bible as it is in all the Mediterranean world."

[84] Lucien Richard, "On Evangelization, Culture, and Spirituality: A Post–Vatican II Perspective," *The Catholic World* 234 (March/April 1991): 65; also cf. Shirley Guthrie, "The Narcissism of American Piety: The Disease and the Cure," *The Journal of Pastoral Care* 31 (December 1977): 220–29.

[85] Bernard Lee, "Intentional Christian Communities in the U.S. Church," *The Catholic World* 234 (July/August 1991): 182.

[86] Viktor Frankl, *The Will to Meaning* (New York: American Library, 1969).

[87] Tex Sample, *U.S. Lifestyles and Mainline Churches* (Philadelphia: Westminster/John Knox Press, 1990), 48.

[88] Sample refers to Alvin Toffler's suggestion in *Future Shock* that many people live "life in modules, meaning that we live our lives in different segments or stations and may do different things at different degrees of maturity or quality or importance" (*U.S. Lifestyles*, p. 46). He suggests, therefore, that journey language and theology appeals to this group; obviously, that is the language of Christian initiation (cf. RCIA, 4).

[89] The strength of Alcoholics Anonymous (and other 12-step groups) is that they insist that people will keep their sobriety through the 12th step—by "carrying this message to other alcoholics."

[90] In many cases we refer such people to professional counseling. We assure sponsors especially that the needs of some candidates are beyond the competence of most sponsors.

[91] Cf. Lawrence Cremin, *Public Education* (New York: Basic Books, 1976).

[92] I should add, however, that this curriculum is heavily focused on "proclaiming the message" and much is programmatic and terminal rather than rooted in the ongoing life of the primary catechist, the community.

[93] Cf. Boys, *Educating in Faith*, 201–3.

[94] Cf. Malcolm Knowles, *The Modern Practice of Adult Education* (New York: Association Press).

[95] Michael Warren, "Introductory Overview," in *Sourcebook*, 27.

[96] As cited by Richard Neuhaus, *First Things First* (August/September 1992): 73, emphasis added. This is too much even for neo-conservative Neuhaus, who comments, "President Bush's discovery of what Christ has ordained would be of theological interest were it not so patently political balderdash—balderdash spiced with nationalistic hubris, a generous sprinkling of mendacity, and more than a hint of blasphemy."

[97] For example, cf. Ched Myers, *Binding the Strong Man: A Political Reading of Mark's Story of Jesus* (Maryknoll NY: Orbis Books, 1988).

[98] Cf. Joseph Cardinal Bernardin, "The Consistent Ethic: What Sort of Framework?" *Origins* 16 (October 30, 1986): 347–50; also, Ronald Krietemeyer offers reflections on such ethical consciousness-raising in Ronald Krietemeyer, "Policies and Priorities," *Church* 7 (Fall 1991): 14.

[99] George Albert Coe, "A Possible Role for Biblical Religion in Public Life," *Theological Studies* 40: 706. Robert Bellah and associates agree in Robert Bellah et al., *Habits of the Heart* (Berkeley: University of California Press, 1985).

[100] Weigel, *Freedom*, 63.

[101] Mitchell, "The Kingdom Journey," 7–8.

# CHAPTER FOUR

## Catechesis in the Catechumenate:

Reflections on the Rite of Christian Initiation
of Adults, #75

*The general principles of any study you may learn by books at home; but the detail, the colour, the tone, the air, the life which makes it live in us, you must catch all these from those in whom it lives already.*[1]

• Cardinal John Henry Newman

IN THIS CHAPTER, we sharpen our focus from catechesis in general to catechesis specific for initiation into community. We focus even more closely on catechesis in the catechumenate period with the dynamics given in paragraph 75 of the *Rite of Christian Initiation of Adults*.

Newman echoes in the nineteenth century what Paul wrote in the first century: "How are they to call on one in whom they have not believed? And how are they to believe in one of whom they have never heard? And how are they to hear without someone to proclaim him? And how are they to proclaim him unless they are sent? . . . So faith comes from what is heard, and what is heard comes through the word of Christ" (Romans 10:14–17).

Like us, Newman lived in the time after Johannes Gutenberg. After catechisms began to roll off the presses, their printed messages sometimes seemed more important than Paul's living messengers. We forgot that catechisms are not our earliest tradition. They are a relatively recent innovation. Martin Luther originated the catechism in the year 1529.[2] The Council of Trent (1545–1563) expanded the idea, and the United States bishops at the Council of Baltimore (1885) copied Trent. In schools, CCD and inquiry classes, people were fed a diet of catechisms, but they came away malnourished. But the first editions of the Baltimore catechism stated that it was a summary of doctrine for teachers, not a text for those being catechized.[3] Apparently, that is also the purpose of the new universal catechism. It is a summary of the Catholic tradition, and it will need adaptation for various cultures by skilled and faithful catechists.[4]

We most remember our best teachers, not the books they taught. The priests and catechists whom I most cherish were far better than their doctrine, theology or catechisms.[5] Andrew Greeley's study of young adults documents this experience: "The principal 'sacrament' by which loving goodness is revealed to us is other human beings. . . . It is not the quantity of the education that matters but the quality; it is the relationship with an excellent teacher that affects the religious imagination."[6]

**Conversation Starter:** What religion teachers or catechists do you remember? What were their special gifts to you? Tell a story of how you have given these gifts to others.

Books are not the great messengers. People are. We know the message through the messengers. This is true of all wisdom, including and especially our knowledge of God. Faith is not jut knowledge *about* God. Faith is knowing God as a beloved. Faith is a loving friendship with the risen Christ in the community, present through the Spirit, especially where Christ promised to be: in the hungry, the thirsty, the naked, the stranger, the sick and the prisoners, and where two or three gather in his name.

*Credo* means "to give the heart." We learn faith from those who give their hearts, from those who know God and Christ as beloved and friend, from messengers in whom God's Spirit lives already. Faith comes from hearing the messengers. In Marshall McLuhan's classic phrase, the medium is the message. This is true because the message was first a person, not a book. Recall our vision of ministry of the word in chapter two. That message, that word, "became flesh and lived among us . . . full of grace and truth" (John 1:14).

Take these lines as a job description of catechesis for today's Christian community and for catechists and homilists within that community. Take them as a description of the process of initiation:

> We declare to you what was from the beginning, what we have heard, what we have seen with our eyes, what we have looked at and touched with our hands. . . . We declare to you what we have seen and heard so that you also may have fellowship with us; and truly our fellowship is with the Father and with his Son Jesus Christ (1 John 1:1, 3).

In the centuries before printing presses, Christian initiation happened through family and neighbors; through stories of faith enfleshed in lives; through music, drama, mystery plays and processions; in churches, cathedrals and stained-glass windows; and especially in the liturgies, the feasts and seasons of the church year in the local community's life of worship and witness. Just as it means in the so-called primitive tribal cultures, in Christendom, initiation meant learning the life of the community.

In our century, Christendom is dead in secularized Europe. It is less clearly so in secularized, pluralistic North America, where a galaxy of religions and worldviews compete for allegiance. Americans profess religious belief, but we celebrate Superbowl Sunday as our real feast day. We absorb our values from hours in front of the tube and surrender our lives and our pocketbooks to an advertising blitz that proclaims "GE, we bring good things to life," and "Seagrams Crown Royal—the World's Greatest Dad," "This baby won't keep you up at night" (Volkswagen) and "We don't love you and leave you" (Xerox).

George Gallup reports that 98 percent of Americans believe in God or in a universal spirit. But he also claims that

> There is a profound gap between religious belief and practice. Roughly three out of four among the public . . . do not consciously connect religion with their judgments of right and wrong. . . . It would accordingly be at once possible for almost all American people to 'believe in God' and yet for society to be essentially materialistic.[7]

A pastor laments,

> I do not know a culture with the trappings of Christian appearances as underdeveloped in the ways of the gospel as our own United States and, if I may be so bold, our neighbors to the north. If any church needs a conversion to the demands of the gospel and to the cries of the prophets more than ours with our superficial, individualistic evangelism or our Catholic piety of a real presence in the sacraments and a real absence elsewhere, I want you to show me.[8]

> **Conversation Starter:** Cite examples from your experience of how catechumens are influenced by the individualism, materialism, consumerism and pluralism that compete with Christian faith for their allegiance. Where do you see secularism in the midst of professed belief? How do you help catechumens face the challenge?

Church life is quaking even in such solidly Catholic countries as Ireland. Bishop Donal Murray of Dublin writes, "In a supportive culture, allegiance to the church and the values of a Christian way of life were almost part of the atmosphere people breathed. Today's catechesis must devote a far greater proportion of its efforts to strengthening of personal commitment." Echoing Newman in our times, Murray adds, "Commitment cannot be taught from textbooks and syllabi; it can only be communicated by a person who already has it."[9]

Perhaps in North America, mobility affects church life more than it does in Ireland. Many people say that they believe in God, but that they dropped out of church simply because they moved.[10] They no longer have the support (and pressure) of family for church membership. The West Coast, where most people who live there have moved from other regions, has the highest number of unchurched people in the United States. They have lost their roots in family, neighborhood and community. Mobility can be a plus, however. People who feel lost and rootless sometimes search for a new community. Will they find these new relationships (and faith) in the local church or in a local social or self-help group?

Didier Piviteau calls for a shift in catechesis from a schooling model to catechesis within a community of believers:

> The church has developed tremendously the schooling approach to religious education (formal catechetics) but has used the structure to try to foster initiation, a task for which it was never intended. . . . The most urgent task nowadays is to work at building a church where initiation is possible. It means we have to find what *type of community* can be valid for the church today.[11]

## A Vision of Catechesis in the Order of Initiation

One way to describe a community is in terms of its mission. We become who we are by doing what we are. Before there were church structures, there was mission—"Go therefore and make disciples of all nations" (Matthew 28:19). The disciples who were sent forth became a community whose life came from sharing the good news. Mission makes church.

In the national catechetical directory, *Sharing the Light of Faith* (1979), the United States bishops see the church's catechetical mission in four dimensions: message, community, worship and service. "The fundamental tasks of catechists are to proclaim Christ's message, to participate in efforts to develop community, to lead people to worship and prayer, and to motivate them to serve others" (#213).[12] That vision harkens back to themes from biblical times: *kerygma, koinonia, leiturgia* and *diakonia*. The *Declaration on Christian Education* (1965) of Vatican II says that catechesis "gives clarity and vigor to faith, nourishes a life lived according to the spirit of Christ, leads to a knowing and active participation in the liturgical mystery and inspires apostolic action" (#19).

The *Rite of Christian Initiation of Adult* (1972) identifies the same four dimensions in #75:[13]

> The catechumenate is an extended period during which the candidates are given suitable pastoral formation and guidance, aimed at training them in the Christian life. In this way, the dispositions manifested at their acceptance into the catechumenate are brought to maturity. This is achieved in four ways.
>
> 1. A suitable catechesis is provided by priests and deacons, or by catechists and others of the faithful, planned to be gradual and complete in its coverage, accommodated to the liturgical year and solidly supported by celebrations of the word. This catechesis leads the catechumens not only to an appropriate acquaintance with dogmas and precepts but also to a profound sense of the mystery of salvation in which they desire to participate.
>
> 2. As they become familiar with the Christian way of life and are helped by the example and support of sponsors, godparents and the entire Christian community, the catechumens learn to turn more readily to God in prayer, to bear witness to the faith, in all things to keep their hopes set on Christ, to follow supernatural inspiration in their deeds and to practice love of neighbor, even at the cost of self-renunciation. Thus formed, "the newly converted set out on a spiritual journey. Already sharing through faith in the mystery of Christ's death and resurrection, they pass from the old to a new nature made perfect in Christ. Since this transition brings with it a progressive change of outlook and conduct, it should become manifest by means of its social consequences and it should develop gradually during the period of the catechumenate. Since the Lord in whom they believe is a sign of contradiction, the newly converted often experience divisions and separations, but they also taste the joy that God gives without measure."[14]
>
> 3. The church, like a mother, helps the catechumens on their journey by means of suitable liturgical rites, which purify the catechumens little by little and strengthen them with God's blessing. Celebrations of the word of God are arranged for their benefit, and at Mass they may also take part with the faithful in the liturgy of the word, thus better preparing themselves for their eventual participation in the liturgy of the eucharist. Ordinarily, however, when they are present in the assembly of the faithful, they should

be kindly dismissed before the liturgy of the eucharist begins (unless their dismissal would present practical or pastoral problems). For they must await their baptism, which will join them to God's priestly people and empower them to participate in Christ's new worship.

4. Since the church's life is apostolic, catechumens should also learn how to work actively with others to spread the gospel and build up the church by the witness of their lives and by professing their faith.

The catechetical vision flows from who we are as church: the real presence of the risen Christ, through the Spirit, in the world. "The church is a kind of sacrament or sign of intimate union with God and of the unity of all people."[15] Mission flows from that sacramental presence.

In its most powerful paragraph, the *Constitution on the Sacred Liturgy* (1963) expands the understanding of Christ's presence far beyond the consecration of bread and wine.

Christ is always present in his church, especially in her liturgical celebrations. He is present in the sacrifice of the Mass, not only in the person of his ministers . . . but especially under the eucharistic species. . . . He is present in his word, since it is he himself who speaks when the holy scriptures are read in the church. He is present, finally, when the church prays and sings, for he promised: 'Where two or three are gathered together for my sake, there am I in the midst of them' (Matthew 18:20) (#7).

The rites of initiation celebrate an even wider sacramental presence throughout the journey. At the very beginning, in the rite of acceptance into the order of catechumens, "God showers his grace on the candidates" (#41) who already have entered "a relationship with God in Christ" (#42) and in that rite become "part of the household of Christ" (#47)—before baptism.

> **Conversation Starter:** Recall a liturgical celebration and how you did or did not experience Christ's real presence in the word, in the ministries, in the ritual actions (such as eating, immersing, anointing, processing or laying on hands) and in the community.

Our ministry to catechumens and their ministry to us is grounded in the real presence of Christ in the community, which is the body of Christ. That community lives and shares Christ's presence by proclaiming his message, developing community, offering worship to God and service to God's people[16]—the dimensions and dynamics of catechesis found in #75.

These four dimensions of catechesis are interdependent and intertwined. For example, although #75.1 focuses on proclaiming the message through scripture and doctrine, the message came to us from communities of faith in the past and takes life from the community in the present, which is the medium of the message (#75.2). It is best proclaimed when the community gathers for liturgical worship (#75.3). The community lives the message when we witness and give our lives in service especially with the hungry, thirsty, naked, stranger, sick and prisoner (#75.4). None of these dimensions of catechesis is complete without the others. They must be put together and kept together.

The focus in this book is on proclaiming the message (#75.1) in the liturgy of the word of the Sundays and feast days of the liturgical year (#75.3). We shall call that liturgical catechesis—echoing God's word in the liturgy. But before we narrow our focus to that one dimension, we take an overview of all four dimensions of catechesis for the catechumenate period.

***Proclaiming the Message (#75.1)*** The *Constitution on the Sacred Liturgy* announces Christ's presence in the word. That is something new for contemporary Catholics who were taught that they followed the law of Sunday obligation if they arrived at Mass in time for the offertory. Our ancestors knew better. A sixth-century theologian wrote, "Tell me which seems the greater—the body of Christ or the word of Christ? If you wish to answer accurately, you must say this: The word of God is not less than the body of Christ."

PREACHING  We gather around Christ's real presence in the word. We proclaim that word and preach Christ's message so that faith may come by hearing through living messengers who are also Christ's real presence in his body. That word most especially is stories of God's dealing with people—the story of God and Israel (and within that story, the stories of God and Abraham, Sarah, Moses, Ruth, David and all the others) and the story of God and Jesus (and within that story the stories of the community of disciples and of Mary, Peter, John, the Samaritan woman,

Lazarus, the workers in the vineyard, the prodigal son and all the others). We proclaim those stories in ways that allow the word of God to become our story. "Scripture is not the word of God (though it once was—in another time and place and community). And our stories are not the word of God (though God may be active in them). The word of God happens when scripture story and our story meet. . . . When past word meets present situation, the word of God happens."[17]

The privileged place for that preaching is not the classroom but in the church where that word becomes flesh once again in the community of God's people. Paragraph 75.1 speaks of "suitable catechesis . . . accommodated to the liturgical year, and solidly supported by celebrations of the word." The primary place for that catechesis will be the liturgy of the word on Sundays and feast days, followed by catechesis after the catechumens are dismissed. In the liturgy of the word, we proclaim the message in ways that no theology class or inquiry class can match: in scripture (proclaimed, not just read); in prayer and song; with vesture and gesture; in sight, sound and silence; in story, image and symbol; within a community of believers.

The liturgy of the word is the special place for the homily, which brings God's stories in the present to meet God's stories in the past. Homilists should not "transmit meaning in messages" but rather create conversations "that evoke meaning."[18] Priests who mourn the loss of private instructions or of teaching the inquiry class should know that their ministry is now even more important as homilists.[19] The United States bishops define the homily as "a scriptural interpretation of human existence which enables a community to recognize God's active presence, to respond to that presence in faith through liturgical word and gesture, and beyond the liturgical assembly, through a life lived in conformity with the gospel."[20]

In a startling shift from a vision of priest as "sacrament maker," Vatican II names preaching and teaching God's word as the primary duty of both priests and bishops.[21] Without the faith that comes from hearing that word proclaimed, there is a "real absence" rather than the real presence of Christ active in God's people in both liturgy and life.

Because homilies bring life to meet word, there is a new emphasis on the critical role and influence of the life of the community in shaping how we both proclaim and hear the word. In scripture studies, we have learned, for example, how Matthew's message differs from Mark's because Matthew preaches to a different community with different needs. Today's homilists also are shaped by what is happening in the lives of people, families, neighborhoods and in the local and world communities of which we are a part. That is where God continues to reveal. We preach with the Bible in one hand and a newspaper, novel, diary or weekly journal in the other.

The bishops' document on preaching suggests that one way to prepare a homily is to meet with a small group to reflect on both the scriptural story and the people's stories and then to bring both into preaching.[22] Homilists then can preach dialogically, even without a "dialogue homily," so that what they say is in dialogue with what they heard from the community. In fact, the Greek *homilein* means "to have a conversation." Our bishops note, "The New Testament usage suggests that a homily should sound more like a personal conversation, albeit a conversation on matters of utmost importance, than a speech or a classroom lecture."[23]

Fred Baumer says that, like conversation, a homily is transactional, not transmissive, speech. Transmissive speech is the "jug and mug" approach in which a speaker pours from his or her jug of knowledge into the mugs of the hearers' minds. It is a monologue. Transactional speech invites hearers into dialogue within themselves by giving them access to truth (as Mary Boys envisions good religious education should) and by inviting people to find their own meaning.[24] Genuine homilies will raise questions so that hearers discover their own meanings and come to their own decisions.[25]

A model for such preaching is found in Jesus' conversation with his followers on the road to Emmaus (Luke 24:13–35). He first listens to their stories—"What are you discussing with each other while you walk along?" Then "he interpreted to them the things about himself in all the scriptures." The message was told in dialogue with the things that happened to him and that would happen to them in Jerusalem. Today's homilists need to be in dialogue with what happened and is happening in Jerusalem, Jersey City, Johannesburg—anywhere in our world. We interpret human life, primarily, not texts. "The preacher does not so much attempt to explain the scriptures as to interpret the human situation through the scriptures."[26]

In light of the Emmaus story, many describe homilies as "breaking open the word." Before those disciples recognized him in the breaking of the bread, Jesus broke open the scriptures for them. They came to faith through hearing the word opened up so that the scripture stories became their own stories. Their hearts first needed to burn within them "while he was talking to us on the road, while he was opening the scriptures to us." Then they could recognize him in the breaking of the bread, in Jesus' body broken for the life of the world, in the broken lives of those who are the new body of Christ.

Therefore, breaking open the word in homilies does not mean explaining the scripture story and applying it to today. It means finding today in the scripture and the scripture story in today's story. Homilies move from life to symbol/text and back to life. (Chapters six through ten will explore methods of doing that.) Homilists must listen for God's presence in people of present and past, in life and in scripture. They do so "not merely to make a homily relevant—but to hear God's word today . . . in the depths of human experience, . . . at the limits or boundaries of our experience where the ultimate questions of life are raised."[27]

Who preachers are and what they say are shaped by the communities in which they listen and live outside the liturgy, and how they live and pray into and from the liturgy. "The crucial proving ground for effective preaching [and catechizing] remains in the arena of personal and spiritual formation. Maturity of character, sound pastoral experience, depth of spirituality—these give a license for authentic preaching that is capable of stirring the soul."[28] Homilists also are shaped within the liturgy by the community assembled for worship: the faith and the faces of the people that remind homilists of "the joys and the hopes, the griefs and anxieties of the people of this age"[29] that are part of the conversation between God and the community.

The community also enters the dialogue by listening, praying and responding. Within the liturgy, the assembly not only listens but also proclaims its faith. Outside the liturgy, the community proclaims what

God is doing today, who is dying and rising today, how the word becomes flesh today.

What is true for homilists and homilies is true for catechists and catechesis. Catechesis echoes the word. Like homilists, catechists listen to and proclaim that word. The catechetical session with catechumens after the homily is not an "add-on" to the liturgy. It is part of and continues the liturgy of the word with catechumens. It continues to break open the word that breaks open our lives with the same dynamics as the homily.

CATECHESIS    Like the homily, catechesis is an act of faith and worship, not just of instruction. Catechists and catechumens listen and proclaim, evoke faith and respond in faith. A typical session with the smaller group of catechumens continues the dialogue begun with the larger assembly—in scripture proclaimed; in prayer and song; with vesture and gesture (in the blessings, anointings and exorcisms, for example); in sight, sound and silence; in story, image and symbol; within a community. Catechesis continues the dynamics of church, not those of the classroom.

Having said that, I must add that at times catechesis will turn to the disciplines of religious education and theology to critique, analyze and interpret the connections between our lives and times, and God's word. For example, when the gospel of Mark discusses absolute fidelity in marriage (Mark 10:2–16—Twenty-seventh Sunday of Ordinary Time, Year B), the homilist might need to share some scriptural interpretation with the entire assembly during the homily. During the catechetical session with catechumens, the catechist also might interpret that text through history, theology and canon law—material not usually appropriate for a homily. These interpretations never are simply facts or information, but a call to conversion to a faithful God who makes our faithful love possible.

In #75.1, catechesis is called "suitable, gradual and complete, leading to an appropriate acquaintance with dogmas and precepts and a profound sense of the mystery of salvation in which catechumens desire to participate." These are words more about quality than quantity. Other paragraphs in the document flesh them out and make clear that the goal of catechesis is not just quantified religious knowledge about doctrine (although knowledge is a goal).

SUITABLE   The candidates receive "pastoral formation" (not just information) "aimed at training them in the Christian life" (#75). They are "initiated into the mysteries of salvation and the practice of an evangelical way of life" (#76). Instruction is not just about facts. Catholic teaching "enlightens faith, directs the heart toward God, fosters participation in the liturgy, inspires apostolic activity and nurtures a life completely in accord with the spirit of Christ" (#78). (We might demur at the word "completely." At the end of the catechumenate period, we celebrate God's loving choice and election of the unworthy, not the perfection of the worthy.)

Indeed, in our pluralistic culture where we cannot depend on a community to pass along shared understandings or a common set of values, new members need knowledge of the Catholic tradition. Especially with youth, we need not contribute to "the closing of the American mind"[30] by closing the religious mind to the basics of Catholic Christianity.

> **Take a Stand:**   What are the "basics" of the Christian message?

If tradition means only information, such tradition is, as was said earlier, the "dead faith of living people." The goal of all religious knowledge is transformation—faith lived in response to the revelation of God's love. "What is learned is no more and no less than that it is the love *of* God *through* Jesus Christ and *in* the Holy Spirit. All the doctrines of Christianity are but explications of that one statement."[31] The goal of that learning, as stated in the *General Catechetical Directory* (1971), is that people "may be converted to God through Christ [and] that they may interpret their whole life in the light of faith" (#37).

When some call for a return to "the basics," they usually mean religious knowledge and doctrines.[32] In those terms, Cardinal Joseph Ratzinger defines the basics as the creed, the Lord's Prayer, the Ten Commandments and the sacraments.[33] The rites of initiation hint that we celebrate the basics that are "suitable" and "appropriate" for fledgling

Christians in the two presentations—of the creed and the Lord's Prayer. But these celebrations stress that knowledge and words are not the basics. The *community* presents not just words but its own life. It presents a faith living in a community in the present and prayed in words from the past that express "tradition as the living faith of dead people."

The concept of "faith" as a personal relationship with God present through the Spirit in the communities of past and present is basic. "The creed presupposes an *act of faith* that is highly personal and antecedent to any verbal formulation. Before saying out loud 'I believe in God,' I must say in my heart, 'My Lord and my God, I believe in You' in order to say it sincerely."[34] Without the faith experience of God revealed in Christ, we have a Catholic version of fundamentalism: doctrinal texts, literalist mouthing of words without the experience of their meaning. In William Shakespeare's images, we have Matthean, Nicene, Thomistic or Rahnerian words flowing "trippingly on the tongue," but they are "full of sound and fury, signifying nothing."

Therefore, the "quality control" in #75.1 is "a profound sense of the mystery of salvation in which they desire to *participate*." We invite catechumens to participate in the mysteries of Jesus' dying and rising. Catechesis is "suitable" and knowledge of doctrine and precepts is "appropriate" if they lead to those mysteries.

We also speak of what is "suitable" for the initiation of new members. We must distinguish between sacramental formation (before, during and after the sacramental celebrations) and ongoing catechesis. Paragraph 75 explores what is suitable for the beginnings of the journey. After initiation we invite new members to a lifelong exploration of God's love in Christ Jesus. That may well include degrees and courses in theology. Even then, the goal is not just a PHD but a deepening of conversion.

GRADUAL    "Gradual" means that catechesis is adapted to the unique journey of each person and "varies according to the many forms of God's grace, the free cooperation of the individuals, the action of the church, and the circumstances of time and place" (#4).

COMPLETE    What about "complete" catechesis? That sounds like a survey of all the tomes of Vatican II, St. Teresa of Avila or Bernard Lonergan.

**Take a Stand:**   How do you understand "complete"
catechesis for catechumens?

"Complete" also describes quality, not quantity. It refers to the
hierarchy of truths. Certain doctrines are basic to our expressing God's
love for us through Christ in the Spirit, and these must be completely
presented. John Paul II in *Catechesi Tradendae* (1979) states, "Integrity
[completeness] does not dispense from balance and from the organic
hierarchical character through which the truths to be taught, the norms
to be transmitted, and the ways of Christian life to be indicated will be
given the proper importance due to each" (#31). The *General Catechetical Directory* (1971) also affirms, "On all levels, catechesis should take
account of this hierarchy of the truths of the faith" (#43). What are
these truths? In commenting on the Directory, Berard Marthaler states,

> the church also recognizes 'a certain hierarchy of truths' in which such tenets
> as found in the ancient creeds are considered basic (#43). Catechesis must
> necessarily be Christocentric (#40) and at the same time Trinitarian. To
> neglect the integrity of mystery latent in the phrase "through Christ, to the
> Father, in the Spirit," is to rob the Christian message of its proper character.[36]

**Take a Stand:**   Name all the "Catholic differences" that
distinguish Catholics from Protestants, especially from the
evangelical churches. What is a key Catholic difference that
grounds all other differences?

COMPLETE CATHOLICISM   That hierarchy of truths that Marthaler
describes may be complete and integral Christianity. What about "complete Catholicism"? People from other churches who are joining the
Catholic church want to know "the Catholic difference."

Some claim that the Catholic difference lies in doctrines and
practices regarding, for example, sacraments, Mary, the pope and devotions. But doctrines and practices differ because the Catholic *experience*
of God differs. Once again, doctrine is not basic. Faith is.

*The* Catholic experience of God in faith is the *incarnation*—not just
the experience of Jesus as the presence of God in human flesh but the
enfleshment of God in the Spirit throughout creation in a sacramental
world.[37] Catholics experience the beyond in our midst, the extraordinary
in the ordinary. "Sacraments are not exceptional and extraordinary

events; they are standard and ordinary—like baths and dinners, kisses and loving touches, hugs and perfume, prayers and celebrations."[38]

The Catholic experience of God (shared by other sacramental churches) is that all of God's creation can be "visible signs of invisible grace." Therefore, Catholics celebrate seven sacraments (and seventy times seven sacramentals), not just two. Therefore, Catholics celebrate God's presence with all kinds of smells and bells, sights and sounds, gesture and vesture. Therefore, Catholics celebrate God's presence in Mary and the saints. Therefore, Catholics find God's presence in the community of the faithful, in a multitude of ministers, including the pope.[39]

We invite people to enter the Catholic difference not just by learning doctrines, but also by experiencing God's presence in community, in the people and in the events of their lives. If their experience has been hurtful and oppressive, learning truths usually will not heal. Healers (such as the sponsors and the catechumenal community) heal. Then those who have been healed can enter into the Catholic difference when they celebrate with that community our shared experience of God through water, oil, bread and wine, and the laying on of hands in reconciliation.

Will catechesis based on the liturgical year and the liturgy of the word be "complete"? Our church says that it will be. In its document on the liturgy, Vatican II noted that "within the cycle of a year, moreover, [the church] unfolds the whole mystery of Christ, not only from his incarnation and birth until his ascension, but also as reflected in the day of Pentecost, and the expectation of a blessed, hoped-for return of the Lord."[40] Paul VI adds: "According to the hope of the Second Vatican Council, sacred scripture will then be a perpetual source of spiritual life, the chief instrument for handing down Christian doctrine, and the center of all theological study."[41]

The liturgy of the word, especially the readings of the lectionary, can lead to exploring the basics of Catholic Christianity, including the 1,900 years of postbiblical tradition. A Roman Catholic position on the development of doctrine, while affirming that no doctrine contradicts scripture, would not claim that all doctrines are explicitly in the Bible. We do not exhume doctrines buried in biblical stories and images. Catholic tradition affirms, however, that the scriptures are the primary expressions of Christian faith. "Whatever else is shared about life in Christ [in this case Catholic life], be it ethical or doctrinal or disciplinary, the biblical message is its bedrock. All other teaching is built on the word of God."[42]

That does not mean that we preach doctrine or precepts from the pulpit. Dogma is very limited. Much of it is in language that only historians understand or that theologians can pronounce.[43] Much was directed against a particular heresy that may or may not be alive today. I noted in chapter three that popularized theology, more than defined doctrine, can remove obstacles to faith and deepen faith by giving us a language from our culture. At times, we can use that language in preaching and more often in the catechetical sessions. Yet "doctrine informs, disciplines, protects and enriches the preaching of the kerygma—but never replaces it. . . . Doctrine is second-order language designed to clarify the boundaries of belief in polemical contexts or to clarify, rather than to evoke, the community's religious experience."[44]

Therefore, I repeat that the first-order symbolic language of contemporary stories in dialogue with scripture stories and images are more concrete than theological texts or catechisms, and they more immediately connect with our individual and communal experience. The great questions of meaning—not abstract questions—generate the skeleton of the lectionary stories: Where is your brother or sister? Have you seen the place where the world began? But you, who do you say that I am? Were you not born blind? How is it then that you see? Why do you look for the living among the dead?

The catechumenate team should keep a checklist of teachings that have been covered to assure that catechesis has been complete, aware that what is sufficiently "complete" for the initiation of new members does not "cover" everything and, indeed, leaves them with inquiring minds eager to explore the Catholic heritage for a lifetime. Those teachings, however, should emerge organically from the liturgy of the word and the life of the community. "Delineating a 'theme' places the focus on didactic concepts to be derived from a passage rather than on evoking and celebrating the presence of Christ with us."[45] Our post-biblical tradition of focusing on incarnation during Advent-Christmas-Epiphany, redemption during Lent, Spirit during Easter-Pentecost, discipleship and mission during Ordinary Time, saints on All Saints' Day and Mary on Marian feasts arises quite naturally from the scriptures and the liturgical year.

At times, we might need to schedule additional sessions during the week, for example, to cover both our biblical and postbiblical tradition on marriage and sexual morality prompted by Matthew's treatment of marriage on the Sixth Sunday of Ordinary Time, Year A. Rather than using a catechism, more flexible publications such as *Living the Good News* on scripture and liturgy,[46] and *Catholic Update* on the Catholic tradition[47] offer additional sources for both private and group reflection when a particular Christian Catholic teaching arises in discussion.

COMPLETE BIBLE   A final note on completeness. In terms of the totality of biblical history, Mary Collins contends that the lectionary itself is not complete. She proposes, "The lectionary is a collection of pericopes (Greek for 'snippets' or 'cuttings'); it serves a church already familiar with the story of salvation that can recall the larger episodes and patterns through the reading of snatches of a story."[48] Catherine Dooley adds that some of the most important stories of the Hebrew Scriptures are not in the lectionary because these "fundamental biblical passages cannot be easily correlated with the gospel."[49] Some of the key Christian Scriptures are proclaimed during summer months when the catechumenate might not be meeting weekly.

Indeed, critiques of the present lectionary abound; and some suggest that rather than connecting the first reading to the gospel, sometimes artificially, there should be a continuous reading from the Hebrew Scriptures that proclaims the broad scope of God's dealings with Israel.[50] If, however, we proclaim the most important stories of scripture and the grand sweep of biblical literature to evangelize candidates during the precatechumenate period, they should have some sense of the "big story" that is the context for the pericopes of the lectionary.

During the breaking open of the word in homily and catechesis, we also situate those texts within that larger story. An impoverished notion of homily limits preaching to just the individual scriptural texts. We can homilize and catechize those "smaller stories" of Mark, for example, within his "big story" (see the sample homily in chapter eight).

We also hear the texts within the larger stories of the entire liturgy and the liturgical season. In light of that, the popular phrase "lectionary-based catechesis" is a misnomer. We are doing liturgical catechesis centered on the entire liturgy of the word. In addition, many candidates bring a biblical background from their Protestant churches stronger than that of Catholics.

> **Conversation Starter:** What is your experience of catechumens' knowledge or lack of knowledge of scripture? How have you responded to that in the precatechumenate?

For baptized Catholics (and I suggest also for catechumens and baptized candidates for full communion), preaching from the lectionary, and from the entire liturgy at the liturgical season, is the normal fare that nourishes us on the basics of both biblical and postbiblical Christianity. Gerard Sloyan agrees:

> My first argument for preaching uninterruptedly from the lectionary is from tradition. . . . The church has never put any argument before it. We do and pray and think what has been done from apostolic times insofar as this can be discovered from its best witness, the books of the two testaments. . . . The Bible is the great corrective to all the false starts and near misses of Christian history. It does nothing to threaten the valid developments of genuine tradition. It does everything to threaten the ephemeral doctrines, the ephemeral pieties, the human traditions we so readily confuse with the divinely authored tradition.[51]

Walter Brueggemann adds that preaching from the Bible threatens ephemeral ideologies and worlds in which there is "no danger, no energy, no possibility, no opening for newness! . . . [Biblical preaching] is the ready, steady, surprising proposal that the real world in which God invites us to live is not the one made available by the rulers of this age."[52]

SUMMARY    Thomas Morris summarizes the "building blocks" that we have surveyed to construct a liturgical catechesis based on #75.1 and connecting with #75.2, 75.3 and 75.4:

1. scripture interpretation (moving beyond fundamentalism and beyond individual texts to the "big stories" of scripture)

2. celebration of the word (moving beyond the lectionary texts)

3. faith sharing (moving beyond lectures and also beyond religious narcissism to hearing other individual and community stories)

4. life experience (moving from past to present)

5. Catholic tradition (moving beyond the biblical message)

6. ritual and prayer (moving beyond religious information to formation in faith, and beyond words to rituals and the rhythms of the liturgical seasons)

7. servanthood (moving beyond the inner life of the community to service in the world) and

8. spiritual-community (moving beyond the catechumenal group to shared life with the wider living, praying, serving Christian community)[53]

***Developing Community (#75.2)***   "Community" is a slippery term. In our North American culture, many people identify community with intimacy, friendship and "warm fuzzies." "Community" often connotes encounter groups, not mission groups; self-help, not "other-help"; more cocoon for comfort than motivator for mission. Some in catechumenate ministry fear that some catechumens meet not God but the group, that they are being initiated not into the church community but into the catechumenate team. For people to come to depth in faith they do need a small community of people who know each other well enough to share their values, but the focus of such a community is on faith and values, not just intimacy.

In fact, values are at the heart of community; ultimately, they make or break even friendship and marriage. "A community is a group of people who share meaning and value. To put it the other way around, wherever there are common understandings, common views, common beliefs or judgments, common expectations or goals, there is at least a rudimentary community."[54] Bernard Lonergan adds, "Community coheres or divides, begins or ends, just where the common field of experience, common understanding, common judgment, common commitments begin and end."[55] Therefore, all that we have said about proclaiming the message (#75.1) also develops community, because that message is about not just facts, but discipleship and common understandings of and commitments to the reign of God.

COMMUNITY AS COMMUNION IN THE COMMUNAL LIFE OF GOD   If we are to distinguish Christian community from psychotherapeutic groups, we need to meet God, not just the group. We need to rediscover the life of the Spirit and the divine life of the Trinity into which we enter through that Spirit. That is not wrong, just inadequate. In Western Christianity, we focus on *Christ's* presence in the eucharist, especially in the community. The emphasis is on union with Christ. In the East, the focus is on the *Spirit* of Pentecost. That Spirit unites us in covenant to the inner, self-giving life of God, which is three Persons living in community. That divine community of self-giving love is the life that all the baptized share. Therefore, all the baptized, not just the hierarchy or magisterium, gather to listen to our lives, to listen to God's word and to interpret our lives in light of that word. All the baptized have a part in shaping those common *understandings* and *commitments* that constitute community. All the baptized enflesh those understandings and commitments in mission and witness to all peoples with whom God longs to be in covenant.

It is the Spirit of Pentecost who unites us in that covenant and sounds the death knell of the babble of Babel; all peoples now can understand each other (Parthians, Medes, Elamites, Egyptians, Libyans and Romans in early times; African Americans, Hispanics, Asians, Native Americans and Europeans in our times). That is the wondrous "common understanding" of the Spirit's covenant. That Spirit sends us forth, all the baptized, to give ourselves to others just as Jesus was sent forth from God and sacrificed himself for his sisters and brothers. That is our "common commitment." We live and celebrate the life of God in the Spirit, and that Spirit empowers us for mission especially when we gather for liturgy.

A rekindling of our faith in the real presence of the Spirit might intensify our belief in the immersion of all the baptized into our communal life in God and into our ecclesial mission as church. It might free us from that North American mind-set that limits community to friendship, warmth, intimacy and bonding. It might free us from distorted Christologies that envision a monarchical God who is mediated by a monarchical Christ the King, who is mediated by monarchical popes, bishops and priests to a subservient and receptive people. The rediscovery of *our* Spirit might free us for the shared life and mission that is the gift and vocation of all Christians. Such a rediscovery might unite us with believers in other religious traditions who live in the Spirit and invite us into the "sacramental" vision of the Native American peoples, who celebrate the Spirit not just in humankind but in all living things and in the good earth.

COMMUNITY LIFE OF PRAYER AND MORAL VALUES    This communal life in the Spirit is the context for proclaiming the message and for all catechesis. However, #75.2 looks especially at the community of faith in terms of its life of prayer and moral values, from past and present. I suggest that *prayer* is, ultimately, our way of entering into the "common understandings" of the community. The *moral values* of the community invite us into the "common commitments" of that community. In the words of the document on adult initiation, the catechumens "become familiar with the Christian way of life and are helped by the example and support of sponsors, godparents and the entire Christian community."[56] They learn "to turn more readily to God in prayer, to bear witness to the faith . . . to keep their hopes set on Christ, to follow supernatural inspiration in their deeds, and to practice love of neighbor . . . with a progressive change of outlook and conduct . . . manifest by means of its social consequences" (#75.2).

Cardinal Newman affirmed that we learn such faith from those in whom it lives already. In light of that, Aidan Kavanagh asserts that "Catechists of the new sort might better be old people who know how to pray, the ill who know how to suffer, and the confessor who knows what faith costs than young presbyters with new degrees in religious education."[57] We need trained catechists and homilists to avoid biblical and doctrinal fundamentalism and to resource and facilitate the conversation, but praying and living more often are caught from disciples of Jesus who know how to pray and live the life of the Spirit than taught by professionals.

Therefore, in formal sessions and more often in informal meetings, catechumens must meet people who know how to *pray*. That includes liturgical prayer and the wide spectrum of ways that Catholics pray, such as formal prayer, spontaneous prayer, biblical prayer, the rosary, prayer groups, meditation, prayer using the imagination and contemplative prayer. To pray with the church throughout the world, catechumens might reflect and pray over the daily readings of the lectionary. We can introduce them to a simple form of the liturgy of the hours. We must take care not to require them to pray in just one way. There are many "prayer mansions" in the Father's house.[58]

> **Conversation Starter:** How have you introduced catechumens to prayer and to people who pray in different ways?

In formal and informal meetings, catechumens also meet Catholic Christians to share their *moral values*, both in conversation and, more importantly, in action. Married people who know sacrificial love and fidelity, families who know the struggles of communication, shut-ins who share the frustrations and the meaning of their suffering, divorced or separated people who know loneliness, employers and employees who see work not just as job but as vocation, old people who have dreams, and young people who have visions—all these have moral values to share.

Catechumens might visit the sick with the eucharistic ministers, serve the poor with the St. Vincent de Paul Society, assist new immigrants and refugees with the social-concerns committee. They will talk with and see the example of Christians who believe that the "seamless garment of life" clothes the issues of abortion, capital punishment, the arms race, care for the handicapped and disabled, abuse in families, care for the aged, care for the poor, and care for our ravaged and polluted land and waters.[59] They meet parish leaders to hear and assess how the parish is about gospel mission and not just about budgets and bureaucracies.

> **Conversation Starter:** How have you helped catechumens meet the people of the parish and of the Catholic church and not just the catechumenate team?

Although the Catholic church, like most churches, seems preoccupied with sexual morality, #75.2, like the gospels, stresses morality with its "social consequences." If we get to the basics with moral issues, it is clear that although catechumens need moral guidance and example in the area of sexuality, the gospels center on justice as more basic. "One out of every ten verses in the synoptic gospels is about riches and poverty, one out of seven in Luke."[60] The 1971 synod of bishops put justice at center stage: "Action for justice and participation in the transformation of the world appear to us as a constitutive dimension of the preaching of the gospel."[61] Like other values, however, justice will be caught, not taught, by being with the oppressed and the victims of injustice. We will return to that when we explore apostolic witness in #75.4.

If initiation is not a program that ends with the sacraments of initiation, then *during* the catechumenate we need to integrate the new members into the life of the community. *After* initiation, these new members, who experienced church precisely as a community within the larger community, will need integration into a small Christian community in the parish so that they are not lost in the crowd.[62] Such integration is the special ministry of their sponsors (godparents) and their sponsoring communities. It does assume that there are some attempts to restructure the parish into small communities.

I do not intend to explore the ministry of sponsor and godparent.[63] The sponsor or sponsoring community (some parishes offer a small group) often will be the catechumen's best experience of church as community and his or her guide and witness into the community during and after initiation.

I close this section with a story about a sponsor. Jim O'Connor was in his late 20s when he came to one of our institutes battling cystic fibrosis. He returned to his parish and became a sponsor with his wife, Judy, who married him knowing that he was dying. She wrote to me about his final days:

> Roger [their catechumen] came to see Jim the day before he died. When he was leaving, he told Jim to "feel better." Jim told him, "If not in this life, in the next." This really upset Roger, and he told Jim to stop talking like that. Jim just told Roger that it was OK and reminded him, "That's what your faith is for." As I told Roger, when he said that he only had one sponsor now, "That is just not so. Jim is in an even better position to support you if you direct your needs through him in prayer." . . . The catechumenate meeting we had after Jim died was very inspiring. Each person talked about their feelings, where they were when Jim died, and the joy of knowing Jim is at peace.

Again, to paraphrase Cardinal Newman: The detail, the color, the tone, the air, the life that makes faith live in us—you must catch all these from those in whom it lives already.

*Celebrating Liturgy (#75.3)*    The order of Christian initiation offers a galaxy of liturgies to celebrate what God is doing in the lives of both the catechumens and the community. We celebrate the journey in a myriad of ways: through greeting and welcoming by the community, hearing and proclaiming the word of God, signing the senses, accepting the cross and the scriptures; in blessings, exorcisms and anointings; through calling catechumens' names and signing the book of God's chosen ones; in prayers, litanies, music, laying on of hands; through immersing, chrismating, eating and drinking, with lots of touch, water, oil, bread and wine.

ROBUST SYMBOLS AND IMAGES    The United States bishops' document on music states in strong language, "Good celebrations foster and nourish faith. Poor celebrations weaken and destroy faith."[64] Good celebrations are full of strong, robust, full-hearted images and symbols. Poor celebrations falter with weak, flabby, halfhearted images, words and rituals.

The primary place of Christ's presence is the community where two or more gather in his name. However, if the assembly does not believe, for example, that they are the body of Christ welcoming new members with enthusiastic joy and gracious hospitality, if they watch their watches and dread that one of these rites might add 15 minutes to their time in church, they are hardly a sacrament of Christ's welcoming, accepting, healing, unifying presence.

A few drops of water is hardly a robust image of immersion into Jesus' dying and rising. People are not sprinkled to death. "Little dabs" of oil will not "do ya." Mumbled scriptures obscure a word that should open our hearts like a two-edged sword. It is, to say the least, difficult to do what we are told to do—"take and eat"—with the wafers that we misname "bread."

Some claim that the state of the liturgy in North America simply cannot bear the burden of the liturgical catechesis that is envisioned in these pages. We need not be Pollyannas about the clergy and the assemblies who do not see initiation (or eucharist or any other sacrament) as the responsibility of all the baptized (#9) and who reduce "full, conscious and active participation in the liturgical celebrations" (*Constitution on the Sacred Liturgy*, #14) to mouthing a few prayers and hymns. Mark Searle comments:

> Is the concept (and practice) of "active participation" a genuine step toward the redistribution of responsibility in the church, or is it a means to heading off

more radical forms of participatory democracy? . . . Is the revised liturgy serving the pedagogical role of fostering a genuinely new consciousness, or is it a way of perpetuating the old imperialist theology in more attractive packaging?[65]

Nor need we be Pollyannas about the present state of liturgical affairs. We also need not be paralyzed. The Sunday liturgy remains the place where most people will hear the word of God echoed and the place where bodies are broken and blood shed for the life of the world. If done with vigor and integrity, the galaxy of rites in initiation can themselves awaken the "responsibility of all the baptized" and "active participation."

A community alive to worship and witness, which goes out to welcome candidates; signs them with the cross from head to foot; proclaims the word with fidelity; testifies at election to what God has been doing in their lives; lays on hands in solidarity in the Spirit for healing; immerses in water that recalls the waters over which God's Spirit bent low at creation and flood and exodus; generously anoints them with the oil of priests, prophets, kings and martyr-witnesses; and shares their brokenness in broken bread and shared wine—all these strong and authentic images can invite catechumens into worship, into exodus, into death and resurrection.

In other words, the liturgies of all sacraments find their roots in the ordinary events of human life made extraordinary by God's presence.[66] If baptism is immersing and going down into waters of dying and rising, it must look like an immersion, not like a sprinkling nor a dousing. If eucharist is to be a community banquet of the Lord, it must first be a shared meal, not fast food from a drive-through. It must "look like and behave like a shared meal if it is to be anything else that faith claims for it."[67] If a Martian came into Mass, would she immediately cry, *"Yaya, fragon do un hyfleschuffer!"*? (That's Martian for, "Hey, that's a meal!")

The power of sacraments to foster and nourish faith resides, in large part, in their human integrity. At that level, are they truly what we say they are? A rose is a rose is a rose, Gertrude Stein wrote. If it looks like a duck, walks like a duck and quacks like a duck, it's a duck. And a meal is a meal is a meal. Immersing is immersing is immersing. Welcome is welcome is welcome. Reconciling is reconciling is reconciling. If we celebrate these liturgies with integrity, with fidelity to their roots in God's creation and our humanity, then they speak a message. In their own way, they echo God's word. They catechize. They are liturgical catechesis at its best.

**Conversation Starter:**    Recall a good celebration that "fostered faith" and a poor celebration that "destroyed faith."

LITURGICAL CATECHESIS    Liturgical (or ritual) catechesis is a term that unites liturgists and catechists. It heals the divisions between those two ministries. Some liturgists thought catechists used liturgy merely for "instruction."[68] Some catechists saw liturgy as empty, mechanical ritualism or fussy rubricism. Liturgical catechesis, which unites both liturgy and catechesis in one phrase, is an attempt to affirm the wedding between good liturgy and catechesis. One not only flows into and out of the other but takes place within the other.

Robert Duggan and Maureen Kelly define it this way: "Ritual catechesis names the activity of bringing faith to consciousness through participation in and celebration of the rites of the community."[69] Gilbert Ostdiek adds, "The classical theological dictum that liturgy is 'first theology' and that what theologians do is 'second theology' offers us a parallel. Liturgy with its formative power is a 'first catechesis,' while the systematic reflection on that experience done under the guidance of a catechist is 'second catechesis.'"[70]

Liturgical catechesis reverberates with, but significantly nuances and expands, currents and trends in modern catechetics. In almost all contemporary catechesis, including that for initiation, the catechist helps people reflect on their experience.[71] Catechesis listens to people's experiences and stories of God's absence or presence on their own Emmaus journeys and searches for their meaning in the light of the Judeo-Christian stories. This assumes that human life — in birth, meals, reconciliation, wedding, healing, leading, dying — can be a sacrament of God's presence.

Catechesis helps people to reflect back on these "sacraments" to discover a God always present to them but to whom they may not have been present. We invite them to discover not a God out in the heavens but a God incarnate in the people and events of earth, in John Robinson's phrase, "the beyond in our midst."

Perhaps no theologian influenced this approach more than Karl Rahner. He insists that all people in their very being are open to and searching for this "beyond in our midst" and that they experience God's presence and mystery in ways that are preconscious and unexpressed. In the depths of our being and in the depths of our desire, there is openness to, thirst for, thrust toward the experience of God. In the depths of our own mystery as persons, which we grasp with increasing awe and wonder with the passing of the years, there is a hint of an even more wondrous Mystery that enfolds us and that we call God. In Rahner's words, "The grace of God has always been there . . . ahead of our preaching. . . . Our preaching is not really an indoctrination with something alien from outside but the awakening of something within, as yet not understood but nevertheless really present."[72]

Awakening happens especially when persons or events (sacramental moments) send us into our depths to discover that presence. John Shea puts that into everyday language: "There are moments which . . . cut through to something deeper. . . . It may be the death of a parent, the touch of a friend, falling in love, a betrayal. . . . But whatever it is, we sense we have undergone something that has touched upon the normally dormant but always present relationship to God."[73] In this perspective, all humans have the same experience of God at the inner core of their being; they simply express it in different stories and rituals. The task of catechesis is to bring that *inner world into the outer world*, especially by looking back at those sacramental moments.

From this perspective, however, first, people have difficulty reflecting on or expressing experiences that they have not had. Second, we usually cannot create such experiences (such as a parent's unconditional love for prodigals or the awareness that we, too, are entombed like Lazarus). Third, catechesis is frustrated because there sometimes is little to look back on. We must wait for life, the person and God to interact.

George Lindbeck disagrees. His works suggests that the power of liturgical catechesis is not only to reflect back on or express experience but also to create the experience—in church, not in the classroom.[74] Lindbeck insists that the principal task of catechesis is not to bring the inner world to expression in the outer world but to bring *the outer world to shape the inner world*. The inner world (experience of God) is created by an outer world (the stories and rituals of a religious tradition). He asserts that rituals have the power to form, generate and create our experience of God especially through the people of God gathered around us as the welcoming, initiating, reconciling, healing, real presence of Christ.

**Conversation Starter:**  Tell a story of a catechumen who had not experienced God's healing, unconditional love through the people of his or her life.

On the one hand, if everyone has basically the same experience of God (as Rahner asserts), why is it that this experience finds such wondrously diverse expressions, for example, from the concern for the dignity of the human person in many Western religions (with the attending danger of individualism) to the goal of the absorption of the person into the One in many Eastern religions (with the danger of loss of personhood). Perhaps the stories and rituals of those religions create different experiences in their members.

On the other hand, as liturgists and catechists, we need not wait for life experience to awaken the awareness of God in the depths of the person before we can express and reflect on that awareness. In the public rituals of a community, the stories, images, actions and symbols can generate that inner experience and give us a language to express it and to name what has been happening to us, as prodigals or as Lazaruses, for example. "It is necessary to have the means for expressing an experience in order to have it, and the richer our expressive or linguistic system, the more subtle, varied and differentiated can be our experience."[75]

The galaxy of rites and the myriad of images and stories offered throughout the journey of initiation provides that "rich linguistic system" that gives both the catechumens and the community "the means for expressing our experience of God in order to have it." If our culture replaces the holy days with Superbowl Sunday and the scripture stories with the soaps, "Beverly Hills, 90210" and "Terminator 2," people (especially youth) no longer have the language that makes the experience of God possible.

Religious faith emerges not just from an identical experience of God available to all humans. Experience of God also is formed by, created by, shaped by, revealed in, and being grasped by us in the very rituals, symbols, images, language, movement, music and stories of each religion's unique tradition. Mary Collins asserts,

> The liturgy "condenses" what the church believes in, what it knows of praying, what it hopes for, what it is committed to in love and what it knows about

human possibility. These profound religious meanings are "stored" in the gestures, words, the transactions, the elements of the liturgy, even in the space in which the church assembles.[76]

We open that storehouse to learn our language of faith and to let it shape us. It is like a child learning a language. The child learns it by osmosis within his or her family and community. He or she thinks, plays, sings and works somewhat differently than others because he or she learned that language and not another. Children become human by learning a language. We become born-again humans by learning the language of Christ.

Rituals are the most important language of a religious community, especially initiation rituals in which people express their identity and what they most cherish and hold dear.[77] They invite us into the vision and values of that community. Because rituals are rich experiences in themselves, they can create that life in others. That is the power of liturgical catechesis in Christian rituals of initiation. Robert Duggan and Maureen Kelly assert that "ritual experience itself is catechetical and formative, at a level and with a power that no formal instruction can emulate."[78] They reflect the vision of pioneer liturgist Josef Jungmann: "The most effective form of preaching the faith is the celebration of a feast."[79]

Mystagogy, at the time of the sacraments of initiation, is closest to what we are calling liturgical catechesis. There is a "before, during and after" to mystagogy and to liturgical catechesis. For reasons just discussed, the most powerful catechesis happens *during* the rites. *Before* the rites, we do not explain liturgies; for example, we do not tell people what they will experience at the water during baptism. We simply let the water (lots of it) flow and speak for itself. We do connect personal and communal stories to biblical stories of chaos and creation, flood and rainbow, slavery and exodus, dying and rising, and to the stories of the Samaritan woman, the blind man and Lazarus before baptism; but we also leave people free to respond in faith to whatever God is doing to them in the waters.

At sessions *after* the Easter vigil, the newly baptized do mystagogy: They reflect on, ponder and savor the mystery of God's presence when the community immerses, anoints, eats and drinks at font and table. If the initiation that they experienced has had integrity, with rich and robust symbols and abundant faith, the candidates experience initiation into community and mission. They will learn all they need to know about baptism, confirmation and eucharist.

We follow the same process during the catechumenate period: We prepare the catechumens for the two major rites of transition, the rite of acceptance into the order of catechumens and the rite of election. We do not practice with them. We do practice with the sponsors so that they know where to lead the catechumens, who are left free to be grasped by the ritual. Prior to the celebration, we help them reflect back on their journey to see what God has been doing in their lives. We reflect on questions based on core images and symbols of the rites—the cross in their lives and in our world, their favorite scripture stories, how and for what they have been called and chosen, for example. After the celebration, we reflect back on the rites as we do after the Easter Vigil.[80]

> **Conversation Starter:**   How have you done liturgical catechesis before and after the rites of acceptance and of election?

Throughout the journey of initiation, *the* time for liturgical catechesis takes place every Sunday and feast day of the year during the liturgy of the word and the breaking open of that word. What we have said about #75.1 happens during those gatherings. Most of this book offers a vision and some methods for liturgical catechesis when catechumens meet with a catechist from the time that they are sent forth after the liturgy of the word until the end of Mass, and then joined by their sponsors and family members for extended breaking open of the word for one to two hours.[81] I already have stressed that this time is not an add-on to liturgy. It continues the liturgy of the word and is marked by all the dynamics of church, not classroom—images, symbols, stories, music, prayer and ritual action. Every session should include one or more of the rites that belong to the catechumenate period—celebrations of the word, rites of exorcism, blessings, anointings and, perhaps, the presentations and ephphetha rite (#81–104). And this session might include theology and reflective interpretation of our lives and religious tradition in ways that invite to prayer and conversion.

**Take a Stand:**   What objections have you heard to the sending forth of catechumens after the homily? How have you responded?

DISMISSAL    This discussion of liturgical catechesis brings up the "D" word—dismissal. Unless there are pastoral problems, we "kindly dismiss" catechumens before the liturgy of the eucharist (#75.3). That unleashes a cacophony of complaints, more often from baptized Catholics than from catechumens.

"You are judging catechumens as inferior!" Catholics too often feel judged; they transfer that feeling to the catechumens. "You're throwing them out!" Some Catholics feel excluded and thrown out. "They've been coming to Mass for years. Now they have to leave?" If they have come for years, they may not need a catechumenate. We decide that with them. But many people, including Catholics, have come for years without really hearing a word that prepares them for the table. For them, dismissal to the breaking open of the word is appropriate.

"Sunday is family day, and you are dividing families." We invite the family to extended catechesis after eucharist, and we offer the family a unity deeper than they might find on Sunday afternoon watching the football game.

"In egalitarian America you are making distinctions." Yes! Not because people are good and bad, but because they are different. If catechumens need to be nourished on the word before we invite them to eucharist, how rude and inhospitable to make them sit in pews and watch everyone else eat! At what other meal would we do that? We respect differences and nourish the catechumens on Christ's real presence at the table of the word through ministers and the community (cf. *Constitution on the Liturgy*, #7) until we can rejoice with them at the table of the eucharist. When they finally come to the table, catechumens testify that eucharist is the heart of initiation (as it should be) precisely because they hungered for so long.

"You're forcing shy catechumens to go on public display when they leave." Shyness is rarely the issue. For both catechumens and Catholics, vulnerability may be the problem—perhaps they can't appear before people because they have been hurt by people. They need and deserve gentleness, time to heal. More often, the enemy is American individualism and privatism. Brought into the religious realm, these traits leave us devoid of any communal responsibility to witness to conversion and faith or to prepare for a communal meal with the church understood as body of Christ broken for our sisters and brothers. That is grist for conversion.[82]

"You're asking more of catechumens than you are of everyone else. How about others who stay at Mass but do not come to communion? How about those who do come but who do not see eucharist as communal meal summoning commitment and sacrifice?" Tom Conry comments,

> Since the principal disease of our assemblies seems to be an insufficient understanding of its own baptism, the ritual remedy of sending out those who are not baptized dramatizes and delineates in shockingly prophetic manner—especially for American Catholics, who tend to overvalue a juvenile inclusiveness-at-all-costs—the actually crucial sacramental charism.[83]

Now we are getting to the real issues—what these rites of initiation can be for the whole community, not just the individual catechumen.

In a culture affected by narcissism and privatism, it is hard for some Catholics to hear that sacraments are for the church community and not just for the person. Catholics differ from Pentecostals because we see the community not just as a support to the Spirit but as the very place of the Spirit's presence. Catholics are born again and again through the Spirit who is present within the community. God's life is mediated to persons in sacraments of the Spirit-touched community that is sacrament of Christ.[84]

Centuries ago, Thomas Aquinas asserted that the purpose of eucharist is communal—building up the mystical body of Christ in whom the Spirit lives. In our century, Vatican II states that the preferred form for all sacramental celebrations is communal.[85] Just as the communal celebration of eucharist gradually is raising Catholic consciousness about eucharist as the communal meal that unites us in Christ's body, so these rites move sacraments of initiation away from private ceremonies in dark church vestibules with a few members of the family present on some Sunday afternoon. Like eucharist, initiation also comes front and center—in communal celebrations, in the light of the church nave and sanctuary, with the parish community. And if the principal time of ongoing catechesis is the liturgy of the word followed by breaking open the word, on every Sunday and feast day of the year, then like eucharist, this sacrament finds its purpose—the building up of the body of Christ, Sunday after Sunday, season after season, year after year.

By dismissing catechumens, are we asking more of them than we do of baptized Catholics? Yes. We hope that request is for their sake and that it is not oppressive.

In our culture, we need to change the word "dismissal." It says ejection and rejection. The order uses this word in the introductory explanation in #75.3. It does not use dismissal in the actual ritual of sending forth (#67). "Inviting" and "sending forth" are better terms. They say what we mean. We *invite* catechumens to the table of the word, as an act of hospitality, to receive nourishment in faith until we invite them to the table of the eucharist. We *invite* them to prepare to pray the eucharist in all its parts: the prayer of the faithful, which is intercession for the whole world; the eucharistic prayer of praise for God's deed in Jesus, which is a responsibility of all priestly people; communion with bodies broken and blood shed throughout the world. We invite them to a maturity of faith for the sake of their own healing and that of all God's people.

> The catechumens are being formed for this priestly ministry of public prayer on behalf of the whole world. . . . Letting go of everything that is unsuitable to a maturing disciple is one of the tasks of catechumens.[86]

When catechumens are *sent forth*, they minister to the community.[87] With poor catechesis, they might "slink out" (as one pastor calls it) as if thrown out. With good catechesis, they become aware of their ministry to us. Perhaps they are only gradually entering that "priestly ministry for the whole world," but already they minister to the assembly that sends them forth. They should not slink out but leave with words of support and gratitude by the presider who in our name sends them forth to foster the faith that one day they will witness to us. In many parishes, they leave with the entire assembly extending hands toward them and singing music[88] that promises that we go with them in faith. They leave with smiles on their faces because they see that they are a gift to us.

They are a gift to us because they *invite* those who remain for eucharist to enter more deeply their own conversion journey. They invite visitors or those who frequently come to eucharist without membership to make a decision. Each Sunday, they are a reminder, challenge and invitation to visitors to join this community. They give visible witness that this community is serious about the ministry of initiation.

Catechumens also challenge and *invite* members to deeper faith. Yes, in the past we asked much less of members. Many yawn through the prayers of "priestly people," leave the praying to the priest and drift up to communion with little sense of those with whom they commune. When catechumens leave, they challenge and invite those who stay to wake up—to see what a privilege it is to come to table. Others hide in the back pews and dare not come to communion because they feel unworthy. Their God is not good enough to accept them. Catechumens and sponsors challenge the fearful to cheer up and look up. By their words and witness, they testify to a God who welcomes them precisely because they know they are *not* worthy. They are the elect by God's mercy, not the perfect.

In that regard, I offer a special note to homilists. My bias is that when we open up the scriptures and the liturgy, the bedrock of our tradition, we discover afresh the God of Jesus Christ. We hear again both Jesus' acceptance of outcasts, sinners and the unworthy and his challenge to those who thought they were worthy. In the wrong hands, what we ask of catechumens could be a new elitism. We need to preach with constancy and fidelity that those chosen and elected—the "elite" of Jesus' time—were those able to accept God's unearned love and mercy. That is the message we preach to catechumens and to the community Sunday after Sunday.

> **Conversation Starter:**   What is your experience of the impact on the larger parish community of the sending forth of catechumens?

We know that catechumens leave each Sunday to reflect on the homily. This means that some of those faces in the assembly are not just yawning or fearful. They look up in expectation and hope. They eagerly await a message of good news that calls them to conversion. If homilists preach to them, in the simple, clear, convincing language that "babies in the faith" can hear, in stories that link today with tradition, perhaps we can preach through them to the yawning and the fearful. We shall be preaching conversion Sunday after Sunday to the whole community. Who knows what might happen? If we are born again (and again), catechumens have again ministered to us.

Through the liturgies and liturgical catechesis, initiation ceases to be one more program at the periphery of parish life. It becomes a sacrament at the heart of parish life with potential impact on the entire community, as eucharist is. Take your time. This sacrament will be there until Jesus comes again. The opposite is also true. As Marshal Lyautey said when his orderly protested at watering the century plant in his garden because it wouldn't bloom for a hundred years, "Then we haven't a moment to lose!"

*Witness to Faith (#75.4)*    In 1972, the United States bishops published a pastoral letter, "To Teach as Jesus Did." If we teach as Jesus did, we learn to eat as Jesus did. We give witness to the good news by washing feet. We break not only bread at table. We break open our lives for all God's broken and wounded people and recognize Christ in that shared brokenness.

Xavier Leon-Dufour claims that the scriptures tell two tales about how Jesus eats his final meal.[89] The first is in the synoptic gospels and in Paul who tell us Jesus' words, "This bread is my body broken for you; this cup is the new covenant of my blood shed for you." Too much of church life focuses on bread and cup. We forget the "broken" and "shed." We forget that when we eat and drink that bread and cup, *we* become body broken and blood shed for all our sisters and brothers. We forget the second story about Jesus' final meal in John's gospel—the story of Jesus washing feet. We share the lives of broken people by washing feet, by giving our lives in service. Leon-Dufour says that is why the washing of feet was considered a sacrament until the thirteenth century.

The Last Supper was like all the meals that Jesus ate. His meals offer life and healing for those most rejected and alien: the woman "who had a bad name in the town" (Luke 7:36–50); prodigal sons and daughters; the poor; the sick; the hated foreigners at wedding feasts (Luke 14:15–24); Zacchaeus, the wretched and puny tax collector (Luke 19:1–10); all these are brought to a climax by broken disciples who recognize the Lord in shared brokenness when they break bread (Luke 24:13–35). At those meals, Jesus catechized, not by lecturing about love but by eating with love. He did it by doing it, and he told us to "do this in memory of me." Within that command is the invitation to apostles to give witness to Jesus' love by washing feet: "I, your Lord and Teacher, have just washed your feet. You, then, should wash one another's feet" (John 13:14). He commands us to eat as he did.

Very early, Christians forgot how to eat as Jesus did. Paul admonished the Corinthians, "When you come together as a church, I hear that there are divisions among you. . . . When you come together, it is not really to eat the Lord's supper. For when the time comes to eat, each of you goes ahead with your own supper, and one goes hungry while another becomes drunk" (1 Corinthians 11:18–20). In modern terms, "the well-off came . . . with their smoked pheasant and 'Ile de France' bread, their chilled 'Chateauneuf-du-Pape' wine and linen in wicker baskets. . . . And the poor brought their baloney sandwiches and Diet Cokes in brown paper bags."[90]

So very early, Christians were reminded how to eat as Jesus did. St. John Chrysostom urged, "Do you want to honor Christ's body? Then do not honor him here in the church with silken garments while neglecting him outside where he is cold and naked. . . . Of what use is it to weigh down Christ's table with golden cups when he himself is dying of hunger? First fill him when he is hungry; then use the means you have left to adorn his table."[91] In the earliest tradition of Hippolytus, the criteria for conversion centered on such a change of life-style; in the tradition of James, the question was, "Have they cared for the orphans and the widows?" (James 1:26).

In early American times, Bartholome de las Casas, the first priest ordained in the Western Hemisphere, refused to celebrate eucharist in Cuba because the wheat used for the eucharistic bread was harvested by slaves. He knew the link between liturgy and justice. In our times, Robert Hovda, one of the pioneer liturgists of this century who, like Virgil Michel or H. A. Reinhold, never lost the connection between liturgy and justice, writes about eucharist:

> Where else in our society are we all addressed and sprinkled and bowed to and incensed and touched and kissed and treated like *somebody*—all in the very

same way? Where else do economic czars and beggars get the same treatment? Where else are food and drink blessed in a common prayer of thanksgiving, broken and poured out, so that everybody, everybody shares and shares alike?[92]

DOING EUCHARIST    At Easter, we are initiated into a community that is filled with the Spirit's gifts and sent as apostles at Pentecost to eat as Jesus did, to wash feet and to give away those gifts to our sisters and brothers. Therefore, the order of initiation states that catechesis after initiation happens especially at eucharists of the Easter season (#244, 247). It is there that we learn how to follow Jesus' command: "I have set an example for you, so that you will do just what I have done for you" (John 13:16).

At eucharist where we treat czars and beggars like somebody, we call the Christian community to subversion and conversion. We are sent to subvert a culture that does not know how to eat and to convert all meals into places of communion, care and justice.

"Mass" comes from the Latin *missa*, which means "sent." An apostle is "one sent forth" (*apostellein* in Greek). Like Jesus, we are apostles anointed and sent by the Spirit to bring "good news to the poor . . . liberty to captives and recovery of sight to the blind, to set free the oppressed and announce that the time has come when the Lord will save his people" (Luke 4:18–19). We already noted that in Greek, "martyr" means witness. Early martyrs witnessed by their physical death. All Christians are called to die, to sacrifice, to give our lives for each other. In the sacraments of initiation, we all are anointed with chrism, which is blessed as the oil of "priests, prophets, kings and martyrs." If we eat as Jesus did, we are sent as witnesses from eucharist to give ourselves literally away—in our marriages, families, friendships, work, neighborhoods, communities, especially in being with and for the poor. This is the "apostolic witness" that begins in the catechumenate, not just after initiation.

Reports from all over North America indicate that in many parishes, mystagogy is a disaster. Apparently, the neophytes did not come to see initiation as incorporation into a church of Spirit-filled missionaries. They may "attend" Mass, but they fail to "do" eucharist. At least they fail to participate in sessions that reflect on the meaning of eucharist for mission and witness, and they fail to meet in small groups of fellow missionaries to support each other in living the gospel.[93]

STRONG ON SERVICE    The seeds of that disaster are sown during a catechumenate period that ignores #75.4. Some are concerned about catechesis being "soft on doctrine." Without denying that concern, would that there was equal concern about being "soft on service"! Do we really believe that catechumens come to know Christ where he said he would be? That we shall be judged on whether or not we knew him there—in the least of his brothers and sisters?

Yes, we need to know creeds and commandments. Ultimately, however, creeds are about what God has *done* to love us—create, die and rise, send the Spirit. Commandments are about how we respond in love—love God and love neighbor as ourself (Mark 12:29–31). We learn about God by receiving and giving justice and love. "To experience God is to do justice" (Jeremiah 22:15–16; Matthew 7:21; 1 John 4:7–8).[94]

If one out of ten verses in the synoptic gospels (one out of seven in Luke) is about poverty and riches with the call "to bring good news to the poor" (Luke 4:18), we invite catechumens to the heart of the gospel not just by talking it but by doing it. They will learn Catholic precepts (#75.1), such as the corporal works of mercy, by doing them (#75.4).

We know God in Christ by doing what God did in Christ. "We do not first know Christ and then follow him. Like the disciples, we come to know him *by* following him."[95] Therefore, we do not wait until after Easter to involve candidates in mission ("Surprise! Have we got a ministry for you!"), often reduced to handing them a list of parish groups. *During* the catechumenate period, catechumens, as apprentice Christians, practice their apprenticeship by discipleship (from the Latin *discere*, to learn) and apostleship. *During* the catechumenate, they come to know Christ by following him as disciples and by being sent forth in apostolic witness. If that happens, they learn by osmosis and simply take it for granted that they are being apprenticed into a lifetime mission for which they need support during mystagogy and beyond.

How might the catechumenate period foster that apprenticeship? First, the normal turf for witness is not in some church group with Catholic letters (CCD, CYO, CFM or even OCIA) but in lives that all those Catholic letters exist to support: in family, neighborhood, work, community and world. During mystagogy, we usually do not invite neophytes to the catechetical or liturgical ministries first. The neophytes prepare for the ministry of word and table by washing feet. Parishes are tempted to fill "churchy" ministry slots with these enthusiastic new members. Catechumenate teams pounce on them as a ready source for new sponsors because they know the process. Neophytes themselves sometimes want to stay in the cocoon as sponsors, especially if in reality they joined the team, not the church.

During the catechumenate period, therefore, they need to learn that they are initiated into a church whose reason for being is not self-service or self-help, but service in and to the world. That is where God's reign of justice and peace happens, not at church meetings. All church meetings and ministries exist to serve the reign of God. One pastor puts it this way:

> If the catechetical enterprise in your parish covers womb to tomb, we may have a good parish. Add to that well-trained music ministers, liturgy planning committees for principal Masses . . . and on-the-job training for lectors, folk groups and choirs, we may have a better parish. The best parish includes all the aforementioned plus two out of three decent homilies and a parish council that engenders total parish participation in all decision making. Wonderful! Except for *one* thing. We may be on the road to hell. If Matthew 25 is not integral to your parish organization and ministries and, in fact, the real reason for all the self-nurture, then what's the church for? We are put here to work toward the reign of God. Show me in your budget and parish directory how you are doing that.[96]

Fidelity to Matthew 25 ultimately is an act of faith in a God revealed in and committed to the poor. In seeing the hungry, thirsty, sick, naked, prisoner and stranger, we see the Christ. Commitment to the poor reveals the kind of God in whom we believe. Gustavo Gutierrez writes: "We must be committed to the poor, not necessarily because they are good, but because God is good. According to Karl Barth, God always takes the side of the lowly. As Bishop Desmond Tutu said, . . . 'God is not neutral.'"[97]

We invite catechumens to see what some Catholics do not see: that their daily lives are the place of their Christian vocation to live Matthew 25. That is where faith emerges into relationships, responsibilities, lifestyle, behavior, values and action.[98] The inquirer comes from the world, into the parish community, into the small catechumenal community, to be empowered to leave that catechumenate, to go back into the world to make it the reign of God. That is why, when Dolores Leckey was executive director of the United States bishops' Committee on the Laity, she loved to say that 98.5 percent of the baptized live their Christian vocation not in some explicit church group but in their families, neighborhoods, work and civic communities.

David O'Brien adds, "Let us remember that all the works of the church, from sacraments to church suppers, have public implications. . . . Will we form a people for the church, or will we form a people for a world, this world, our world?"[99] Unfortunately, catechumens join a church in which many Catholics have little sense of mission or vocation to share Christ's love. "Only 34 percent of Catholics say that sharing the love of Christ with others is very important to them, compared to 51 percent of Protestants and 86 percent of Evangelicals." Furthermore, only two percent of church-going Catholics are personally involved in evangelization; 38 percent have what the Notre Dame study on the parish calls an "agentic religion" (primarily concerned about their own salvation). Only 32 percent of parishes have outreach programs. The good news is that Gallup reports that 64 percent of the churched (versus 40 percent of the unchurched) are involved in volunteerism in the civic community. Apparently, some churches help people make connections between gospel and world.[100]

Therefore, the call of #75.4 to apostolic witness does not mean that catechumens necessarily join some parish ministry group. The primary task of catechists is to help catechumens break open the word of God in ways that make practical connections between the word and their lives. Research before the 1987 synod on the laity with some 100,000 people revealed that many Catholics seek those connections:

> Marriage and family life are cited most often by these faithful as the area where they experience God most (along with the parish) and also the area where they seek further guidance and resources. Marriage and family is where the relevance of their faith is primarily tested for these faithful. . . . There is widespread recognition that the Christian life includes areas customarily called secular, i.e., work, civic obligations, political activities, neighborhood and family life, public education, culture. However, people frequently admit that this integration does not occur often enough or well enough. . . . Next to family and parish, most people say they experience God and exercise their vocation in the workplace, but it is a distant third.[101]

That is tragic, because work occupies so much of people's lives and is the turf where so much of the gospel is lived. Therefore, homilists and catechists will empower both catechumens and the baptized to connect word, worship and world.[102]

Second, we might invite catechumens to join church ministry groups. Many will need the more formal structure of a group that is making links between gospel and world. Catechumens often gravitate toward what their sponsors have been doing to witness to their faith. Usually, that will not be catechetical or liturgical ministry but ministries of justice and social concern with groups committed to sharing good news with the poor and oppressed. Catechumens usually move gradually toward this involvement. Apostolic witness is built into the curriculum. We avoid focus only on the "service project" approach taken by some programs for youth. We are not inviting catechumens to a project, but to a life of mission and witness that will continue after initiation.

> **Conversation Starter:** How have you invited and involved catechumens in Christian witness, service and mission to and in the world during the catechumenate period?

Third, as we have seen, catechumens witness to the community during the liturgy of the word and especially at the major rites of initiation. Even when they shake with fear or fumble and stammer their words—perhaps especially when they shake and stammer—they give witness to the faithful that God does wonderful things in the lives of wonder-filled, ordinary people like you and me.

This is the holistic vision of catechesis of #75—proclaiming the good news through message, community life, worship and witness. All of these dimensions of catechesis are interdependent. They come together in a poem by a catechumen, a Native American from the Cherokee nation, written after her rite of election:

> Lord of the valley, Lord of the mountaintop,
> Lord of timelessness and our times,
>
> We have walked with you a year around
> And shared a year of grace.
> We have looked into each others' eyes
> And shared an honest year.
> . . . . . . . . . . . . . . . . . . . .
> Fresh pages of your calendar
> Bear the marks of our response.

We touch the rhythms of your seasons
And carry deep within
The patternings of changing and of love.

We kneel
   Tremble
   Shivering in the chasms
   Shivering on the heights
   Grateful for companions.

Will you take us now and make us useful?
Can we share these treasures?
Water and wine for a thirsty time—
Bread and roses for hungry hearts.

As you gave life for life
As life has been shared with us for life
So now we give our days and strength
To walk each gifted year around
In joy.

# Endnotes

[1] F. X. Connolly, ed., *A Newman Reader* (Garden City NY: Image Books, 1964), 81, 187.

[2] Martin Luther wrote in his letter of introduction to the *Small Catechism*, "Be faithful to that text, word for word in such manner that your hearers will be able to repeat it after you and to commit it to memory. If any refuse to learn it in that way, you must tell them they are renouncing Jesus Christ, and they are no longer Christians. . . ."

[3] Cf. Mary Charles Bryce, "The Baltimore Catechism—Origin and Reception," in *Sourcebook in Modern Catechetics*, ed. Michael Warren (Winona MN: St. Mary's Press, 1983), 140–45.

[4] For John Paul II's comments on the need and place of catechetical works and catechisms, see *Catechesi Tradendae*, #49–50.

[5] Berard Marthaler comments on the pitfalls of catechisms: "The better the catechism is as a manual of instruction, the more likely it is to take on a life of its own. . . . Mastery of the catechism text becomes a goal in itself. . . . The short, concise answers with their rhythmic cadence, especially in the hands of untrained catechists, put greater emphasis on orthophony than orthodoxy." "Catechetical

Director or Catechism?" *Religious Education and the Future*, ed. Dermot Lane (New York: Paulist Press, 1986), 58.

Graham Greene complains about a priest who was unable to help him into faith, who could only give him "a penny catechism with its catalogue of preposterous questions and answers, smug and explanatory: mystery like a butterfly killed by cyanide, stiffened and laid out with pins and paper-strips." "A Visit to Morin," in *The Substance of Things Hoped For*, ed. John Breslin (Garden City NY: Doubleday, 1987), 284.

[6] Andrew Greeley, *The Religious Imagination* (New York: Wm. H. Sadlier, Inc., 1981), 49.

[7] George Gallup, "What We Know and What We Do Not Know: A Statistical Analysis of Unchurched Americans," *New Catholic World* (July/August 1976): 148–54.

[8] Raymond Kemp, "The Rite of Christian Initiation of Adults at Ten Years," *Worship* 56 (July 1982): 314.

[9] Bishop Donal Murray, "The Language of Catechesis," in *Religious Education*, ed. Dermot Lane, 131.

[10] According to a Gallup poll, 28 percent of those who ceased church membership in 1978 and 22 percent in 1988 did so because they moved; Gallup says that it would not take much for them to return, especially if they are invited and bonded with a community. George Gallup et al., "The Unchurched American—Ten Years Later" (Princeton: Princeton Religion Research Center, 1988), 45.

[11] Didier Piviteau, "School, Society and Catechetics," in *Religious Education*, ed. Dermot Lane, 24–25, 27.

[12] Thomas Groome expands this approach to church ministry in his "pedagogical creed" at the end of his masterful *Sharing Faith* (San Francisco: Harper & Row, 1991), 444–46.

[13] In appendix II, I offer an exercise that extends these dimensions of catechesis to other dimensions of parish life.

[14] See Vatican Council II, *Decree on the Church's Missionary Activity (Ad Gentes)*, #14.

[15] *Constitution on the Church*, #1.

[16] I treat these dimensions of mission in *Ministries: Sharing God's Gifts* (Winona MN: St. Mary's Press, 1980).

[17] Thomas Harding, "Preaching: Let the Word Happen," *Modern Liturgy* 16 (December 1989): 10.

[18] Fred Baumer, *Toward the Development of Homiletic as Rhetorical Genre*, unpublished doctoral dissertation (Northwestern University, 1985), 227.

[19] About homilies in general, Andrew Greeley concludes from his study of young adults: "The most important influence on the religious behavior of American Catholics is the religious behavior of their spouses. The second most important factor is the quality of Sunday preaching in the local parish. Nothing much else matters." *The Catholic Myth* (New York: Charles Scribner's Sons, 1990), 145.

[20] *Fulfilled in Your Hearing* (Washington DC: USCC, 1982), 29. I shall suggest later that although homilies most often deal with the scriptures, the focus is more correctly on the entire liturgy of the word and its place in the season of the liturgical year.

[21] *Decree on the Ministry and Life of Priests, #4; Decree on the Bishops' Pastoral Office in the Church, #12*

[22] *Fulfilled in Your Hearing*, 36–38.

[23] *Fulfilled in Your Hearing*, 25.

[24] Baumer, *Toward the Development*, see chapter six especially.

[25] Cf. "A Shared Praxis Approach to Preaching," in Groome, *Sharing Faith*, 372–78.

[26] *Fulfilled in Your Hearing*, 20.

[27] Mary Catherine Hilkert, "Preaching and Theology: Rethinking the Relationship," *Worship* (September 1991):400. She adds that M.-D. Chenu once claimed that every thinking Christian is an "unwitting theologian." "Preachers need to become 'witting ones.' To take on the life of the preacher is to commit oneself to becoming a contemplative . . . not only [by engaging in] ongoing academic study but also [in] serious, daily and sustained reflection on experience . . . in the tradition of Thomas Aquinas who described the theological task as reflection on all of reality in relationship to God," 404–5. Cf. *Summa theologiae* Ia, q.1, a.7.

[28] Donald Senior, "Scripture and Homiletics: What the Bible Can Teach the Preacher," *Worship* 65 (September 1991): 397.

[29] *Pastoral Constitution on the Church in the Modern World, #1.*

[30] Cf. Allan Bloom, *The Closing of the American Mind* (New York: Houghton Mifflin, 1987).

[31] Charles Hefling, *Why Doctrines?* (Cambridge MA: Cowley Publications, 1984), 69.

[32] "Let's face it, let's own up to it. It is about time that we become deadly serious and admit what is being admitted in a number of secular fields of education, namely that there is an absolute necessity to return to the basics in these fields and if this is the case in these fields, all the more reason for doing so in this most important field of religious education." Michael J. Wrenn, "Religious Education at the Crossroads," in *Religious Education*, 46.

[33] Cardinal Joseph Ratzinger, "Sources and transmission of the faith," *Communio* 10 (Spring 1983):18. The bishops of the United States also identify the basics of religious knowledge in *Sharing the Light of Faith*, chapter V, and in "The Basic Teachings of the Catholic Church."

[34] Berard L. Marthaler, *The Creed* (Mystic CN: Twenty-third Publications, 1987), 393.

[35] "Book Review" of Robert Duggan and Maureen Kelly, *The Christian Initiation of Children*, in *The Living Light* 28 (Fall 1991), emphasis added. I do not intend to enter or try to resolve the controversy between Groome and Duggan and Kelly as to whether catechesis based on the liturgy of the word without additional religious education sessions is sufficient to hand on both our biblical and postbiblical tradition with young children; cf. Thomas Groome and Robert Duggan, "Lectionary-based Catechesis: Conflicting Views," *Church* 8 (Spring 1992): 14–20. I do affirm that given the qualifications and suggestions of this book (e.g., adding sessions on particular doctrinal or moral issues when necessary), it is largely sufficient for the initiation of adults.

[36] Marthaler, *The Creed*, 68–69.

[37] For treatments of "the Catholic difference," see Rosemary Haughton, *The Catholic Thing* (Springfield IL: Templegate, 1980); David Tracy, *The Analogical Imagination* (New York: Crossroads Publishing Co., 1981); Andrew M. Greeley and Mary Greeley Durkin, *How to Save the Catholic Church* (New York: Viking Penguin, Inc., 1984). For a pamphlet suitable for candidates, cf. Joanne McPortland, "Catholics: Christians with a Difference" (Los Angeles: Franciscan Communications, 1984). Richard McBrien, "The Theological Foci of Catholicism: Sacramentality, Mediation, Communion," *Catholicism, Volume II* (Minneapolis: Winston Press, 1980), 1180–83.

[38] Aidan Kavanagh, "Principles for Sacramental Catechesis," *The Living Light* 23 (Summer 1987): 322.

[39] That sacramental experience appears in that wonderfully Catholic poet Gerard Manley Hopkins's "dearest freshness deep-down things" and novelist Walker Percy who writes of "bread, wine, water, touch, breath, words, talking, listening . . . a world which is a sacrament and a mystery" (cited in *America* 164 [May 26, 1990]:1). Another Catholic writer, Hillaire Belloc, writes in homelier fashion:

> Where ere the Catholic sun doth shine
> There's music and laughter and good red wine.
> At least I've heard them tell it so:
> *Benedicamus Domino.*

[40] *Constitution on the Sacred Liturgy*, #102. The Council goes on to mention Mary, the saints and the panoply of Catholic devotions celebrated during the liturgical year, #103–5.

[41] "Apostolic Constitution on the Promulgation of the Roman Missal," 1969.

[42] Gerard Sloyan, "Forming Catechumens through the Lectionary," in *Before and After Baptism*, ed. James Wilde (Chicago: Liturgy Training Publications, 1988), 32.

[43] Supposedly, Karl Rahner's mother once said, "I never could understand Karl!"

[44] Hilkert, "Preaching and Theology," 403–4. Gerard Sloyan insists that biblical and liturgical preaching does express the fundamental doctrine and teaching of the church but in images and narrative appropriate to liturgy. "Is Church Teaching Neglected When the Lectionary Is Preached?" *Worship* 61 (March 1987): 126–40.

[45] Catherine Dooley, "The Use and Misuse of the Lectionary in Catechesis for Children," *The Living Light* 27 (Spring 1991): 223.

[46] Episcopal Diocese of Colorado, 1-800-824-1813.

[47] St. Anthony Messenger Press, Cincinnati, Ohio. However, the *Come and See* materials by Karen Albertus, also available from St. Anthony Press, do impose a theme on given Sundays and feasts by using a particular issue of *Catholic Update*.

[48] Mary Collins, "Becoming a Priestly People," *Catechumenate* 13 (May 1991): 5. In terms of biblical illiteracy, Gallup reports, for example, that only 50 percent of American adults could name any one of the four gospels. *The Role of the Bible in American Society* (Princeton: Princeton Religion Research Center, November 1990).

Television personality Steve Allen's research found that in one parish, even in the "religious" 1950s, "nearly one-fourth of adult members . . . could not identify Calvary as the place of Jesus' death. Over one-third did not know that Nazareth was the town where Jesus was brought up. Gethsemane rang no bell for 43 percent, and

Pentecost had no significance for 75 percent." Their answers about the number of converts baptized by Jesus ranged from none (correct) to 300,000. *Steve Allen on the Bible, Religion and Morality* (New York: Prometheus Books, 1989).

[49] Dooley, "The Use and Misuse," 222.

[50] Gerard S. Sloyan, "Some Suggestions for a Biblical Three-Year Lectionary," *Worship* 63 (November 1989): 521–35; Sloyan, "Forming Catechumens, 27–30; Jim Wilde, "The Lectionary: Some Problems and Remedies," *Catechumenate* 9 (July 1987): 25–30.

[51] Sloyan, "Is Church Teaching Neglected," 130, 134.

[52] Walter Brueggemann, *Finally Comes the Poet* (Minneapolis: Fortress Press, 1989), 2–3.

[53] Thomas Morris, "Lectionary-based Catechesis: Is It Enough?" *Catechumenate* 13 (September 1991): 22–27. Note: Morris now prefers the title "Catechesis Based on the Liturgy of the Word," because the content of his article clearly includes more than lectionary texts as building blocks.

[54] Hefling, *Why Doctrines?*, 45.

[55] Bernard Lonergan, *Method in Theology* (New York: Herder and Herder, 1972), 79.

[56] Although the document does not mention it, the catechumens also might "become familiar with the Christian way of life" and learn to pray through the ministry of a spiritual director; cf. Thomas H. Morris, *The RCIA: Transforming the Church*, (New York: Paulist Press, 1989), 173–81.

[57] Aidan Kavanagh, "Initiation," in *Simple Gifts*, vol. 2 (Washington DC: The Liturgical Conference, 1974), 12–13.

[58] A book of prayer written explicitly for catechumens is *Teach Us to Pray* by Gabe Huck (New York: Wm. H. Sadlier, Inc., 1982). *Catholic Household Blessing and Prayers* is an excellent resource for prayer. It offers the "traditional" Catholic prayers and provides models for prayers and blessings at various moments of life (Washington DC: USCC, 1988).

[59] Cf. Cardinal Joseph Bernardin, "The Consistent Ethic: What Sort of Framework?" *Origins* 16 (October 30, 1986): 345–50.

[60] Kathleen R. Fischer and Thomas N. Hart, *Christian Foundations* (New York: Paulist Press, 1986), 85–86.

[61] 1971 Extraordinary Synod, "Justice in the World," introduction.

[62] Cf. *Rite of Christian Initiation of Adults*, National Statutes for the Catechumenate, #24.

[63] Cf. Ron Lewinski, *Guide for Sponsors* (Chicago: Liturgy Training Publications, 1980); Thomas Morris, *Walking Together in Faith* (New York: Paulist Press, 1992).

[64] *Music in Catholic Worship*, #6.

[65] Mark Searle, "The Pedagogical Function in the Liturgy," *Worship* 55 (July 1981): 347. Tom Conry adds: "There is an announcement that everyone should 'stand and greet our celebrant' and he walks solemnly to the front of the room . . . in a procession that is clearly the remnant of court royalism. He turns to the assembly from his point in front of everyone where only he has access to the important ritual furniture and his first substantial ritual action is to forgive the assembly for being in its own space: 'For all the times we have gotten out of line, Lord have mercy.' . . . A mere two minutes and thirty seconds into the liturgy we have already said everything about that parish's theology of the importance of baptism that there is to say." "How Can We Keep From Singing?" *Pastoral Music* 13 (October/November 1988): 33–36.

[66] Like many of us, Woody Allen wants not ordinary experience but signs and wonders proving God's presence: "How can I believe in God when just last week I got my tongue caught in the roller of an electric typewriter? I am plagued by doubts. What if everything is an illusion and nothing exists? In that case, I definitely overpaid for my carpet. If only God would give me some clear sign; like making a large deposit in my name at a Swiss bank." Cited by Kathleen Fischer and Thomas Hart, *Christian Foundations* (New York: Paulist Press, 1986), 29–30.

[67] Peter Fink, "The Language of Sacraments," *Worship* 52 (November 1978): 568.

[68] One liturgist always knew better. Aidan Kavanagh, with his customary poetic flourish, writes, "Sacraments don't teach; they seduce. . . . Sacraments are not 'bottom lines'; they are grand opera. Sacraments are not 'white papers'; they are love poems (How do I love thee? Let me count the ways . . . ). Sacraments are not single tones; they are symphonies filled with fugues, themes, codas and repeats." "Principles for Sacramental Catechesis," 322.

[69] Duggan and Kelly, *The Christian Initiation of Children*, 48.

[70] Gilbert Ostdiek, "Catechesis, Liturgical," in *The New Dictionary of Sacramental Worship*, ed. Peter Fink (Collegeville: The Liturgical Press, 1990), 169.

[71] For a survey of principles of catechesis for all four periods of the catechumenate, see James B. Dunning, "Prebaptismal and Postbaptismal Catechesis for Adults," in *Before and After Baptism*, 53–65.

[72] Karl Rahner, *Mission and Grace*, vol. I (London: Sheed and Ward, 1963), 156.

[73] John Shea, *An Experience Named Spirit* (Chicago: Thomas More Press, 1983), 98.

[74] "Experiential-expressivism has lost ground everywhere except in most theological schools and departments of religious studies where, if anything, the trend is the reverse," George Lindbeck, *The Nature of Doctrine* (Philadelphia: The Westminster Press, 1984), 25.

[75] Lindbeck, *The Nature of Doctrine*, 37. Lindbeck adds, "[This] reverses the relation of the inner and the outer. Instead of deriving external features of a religion from inner experience, it is the inner experiences which are viewed as derivative. . . . To become a Christian involves learning the story of Israel and of Jesus well enough to interpret and experience oneself and one's world in its terms. A religion is above all an external word . . . that molds and shapes the self and its world, rather than an expression . . . of a preexisting self" (p. 34).

[76] Collins, "Becoming Priestly People," 6–8.

[77] Although Lindbeck titles his book *The Nature of Doctrine*, his treatment makes clear that it is not abstract doctrine but the power of myth and ritual that most forms and shapes us. Our *experience* of God in sacrament and ritual, through liturgical catechesis, is once again the best way to help catechumens learn "the Catholic difference."

[78] Duggan and Kelly, *The Christian Initiation of Children*, 34.

[79] Josef Jungmann, "The Kerygma in the History of the Pastoral Activity of the Church," in *Sourcebook*, ed. Michael Warren, 200.

[80] For example, Linda Gaupin, CDP, associate secretary to the United States Bishops' Committee on the Liturgy, suggests that in addition to word, there are nine primary symbols for Catholic Christian identity and worship—assembly, water, light, touch (laying on of hands), salt, bread and wine, oil, new garment, cross. She offers ways to reflect on these core images before and after a liturgy.

[81] Aside from the liturgical/catechetical reasons discussed in the text, many parishes find Sunday morning the most practical time for catechesis. In rural parishes, people

need to travel only once; in some urban areas, people fear to leave home on a week-night; and in suburban areas, with meetings and sports scheduled every night of the week, Sunday morning might be the uncluttered time. In addition, if we do our cate-chesis with #75.1 (word) and #75.3 (ritual) on Sunday, that leaves the rest of the week for #75.2 (community) and #75.4 (apostolic life); too often, those dimensions get short shrift. For another treatment of reasons for dismissal, see James B. Dunning, "Don't Dismiss the Dismissal: But Change the Name," *Church* 5 (Summer 1989): 34–37.

[82] Psychologist Robert Coles writes a devastating critique of middle- and upper-class church privatism: "You enter churches of the privileged full of yourself. . . . There will be—and this is important—no surprises. The format is fixed and the words and music are modulated, no extremes. . . . Without having been told, you understand that if anything happens to you of a spiritual nature, you are to keep it to yourself." Robert Coles and George Abbott White, "The Religion of the Privileged Ones," *Cross Currents* 31:1, 7.

[83] Tom Conry, "A Short Technical Organum for the Liturgy" (Unpublished paper, 1986), 11.

[84] The paradox is that Pentecostals, for whom the community is a luxury and simply a support to faith, often have more fellowship and community than Catholics for whom the community (in theory) is a necessity, the incarnation of the risen Christ through the Spirit. The theory, as voiced by Aidan Kavanagh, proclaims: "As Jesus is the sacrament of God, so the church is the sacrament of Christ; and all its liturgical rites are sacraments of the church. Know the sacraments and we know the church; know the church and we know the Christ without fail; know the Christ and we know God with absolute certainty." "Principles for Sacramental Catechesis," 322.

[85] *Constitution on the Sacred Liturgy, #27.*

[86] Collins, "Becoming Priestly People," 7.

[87] One author contends that more important than the catechesis following the sending forth is the sending forth itself. It challenges those who stay to question their own faith and preparation for the eucharistic table: "On a brutally practical level, what happens during the time that the catechumens are together outside of the liturgy . . . is ritually beside the point. The prophetic action is in the dismissal rite itself. . . . That is why the dismissal rite is widely resisted, even disregarded in 'liberal' parishes." Tom Conry, "A Short Technical Organum," 5.

[88] Music written for the rites of initiation is becoming available, including acclama-tions to accompany the sending forth of catechumens, see David Haas, *Who Calls You*

*By Name*, vols. I and II (Chicago: GIA Publications) and Lynn Trapp, *Rite of Christian Initiation of Adults: Musical Setting* (St. Louis: Morning Star Music).

[89] Xavier Leon-Dufour, *Sharing the Eucharist Bread* (New York: Paulist Press, 1987), 283–85.

[90] James Dallen, "Liturgy and Justice for All," *Worship* 65 (September 1991): 291.

[91] Cited by David Emerick and James Garcia Ward, "The Relationship between Eucharist and Justice," *Emmanuel* 93 (July/August 1987): 311.

[92] Robert Hovda, "The Mass and Its Social Consequences," *Liturgy* 80 (June/July 1982): 6.

[93] Some drop out completely, perhaps in part because they miss the care and support that the community gave them during the process of initiation. Therefore, the United States bishops ask that parishes invite them to meet at least monthly with other Christians for a year after initiation (*Order of Christian Initiation of Adults*, National Statutes for the Catechumenate, 24). In part, that is to support them in faith. It is also to support them in their witness to that faith. We need to discuss this with catechumens before initiation so that they see clearly that they are baptized for mission.

[94] Lane, "The Challenge Facing," 160.

[95] Mark Searle, "Conversion and Initiation into Faith Growth," in *Christian Initiation Resources Reader*, vol. I (New York: Wm. H. Sadlier, Inc., 1984), 72.

[96] Raymond B. Kemp, "The Mystagogical Experience," in *Christian Initiation Resources Reader*, vol. IV (New York: Wm. H. Sadlier, Inc., 1984), 67.

[97] Gustavo Gutierrez, "The Church of the Poor," *The Month* (July 1989): 266.

[98] That is the vision of John Paul II's exhortation, *Christifideles Laici* (e.g., #5), written after the synod on the laity. For the text with commentary by Peter Coughlan, see *The Hour of the Laity* (Philadelphia: E. J. Dwyer, 1989). Also see the *Constitution on the Sacred Church*, #31, and the *Decree on the Apostolate of the Laity*, #5.

[99] David O'Brien, "The Future of Ministry: Historical Context," in *The Future of Ministry*, ed. Joseph Sinwell and Billie Poon (New York: Wm. H. Sadlier, Inc., 1985), 49.

[100] George Gallup and Jim Castelli, *The American Catholic People: Their Beliefs, Practices, and Values* (Garden City NY: Doubleday, 1987), 38; Joseph Gremillion and Jim Castelli, *The Emerging Parish: The Notre Dame Study of Parish Life Since Vatican II* (San Francisco: Harper & Row, 1987), 180.

[101] Robert Kinast, "Laity View Their Roles in Church and World," *Origins* 17 (June 25, 1987): 95–99.

[102] That includes the oft-disdained political world: "A skeptical attitude toward 'politics' has no reasonable foundation among Christians. . . . It seems particularly important to promote among the laity's vocations a political involvement which places Christian values at the service of the human person and the progress of justice in the life among nations." Vatican General Secretariat of the Synod of Bishops, "Vocation and Mission of the Laity," *Origins* 17 (May 21, 1987): 1–19.

# CHAPTER FIVE

## Hearing the Good News

*I cannot imagine a scrap of argument against a rigorous theological and historical education touching on both East and West to prepare the homilist [and catechist]. . . . [But] one error in pastoral practice I am sure we must not make again is to impose upon the Bible a creedal grid which makes the Bible say those things and only those things that the great doctrinal struggles . . . resulted in. . . . We have made the Bible the handmaid of theology—theology whose sole raison d'étre is to be the handmaid of the Bible. We have put human reflection on the divine word above that word. . . . You know some of the tragic outcomes: purgatory reckoned on a par with the parousia, . . . the undeniable reality of assisting or cooperating grace [actual grace] reckoned superior to the graced life itself [sanctifying grace—the life of the Spirit].[1]*

• Gerard Sloyan

■

WE CONTINUE TO sharpen our focus—from catechesis in general (chapters two and three) to the vision of catechesis in community in the order of initiation #75 (chapter four) to catechesis through the liturgy of the word envisioned in #75.1 and #75.3, with a response to Gerard Sloyan's call for homilies/catecheses centered on the word of God (chapter five).

We also come to the main reason why I am writing this book. I write to respond to the question How do we (homilists, catechists and catechumens) hear the word of God? In this chapter, we explore four ways of hearing God's word.

## A Fundamentalist Hearing of Scripture

I am a product of pre–Vatican II formation in scripture (and doctrine/ theology). I was formed (deformed and misinformed) by four years of a Catholic fundamentalist/literalist reading and hearing of scripture. I assume that some homilists and catechists have been blessed by exposure to contemporary biblical studies and have moved beyond fundamentalism. I also assume, however, that most have not. They not only misread scripture as fundamentalists. They also live in a culture infected with privatism, psychologism and romanticism, which distort scripture's communal message.[2]

My concern in this and succeeding chapters is not only to address these distortions. I also hope to open up the thrilling message of scripture as a two-edged sword that opens our hearts to God's word of covenant and promise to all people. That message is made more accessible to us by many contemporary scripture scholars who are the true radicals in our church. They send us back to our biblical roots, to which we always need to return if we are to hear and homilize/catechize God's word with fidelity.

In this chapter, we explore four ways of hearing God's word in the liturgy of the word: fundamentalist, historicist, doctrinal/psychological and pastoral/theological.[3] We shall take a brief look at how the lectionary is a text distinct from the Bible and at how to mine the meaning of that text as the church prays the Bible in the liturgical seasons. Finally, we look at the entire liturgy of the word (including the prayers and liturgical seasons) as a source for catechesis. In later chapters, I focus on the gospels, acknowledging that homilists and catechists might choose to focus on other readings. However, many will choose the gospels, because the first readings were chosen in light of the gospels.[4] In hearing those gospels and our entire Christian heritage, let Albert Nolan of South Africa keep us centered on how to preach and listen:

> The problem with what is preached in our churches today is that it no longer has the shape or character of good news. . . . Good news can wake us up, shake us out of our lethargy and enable us to respond to the challenges of life. . . . Good news is not a statement about hope, it is the kind of news that will generate hope . . . Like all prophetic messages the gospel is not about "the former things" but about "the new thing" that God is doing today, about the God who is "making all things new" in South Africa today. What we are searching for is not a new gospel but a gospel that is news.[5]

**Conversation Starter:**   Recall a time when the proclamation of God's word in scripture and homily was truly news.

## A Fundamentalist/Literalist Hearing of Scripture

In the broad sense, fundamentalism[6] confounds and crosses denomina-tional, religious and ideological boundaries. It is a mind-set besieging all religions and ideologies. We find it wherever a book has authority—the Bible, the Koran, *Das Kapital*. It is not so much a particular interpretation of the book as an apparent lack of any interpretation in favor of a literalist reading—a rigid adherence to a text for its own sake without unveiling its meaning or purpose. It is not really a teaching or doctrine but an uncritical imbibing of text, teaching and doctrine. On final analysis, however, the lack of interpretation is only apparent. There is interpreta-tion, often through the filters of one's own culture and worldview accepted uncritically as the way people always and everywhere see and think.

Classical fundamentalism often occurs when people feel excluded from social or political power or when they cannot deal with cultural changes that threaten to corrupt the good old days when everything was done by the good old books.[7] They cry, "Back to the basics! Back to the faith of our fathers (and mothers)!" Witness the Muslims who brandish the Koran when the Shah imposes modernity on Iran. Witness the youth of the Red Guard waving Mao's little red book to reclaim Communist purity in the People's Republic of China. Witness the North American evangelists who confront a thoroughly corrupt culture with God's word of judgment during the last days of "the late great planet Earth."[8]

José Ortega y Gasset describes the fundamentalist angst and mind-set:

> Take stock of those around you and you will . . . hear them talk in precise terms about themselves and their surroundings, which would seem to point to them having ideas on the matter. . . . Quite the contrary: through these notions the individual[s are] trying to cut off any personal vision of reality, of [their] own very life. . . . It does not worry [them] that [their] ideas are not true, [they] use them as trenches for the defense of existence, as scarecrows to frighten away reality.[9]

Søren Kierkegaard adds:

> [Partisans] of the most rigid orthodoxy . . . know it all, bow before the holy; truth is an ensemble of ceremonies. . . . [They] know everything the same way as does the pupil who is able to demonstrate a mathematical proposition with the letters ABC, but not when they are changed to DEF. [They] are therefore in dread whenever [they] hear something not arranged in the same order.[10]

How often have we heard since Vatican II, "I can't handle all these changes!" One parishioner exclaimed, "If Jesus knew what was going on in this parish, he'd turn over in his grave!" A woman wrote to me in the 1960s, "Everything was falling apart. The only stable thing in my life was the church, and then *you* arrived!" The issue is change, cultural and personal turmoil—not "the changes." For such turmoil, we certainly can have compassion.

> **Conversation Starter:** Tell stories of Catholics (including yourself) and catechumens for whom the real source of turmoil and conflict was not changes in the church but changes in their lives.

In light of that, Patrick Arnold writes,

Fundamentalism is a historically recurring tendency within the Judeo-Christian-Muslim religious traditions that regularly erupts in reaction to cultural change. . . . [Fundamentalists tend to be] authoritarian personalities: individuals who feel threatened in a world of conspiring evil forces, who think in simplistic and stereotypical terms and who are attracted to authoritarian and moralistic answers to their problems.[11]

Obviously, these characterizations do not apply to those of us who read texts literally simply because we have not learned how to read texts from another culture, like the six-year-old who asks about the Ascension, "How fast did Jesus go up?" They do apply, however, to authoritarian leaders who deliberately keep people unlearned so that they can control the meaning of texts. And they apply to those who refuse to learn, such as the woman who, after a tedious, frustrating conversation about the historical meaning of the Bible, retorted, "Well, if the King James Bible was good enough for St. Paul, it's good enough for me!" On all matters, such people's minds may be stuck at the concrete thinking of a six-year-old. They are unable to hear the language of image, poetry, symbol or story. They may well read Art Buchwald or Gary Trudeau literally. I find that it is usually fruitless and frustrating to dialogue with literalists. We speak different languages.[12]

My favorite story of literalism concerns a woman in California who complained about all this symbolic interpretation of the Bible. She proclaimed, "I take the Bible literally!" Her adversary responded, "Well,

then, I guess that you have sold all that you have and given to the poor."
She retorted, "I'm not that literal!"

> **Conversation Starter:**   Tell some stories of times when
> people (including yourself) gave a literalist/fundamentalist
> hearing of scripture.

The fundamentalist rejects the idea, affirmed by Vatican II, that
revelation is not in books, not in the Bible, not in defined doctrine.
Revelation is in a person—Jesus, the Christ. That person and the
community's witness about him precede the book, and that witness is
different from (though not contradictory to) the scriptures written about
him. Protestant and Catholic biblical fundamentalists imagine God
dictating truths word by word into minds of biblical authors. The
Catholic fundamentalist also imagines God dictating doctrines into the
minds of popes. Therefore, each sentence must be accepted literally.

Because some people who enter the Catholic church come from
fundamentalist churches, I offer a brief survey of that tradition. I
center especially on how Protestant *fundamentalism* differs from Catholic
*fundamentals*—the "Catholic difference" of the incarnation of God in a
sacramental world. We catechize about these fundamentals not so much
by teaching doctrines (which could lend itself to doctrinal abstractions
and literalism) but by inviting people to the *experience* of God enfleshed
in humans and to the Catholic world of "visible signs of invisible grace."

*Christian Fundamentalism and Catholic Fundamentals*   Christian
fundamentalism came out of the evangelical movement at the beginning
of the twentieth century, partly in reaction to scripture studies that
questioned the Bible's literal meaning. This kind of biblical criticism
especially threatened those Protestants who lived by the literal meaning
of the book. A 12-volume work, *The Fundamentals*, was published, and
millions were distributed free of charge. The movement collapsed in 1929
with the depression and re-emerged during the 1950s.

There are basically three groups of evangelicals. There is the
mainstream, the most well known of whom is, perhaps, Billy Graham.
They are ecumenical, and they are regarded by the fundamentalists as
traitors to the cause of evangelism. There are the pure fundamentalists,

such as Jerry Falwell, for whom the only authority is the Bible. And there are the Pentecostals who add to the Bible the ongoing influence of the Spirit, especially in the gifts of tongues and healing.

Five basic teachings, first presented in this form in *The Fundamentals*, unite the fundamentalists: first, the inerrancy, infallibility and literal inspiration of the Bible; second, the divinity of Christ as attested to by the virgin birth; third, the resurrection (resuscitation) of the body of Jesus; fourth, the literal return of Jesus in a second coming (often seen as being imminent); and fifth, the vicarious satisfaction by Jesus for the debt of our sins—we can do nothing toward our salvation.

I suggest that beneath these fundamentals is what separates classical, evangelical Protestantism from Catholicism and other sacramental churches. Unlike fundamentalism—with a radical dualism that separates God and humankind, divine and human, spirit and flesh—Catholics experience God's presence mediated in the human and in our created world, the experience of God incarnate in Jesus, incarnate in the human, incarnate in all creation, in a sacramental world that mediates God's presence in human flesh and in the good earth.

That mediation directly assaults a literalist understanding of the five teachings of fundamentalism. First, regarding scripture: Literalists believe that "the human literary abilities of the authors were suspended and those who were inspired merely functioned as secretaries of God."[13] For Catholics and members of other sacramental churches, God's message is mediated through the humanity of Jesus and then in all the human ways that the biblical authors give witness to Jesus: "catecheses, stories, testimonia, hymns, doxologies, prayers—and other literary forms of this sort which were in Sacred Scripture and were accustomed to be used by people of that time."[14]

Second, regarding the divinity of Christ and the virgin birth: For fundamentalists, there is a not-so-subtle disdain for the human, especially human sexuality. They say that Jesus is divine on the Father's side, human on his mother's side (which in application can lead to the subordination of women to men) and that we are saved because Jesus is God. Catholics, on the other hand, affirm that we are saved in Christ's humanity. He takes our journey and, as flesh of our flesh and bone of our bone, leads us through death to God's gift of life.

Third, regarding the bodily resurrection of Jesus: Catholics affirm not the resuscitation of a corpse, which would mean that Jesus would have picked up where he left off—as a Jewish male of the first century. Rather, we believe that Jesus in a risen, spiritualized body (cf. 1 Corinthians 15:42–49) is one with all Jews and Gentiles, male and female (cf. Galatians 3:28), of all times and seasons. He transcends all the divisions, including race and sex, and even the divisions between the saved and the unsaved.

Fourth, regarding the imminent second coming of Jesus: For the fundamentalist, the world is evil, beyond redemption from the inside. God will have to come from the outside in the person of Jesus the judge and wipe it out. In the meantime, God is outside this world and jumps in occasionally to keep this sinking ship afloat with miracles.[15] In contrast, the Catholic vision is one of a sacramental world with seven sacraments, seventy times seven sacramentals and a galaxy of "visible signs of invisible grace" in and through which God is mediated, really present and coming to us now, not just in a final cataclysm.

Finally, regarding substitutionary atonement: Fundamentalist teaching regards humans as thoroughly despicable, evil wretches saved by amazing grace. In this view, Jesus doesn't save through defiled mediators. He saves directly through the Spirit, without go-betweens. In contrast, Catholics celebrate community meals, initiations, reconciliations, healings, weddings and any number of occasions in which God is present through people, including popes and presbyters. We know that these celebrations and persons are not God, but they are the best hints of God that we have. In the humanity of Jesus, we have the best hint of all, and these glimpses of grace continue in a mediating, Spirit-gifted community.

Therefore, while Catholics agree with fundamentalists about basic truths, we give each a quite different meaning based on our experience of God's incarnation in a sacramental world. The paradox is that some Catholics, including some homilists, catechists and sponsors, have not had this incarnational experience and hang onto texts and doctrines as life preservers. They flee Jesus' stormy, human journey and try to moor their boats behind the protecting seawalls of divine, unchanging words from the Bible and the pope. Unfortunately, some catechumens also have an image of an authoritarian, unchanging Catholic Church that hands down truths given directly to popes by God, and it is precisely this unsinkable bark that they want to board.

> **Conversation Starter:**   Recall people who are prone to negative attitudes about the world, human life and especially themselves. How might such attitudes shape, for example, views of Jesus' humanity, of the end of the world, of sexuality or of praying and worshiping in human ways such as at a meal or through the exchange of peace?

If we invite catechumens and candidates to the experience of incarnation and sacrament, if we move beyond the incarnation as a past fact about Jesus to its present meaning for all humans and all creation, then we move beyond a fundamentalist/literalist hearing of both scripture and doctrine. When catechumens enter the catechumenate as literalists, they may be simply uninformed or they may come with closed minds. In either case, hope for conversion and change lies in inviting them through story, image and symbol into the experience of faith that gives birth to scriptural and doctrinal texts. Such movement, however, often is impossible for minds closed to such realities.

I conclude our reflections on fundamentalism with a challenge from Richard McBrien:

> A prominent biblical scholar once observed that the number of Catholics who have been lost to the Catholic church because of the dissenting views of Hans Küng could hold a convention in a telephone booth, but the number lost because of biblical fundamentalism is in the hundreds of thousands. . . . But the Catholic Church's most effective response to the challenge of biblical fundamentalism is not one of condemnation or ridicule. The church will have to commit itself anew to the best biblical education it can provide. Everything it does must have a solid biblical foundation: courses, workshops, conferences, retreats, days of prayer, programs of spirituality, homilies, lectures and educational publications of every kind.[16]

## A Historicist Hearing of Scripture

At their best, historical/critical methods of Bible study interpret the original historical meaning of the stories, images and symbols of scripture and put them into dialogue with the stories, images and symbols of our communal and personal lives. These methods unleash the call of our ancestors in faith to conversion, change and transformation.

At their worst, however, these methods are purely academic exercises that unearth a plethora of historical and literary data but that are, supposedly, so objective and neutral that they leave the Bible sterile and us empty. The scholars critique and demythologize the message into oblivion. There is a deluge of information but no call to transformation. There are no "so whats" for our lives and times.

We will return to the best of historical criticism when, later in this chapter, we discuss the pastoral/theological way to hear scripture. At this point, we name and exorcise the worst.[17]

In a devastating critique, Walter Wink, who uses historical Bible studies in ways that call to conversion, decries the present state of many of those studies:

> Historical biblical criticism is bankrupt . . . not because it has run out of things to say or new ground to explore. It is bankrupt solely because it is incapable of achieving what most of its practitioners considered its purpose to be: so to interpret the scriptures that the past becomes alive and illumines our present with new possibilities for personal and social transformation.

The writers of the Bible always saw their past of exodus and covenant as a message for the present. "Their past was a continual accosting, a question flung in their paths, a challenge, and a confrontation. But because [scholars remove themselves] from view, no shadow from the past can fall across [their] path. [They insulate themselves] from the Bible's own concerns. [They examine] the Bible, but [they themselves are] not examined—except by [their] own colleagues in the guild!"[18]

Wink suggests that the sterilization of biblical studies is rampant in schools of liberal Protestantism that seek to remove themselves from the censorship and interference of the church community. The community is thus deprived of critical and constructive contributions. The scholars talk to themselves and seldom ask of texts the questions on which human lives hinge.

Perhaps that is less true of Catholicism, in part because of our church's reaction against modernism and biblical studies and because of our silencing of biblical scholars early in this century. We were latecomers to these studies when Pius XII finally gave us an opening to modern biblical studies with his encyclical *Divino Afflante Spiritu* in 1943. Even so, most of us probably have, on the one hand, endured homilies from young presbyters fresh from the seminary or catechesis from catechists who just returned from some summer school with the titillating disclosures that there were no Adam and Eve, no Jonah in the whale, no diving through the depths of the Red Sea but sloshing through the pools of the Reed Marsh, no Magi with gold and incense and myrrh. We wondered if they also would leave us with no Jesus, no resurrection and no "so whats" that made any connection between us and God.

> **Conversation Starter:**   Recall an "historicist" homily
> or catechetical session that you have experienced.

On the other hand, we also have experienced what happens when we deprive people of modern biblical insights. For example, many in the Charismatic Renewal developed a new love for the word of God. When they received little help from Catholic leadership in interpreting that word, they turned to the fundamentalism and private revelations of Protestant Pentecostals ignorant of or hostile to scriptural scholarship. Some of these people may be ministers in a catechumenate, and they will need more solid biblical formation.

Wink and others attribute the bankruptcy of biblical studies to an exaggerated attempt by scripture scholars for scientific objectivity or a "value-neutral" exegesis. Like Sergeant Joe Friday in "Dragnet," they want just the facts. Such objectivity might, indeed, free interpretation from the religious biases of the scholars (although most have racial, sexual and class interests that are unconsciously reflected in their work), but, as John Baldovin comments, "It limits itself purely and simply to the best and most accurate understanding possible of the texts in question as well as their historical and social background. The trouble with such an 'objective' or objectivist approach . . . is that it encourages people to believe that only what can be stated as literally true in scripture is really true." Some people may conclude, for example, that if the Magi did not really bring gifts, then there is no truth in the story. "Taken to its extreme, the vast majority of the biblical writings would have to be considered as nothing more than pious twaddle."[19]

Wink concludes that the scholars separate "theory from practice, mind from body, reason from emotion, knowledge from experience. Is anything but intellectualism possible when our questions do not arise primarily out of the struggle with concrete problems of life and society, from the blistering exposure to trial and error, from the need for wisdom in the ambiguous mash of events?"[20] In our discussion of a pastoral/ theological hearing of scripture, we shall see that a more adequate use of biblical studies arises precisely from such struggles, exposure and mash of events in biblical communities and in our communities.

## A Doctrinal/Psychological Hearing

Baldovin says that in the doctrinal/psychological approach, we search the Bible for doctrines or truths about salvation and for maxims about how to live our lives. An extreme case is the "instant inspiration" that some get when they open the Bible, place their fingers on a passage and get a message. This is more akin to magic and superstition than to faith. The Bible becomes a collection of proof texts for preconceived religious biases and opinions.

Sometimes the Bible is used to prove something else. Allegory, for example, uses the text for a totally different kind of truth. Baldovin cites the fourth-century theologian, Gregory of Nyssa, who takes the life of Moses as an allegory for the progress of the human soul to God. That certainly would come as a surprise to the authors of the Pentateuch.

A more common use in catechumenates is the selection of a single theme or doctrine from the lectionary readings (which have multiple themes). We then use the scripture as a launching pad from which to soar into preaching and catechizing at length on a predetermined Catholic teaching. That often ignores what is proclaimed in the liturgy of the word on a given day and in a given season. It ignores questions that the liturgy might raise for the catechumens. It might even ignore the vision and message of the scriptural readings about the doctrine that does emerge. For example, if we are faithful to our biblical heritage, on All Souls' Day, we preach and teach a God who never gives up on us, not the images of fire and purgation that mark too much of the teaching on the doctrine of purgatory.[21] Indeed, the liturgy of the word quite naturally raises questions that prompt reflections on our 1,900 years of postbiblical tradition. We violate good catechetical method, however, by imposing a single doctrine on the scriptures.

An even more common method in catechumenates is a psychological approach in which texts are made to connect with our inner psychological states: How am I like the Samaritan woman; the prodigal son; the Canaanite woman; Jesus tempted in the desert, weeping in the garden, abandoned on the cross? When have I felt like the disciples on the stormy sea? Elisabeth Schüssler Fiorenza contends that the liturgy itself is a good example of this, because it forces scripture texts into themes not warranted by the text. In general, she rejects this doctrinal/psychological approach to scripture.

John Baldovin does not. He says that the Bible contains facts and doctrines and can lead to reflection on postbiblical facts and doctrines. The Bible "can be an excellent starting point for themes that may not have been the original author's concern. It has, in the great spiritual classics of writers like Origen and Gregory of Nyssa, provided the basis for profoundly moving reflections on the Christian faith and human life."[22] Others, from Ignatius of Loyola to Jean Jacques Olier, offer methods of prayer that invite people to enter into the experience of the characters in biblical stories.

At the same time, Walter Wink warns against a psychological focus that infers meaning or motivation from inadequate data or reduces scripture to nothing but psychodynamics and feelings. He insists, however, that "virtually every narrative requires psychological analysis to be understood: *Why* did she do this, or *why* did he say that? . . . Psychological insights simply are drawn on where appropriate—and that is determined by the nature of the text, not by psychological theory." The application of psychological insights to ourselves is one way to make the text our own. "*Not the text, but we ourselves are the object of analysis,* and it is precisely the objectivity of the text, its very alienness and opposition to us, which is most able to help us discover those aspects of ourselves lost to consciousness and allowed to languish in the dungeons of the soul."[23] Wink himself makes particular use of Carl Jung in probing biblical and contemporary archetypes and images of ourselves.

Baldovin concludes with a caution against "instant inspiration," and he insists that the doctrinal/psychological approach "does not render *the* meaning of a biblical text."[24]

Bless me, church, for I have sinned. In the past, I have most often used a doctrinal/psychological approach to scripture. In making the scriptures our own, I often use the language, "Put yourself into the story." I invite people to identify with a person in the story such as the prodigal son or the outlandishly merciful father or the pouting elder brother. I then ask, "How is your relationship with God like that person's relationship with God? How is your experience of God like that of the person in the story?" The story asks and reveals much more than that.

In self-defense, I must say that I have come closer to the meanings of texts by insisting that biblical stories are stories of communities. We also are called to put our community into these stories: How does our church welcome prodigals home? How is our community's treatment of outcasts, minorities and women like the treatment the Samaritan woman received from the community in which she lived? I also have tried to move beyond feelings and inner psychological states to behavior, personal and communal change, conversion and transformation.

I still believe that this approach is valid. I also have come to a strong conviction that it can play right into the hands of North American privatism and narcissism ("the texts are just about me and my story") and romanticism and psychologizing ("it's good news if I feel good; it's good news if it's therapeutic for me").[25] I agree with Baldovin not just that this approach misses core meanings in the biblical text. I also agree that the historical/critical approach, when used pastorally and theologically to interpret contemporary times and communities in the light of past times and communities, is not only more faithful to God's word. It is more exciting and literally world-shattering for God's people. To that approach we now turn.

> **Conversation Starter:** Tell of a time when a psychological approach to scripture (put yourself in the story; how are you like a character in the story) was helpful for you or for catechumens.

### A Pastoral/Theological Hearing

For those fed in the past on a diet of biblical fundamentalism, as I was, today there is exciting good news. Contemporary pastoral biblical interpretation does not begin with dry facts from the past. We begin as the biblical authors began—with questions from the present. To those questions we bring the wisdom of our ancestors in faith who, in their communities, faced similar questions that arose from their "struggle with the concrete problems of life and society, from the blistering exposure to trial and error, from the need for wisdom in the ambiguous mash of events," to use Wink's phrase.

For those concerned about a catechumenate soft on doctrine, there is challenging good news. The primary doctrine that we proclaim and that all postbiblical teaching unfolds and develops is scriptural doctrine—the teaching about God in Christ Jesus that is closest to the actual experience of God in Jesus. Contemporary biblical studies grant new access to that doctrine, and I find it more exciting and more prophetic than any modern theologian or church document, including those of Vatican II. In some cases, biblical doctrine confronts and challenges contemporary church teaching and practice, such as the current norms about who is welcome in our church and who can be reconciled. Therefore, I once again call homilists and catechists not to be soft on biblical teaching but to give people access to the wonderful insights of scripture scholarship so that we can move beyond fundamentalism and hear a word of God alive in our times.

Scripture studies in the Catholic church have passed through three main phases. Many Catholics began this century as fundamentalists embroiled in the sometimes vicious attacks by church authorities on Catholic scripture scholars who supposedly were "tainted" by questions about the historicity of biblical events. In the second phase, Catholics were encouraged to take up that historical/critical scholarship. Sometimes that led to the historicism already discussed or the dehistoricization of biblical events feared by the Vatican.

The best-known name in historical/critical scholarship is Rudolph Bultmann, who claimed that we have no access to the historical meaning of Jesus' teaching and experience of God. Among many others, Kenneth

Bailey disagrees. For example, Bailey visits some tiny, isolated, conservative peasant villages throughout the Middle East where he finds life much as it was in the first century. He sits at the city gates with the elders and tells them Jesus' parables. Then the elders tell him what the parables mean. Bailey then draws forth from all of Luke's parables incisive, theological motifs with implications for our times.[26] Enter the third phase, the post-Bultmann phase, peopled with scholars such as Bailey who do their historical homework but are motivated by contemporary pastoral concerns, issues and questions.

An exciting part of this third phase is what is called a "literary" reading or hearing of a text. *Historical criticism* centers on what we could learn of the history of Jesus, his community and the communities of the authors of scripture. *Redaction criticism* explores the editorial work that the writers perform on their sources and acknowledges that these authors are true pastoral theologians who modified and adapted texts in response to the needs of their communities. *Literary criticism* of scripture approaches each gospel as one would approach a short story or novel. "It is the very nature of the biblical narrative to recast historical events into a fictional mode. Historians are not objective reporters, but they re-create events to make them intelligible to their faith communities. They fill in the gaps. They fictionalize as part of communicating history as story; . . . the rules that govern fiction also govern biblical narrative."[27]

Therefore, in literary criticism, we do not look first for the historical sources of texts nor for the theological motivation of the author. We look for the plots, the settings, the characters, the interactions and the conflicts. We find in a text a world that, once created by the author, takes on an existence of its own that goes beyond the meaning of the author or his or her community. The authors of the scriptures lure us into the drama just as William Shakespeare lures us into the intrigues of *Macbeth* and Flannery O'Connor catches us up into Mrs. Turpin's "Revelation."[28] A pastoral/literary hearing, however, ends not only with the hearers identifying with the feelings or inner psychological states of characters in the drama (the psychological approach to scripture) but the hearers also enter into the pastoral issues of communal conflict and liberation that are part of the plot.

**Conversation Starter:**   Tell how a short story, novel or play lured you and your family, friends or community into the drama.

Enslaved people are drawn into the drama of the Exodus of Israel and into the dying and rising of Jesus in ways that the authors could not foresee.[29] Therefore, a

> text should not simply be understood as a window through which the reader views the historical author and his or her contemporaries. The text is a world in itself apart from the author and the original audience for whom the author wrote. It is a kind of mirror in which the reader sees himself or herself reflected in the world of the story.[30]

I would add that the reader also sees the community reflected in the world of the story.

If the authors of scripture are more homilists than historians, what we said earlier of homilists is true for them. They do not preach a message *at* us. They enter into conversation *with* us. What we see and hear is more important than what they say. We can hear more than what they say. For example, David Rhoads and John Michie claim that Jesus and the disciples in Mark's story are round characters, with changing traits, who are complex and unpredictable, whereas the religious leaders are flat, predictable characters with fewer, usually consistent, traits. The disciples are round because of their conflicting traits. "On the one hand, they are loyal and courageous, with a capacity for sacrifice and enough fascination with Jesus to follow him. On the other hand, they are afraid, self-centered and dense, preoccupied with their own status and power."[31] Literary critics do not solely identify these characters with their historical counterparts. They first want to learn about them and *about us* within Mark's story world.

The literary critics believe that the gospel authors are influenced by Greek drama, which draws the audience into the story to participate in the tragedy and to share the experience of its characters.[32] These critics stress less what a text means in itself, and more how the text, when heard as story or drama, draws hearers into an interaction that is not "a subjective fabrication of the reader, for the text itself guides the reader in its realization."[33] The readers then can go back to discover something about the historical Jesus and the early church, but they do not begin there.

They go back in a stronger position to discover what the text has to say about the Jesus and the church of history because they now can distinguish between the author's literary and historical intentions. "Literary criticism would thus be either a fundamental stage of historical criticism or a stage which in this respect must precede historical criticism."[34]

If this is true, hearing the story will be the first task of a pastoral/theological hearing of scripture—to move through the story world of the text to understand the plot, setting, conflicts, questions and characters, and to see what light they shed on our plot, setting, conflicts, questions and characters. In that way, when we form our theology, we will seek not just historical facts and not just the psychological inner states and feelings of the characters but also a pastoral understanding that cares for and liberates people in practical ways.

Pastoral theology "seeks to understand the implications of faith for the actual situation of the church."[35] A pastoral/theological/literary hearing of scripture, therefore, looks at the life issues in our times and in the stories of Israel and Jesus, makes connections and enters into conversation. As in any conversation, we are open to surprise, conflict and a changing of our minds. Biblical texts from another culture might be so foreign and alien that we cannot hear them. They also may seem strange because they so accost and assault our cultural stories (e.g., of power and control), that we must change if we are to continue the conversation and enter the story world of Jesus and the dramas facing the early Christian communities.

A pastoral/theological/literary approach to scripture offers us a new respect for the biblical authors. They are far more than mere collectors and compilers of the sayings of Moses or Jesus. They are true storytellers whose stories can go far beyond their original intentions and speak in new ways to later generations. "The biblical texts are given their due as documents that respond to pastoral problems in a theological way. In other words, the biblical critic tries to understand the original context for this or that portion of scripture and then to apply it to appropriate parallels in contemporary life."[36] The biblical critic then invites people into the drama.

For example, chapter 15 in Luke is more than stories about how God searches and finds individual lost sheep, coins and sons. Luke gives us the plot, setting and characters that bring him to tell these stories: "The

Pharisees and the scribes were grumbling and saying, 'This fellow welcomes sinners and even eats with them!'" When we look at the gospel of Luke in chapter nine of this book, we shall see that conflicts about meals and who is welcome play a big part in Luke's plot line. So Luke inserts three stories of Jesus that call Luke's community (and us) from grumbling to rejoicing when the lost are found. They are stories that call his church (and ours) not only to welcome outcasts but also to search zealously and vigorously for them, to run down roads to embrace them and to rejoice and throw parties for them when they return. That message confronts and challenges our church and society, which still have problems welcoming and eating with outcasts and outsiders in a world of new immigrants, new refugees, new "Gentile" nations that Luke never could have imagined.

Some scripture texts tell the story of a particular community in a particular plot and setting of their time, and because times and issues change, not all texts speak to our times. "It is therefore necessary for the minister to learn how to determine the situation and needs of his or her congregation with the same sophistication he or she applies to the study of biblical texts."[37] We need sociological, psychological, cultural and political wisdom to interpret not only biblical times but also our times to find the parallels or the lack thereof. Then the word of God ceases to be just words but a living word that "shall not return to me empty, but shall accomplish that which I purpose, and succeed in the thing for which I sent it" (Isaiah 55:11).

Thomas Groome, expanding in part on Paul Ricoeur,[38] calls for three kinds of interpreting: "hermeneutics of retrieval, suspicion and creative commitment to the text."[39] All three will tap the resources of the official church magisterium, the research of scholars and the faith of the people (sensus fidelium) down through the centuries, plus our own personal and communal experience.

First, a "hermeneutic of retrieval" will discern, affirm, cherish and make accessible the Christian tradition in ways that cast light on our lives today and summon us to live our faith in our world as the place of God's reign.

Second, a "hermeneutic of suspicion" critiques in a positive way both distortions within texts and false, perhaps dominant, interpretations of texts by ecclesial communities in the past and present and by ourselves. "Much that has been proudly told must be confessed as sin; and much that has been obscured and silenced must be given voice."[40] In later chapters, we shall see many examples of how the dominant interpretation tames, conceals, conveniently forgets or excludes what Johann Metz calls the "dangerous" or "subversive" memories of the scriptures, especially the parables.[41]

Third, "creative commitment to the text" is "creative" when, prompted by contemporary events and needs, we pose constructions beyond the present dominant interpretations (as in a literary hearing of the texts). This includes "reconstruction," when we reclaim interpretations that have been dismissed or conveniently ignored. This hermeneutic is "committed" because the intent of these constructions and reconstructions is to summon us to the reign of God.

We shall be exploring and applying this pastoral/theological approach to scripture especially through a literary reading and hearing in succeeding chapters of this book.

## Hearing the Lectionary

Although I am focusing, for practical reasons, on a pastoral/theological hearing of only the gospels of the three-year cycle of the lectionary, a quite different approach also is an option.[42] That approach is to mine the meaning of all the scriptures in the lectionary and to take the lectionary as an independent text different from the Bible, although this approach will nonetheless appreciate the gems of biblical research.

.The lectionary is the church's way of praying the Bible. We can break open this liturgical/literary text in ways that go beyond pure biblical interpretation. We can see the lectionary readings as blocks of material, such as all the readings of Advent or Lent. We see each block as a text that we interpret and that has a meaning that is not dependent on the reasons why the compilers chose the texts. Like scripture and doctrine, the lectionary as a text takes on a wider meaning than that known to the compilers. It becomes its own story and world. When a community prays and homilizes/catechizes on these texts, it can find meanings beyond the intentions of the biblical authors or of the liturgical compilers, because each community brings its own issues and questions to these texts.[43] I say this acknowledging the dangers of falling into fundamentalism and private revelations.

In Year B, for example, Advent begins with a lamentation: Where is God now? When is God coming? The rest of Advent is God's response in Jesus: "I come to inaugurate the reign of God." In Lent of Year B, the first readings are stories of the covenant, which in Lent is fulfilled in Christ and in Eastertime continues in the church. In the summer, on the Sixteenth Sunday of Ordinary Time, the gospel of Mark says that Jesus "began to teach them at great length" (Mark 6:34). Then for several Sundays following, the lectionary provides Jesus' teaching "at great length" on the bread of life from the gospel of John.

This approach suggests that just as the synoptics differ in their vision of Jesus because of the particular concerns of their communities, so also each of the three years of the lectionary cycle offers a different vision of Christ, church, God and discipleship. We can ask, What is the image of Christ during Advent in Year A? What is the image of discipleship in the Sundays of Ordinary Time during Year B? Those images are not exhausted by the intentions of the biblical authors or the liturgical compilers. They take on new life and meaning within a living, praying community that brings issues from its life and time to interpret the lectionary texts. For example, Year C with the gospel of Luke is the favorite course of readings for many Latin American base communities who perhaps hear a stronger message about liberation than did Luke's community.

## Hearing the Liturgy of the Word

Our hearing of all the lectionary readings for an entire season correctly moves us beyond a narrow focus only on the gospel of a given Sunday. Although I offer interpretations only of the gospels, our preaching on the gospels needs to take place in the context of the entire liturgy of the word and of the liturgical season. We situate individual gospel stories within the big story of the entire gospel and within the church's story and journey in Christ in the liturgical seasons. We have pondered the larger scriptural story during evangelization in the precatechumenate with inquirers. In the catechumenate period, we return to that story and to the living community's story during the liturgical year so that we know whence we come and where we are going.

This is also to say that although most homilies preach the scriptures—especially the gospels but rarely the psalms—the entire liturgy (both of word and eucharist) is a source for preaching: the prayers, the ritual actions, the liturgical seasons, the ministries (especially that of the assembly), even the silence. In that sense, the common phrase, "lectionary-based catechesis," is too limiting. We preach on all that reveals Christ's real presence.[44]

## Endnotes

[1] Gerard S. Sloyan, "Is Church Teaching Neglected When the Lectionary Is Preached?" *Worship* 61 (March 1987): 133–34.

[2] One scripture scholar critiques institutes offered by the North American Forum on the Catechumenate for not sufficiently moving participants beyond fundamentalism; see Margaret Ralph, "Does 'Breaking Open the Word' Promote Fundamentalism?" *Forum Newsletter* 7:1, 4–9.

[3] For this approach, I am indebted to John Baldovin, "The Bible and Liturgy, Part One: The Status of the Bible Today," *Catechumenate* 11 (September 1989): 12–19; Baldovin acknowledges his own debt to Elisabeth Schüssler Fiorenza, *Bread Not Stone* (Boston: Beacon Press, 1984).

[4] For suggestions regarding a continuous reading of the Hebrew Scriptures, see Gerard S. Sloyan, "Some Suggestions for a Biblical Three-Year Lectionary," *Worship* 63 (November 1989): 521–35.

[5] Albert Nolan, *God in South Africa* (Grand Rapids: Wm. B. Eerdmans, 1988), 9, 11, 16.

[6] For a popular treatment of Protestant fundamentalism, see Anthony Gilles, *Fundamentalism: What Every Catholic Needs to Know* (Cincinnati: St. Anthony Messenger Press, 1984).

[7] For a description of contemporary developments giving rise to the growth of fundamentalism in the United States, see Nathan Kollar, "The Mediating Church and the Future of Christian Fundamentalism," *PACE* 20, 278–81. For an overview of the phenomenon, see James Barr, *Fundamentalism* (Philadelphia: The Westminster Press, 1978).

[8] For a modern classic proclamation of divine wrath at the end-time, see Hal Lindsey and C. C. Carlston, *The Late Great Planet Earth* (Grand Rapids: Zondervan Publishing Co., 1970).

[9] José Ortega y Gasset, *The Revolt of the Masses* (New York: W. W. Norton & Co., Inc., 1957), 156–57.

[10] Søren Kierkegaard, *The Concept of Dread* (Princeton: University Press, 1957), 110 ff.

[11] Patrick Arnold, "The Rise of Catholic Fundamentalism," *America* 156:14, 298, 301.

[12] Gallup reports that 37 percent of Americans in 1984 were biblical literalists (down from 65 percent in 1963), "Gallup Report," no. 216 (Princeton: Princeton Religion Research Center).

[13] Dianne Bergant, "Fundamentalists and the Bible," *New Theology Review* 1 (May 1988): 39. (This entire issue is on fundamentalism.)

[14] "The Historical Truth of the Gospels," *Instruction of the Roman Pontifical Biblical Commission*, 1964, viii.

[15] Zachary Hayes, "Fundamentalist Eschatology," *New Theology Review* 1 (May 1988): 21–35.

[16] Richard McBrien, "The Future of the Church," Warren Lecture Series in Catholic Studies, no. 14. Available from The University of Tulsa, Warren Center.

[17] My purpose is not to give a detailed description of the various kinds of biblical criticism. For overviews of that discipline, see Alexa Suelzer and John Kselman, "Modern Old Testament Criticism"; John Kselman and Ronald Witherup, "Modern New Testament Criticism"; and Raymond Brown and Sandra Schneiders, "Hermeneutics," *The New Jerome Biblical Commentary* (Englewood Cliffs NJ: Prentice Hall, 1990), 1, 113–65.

[18] Walter Wink, *The Bible in Human Transformation* (Philadelphia: Fortress Press, 1973), 1, 2, 4.

[19] Baldovin, "The Bible and the Liturgy," 17–18.

[20] Wink, *The Bible*, 6.

[21] Gerard Sloyan comments, "A biblical homily on the feast of All Souls . . . is assured a marvelous centrality as the gospel of Jesus Christ. Preaching in any other mold but that will shortly prove erratic, eccentric or, God forbid, heretical. It can do worse. It can be trivial." "Is Church Teaching," p. 140. I would say the same of catechizing.

22 Raymond Collins agrees. Although he gives priority to a historical-critical reading of scripture, he admits other approaches, including the doctrinal and psychological; cf. "On Reading the Scriptures," *Emmanuel* 96 (March 1990): 70–73, 98–101.

23 Walter Wink, *Transforming Bible Study* (Nashville: Abingdon Press, 1980), 163–64.

24 Baldovin, "The Bible and the Liturgy," 17.

25 Researcher Daniel Vankelovich comments on the culture of narcissism: "In the past, the purpose of self-improvement was to better oneself in . . . ways associated with worldly or familial success . . . based on the ethic of self-denial." In the new quest, the object is the self. "I am my own success story and work of art." "New Rules in American Life," *Psychology Today* 15: 51.

26 Kenneth Bailey, *Poet and Peasant and Through Peasant Eyes* (Grand Rapids: Wm. B. Eerdmans, 1976).

27 Marie-Eloise Rosenblatt, "New Testament Scholarship Twenty-Five Years After Vatican II," *The MAST Journal* (Spring 1991): 5. I assume that Rosenblatt uses "fictional" not as necessarily totally nonobjective history but as story form.

28 "Revelation," in *Flannery O'Connor: The Complete Stories* (New York: Farrar, Straus & Giroux, Inc., 1981), 488–509.

29 In fact, the Christian authors approach the Hebrew stories just as we do; for example, Luke sees Jesus' final journey to Jerusalem and his dying and rising as participating in the drama of the Exodus from Egypt.

30 Frank Matera, *What Are They Saying about Mark?* (New York: Paulist Press, 1987), 86.

31 David Rhoads and Donald Michie, *Mark as Story* (Philadelphia: Fortress Press, 1982), 117.

32 Cf. Augustine Stock, *Call to Discipleship* (Wilmington: Michael Glazier, Inc., 1982).

33 James I. Resseguie, "Reader-Response Criticism and the Synoptic Gospels," *Journal of the American Academy of Religion* 52 (June 1984): 308.

34 Norman Petersen, *Literary Criticism for New Testament Critics* (Philadelphia: Fortress Press, 1978), 21; see also Leonard Doohan, *Mark: Visionary of Early Christianity* (Santa Fe: Bear and Company, 1986), 22–24.

[35] Richard McBrien, *Catholicism*, vol. I (Minneapolis: Winston Press, 1980), 57.

[36] Baldovin, "The Bible and the Liturgy," 18.

[37] Elisabeth Schüssler Fiorenza, *The Challenge*, 35–36.

[38] Cf. Paul Ricoeur, *Freud and Philosophy* (New Haven: Yale University Press, 1970), 28–36.

[39] Thomas Groome, *Sharing Faith* (San Francisco: Harper & Row, 1991), 230–35. "Hermeneutics: The science of interpretation; the body of principles which governs the interpretation of any statement or text," Richard McBrien, *Catholicism*, vol. II (Minneapolis: Winston Press, 1980), xxxi.

[40] Joseph Hough and John Cobb, *Christian Identity and Theological Education* (Chico CA: Scholars Press, 1985), 98.

[41] Johann Metz, *Faith in History and Society* (New York: Seabury Press, 1980), 110, 56.

[42] For this entire section, I am indebted to Richard Fragomeni who, with students at the Catholic Theological Union in Chicago, is exploring this approach to the lectionary. See his article "Revisiting Lectionary Catechesis," *Modern Liturgy* 19 (April 1992): 46. He distinguishes between "lectionary-based catechesis," which utilizes biblical interpretation to unpack the meaning of lectionary readings in their biblical contexts (see preceding section) and "lectionary catechesis." I disassociate myself from his description of "lectionary-based catechesis" as "Bible-study." I also disagree with his apparent exclusion of lectionary-based catechesis. I see his approach to "lectionary catechesis" as described in these paragraphs as one helpful option that is in the early stages of development.

[43] Cf. Paul Ricoeur, *Interpretation Theory: Discourse and Surplus of Meaning* (Fort Worth: Texas Christian University Press, 1976).

[44] Cf. *Constitution on the Sacred Liturgy*, #7.

# CHAPTER SIX

# Conversing with Scripture:
## A Pastoral/Theological Method
## of Hearing the Word

*The Word of God is not primarily a voice speaking from an ancient text about a past time. True, the sacred text is a voice uttered once upon a time, but it is also a voice that has been turned loose from its original speaker and its original time. When the Word is heard again—and really heard—it levies a claim upon immediate lived experience. Whatever levies a new claim now on behalf of a better tomorrow puts today at risk. Did it not do that, it would not yet be God's Word but only a voice from the past. The question is how to be with the words of the Scriptures to give them the best chance to become Word in conversation with us.*[1]

• Bernard Lee

WE NOW EXPLORE one method for our conversation with scripture. This method has several desirable qualities: First, it is *pastoral*; it deals with the questions and issues in our contemporary communities. Second, this method is *theological*; it seeks to discover who the God of Jesus Christ is and what that God reveals about the meaning of human life lived in the Spirit. Third, it enables a conversation that makes accessible the *historical criticism* of modern biblical studies in ways that move us beyond fundamentalism and historicism and put us in dialogue with the pastoral questions and concerns in the biblical communities. Fourth and finally, this method uses *literary criticism* to invite us into a drama that is larger than the original story. We explore this method of conversation with the scriptures with the conviction of Karl Barth that "those involved in active ministry may not leave theology to others."[2]

More than interpretation, conversation implies two-way communication and dialogue. We not only interpret texts; texts also interpret us. The word of God forever calls us to change, to conversion, to transformation. Therefore, we begin this exploration of a method of conversing with God's word by reflecting on the dynamics of human conversation. We shall then apply those dynamics to our method. Then we shall focus on how that method might be used by homilists and catechists to prepare for and converse with the Sunday liturgy of the word.

## About Conversation

Bernard Lee discusses the nature of conversation when he writes about a "shared homily" within the liturgy of the word. He distinguishes a shared homily from what often happens in a "dialogue homily," which can be a freewheeling, on-the-spot response by the homilist and the gathered community to the proclaimed text. That type of response may be part of the exchange, but Lee's shared homily is a much more disciplined conversation. It requires doing the hard work that allows a conversation to communicate and to lead to friendship.[3] The dynamics he suggests also apply to our preparation for liturgical catechesis.

> **Conversation Starter:** Tell how a relationship and conversation with a friend or beloved has changed you. Tell of times when conflict and misunderstanding brought about those changes.

"When I meet a new person, I bring with me to that first encounter my own history, expectations, needs, hopes and aspirations. In other words, I already exist in a world of meaning that has been long in the making."[4] That world forms and shapes our first impressions of a new person. We also may assume that everybody's world is like our world and that everyone thinks as we do.

If we choose to deepen relationships, however, we soon discover that other people's worlds and stories are different from ours. For a time, that can create a distance between us, and that can be painful. But if we want relationships to develop, we learn to hear. We do "active listening" and acquire "listening hearts" that hear not just events and words but the fears or hopes, pain or gratitude that lie beneath and beyond the words. Gestures, facial expressions, tones of voice, pauses and silences are all part of the conversation, and they may say more than words.

We cannot listen to a different life, especially that of a beloved, and come away unchanged. Authentic conversation means threat, risk, vulnerability, loss of control, understanding in new ways and reconstructing our friends and ourselves. We not only discover how we were the same and how we differed at the beginnings of a friendship but we also become co-creators of each other's identity. That means letting go as we allow ourselves to be shaped by another. It also means being open to new possibilities. God and our friend are not through with us yet. We don't know where this relationship will lead. Friendship remains ahead of us as a gift, as a new future with new surprises. Our friend is never totally fused with us but remains different from us with a life still in the making. We also are in the making, and on a given day we may believe that a friend has not understood us. So we go back to the hard work of interpreting and conversing.

New experiences bring new interpretations, and new interpretations and conversations shape new experiences, identities and surprises; the cycle never ends. "This conversation is not a preface to a good relationship; interpreting is the whole story. Tomorrow's possibilities are created by today's conversations. Understanding is never something done once and for all. Understanding is not a noun, it is a verb."[5] James Fowler envisions faith as relationship with God, and so he sees faith, too, not as a static noun but as an active verb.[6] Buckminster Fuller saw God, the other partner in conversation, not as noun but as verb.


## About Conversation with Scripture

We believe that God, through Jesus Christ, in the Spirit, is really present in the scriptures. When we come to make friends with that real presence, we also come with our own histories and ways of thinking, feeling and valuing that may connect with shared meanings in scripture.

The worlds of scripture also have many sharp contrasts with our contemporary world. Some books come from thoroughly Jewish communities, others from Jews who had long lived in a Greek-thinking world, and others from those who were never Jews and who came to conversion in a pagan Greco-Roman culture. As with a new friend, we soon discover a distance and strangeness from the worlds of scripture. We find that we have to remove our modern presumptions from the ancient texts. We walk in the sandals of Jesus' disciples, on their ground, with a listening heart. Then we begin to hear texts with meanings quite different from those we heard during our first meeting.

At that point we began to ask what new possibilities are arising? How is this new understanding reinterpreting and restructuring our lives? What threats, risks and challenges do we hear? What new identities?

What surprises? How are we and the real presence of Christ in the text "co-creating" each other?

> **Conversation Starter:** How have you been surprised by scripture and by the God who is revealed there?

Lee identifies three movements in a method of conversing with a biblical text. He presumes a group of five to fifteen people who focus on one text; in this book we presume the same, and we have chosen the gospels as our text. If the group is larger than fifteen, it is better to break into smaller groups so that all can have the opportunity to participate in the following movements.

*First Movement: Initial Understandings*  As we begin a disciplined conversation with a text, the method may seem, at first, artificial or self-conscious. With time it becomes as natural as the first steps in a developing friendship.

First, we meet the text. We proclaim it two or three times. We take time for silent reflection. Then we share our immediate reactions to what we heard. This is not an analysis about the text; it is about us. Lee suggests that a facilitator might raise such questions as, "What impression did you have; what words grabbed your attention; what feelings were experienced; what mood did the text evoke in you?"[7] Hearing similar interpretations from others in the group reassures us. Hearing different interpretations confronts us. Contrasting interpretations loosen up the conversation. At this point we simply listen without agreeing or disagreeing with anyone's interpretation.

Sharing our preliminary understandings reveals our history, our story and our world. Revealing them in a group may reveal how we often bend and shape texts to fit our own biases. We have not heard the text in its own world. We made it say what we wanted said. At this stage the facilitator simply helps us to see and name the assumptions and biases — the world out of which we speak.

However, sharing initial impressions in a group also moves us beyond scripture as private revelations for our own lives into a conversation within a community. That community together has a mission to hear the word and to live that word in the reign of God. We bring shared vision and shared commitments to that mission. Carroll Stuhlmueller notes that for Jews, scripture study is a communal effort, not a private endeavor leading to private revelations. "If we recall a visit to a rabbinical school or yeshivah, seldom does one see a solitary student hunched over a book in a quiet corner of a library. Rather two or three are always looking over the shoulder of a fellow student, all mumbling and conversing."[8]

*Second Movement: Listening to the Text on Its Own Grounds*   In my visits to South Africa, New South Wales, South Carolina and the South Bronx, I have found this second movement the one most lacking in our homilies and liturgical catechesis with the scriptures. This is so, in some cases, because of a fear of intellectualizing. In North America it is due more to the culture of privatism, romanticism and psychologism and to the religion of fundamentalism. Here we presume to think that we can automatically understand texts written in a different world, as if our world were the only world. Admittedly, the problem also has been caused by the refusal of the Catholic church for so many years to encourage the prayerful study of scripture and by the woeful preparation in scripture of both homilists and catechists.

If we truly converse with scripture and allow the texts in their strangeness to interpret, change, challenge and call us to conversion, we need some guides to invite us into their world. Lee insists that the model for such guides is not the scholar who knows all the nuances of form criticism, redaction criticism, literary criticism and structural analysis, but who cannot lead us toward any pastoral "so whats." We require, rather, a new kind of minister of the word and a new sense of community urgency to have someone prepared to help us converse with the word in its own world. Lee submits that the traditional Jewish model of Torah study is a better image than that of Western scholarship. "The study of the Torah for a Jew is not primarily a quest for knowledge but an act of worship. Studying the scriptures *is* worship."[9] The purpose of this book is to offer a vision, a method and an access to the world and the story of the gospel authors so that ministers of the word can help homilists and catechists enter into conversation with God's word.

Lee cites the different meanings of "good Samaritan" in Jesus' world and ours as one example of what ministers of the word might do to enrich our conversation. We tame the image of a good Samaritan into doing a good deed for someone or caring for the sick, as at Good Samaritan Hospital. That usually surfaces during initial understandings of that passage. The minister of the word would then gently lead the group into the world of the text. That world has a long history of bitterness, distrust and hatred. Samaritans were considered by Jews to be worse than pagans because they were considered heretics. Drawing on his personal experience of racial hatred and on his biblical studies, Martin Luther King changed the characters when he preached this text. The man in the ditch was a member of the Ku Klux Klan, and the Samaritan was the black porter from the railroad station. Conversation with the gospel's world might create a new identity and a new sense of who our neighbor is in our world (Luke 10:25–37—15th Sunday in Ordinary Time, Year C).[10] Our top-of-the-head hearing of the parable of the good Samaritan as a call to immense generosity is not bad or incorrect. It simply fails to plumb the astonishing meaning of a story that summons us to reach over chasms of hatred and to retire the word "enemy" from our vocabulary.

Later in this chapter I shall suggest a way to structure this kind of hearing of the texts in our method of preparing homilists and catechists. For now, to ease the fears that some may have both about not having enough professional expertise and about this being too much work, I suggest that this might be a ministry that circulates among several persons during the course of a month. Also, the expertise needed is not a knowledge of all the tomes written on a given text, much of which is not pastorally helpful. I shall offer examples of what I consider to be helpful background in later chapters of this book.

Finally, there are different kinds of expertise. Everyone comes as an expert on his or her own life experience and life with God. The minister of the word comes with expertise on the experience and story of the gospel author. That minister comes not as guest lecturer but as one who, in narrative fashion or through careful questioning, invites the group into the biblical world through dialogue, not monologue; through conversation, not domination. Usually that can be done in five minutes, or even less once we become more familiar with that world.

*Third Movement: Getting the Meaning "Out in Front"*   After hearing the text of the Good Samaritan on its own ground, move to the claims it makes on today and tomorrow in our relationships with contemporary

"Samaritans," "heretics" and "enemies." We first get to the meaning "behind the text" to get "out in front" of the text. We go beyond the intention of the first speaker and the attention of the first hearer. We converse with the word in our world. Some of that old world might be too strange and different to connect with our world. But some of that strangeness may be exactly what we need to hear. The biblical text confronts our limited world, creates new identity and possibilities, sometimes shatters boundaries and often brings surprises—as does a new friend. For example, biblical studies reveal that perhaps for a thousand years we have mistranslated Jesus' words to Simon the Pharisee as "Because she has loved much she is forgiven much." The preferred text of what Luke's Jesus spoke is "Because she has been forgiven much she will love much" (Luke 7:36–50—11th Sunday in Ordinary Time, Year C). The first puts morality and law first, then forgiveness. The second puts forgiveness and grace first; that makes morality possible. That is good news too shocking for some to hear. Does that good news surprise us? Does it raise new possibilities "out in front" of the text in our world about how and with whom we forgive and reconcile?[11]

When the Pharisees interpreted scripture in new ways for their world, they called it *halakhah* (a word related to "road" or "way"). They were pointing out a road to be taken. We shall see that the road of discipleship and the journey to Jerusalem are key images in Mark's and Luke's story of Jesus. One of the earliest names for Jesus' message was "the Way." Lee insists that words do not truly become "word" until some "way" appears. "God's word transforms what it finds, sometimes ever so gently, sometimes like a torrent, sometimes like a fire. But whether it accosts gently or vehemently, accost it does."[12]

*Fourth Movement: Sharing Our New Response*    After sharing our initial understandings, after entering the world of the gospel authors, we share our new response to the text in a world "before the text." That response is not a moralistic demand or burden but a response to the good news revealed about the God of Jesus Christ. The facilitator helps the group do that in concrete, practical ways that challenge our lives, families, churches and neighborhoods, and our civic, national and world communities. At the end of eucharist we say, "Go in peace to love and serve the Lord!" If we do, what old worlds will come tumbling down? What new worlds will be born?[13]

Walter Brueggemann adds that because of their conversation with scripture in community,

> poets, in the moment of preaching, are permitted to perceive and voice the world differently, to dare a new phrase, a new picture, a free juxtaposition of matters long known. Poets are authorized to invite a new conversation, with new voices sounded, new hearings possible. The new conversation may end in freedom to trust and courage to relinquish. The new conversation, on which our very lives depend, requires a poet and not a moralist. Because, finally, church people are like other people, we are not changed by new rules. The deep places in our lives—places of resistance and embrace—are not ultimately reached by instruction. Those places of resistance and embrace are reached only by stories, images, metaphors and phrases that line out the world differently, apart from our fear and hurt.[14]

### About Method

Before I present the method of conversation with the scripture, I wish to offer a few reflections on method in general. "Methods" may mean techniques—role playing, molding with clay or the use of video, for example. "Method" means the dynamics that are part of every catechetical process that invites us into deeper insight and conversion. These dynamics are ingredients and movements that do not necessarily happen in a predictable order. They are bases that catechesis must touch if it is faithful to its mission of transforming persons in community.[15]

For example, a method of Bernard Lonergan offers four imperatives: *Be attentive* to personal and communal history and experience. *Be reflective* and search out the meaning of that experience in the past for the present and future. *Be responsible* and make decisions based on the values discovered in your reflections. *Be loving* and act on your values and do whatever contributes most to the good of persons.[16]

I offer seven imperatives that are somewhat parallel to Lonergan's:[17] Let there be *storytelling* (be attentive to personal and communal experience). Let there be *questioning*. Let there be *a living community of faith* and let there be *tradition* (be reflective on the meaning of life shared in a tradition). Let there be *conversion* (respond to the values that we discover). Let there be *celebration* and let there be *mission* (be loving of God in worship and of neighbor in service).

Is this not the journey taken by all disciples in Luke? They walked toward Emmaus telling stories and asking questions about the events in Jerusalem. They journeyed in a living community of faith (two or three gathered in Jesus' name) and shared the meaning of their tradition (Moses and all the prophets, who also suffered and died because of their fidelity). There was conversion: Their eyes were opened at the breaking of the bread. They celebrated a meal and rushed to mission to share the good news with the other disciples (Luke 24:13–35—3rd Sunday of Easter, Year A). That journey clearly includes the dynamics and dimensions of catechesis in #75, which we explored in chapter four: proclaiming the message, living in community, celebrating the liturgy and witnessing to the world.

Good method always includes these dynamics. If one or more is missing, we lose some aspect of conversion. For example, if we proclaim only our personal story, we have narcissism or parochialism. If we proclaim only the church's story, we have information without transformation. If we have liturgy or witness without the word, that can lead to fundamentalism, ritualism or ungrounded activism. If we have dynamic Word, warm community and great liturgy without witness and mission, we are into self-maintenance, not self-giving for the reign of God.

Some theorists offer various methods for ministry, catechesis, theological reflection and social analysis that tap into these dynamics either in one session or a series of sessions. In Figure 4, I outline and parallel these methods and the dynamics of method just surveyed. I hope that I have not forced apples into orange crates, but I believe that all of these approaches are trying to incorporate this holistic vision of catechesis.

I hope it is clear that method is more important than methods. We need to become so immersed in these dynamics that we do them by instinct. As Lee says about his own method, "With enough use . . . it becomes an instinct and not a program."[18] Doing the hard work of conversing with scripture is time and money better spent than all that is given to the plethora of so-called lectionary-based programs available for everyone from kindergarteners to adult catechumens.[19] We need to get these dynamics of method into our guts so that we make use of all of them by instinct. To paraphrase Marshall McLuhan, the method is the medium is the message.[20]

**Figure 4**

| METHOD IN CATECHESIS AND MINISTRY | | |
| --- | --- | --- |
| **INITIATION PROCESS** | **LONERGAN METHOD** | **THOMAS AQUINAS** |
| Storytelling<br>Questioning<br>Communities of faith<br>Tradition<br>Conversion<br>Celebration<br>Ministries | Be attentive<br>Be reflective<br>Be loving | Observe<br>Judge<br>Act |
| **WHITEHEAD METHOD** | **GROOME PRAXIS** | **MINISTRIES** |
| Attention to experience, culture, tradition<br>Assertion of experience, culture, tradition<br>Decision | What is your present story-experience-praxis?<br>What are your present vision-assumptions behind your praxis?<br>What is the Christian story-tradition-vision?<br>Dialogue between your experience and Christian tradition.<br>What will be your future story-experience-praxis? | Ministries of word<br>Ministries of community building<br>Celebrating service-healing |
| **BERNARD LEE** | **JOHN SHEA** | **TAD GUZIE** |
| Initial understandings<br>The text on<br>its own grounds<br>Meaning "out front" | Meeting with mystery<br>Enlightened by mystery<br>Acting in mystery | lived experience<br>story<br>festing |

**Conversation Starter:** What is your evaluation of the "lectionary-based programs" now on the market?[21]

## About Method to Prepare for the Liturgy of the Word

I offer here a method that utilizes these dynamics in ways specifically tailored for homilists and catechists who are preparing for the liturgy of the word. The method offers a disciplined conversation with scripture that Philip McBrien uses with catechists during 90-minute sessions[22] in a parish that uses the liturgy of the word as a basis for catechesis for the entire parish—kindergarten through the adult catechumenate. The method develops in three stages (facilitator preparation, conversation with catechists, and catechists planning for their group) with three steps for each stage.[23] Figure 5 outlines the three steps for each of the three stages.

**Figure 5**

| A METHOD FOR CONVERSING WITH SCRIPTURE | | | |
|---|---|---|---|
| | Stage 1: Facilitator preparation | Stage 2: Catechist conversation | Stage 3: Planning |
| **Step 1. Initial impressions** | Proclaim text Write impressions | Proclaim text Declare first impressions | Impressions of: learners, materials, exegesis, place in year, options |
| **Step 2. The text** | Consult research | Dialogue with research | Proclaim text again |
| **Step 3. Converse Correlate Decide** | Design catechist session | Group finds meaning for today | Design session for learners |

In all three stages, McBrien follows the three movements suggested by Bernard Lee. He notes, however, that unlike a shared homily in a liturgical setting, this preparation session for homilists and catechists encourages more critical reflection on their initial impressions and pre-understandings because we are preparing to invite catechumens into a critically responsible understanding of our heritage. All sessions begin and end with prayer.

***Stage One: Facilitator Preparation***   The facilitator is a minister of the word who enables the conversation with God's word by reading the sources that help him or her hear "the text on its own ground," but he or she does not function as an expert or lecturer. Facilitators also share their own experience as partners in the conversation. If the homilist or a catechist has a special background in scripture, he or she may serve as the prime facilitator, but it is good if this ministry can be rotated.

McBrien suggests that facilitators ignore both the comments with which most missals and editions of the Bible introduce the readings as well as the interpretations given in program materials. I would add that most popular commentaries do not offer the wonderful and sometimes startling research available from contemporary biblical studies. Such commentaries also tend to define what a text means and thereby short-circuit the conversation.

*Step 1*
The facilitator might prepare with at least one other person. They begin by reflecting on the entire liturgy of the word and the place of this day in the liturgical season, and by proclaiming all the readings of the Sunday or feast day. They decide what dimension of the liturgy to suggest to the homilists/catechists as a focus. (This book offers reflections only on the gospels, so comments here are limited to conversing with the gospel.) In light of the dimension selected, those preparing would proclaim the gospel slowly and carefully a second time, noting their immediate responses and initial impressions of the reading. These responses may be positive or negative, but they must always be honest. If facilitators already have some background in scripture, they may begin to note what they believe the text means on its own ground. If not, they proceed to step 2.

*Step 2*
The faciliator consults what scholars have discovered in the text. (During this step, I invite you to consult the research on the gospels that I offer

in succeeding chapters and to check the resources listed in the endnotes.) Be prepared to be threatened or challenged or surprised, to disagree, to take a risk or to be affirmed as in any conversation with a friend.

McBrien distinguishes between popular and scholarly works. The distinction is not how difficult the commentary is to read. Some popular works are as dry and uninteresting as heavier tomes. The key distinction is that a popular work seeks to inform, inspire, challenge, invite to conversion and, perhaps, to give a meaning to a text, while the scholarly work seeks to equip us to jump into the argument about meaning. Scholars are less interested in drawing a conclusion about definitive interpretations than in offering multiple interpretations with which we can grapple.

In this book, because the focus is on welcome into the community, I have chosen to see most texts through the lens of God's astonishing covenant-love especially for outcasts and outsiders, even though there may be many possible meanings of a text or an entire gospel. Please accept the interpretations that I offer as a partner in the conversation, not as an imposition of meaning. I also want to tease, equip and enable you to do the hard work of consulting the scholarly works referenced in the endnotes, which I do not find referenced in most popular commentaries. McBrien suggests that the facilitator consult at least two scholarly commentaries and seek points of disagreement between authorities. This is hard work. But McBrien quotes his mentor, Nelle Slater: "Do you imagine that any church choir would just show up on Sundays without rehearsal? The results would be disastrous. No one would stand for it. Yet when we allow our teachers just to show up for a religion class, that's like letting the choir do its thing without rehearsal."[24]

## Step 3

During step 3, the facilitator will decide what, how much and how to share with the homilists and catechists: the research on the particular gospel (or other text), its relationship to the entire gospel and its relationship to the entire liturgy of the day and season. Again, this should not be an extended lecture. It could be presented in a brief narrative style (about five minutes) or perhaps through raising questions or in some experiential mode that might take longer.[25] The "how to" always encourages dialogue and does not impose one interpretation of meaning for our lives.

> **Conversation Starter:**   Would you accept the role of minister and facilitator of the word as described above? Why or why not?

*Stage Two: Homilist/Catechist Meeting*   McBrien suggests 90 minutes for this meeting, which will include stages two and three. The first half will be the conversation with the text; the second half centers on planning the homily/catechesis. Groups should be no larger than ten to fifteen people so that all might participate. The facilitator should begin by explaining why the gospel or some other dimension of the liturgy of the word is given special focus. That choice should be open to dialogue and negotiation.

*Step 1*
Proclaim the gospel. The group offers initial impressions. As Lee suggests, the groups eventually will see that at this step they are identifying themselves far more than they identify the text. At this step, members simply listen to each other without agreeing or disagreeing.

*Step 2*
The facilitator provides a background briefing on "the text on its own ground" using materials from this book and other solid resources. The facilitator offers this information in narrative or experiential style, as a fellow believer, not as a guest expert. Step 2 may threaten, challenge or affirm the initial impressions of step 1. It steers clear of the Scylla of fundamentalism by tapping into historical/literary biblical studies, and it avoids the Charybdis of historicism by staying on the course of a pastoral/theological conversation with God's word.

*Step 3*
Proclaim the text a second time. In conversation, the members of the group let go of control and biases, become vulnerable and take the risk of letting the text accost, surprise, confront or affirm them. Although they may become task-oriented and begin to discuss possibilities for catechizing others, the facilitator should lead them back to the conversation.

They converse and allow their personal and communal stories to dialogue with the biblical drama. The group goes beyond the initial impressions and asks How are we and our initial responses affirmed or challenged by what we have heard about the scripture? How might we affirm or challenge and go beyond the biblical meanings? What are the "so whats"?

***Stage Three: Planning the Homily/Catechesis*** The goal of this stage is to focus on specific ways of homilizing/catechizing. The question that the group keeps in mind is How do we engage our catechumens in conversation with God's word?

*Step 1*
The group broadens their initial impressions, going beyond the text to include their experiences of the catechumenate group (catechumens, candidates, sponsors, their families) and of the parish assembly; the strengths and weaknesses of any program materials (or whether any printed resources are needed); what has worked or not worked in the past; the ways that the gospel connects with other dimensions of the liturgy of the word; alternative suggestions for the homily and for open-ended methods of catechesis; discussion of what current issues in church, neighborhood, civic community and world might enter the conversation; discussion of what issues of postbiblical teaching or practice might arise. This should be a freewheeling, brainstorming step; all suggestions should be listed without evaluation.

*Step 2*
Proclaim the text again to let it invite the group deeper into the conversation. Now the group brings the background of its experience, its deepened understanding of the text and its experience with the catechumenate community. What might be the "so whats" for that community?

*Step 3*
The group decides on the concrete shape of the homily and of the catechesis, but those plans always allow for flexibility and surprises. The group decides who leads what parts of the catechesis and whether other members of the parish community should be invited to serve as leaders.

They decide on techniques for homilizing and catechizing. If there are catechists present who minister with groups in the community other than the catechumens, they might separate themselves into one or more groups. In that case, it may be appropriate for everyone to regroup at the end of the meeting to share all the possibilities.

> **Conversation Starter:**   What are your affirmations and reservations about this method? Is it important that homilists and catechumenate catechists use such a method to prepare together? Why or why not?

## Endnotes

[1] "Shared Homily: Conversation that Puts Communities at Risk," in Bernard Lee, ed., *Alternative Futures for Worship, Volume 3: The Eucharist* (Collegeville: The Liturgical Press, 1987), 157 (emphasis added).

[2] Cited by Leonardo Boff, *Church: Charism and Power* (New York: Crossroads Publishing Co., 1985), 138 ff.

[3] Lee relies heavily on the work of Hans-Georg Gadamer and Paul Ricoeur on how small Christian communities might reflect on scripture; cf. Gadamer's *Truth and Method* (New York: Crossroads Publishing Co., 1975); Ricoeur's *Hermeneutics and the Human Sciences* (London: Cambridge University Press, 1981); *Interpretation Theory* (Fort Worth: Texas Christian University Press, 1976); *The Rule of Metaphor* (Toronto: University of Toronto Press, 1984); and David Tracy and Robert Grant, *A Short History of the Interpretation of the Bible* (Philadelphia: Fortress Press, 1984), chapters 16–18.

[4] Lee, "Shared Homily," 159.

[5] Lee, "Shared Homily," 162.

[6] James Fowler, *Stages of Faith* (San Francisco: Harper & Row, 1981).

[7] Lee, "Shared Homily," 166.

[8] Carroll Stuhlmueller, "The Bible and Life: A Mysterious Bond," *New Catholic World* 230 (January/February 1987): 4.

[9] Lee, "Shared Homily," 170.

[10] In these and subsequent chapters, I shall give the references to the lectionary when citing gospel verses, if they occur within the liturgical cycle. All page numbers for references will be in Appendix I.

[11] Cf. Kenneth Bailey, *Poet and Peasant and Through Peasant Eyes* (Grand Rapids: Wm. B. Eerdmans, 1980), 17–18.

[12] Lee, "Shared Homily," 171.

[13] In exploring the gospels we shall see that the synoptics' graphic descriptions of the end of the world focus less on the end of time and more on demolishing the political world of Roman violence and oppression and the religious world of temple elitism and covenant exclusion. We then will hold a conversation about our worlds of political and economic oppression and religious elitism that need to be demolished. Cf. Matthew 24:37–44 (First Sunday of Advent, Year A); Mark 13:24–32 (33rd Sunday in Ordinary Time, Year B); Mark 13:33–37 (First Sunday of Advent, Year B); Luke 21:5–19 (33rd Sunday in Ordinary Time, Year C); Luke 21:25–28, 34–36 (First Sunday of Advent, Year C).

[14] Walter Brueggemann, *Finally Comes the Poet* (Minneapolis: Fortress Press, 1989), 109–10.

[15] For example, the observe-judge-act method, made so widely accessible by Joseph Cardign in the Catholic Action groups in Europe, in the Christian Family Movement (CFM), the Young Christian Worker movement (YCW) and the Young Christian Student movement (YCS) in the English-speaking world, and more recently in the Hispanic *Encuentros*, is rooted in Thomas Aquinas's three steps for a prudent act.

[16] Bernard Lonergan, *Method in Theology* (London: Darton, Longman & Todd, 1971).

[17] "RCIA: Model for Adult Growth," *Worship* (March 1979).

[18] Lee, "Shared Homily," 173.

[19] The worst of these programs give little attention to conversing with scripture. Although they do offer methods that help to connect personal experience with the scriptures, they do so with preconceived lesson plans that may or may not meet the needs and questions of catechumens in a given session. A director of catechetics told me that he had tried most of these programs, tossed them out and simply used the scriptures with methods that stimulated genuine conversation between our tradition (biblical and postbiblical) and people's personal and communal lives. Many of the people he did this with had little education.

[20] Cf. James Dunning, "The Method Is the Medium Is the Message: Catechetical Method in the RCIA," *Christian Initiation Resources Reader, Volume I: Precatechumenate* (New York: Wm. H. Sadlier, Inc., 1984), 86–94.

[21] See criteria for evaluating such materials in Philip McBrien, *How to Teach with the Lectionary: Leader's Guide* (Mystic CT: Twenty-third Publications, 1992), chapter four.

[22] The sessions are offered twice weekly to accommodate both those who can come during the day and those who prefer the evening. For McBrien's description of this method, see *How to Teach with the Lectionary* (Mystic CT: Twenty-third Publications, 1992), chapter four.

[23] Cf. Philip McBrien, "Conversation: A Discipline for Studying and Teaching the Sunday Lectionary," *Religious Education* 85:3, 424–35. I am indebted to Phil and to the catechists of St. Thomas Aquinas Parish in Indianapolis for inviting me to experience their use of this method firsthand.

[24] McBrien, *How to Teach*, 23.

[25] Walter Wink offers experiential methods plus questions that might be used both to prepare homilists/catechists and in sessions with catechumens, e.g., paint pictures; write dialogues with characters in the stories, mime the characters; role-play; make up skits; work with clay; repeat (mantras); move to music; perform physical actions; paraphrase the text; write a prayer; write a parable, psalm, or a poem; read poetry; develop spontaneous rituals; use guided meditations; paint your life-line; work with two sets of texts. Of course, these same methods might be used with catechumens. *Transforming Bible Study: A Leader's Guide* (Nashville: Abingdon Press, 1980), 109–52.

CHAPTER SEVEN

# Conversing with Matthew's Story

*The person who preaches in the context of the liturgical assembly is a mediator, representing both the community and the Lord. The assembly gathers for liturgy as a community of faith, believing that God has acted in human history and more particularly, in their own history. The community gathers to respond to this living and active God. They may also gather to question how or whether the God who once acted in human history is still present and acting today. . . . The preacher represents this community by voicing its concerns, by naming its demons, and thus enabling it to gain some understanding and control of the evil which afflicts it. [The preacher] represents the Lord by offering the community another word, a word of healing and pardon, of acceptance and love.*[1]

• Bishops' Committee on Priestly Life and Ministry

THIS CHAPTER AND those following will focus our attention on one area for a pastoral/theological hearing in homilizing and catechizing. We limit ourselves to how we might break open God's word in the gospels of the liturgical cycle during the catechumenate period (cf. #75.1 and 75.3). In the final chapter, we explore a pastoral/theological hearing of "dogma and precepts and a profound sense of the mystery of salvation" (#75. 1).

Chapters seven through ten, which focus on the "big stories" of Matthew, Mark, Luke and John, offer the grist for the second step in each of the stages of the method of conversing with scripture proposed in the previous chapter. With great hesitancy I have limited this grist largely to the gospels. I offer it as a taste of what might be done with the entire liturgy of the word. A select bibliography of commentaries on the other biblical texts that might be used in this second step may be found at the end of the book.

In this chapter and in the two that follow, I offer you one end product of the process of interpreting and conversing with the gospel—a homily on one gospel reading from each of the three years of the lectionary cycle. For the purposes of this book, I have chosen in each case a pivotal reading, one that opens windows to other gospel readings in that lectionary year and that gives hints of the gospel's "big story." I do so to suggest that preaching the lectionary does not limit us to the one pericope, which is just a snippet of the story. These homilies are, therefore, more lengthy, "heavier" and offer more biblical interpretation than I would offer in most parishes, although I have preached these homilies at Forum institutes. At those institutes and in this book, I am trying to give a much larger dose of this style of preaching.

These homilies give you a chance to see if I practice what I preach (and preach what I practice). You need to decide if you want to follow this particular homiletic road or take a different approach. I am not suggesting this as an absolute but as one pastoral response to our need for biblical literacy.

When adopting this approach in the parish, I assume that some in the assembly have been prepared to hear scripture not just as historical fact but as story, image and symbol revealing God for our times. Many have not. In St. Utopia Parish, which has been restructured into a community of communities, we would invite every parishioner to meet in a community and reflect on the liturgy of the word using the method proposed in chapter six. That would be their spiritual preparation for Sunday eucharist. This follows the dynamics of Thomas Richstatter's and Bernard Lee's "alternative futures for eucharist"[2] in which the liturgy of the word celebrated on a weekday in a small intentional community prepares for the Sunday assembly. Since that will not happen in most of our futures, I suggest that homilists and catechists meet for that preparation. The homilist then shares some of the insights of step 2 in the homily, and the catechist shares even more in the session with the catechumens.

This sharing is not simply didactic; it evokes prayer and commitment. Like step 2 in Lee's shared homily, "this must not be a classroom lecture on historical biblical criticism, yet it must deal as amply as possible with whatever introduces the words' own horizon. An easy narrative style is most helpful—lecturing violates liturgical mood! . . . There can be no genuine conversation if one has not first made an effort to hear what is said upon its own horizon."[3] In lieu of this happening prior to the Sunday gathering, the homilist needs to let the entire assembly in on some of this conversation. If we hear scripture with pastoral/theological ears, how might we speak and preach that good news in ways that move "from hearing a text on its own grounds to what claims it makes on tomorrow"[4] in our communities of today? The ultimate focus is not on texts but on our lives and experience. This is not just our personal experience (a psychological hearing) but primarily for our experience and mission as church (a pastoral/theological hearing).

### Some Assumptions about Gospel and Covenant

Before I begin this process, however, I share with you some assumptions about the gospel writers and how we hear their message. First, the authors of the gospels were more homilists and preachers, storytellers and dramatists than biographers and historians. "Much of the content of the Bible is itself a certain form of 'preaching,' and originated and was shaped by the proclamation of the word."[5] Like preachers and storytellers today, the authors of the gospels voiced the concerns of their communities. In response, they also voiced God's word of healing, pardon, acceptance and liberation. Their messages differ because their communities differed. They were more than secretaries recording word for word what Jesus preached to his communities. They were pastors, storytellers and homilists with passion and compassion—a passionate faith in the God of Jesus Christ and a compassionate commitment to the healing and salvation of their communities. Therefore, they felt obliged to apply the good news of Jesus in ways that met the needs of those communities and invited them into the living story of Jesus in their times.

Second, a pastoral/theological hearing of the gospels shares that passion and compassion. Like the gospel authors, we listen to God's word with a passionate belief in Jesus Christ. Like them, too, our compassionate concerns are for people. We then search the stories of God's dealings with people for theological motifs and understandings that connect with the questions and issues of our times.

We begin by exploring one pressing contemporary issue that apparently was such an overriding concern for our ancestors in faith that it gave our scriptures their name: testament, covenant.[6] "The covenant motif is the haunting melody at the heart of both the Hebrew and

Christian scriptures."[7] "Covenant" is the point of view that I have chosen, as noted in the introduction. One way to hear the gospels in a literary way is to listen for the stories of covenant. Perhaps our word for covenant today is solidarity. For the first time in history, we can be what Karl Rahner calls "world/church,"[8] a church present to and in solidarity with all the cultures and languages of all the continents.

Rahner sees this as our third great cultural transition. The first was the pressing concern of biblical times — the expansion of the community of Jesus' followers beyond Jews to include Gentiles. The second was the transition from the Greco-Roman world to the rest of Europe and eventually through the Europeans to North America. Our challenge is to make the transition to a world/church: Some estimate that 70 percent of Catholics will live in the Southern Hemisphere by the year 2000[9] and that 40 to 50 percent of the Catholics in the United States will be Hispanic.

In that world/church of many cultures, Rahner calls for a depth of faith when faith is no longer supported by the cultural forms of Christendom. He states that

> our present situation is one of transition from a church sustained by a homogeneously Christian society and almost identical with it; from a people's church to a church made up of those who have struggled against their environment in order to reach personally a clearly and explicitly responsible decision of faith. This will be the church of the future or there will be no church at all.[10]

Elsewhere he says that "Christians of the future will be mystics [a genuine experience of God emerging from the depths of experience] or they will not be Christians at all."[11] That church of deeper faith will sing, dance, pray, voice and celebrate faith in ways not just European and North American. It may be closer to the stories, images, experiences and dancing of our Hebrew ancestors than to European philosophies and American psychologies.

The criterion for inclusion in the new covenant of Jesus' blood is not heritage, family ties or male gender. It is faith — living, active faith. Jesus transcends a family based on chromosomes. Mark's Jesus says, "Here are my mother and my brothers! Whoever does the will of God is my brother and sister and mother" (3:35 — 10th Sunday in Ordinary Time,

Year B). In Mark, some women, especially Mary—not by blood but by faith—are the model disciples (his true mother and sisters) who stay with Jesus until the end and hear the good news of the resurrection.[12]

Jesus came not to undo God's covenant of love with Israel. Instead he stood in the tradition of Hebrew prophets and preached fidelity to the God who freely chose Israel in covenantal love. It is a mistake to contrast a supposedly Hebrew God of judgment with a Christian God of love. Jesus' first prophetic word was a summons to fidelity to the prophets' good news of exodus to freedom and covenant in justice. The great commandment was to love God and neighbor as a response to love. What was new about Jesus' covenant was that he fulfilled the prophets' promises to offer God's new covenant to all people, especially outcasts and rejects—women,[13] children, shepherds, the ritually unclean, Gentiles and Samaritans, the poor and imprisoned, tax collectors and sinners—precisely because he chose solidarity with all these outcasts in his times and ours.

Questions about covenant and about who is included were perplexing the communities for whom the gospel authors wrote. These questions dominate the plots of all four gospels. In a culture steeped in the need for separatism from Gentiles and on notions of ritual impurity that created enormous gaps between insiders and outsiders—religious, political and economic—the earliest gospel communities agonized and struggled about who could become followers of Jesus.

These clearly are the great questions for our times as well. One could make a case that not covenant and unity but division often marks our history, not only within Christianity but among all religions. Race, culture, tribe and social and economic class too often prove stronger than covenant and faith—dividing Puerto Ricans from Mexicans, Native Americans from European immigrants, northern Europeans from southern, Brahman from untouchables among Hindus, underclass and homeless from middle class and mortgaged in the United States, Protestant from Catholic in Northern Ireland, Muslim from Hindu in Pakistan, Christian from Muslim in Lebanon, Arab from Jew throughout the Middle East. In 1990, I was in Africa when black tribes slaughtered each other in Liberia, and I heard stories of white police goons leading Zulu followers of Mangosuthu Buthelezi to burn the homes of followers of

Nelson Mandela in South Africa. History is full of so-called religious, racial and tribal "holy wars" fought in the name of God. Isaiah's lion is not yet lying down, except with the lamb inside him.[14]

We bring this closer to home if we explore covenant in light of our built-in drive toward community. Sin is precisely that which divides and alienates. One community-organizer contends,

> All our societal problems . . . stem from the fact that people are alienated. We are alienated from ourselves, resulting in abusive addictions of all kinds. We are alienated from the systems and institutions that affect and control our personal and family lives, making us feel helpless and alienated from one another and keeping us from thinking and acting collectively. [He concludes,] The creation of community is the most radical thing that anyone can do today, and the church is still the best, and in many places, the only vehicle that has a chance to create community.[15]

About such alienated people another writer comments,

> Who do we think those people are who seem to be getting co-dependent on co-dependency books or addicted to 12-step support groups, or are attending New Age workshops? Pagans who dropped from the sky? They are Catholics [and Protestants] just like us. Ordinary people. And they're only looking for answers to the questions: Who am I? How can I get rid of the pain? What is my purpose in life? Where is God in all of this?

He concludes that most are finding more light in communities outside the church than within it.[16]

When we think of the aliens and outcasts, we usually imagine racial or sexual minorities, the poor and homeless, women and children, anyone cast onto the margins. However, Tex Sample offers a fascinating study of the baby boomers (those born between 1946 and 1960) at the center of our society. He claims that those on the "cultural left" with an ethic of self-fulfillment are alienated by the church's ethic of self-denial but would be attracted by a "journey theology." He describes one group on the "cultural right" as "hard livers" who "want more from life and expect more; they plan for it and seek it out; yet they do not trust people, are not happy, and feel excluded from things."[17] According to Sample, they would be attracted by a message of traditional values.[18] Sample suggests strategies and theologies faithful to our tradition that might welcome these strangers home. He also suggests that although most candidates for church ministry come from the cultural right, as do most of our church members, seminaries and universities socialize them out of their cultural roots so that they minister in ways that deepen alienation. Covenant-community needs to offer good news both to the margins and to the center.

If homilists/catechists today truly enflesh the passion and compassion of Jesus and the gospel writers, Sunday after Sunday our first concern will be to ask: Who are the alienated and excluded in our communities, both at the center and at the margins? That is the "big story" within which we hear all year the other stories in the liturgy of the word. We are mediators between our times and God's word when we connect our passion for solidarity and inclusion to the gospel's stories of covenant and inclusion. When in doubt, first look for covenant and for the outsiders whom the God of Jesus Christ brings inside. If we situate all gospel readings—in fact, all Christian tradition—within that big story in homilies and catechesis, we shall respond to the concern that catechumens do not know and that individual pericopes don't present the "big picture."

We make our most liberating moves by interacting with world events. Ninety percent of the Christian scriptures were written after Rome disrupted Israel. These were the signs of the times challenging our ancestors in faith. Those times called them from a Jewish church to a church of the known world. The tragedy is that in spite of Matthew's efforts to integrate both Jewish and Gentile cultures into a church that would be truly catholic, he failed. Apparently, Jewish Christians who had followed the leadership of James in Jerusalem could not make the transition. They bound the way of Jesus to the practices of Judaism. In so doing, they isolated themselves from the "world/church" of their times and, in turn, deprived that church of its Jewish roots. Vincent Donovan contends, "Quite simply, because they made no efforts at cross-culturation, they died. After the year 140 there is not a trace of them left in the world of living human beings."

Donovan adds that in our time of transition we also can

> refuse to admit that we must commit ourselves to an exploration and discovering of a form of the church and its ministry and sacraments, a form of Christianity and of Christ, that we have not known. . . . We can deny that Christ is shackled and trapped in the narrowness of our culture; deny that the Western Christ of ours is a stumbling block for the Holy Spirit.[19]

Or we can we respond with the resilience of the authors of the gospel and expand our community to our known world and especially to the poor and broken sisters and brothers in that world desperately searching for unity and covenant.

I shall keep returning to a "covenantal point of view" of that big story, especially in the three synoptics, as one approach to situating the individual gospels (and the entire liturgy of the Word) of the liturgical year. Once again, when reading the homilies in these chapters, question the approach. In the hope of inviting both the entire assembly and the catechumens into greater biblical literacy, I offer more scriptural inter-pretation than would most theorists on homilies. I have "market tested" these homilies, but that was with somewhat select groups at Forum institutes. The response was generally positive, but a few said they were didactic, not evocative. That is the bottom line. Are they just didactic, informational, interesting presentations of scholarly material—Bible study? If so, cursed be my preaching! I mean them to be evocative—not just of feelings but of faith in a God more powerfully revealed when we unpack the meaning and power of both the biblical message and of contemporary life and times. Do they evoke in us and our communities renewed commitments to welcome the outcast and alienated, within ourselves and in others, with faith in the God of the covenant? If we converse with that message in a pastoral/theological hearing, will it accost our communities as it did those in the early church?

## A Homily on Matthew

> Jesus went away to the district of Tyre and Sidon. Just then a Canaanite woman from that region came out and started shouting, "Have mercy on me, Lord, Son of David; my daughter is tormented by a demon." But he did not answer her at all. And his disciples urged him, saying, "Send her away, for she keeps shouting after us." He answered, "I was sent only to the lost sheep of the house of Israel." But she came and knelt before him saying, "Lord, help me." He answered, "It is not fair to take the children's food and throw it to the dogs." She said, "Yes, Lord, yet even the dogs eat the crumbs that fall from their masters' table." Then Jesus answered her, "Woman, great is your faith! Let it be done for you as you wish." And her daughter was healed instantly. (Matthew 15:21–28—20th Sunday in Ordinary Time, Year A)

When I got off the plane in Adelaide during a visit to Australia in 1985, Michael Trainor, a priest of the archdiocese said, "Hurry up! Throw your port in my boot. We have a crisis." I certainly did not want to be an "ugly American" and violate Australian cultural amenities, so I poured my wine on his shoe. Well, in Australia "port" means luggage and "boot" means car trunk; so after we put port in boot and cleaned his shoe, we sped down the highway.

We headed toward a meeting of the archdiocesan pastoral council, 56 faithful and stalwart Catholics who met monthly with the archbishop. They had been reflecting on reconciliation, with a focus on welcoming home inactive Catholics. The previous month they had heard stories from people who wanted to come home but who wondered if they were welcome. There was a divorced and remarried couple who could not get a decree of nullity of a previous marriage. There was a resigned priest barred from any ministry by the Vatican because he was told he was a public scandal. There was a young gay man trying to leave a fragmented life and enter a stable relationship with one man. Most moving, there was an aborigine, a member of one of the oldest cultures in the world, who asked, "Is my culture welcome in your church?"

The stories left the group paralyzed. On the one hand, they knew what they thought to be church teaching.[20] On the other hand, before them were wounded, fragile, struggling, repentant, fearful, faithful, sinful and graced people who seemed excluded by Catholic teaching and practice. Who can our church welcome?

For two hours, Michael and I shared with the pastoral council the great gospel of the meals—Luke with his astounding stories of how Jesus eats and welcomes people at table. He eats with enemies of the people to begin and end his ministry (5:27–32 and 19:1–10—31st Sunday in Ordinary Time, Year C). Compare the tax collectors Levi and Zacchaeus to organized crime or the Medellín drug cartel.[21] In between, Jesus eats with public sinners and tells stories of banquets for prodigals and outcasts.

Both the gospels of Mark and Matthew include the Jesus' confrontation with the "liberated woman" who demands healing for her daughter. She is a Syro-Phoenician in Mark; but Matthew makes her a Canaanite—the most hated enemy of Israel. Matthew has already told us of Jesus' command to love enemies (5:6—7th Sunday in Ordinary Time, Year A). Now he tells us a story about Jesus doing it.

But Jesus seems to have a hard time doing it. More likely, some in the community for whom Matthew is writing were having a hard time doing it, that is, letting in those Gentile foreigners (today hear Rodriguez, Wong, Muhammed, Kim, Wisnewski or anyone with a name not like ours).

Isaiah 25 (6–10—28th Sunday in Ordinary Time, Year A) and Isaiah in today's first reading (56:1, 6–7) promised that all peoples and nations would join in covenant at a banquet with the richest food and finest wine. But some took those texts and turned them on their heads. Sure, they said, God invites all the nations; but after they get there, God will "deliver them to the angels for punishment"; "they shall be a spectacle for the righteous"; and "his sword is drunk with their blood." These interpreters said that only Jews would eat. Even worse, only perfect Jews would eat. The Qumran sect of Jesus' time also describes this great banquet; but no one gets in who is "smitten in the feet or hands, or lame, or blind, or deaf, or mute."[22]

So here we have this uppity woman assaulting the teaching of Jesus' time. This despised foreigner demands inclusion, and she wants healing for her daughter, who is an outcast on two counts—she is a woman, and she is afflicted by an evil spirit. The woman comes with faith. She calls Jesus "Lord" and "Son of David," a title used by "no-accounts" in Matthew's gospel and astounding on the lips of a Gentile. Matthew's Jesus at first gives her the stock reply: "I was sent only to the lost sheep of the house of Israel." He even compares her to a dog.

But she keeps at him. And, as in every story of Gentiles in Matthew, this outsider gets in. I hope Jesus slapped his knee and guffawed, "Good for you, woman! What great faith you have!"

We might salute this woman as "woman of the year" in Matthew because she gives us a peek at the entire gospel.[23] She appears on the scene right at the center of the gospel. In the first half of the gospel, Matthew is writing to comfort the Jewish followers of Jesus who had been thrown out of the synagogues, and he assures them that they have a teacher far greater than Moses, as evidenced by, for example, the Sermon on the Mount. But the Jewish leaders have rejected that teacher; and just before this story of the Canaanite woman, Jesus gives up on them— "hypocrites," "blind leaders of the blind" (15:7, 13). In her, Isaiah's promise is fulfilled. This woman foreigner and all outsiders and rejects are welcome to the banquet. At the end of this gospel, Jesus sends his followers to *all nations* (28:16–20—Trinity Sunday, Year B).

I mention this history to help us understand that to welcome this despised Canaanite was absolutely appalling for the church of Jesus' time, far more outrageous than for our church to find ways to welcome those people knocking on our door in Australia.

What questions do this woman and Jesus raise for us and our church? Are there hypocrisy and blind leaders of the blind in our family, church and society? In a recent talk, I suggested that the "new" immigrants, many from the South and East and many of them Catholic, could be our church's great gift to our nation as reminders that most of the world is still tired, poor and yearning to breathe free. Yet a man complained afterward that all these foreigners were ruining our country. At a Mass recently, a woman complained to me about a divorced woman "prancing around the sanctuary" as a eucharistic minister. What peoples and cultures do we exclude? Who are the Gentiles and Canaanites of our times, denied acceptance and bread at our table, driven outside to other churches or abandoned outside with all the homeless and table-less? Who is left out in our family, our church, our neighborhood, our society? Who pleads for healing? Do we stand and plead with them in solidarity?

I close with an image and a story. The image, taken from Archbishop Roger Mahoney's homily at his installation in Los Angeles—long before images of L.A. burning entered our homes in 1992—is the infamous California freeway. Mahoney says that those who drive through L.A. on freeways might never see their brothers and sisters in Watts struggling for basic human dignity or the thousands unemployed in East Los Angeles.

> You would overlook them not simply because the poor are often invisible but because the crowds of youth by the liquor stores and the old men shuffling through the streets have become so common. Even more you would overlook them quite literally because the very freeway system that joins the world of culture and opportunity with the world of the great hotels and restaurants allows those who use them to drive right over the poor. The poor are unseen beneath us.[24]

Matthew's Jesus challenges us to look around and to see all the Canaanites (outsiders, rejects, outcasts, foreigners) who ask for healing and whom we drive over on our freeways.

The story is from my mother's funeral in August 1989. She died a good death, a sudden death, but one day too soon. She loved to gather people, amazingly diverse people, at her dinner table. But one person who would not come was her 91-year-old brother, because 25 years before, my sister forgot to ask his wife to pour tea at her wedding reception. The wound festered into total noncommunication. On August 26, 1989, my cousin talked the old man into coming to see my mother to be reconciled. She died the next morning before he arrived. He asked our permission to come to the funeral, and after the funeral my sister presided at a rite of reconciliation. Before the family meal, with seven cousins and my uncle with his wife, she passed around dozens of pictures from the early 1900s, pictures of my mother, her brother and their families. Only he knew the stories behind the pictures. By telling the stories he became part of the family again. He was even able to joke at the end of the meal, "Do you know what Irish Alzheimer's disease is? We forget everything but a grudge!" What grudges and barriers do we need to forget as individuals, as church, as a people? What Canaanites, what outsiders need to share their stories at our tables?

> **Conversation Starter:** In a psychological/personal hearing of this story from Matthew, prepare some questions that might invite catechumens to enter *personally* into the story. In a pastoral/theological hearing, prepare questions that might invite the catechumenal and parish *communities* to enter the story.

## Pastorally Hearing Matthew's Big Story

Michael Garvey writes of a church catholic (universal) enough to have room for everybody.

> [It] knits together a loving family with Mary, the Mother of God, my Uncle Mike, Phil Donahue, Phyllis Schlafly, Bernard of Clairvaux, Mary Daly, Dan Berrigan, Charlemagne, Walker Percy, Joseph Ratzinger, Andrew Greeley, Teresa of Calcutta, Francis of Assisi, and the double-tonsured cosmonaut in the Hawaiian shirt who sits in the pew in front of mine at Mass and flashes a "Sieg Heil" salute during the Our Father.[25]

Matthew wanted a church like that. In a sense Matthew is the first catholic, with a small c. He wants everybody to stay united and together. In that regard, he is more "maternal"—he wants to keep everyone in the family.[26] That is his drama and story of covenant.

Some call Mark the gospel for catechumens, with a sparse outline of the story of Jesus and more action than discourse. Matthew's story of covenant might be called the gospel of a catechist who, in orderly fashion, gathers Jesus' teachings into discourses about the kingdom of heaven,[27] interspersed with narrative actions that bring him to Jerusalem.

Some scholars divide Matthew into five books paralleling the five books of the Pentateuch, each with a discourse (chapters 5 to 7—Sermon on the Mount; chapters 10 to 11:1—mission instruction; chapter 13:1–53—parable instructions; chapter 18—lessons on community life; and chapters 24 to 25—reflections on the end), with the infancy narrative in the prologue and Jesus' passion and resurrection in the climax. Each discourse ends with the phrase "and it happened, when Jesus finished these . . . ,"[28] and the last discourse ends with "when Jesus finished all these words" (26:1), which marks the break between the reflections and the passion story.[29]

Others prefer a threefold division that focuses less on the church and more on Christ: 1) the birth narratives as anticipation of Jesus' life and death; 2) the ministry of Jesus as the gradual unfolding of his life and teachings; and 3) the passion and resurrection as the saving events revealed and taught in the preceding section.[30] In either approach, we would see the lectionary pericope within the literary whole.

## A Jewish-Christian Community

Matthew writes, most likely, as a Jewish Christian[31] in Antioch between the years 85 and 90. After the destruction of the temple by the Romans in the year 70,[32] Judaism lost its center of worship and discipline. Public Jewish worship dispersed entirely into the synagogues, which the Jewish followers of Jesus attended. With Judaism itself at risk of dissolution, however, the teachers of the law decided they needed more control, so they expelled all the heretics and Christians from the synagogues. A benediction prayer from about 85 CE says "let Christians and *minim* [probably heretics] perish in a moment, let them be blotted out of the book of the living."[33] As good Jews, the Jewish followers of Jesus regularly attended synagogue worship. Now they were cut loose from their moorings. What did they have left?

At the opposite pole in Antioch, a bustling center of commerce,[34] were the Gentiles. They had heard about Jesus and wanted to be admitted into the community. How Jewish must they become? Must they be circumcised and follow the Jewish dietary laws? Matthew writes as a liberal conservative in an appeal to all groups in Antioch's conflict-ridden church. Some Jewish Christians insisted on full observance of the Mosaic law. Others wanted some observance but no circumcision. Still others found no need of any Jewish prescriptions, and a fourth group rejected any "abiding significance in Jewish cult and feasts."[35]

Questions bombarded Matthew's community: "How is one to adapt the older, more stringent traditions of a Jewish past to this Gentile future? How is one to wean the church away from strict Jewish observances without letting go of basic morality? What is one to make of a group of 'Jews for Jesus' who have willy-nilly turned into a universal church made up of both Jews and Gentiles?"[36]

Therefore, to establish Jesus' honor—the fundamental Mediterranean cultural value—as a Jew, Matthew begins with a genealogy based on the numerical value of the Hebrew consonants in the name "David" ($D + V + D = 4 + 6 + 4 = 14$). The concern of this genealogy is not so much biology as theology: Jesus is son of Abraham and son of David with a claim to Davidic kingship. And he is a political challenge to the Romans' puppet-king, Herod.[37]

Moreover, as a Jewish "conservative," Matthew says that Jesus "fulfills the law and prophets" (5:17—6th Sunday in Ordinary Time, Year A). Jesus, the Hebrew prophet, fulfills the vision of prophets who proclaimed "the Lord loved you and wanted to keep the promise that God made to your ancestors."[38] However, as a "liberal" Matthew uses the word "fulfill" (*pleroun*), which has nuances of newness, superiority, discontinuity. He keeps both the old coats and the new wineskins (9:16–17), and he calls disciples to be "like a homeowner who takes new and old things out of his storage room" (13:51—17th Sunday in Ordinary Time,

Year A). He is the last gasp of the old age and the first breath of the new. Something beautiful is emerging, but in a community touched by longing for the past and by power struggles. Sound familiar?

Continuity with discontinuity is a hard line to walk, and sometimes later generations stumble off the line.[39] Leonard Doohan contends that our story in the 1980s and 1990s, twenty-five years after Vatican II, is much like Matthew's story in the 80s and 90s, fifty or sixty years after Jesus' resurrection. We were also promised newness and renewal, but

> a few years ago the brakes were applied, renewal began to slow down, and compromise began. Conciliar developments which had given hope were now interpreted restrictively. Instead of a new approach to law, we ended up with a new set of laws simply replacing the old. This is exactly what had happened to Matthew's gospel, which Tertullian had used as "a new law."[40]

That is why Matthew needs a careful reading. At first blush Matthew can sound tough, even legalistic. He is really reassuring the Jewish followers of Jesus that they haven't lost anything. In Jesus they have a prophet faithful to the law who more than fulfills the law, e.g., "You have heard it said . . . but I say to you." Not the smallest detail of the law will be done away with (Matthew chapters 5 through 7—4th through 9th Sundays in Ordinary Time, Year A). Matthew gives hope to his Jewish brothers and sisters, and he situates their hope (and ours) not on law but on love. John Meier comments on the Sermon on the Mount:

> When we read all the stringent moral demands in this sermon, we should remember that they follow, not precede, the basic proclamation of good news in 4:17, 23 [3rd Sunday in Ordinary Time, Year A], and in the beatitudes [4th Sunday in Ordinary Time, Year A]. What comes first is the gospel, the glad tidings of what God has done for us; all that follows is the fitting response of desperate people who have been surprised by joy.[41]

John Pilch suggests that the Sermon on the Mount is the Christian honor code. Since honor and shame are the core concerns in the Mediterranean culture, Jesus proclaims that God honors and makes blessed God's chosen ones. True honor is not a burden but a blessing. The disciples can live with an honor (same as holiness or righteousness in Matthew 5:20) which "must exceed that of the scribes" (described in 5:21–48—6th Sunday in Ordinary Time, Year A) and that of the Pharisees (described in 6:1–18).[42]

Giorgio Gonella adds that the Greek text of Matthew's beatitudes has no verb. "Blessed you!" is a cry of exultation, a "good news," a congratulations. "Jesus is saying 'cheers,' 'here's to you,' 'lucky you.'" The beatitudes are first a statement about God who comes "down" to lift "up," whose "compassion does not depend on whether people are good or bad; it has to do with the fact they are bowed down."[43] The first words of the Sermon on the Mount are about grace, covenant, inclusion and solidarity with each other through the God of Jesus, Moses and the prophets. "Sermon" in Matthew's world meant "epitome"—in Stoic philosophy, a gathering of the characteristic sayings of a mentor. Jesus first characteristic sayings are about grace.

Indeed, among those characteristic sayings is that famous one-liner: "Be perfect, therefore, as your heavenly Father is perfect" (5:48—7th Sunday in Ordinary Time, Year A). To how much Catholic guilt and perfectionism has that line given rise![44] The word in Greek does not mean moral perfection. "Singleheartedness" or "singleness of purpose" is a better translation. God is singlehearted about drawing us and all people into covenant-union, and we are to be singlehearted in our response. Note that Luke changes it: "Be merciful as your Father is merciful" (6:36—7th Sunday in Ordinary Time, Year C). God is singlehearted about being merciful when we are not morally perfect. John O'Grady comments on Matthew:

> The Sermon on the Mount is not a new set of laws but a proclamation of the gospel. God has entered into the believer's life, and now he or she can live life based on that good news. The sermon is not just ethics or morality but a lived faith which is actually experienced, at least sometimes in life. We are not concerned with a perfectionist demand.[45]

Even some demands are less oppressive if heard in their Jewish meaning. For example, Jesus' commands "to offer no resistance to injury" (to take no revenge; 5:39—7th Sunday in Ordinary Time, Year A) and even to turn the other cheek, to give both shirt and coat and to carry the burden a second mile can sound like invitations to be doormats. Some interpret them rather as a call to something akin to Gandhi's or Martin Luther King's militant nonviolence.[46] The first blow with the right hand to the right cheek (in Jesus' culture, the left hand was used only for unclean tasks) was not a punch but a put-down given with the back of the hand by masters to slaves, husbands to wives, parents to children,

Romans to Jews.[47] It is easier to hit the left cheek with the fist of the right hand, but easier to hit the right cheek with a right-handed backhand. Try it. So when turning the left cheek, we are saying to our oppressor, "Use your fist. Hit me as an equal!" In that society, retaliation would have been suicide, so Jesus calls at least for a stance against humiliation.

Only the poorest of the poor would have nothing but an outer garment to give as collateral for a loan.[48] When the powerless could not repay a debt, the creditor hauled them into court to wring out repayment of their last possession by legal means. Even though the powerless could not change the system, they again could take a stand for human dignity. If they surrendered both shirt and coat, they would stand in court naked. Nakedness was taboo in Judaism, and shame fell not on the naked party but on the one viewing or causing the nakedness (cf. Genesis 9:20–27). Jesus calls for clowning and burlesque as a nonviolent protest to humiliation. He stands in the tradition of a later saying from the Talmud: "If your neighbor calls you an ass, put a saddle on your back."[49]

The command to walk the second mile is made in the context of the somewhat enlightened Roman practice of limiting the forced labor that soldiers could demand of subject people. There were mile markers on the highways, and a soldier could force a civilian to carry his pack (about 65 to 85 pounds) for just one mile. More than that meant severe penalties for the soldier. So the Jew, again protesting humiliation, would say, "Oh, kind sir, let me carry the pack a second mile!" And the soldier, to avoid punishment, would plead, "Please give me my pack. Aw, pretty please!" The Jew seizes the initiative and forces the oppressor to make a decision for which nothing has prepared him.[50]

Matthew the conservative directs such teachings—e.g., the gift of the law fulfilled in Jesus who speaks with the very authority of God and who calls them to new heights of human dignity and human love—to Jewish Christians. Matthew preaches "tough love," but his community knows how much they have been loved. We read these texts not so much as laws but as Jesus' dream for the future, his eschatological dream. For Matthew's Jesus, not the smallest detail, "not one stroke of a letter will pass from the law until all is accomplished" (5:18).

With Jesus' death and resurrection, however, all has been accomplished.[51] Jesus sends his disciples "to all nations with baptism, not circumcision, as the initiation rite, with *his* commands, not the Mosaic

Law, as the final norm of morality."[52] This is his vision of how things will be at the end—no anger, no name-calling, peace at the altar, no lust, no divorce, no oaths, no violence, giving to all who want to borrow, love of enemies (Matthew 5—5th through 7th Sundays in Ordinary Time, Year A). This is how it will be in the reign of God.

That reign begins now. It has already begun, but it is not yet complete. Jesus is risen now. We have his Spirit now. We can begin to live that risen life now. The future begins now. "I will be with you always" (28:20—Trinity Sunday, Year B). That is Matthew's last and bottom line. We proclaim that dream now from the housetops and call people to give back the love that they have received with fidelity, forgiveness, compassion and generosity. Remember that this is not law but dream, not commandment but grace. All this comes as vision and call to a dream that in some circumstances may be impossible. We don't cast out from the community fragile, fallen people who fail the dream, either marriage dreams (5:31–32—6th Sunday in Ordinary Time, Year A) or love-your-enemies dreams (5:43–47—7th Sunday in Ordinary Time, Year A). We pick them up and help them to begin again.[53]

That is why these chapters must be balanced by Matthew 16 and 18. It is true that Matthew seems to get tough again in chapter 16 when he gives Peter the power to bind and loose. Remember, though, that Peter in Matthew's gospel stands for the moderate position between those who followed James and those who followed Paul. Peter's mission as "rock" is to keep this somewhat fractious Jewish/Gentile family together (16:13–20—16th Sunday in Ordinary Time, Year A). Remember also that Peter's ministry of binding and loosing should reflect how he has been loosed. He has been picked up from sinking because of his lack of faith (15:21–33—19th Sunday in Ordinary Time, Year A). He tempts Jesus, as Satan does (16:23—22nd Sunday in Ordinary Time, Year A).

In chapter 18, Matthew makes clear that this binding and loosing must take place in a "kinder, gentler" church.[54] He begins by calling his disciples to be humble, like little children. He warns them not to scandalize the little ones and other weak members by their drive for power. He tells them to search out and rejoice at finding lost sheep. He encourages them to correct each other patiently, in dialogue. Then he extends the binding and loosing to the entire community as pastoral care, not as vindictive punishment; because where two or three gather, Jesus is still in their midst to pray for and search out lost sheep. Notice, if an offender will not listen to the community, "let such a one be to you as a Gentile or a tax collector" (18:17—23rd Sunday in Ordinary Time, Year A). John Meier says that in a serious matter, treating someone as a Gentile meant excommunication;[55] but Donald Senior asks, "How did Jesus treat pagans and tax collectors? He didn't give up on them. He went after them!"[56]

The next verses in chapter 18 also balance the Sermon on the Mount. Earlier we saw that, in Matthew's gospel, Jesus tells us to be perfect like our Father in heaven. Here he insists that we are like God if we are compassionate and merciful, more precisely, if we love as God loves, even our enemies, "a love which is not measured and limited by the character of those with whom we have to do, but is poured out in keeping with the love of God."[57] Matthew makes that clear in his dialogue with Peter in chapter 18. Peter asks how often we are to forgive a repentant brother or sister who sins again. Jesus answers with the perfect number seven, multiplied by itself and then by ten—measureless mercy. He says, "Peter (church), don't be too stingy with forgiveness. Forgive as you have been forgiven."

Then Jesus tells a story of measureless mercy versus greedy stinginess. A servant owes a king ten thousand talents—the largest unit of money; ten thousand talents would be like our "billions of dollars." To recover a small portion, the king orders the servant and all he has to be sold. After the servant promises to pay it all back (an impossible task), the king relents, not out of any illusion that the amount will be paid but simply out of compassion for a hopeless cause. However, that servant later demands payment of a denarius (a day's wage) from a fellow laborer and sends him to prison. When the king hears this, he denounces his servant for his abuse of forgiveness. The chapter concludes with harsh words for those who don't forgive. That is precisely how we are not like our Father in heaven and not perfect (24th Sunday in Ordinary Time, Year A).[58]

Ladislaus Orsy, a canon lawyer, contends that this pattern of forgiveness in all Christian scriptures is binding even on those interpreting the law:

The pattern of forgiveness is simplicity itself: The prodigal son is embraced before he can say a word; the woman caught in adultery is protected in her shame and sent home with a few healing words; Peter, who boasted of his strength before the Passion and displayed his weakness three times during it, is asked to make a threefold confession of love. Grace comes to the sinner with a gentleness that knows no recrimination, no imposition, no inquisition, no condemnation—in fact, no limits. *Such a pattern is not there for pious reading only; it is normative for all Christian generations to come.*[59]

I diverge for a moment to ask: Does the gospels' message of an outlandishly merciful God of the covenant speak to our times? Two of our bishops suggest that it does and that we need to be perfect like our Father in heaven, to take a stand for compassion and reject moral perfectionism. They complain that some in our community, as in Matthew's, multiply laws not grace (cf. Matthew 23:1–12—31st Sunday in Ordinary Time, Year A). Archbishop Rembert Weakland declares, "I am sick and tired of perfectionism. I don't think the church witnesses by being a perfect society. I think that's fake. The church witnesses by being a broken society that is seeking healing. . . . We witness because we want to try to help broken people." This is threatened by those who want "to get rid of the divorced, the gays and everybody else that gives us problems."[60] Bishop Kenneth Untener adds,

> There has been a prevailing wind in the church moving us away from softness and toward severity. But John XXIII brought a fresh wind, and it moved us in the other direction. . . . It was a fresh emphasis on mercy and love. But we're not sure how to handle this new breeze. . . . Our tendency will surely be to stifle it. . . . You must pass on the tradition of a church remarkable for its tenderness and mercy.[61]

These bishops' laments might summon us back to the issues in Matthew's community about covenant and law and being perfect as God is perfect—in mercy and compassion.[62]

One entry point into Matthew's big picture, therefore, is to see his pastoral concern to keep the Jewish followers of Jesus in touch with their tradition, in ways that are faithful to the loving, merciful God of the covenant. That is his response to the true conservatives of the law who know that the great good news is about God's love and the great commandment is about our love. Might Matthew's story/plot proclaimed in our times lure into the drama the "conservatives" who feel that "the baby was tossed out with the bath water" after Vatican II? The "liberals" who, if they follow the great commandment, might find room for candles and rosaries in church life? The legalists and purveyors of perfectionism with only laws and restrictions about who gets baptized or married in church or about who can be reconciled?

## A Jewish-Gentile Community

A second entry point into the gospel of Matthew is to see his response to the Gentiles—how his theology of history gradually moves from the Jewish community at the beginning of his gospel toward a Jewish/Gentile (world) community with Jesus' death and resurrection at the end.

Matthew sees three periods of history in the sweep of God's plan: The first period encompasses all the prophets and the law up until but not including John the Baptist (11:13). The second includes only the public ministry of Jesus restricted to the territory and people of Israel (10:5–6; 15:24). All statements about the law not changing and a mission only to Israel are true only "until the end of all things" (5:18). We have seen that for Matthew, that end is not the end of the world but the end of this second period of history with the dying and rising of Jesus. The third period of history begins with Jesus' death and resurrection as the turning point of history (27:51–54; 28:2–3) that inaugurates the new universal mission to all peoples and makes possible his abiding presence in the church (18:20—23rd Sunday in Ordinary Time, Year A, and 28:16–20—Trinity Sunday, Year B).[63]

Even before the third period begins, we get a few hints that a new world is being born. Gentile Magi appear at Jesus' birth (2:1–12—Epiphany). In chapter 8, Jesus heals three marginalized people—a leper (ritually untouchable), Peter's mother-in-law (a second-class citizen as a woman) and most astounding, the servant of the Roman centurion, a hated Gentile. Of him Jesus says, "I tell you, I have never found anyone in Israel with faith like this" (8:11).[64]

All of Jesus' encounters with Gentiles in Matthew are told in the context of healings, in boundary-breaking situations. His healing miracles are with outcasts and outsiders, and many (including the leper) involve touch. Jesus doesn't zap with power; he reaches across boundaries for communion. In the narrative section of chapters 8–9, Matthew offers ten healing miracles to parallel the ten plagues that led Israel to liberation.[65] Only Matthew has the blind and lame being healed in the Temple (21:14). It was illegal for them to be there. These "unclean" rejects were trespassers on "clean" property.

Because of all this scandalous healing, the conflicts and tensions with the Jewish leaders increased. In the parables of 13:1–52, Matthew hammers home the themes of the strange, unpretentious, hidden character (mustard seed, yeast, treasure and pearl) of the kingdom of heaven and of the increasing division from the pretentious, not-so-hidden religious leaders (15th through 17th Sundays in Ordinary Time, Year A).

These set the scene for the leaders' rejection of Jesus in 13:54–58 and his bestowal on Peter and the community the right to interpret his teaching (chapters 16 and 18—21st through 23rd Sundays in Ordinary Time, Year A). His castigation of the Jewish leaders as "blind leaders of the blind" (15:14)[66] immediately precedes that wonderful story of the Canaanite woman who begs for a healing for her daughter, another hint that Jesus is breaking down barriers.[67]

### Hearing Matthew's Parables

In a masterful treatment of all the parables in the synoptics and in the Gospel of Thomas, Bernard Brandon Scott unleashes the powerful message of Jesus in these stories, especially the message about the inclusion of rejects.[68] He gathers the parables into three categories: "Family, Village, City and Beyond," "Masters and Servants" and "Home and Farm." In many cases, he also catches the spirit of the parable in a title such as "You Can't Keep a Good Woman Down" for the story of the unjust judge (Luke 18:2–5—29th Sunday in Ordinary Time, Year C), "Who's That Masked Man?" for the story of the good Samaritan (Luke: 10:25–37—15th Sunday in Ordinary Time, Year C) and "How to Mismanage a Miracle" for the story of the rich fool (Luke 12:13–21—18th Sunday in Ordinary Time, Year C). After exegeting the parable, Scott often concludes with a pastoral/theological hearing of the story titled "From Story to Kingdom." I shall briefly summarize his insights for Matthew's parables that are in the Sunday lectionary.

*What Did the Farmer Sow?* (Matthew 13:1–9—15th Sunday in Ordinary Time, Year A) Scott contends that the synoptic gospels allegorize the story by seizing on the failures of the seeds to grow and thrive and making them symbols of people who fail to respond to the word of the reign of God. This pushes the failure outside that reign so that failure is not part of it. Scott insists that the original story focuses our gaze on the failure of the reign of God itself. "The hearer is left with a kingdom in which failure, miracle and normality are the coordinates. . . . In failure and everydayness lies the miracle of God's activity."[69] He adds that, as in the story of the woman with the ten coins (Luke 15:8–10—24th Sunday in Ordinary Time, Year C), both the ordinary and unclean belong to this miracle. The reign of God does not demand the moral perfection of the law nor the apocalyptic solution of overwhelming harvest.

Two thousand years after Matthew, when contrasting Jesus' call to discipleship and his vision of the God of covenant and inclusion with the life of our church, we see much failure; but God's promise and presence live on. Matthew predicts the failure and renews the promise. He charges, "Don't lose heart"—a message we need to hear in these wintry times!

*One Rotten Apple* (Matthew 13:33—16th Sunday in Ordinary Time, Year A) The rotten apple is the leaven hidden by the woman, to which Jesus compares the reign of God. Most of us interpret the leaven as a positive force that causes dough to rise. In the ancient world, leaven was a symbol of moral corruption. People made leaven by taking a piece of bread and storing it in a damp, dark place until mold formed. The bread rots and decays. Leaven, according to Scott, is used as an image of unholy Israel (Exodus 12:19); unleavened bread is an image of holy Israel (Exodus 12:15–16). Leaven was removed from the house on the holiest days.

Jesus compares God's reign to an unclean woman hiding corrupting leaven. His hearers would have been dumbfounded. Scott concludes that the story serves to subvert the hearers' assumptions about the rules of the sacred and the predictability of what is good; it also warns that what seems evil may indeed turn out to be God's reign. "Such a discourse is corroborated by Jesus' association with the outcast or even those accusations that he has a demon or the beatitude 'Blessed are the poor.' The kingdom is present among the marginal. . . . The parable . . . insists on the kingdom's freedom to appear under its own guise, even if it be the guise of corruption."[70] Might that include the Canaanite woman in Jesus' time and those seeking to come to table in Australia in our times?

**Finders Keepers** Among the "Home and Farm" parables are Scott's titles for the images of the man with the hidden treasure, of the merchant and of the net (Matthew 13:44–52—17th Sunday in Ordinary Time, Year A).

Scott claims that the joy and the rush of the finder to claim the treasure grasp our attention, but they cancel out what the man has done to the real owner. The finder of the treasure is most likely a day laborer who hid the treasure not to protect it from others but to conceal it from the property's owner. "If the treasure belongs to the finder, buying the land [according to law and custom in that culture] is unnecessary. But, if the treasure does not belong to the finder, buying the land is unjust."[71] Because the purchase of the field is for an illegal purpose, if the man reveals the treasure he risks its loss. If he sells all, he is destitute, even though he owns a treasure—ill gotten and of no use. What could Jesus possibly be up to here?

Scott contends that the point of the parable is not the radical choice of the reign of God but just the opposite: The treasure of God's grace and life comes to us as absolute gift; but if we do not receive it as such, grace potentially leads to our corruption. It can tempt us before we are proved. Finding treasure even today is outside the bounds of the everyday, not something earned but found, even sometimes outside the law. Its joy is precisely in its not being worked for. "Even modern treasure hunters who sell stock in their ventures are in search of super returns on their investment and are notorious scams."[72] The paradox is that unearned grace, when it does not call forth virtue, can corrupt. Many parables focus on God's astonishing gift of grace. This one focuses on humans' astonishing and foolish depravity after being so gifted, a focus that can be shared by us and our children, who will be paying the cost of savings-and-loan scams for generations.

**Artifacts** The second image is the merchant who, unlike the man with the treasure, honestly buys a pearl. It involves the merchant's effort. However, the message is the same: possible corruption. If the merchant has sold all that he has to buy the pearl, he will eventually have to sell the pearl to live. The pearl is an image of the great value of the reign of God, but that reign cannot be possessed as a value in itself. It is forever discovered as gift. "That is the kingdom's corrupting power—the desire to possess it."[73] Connect that to our passion to possess or exploit any icon or sacrament of God's presence in people or in the good earth that comes to us as gift, such as the need to control or posess friends or spouses or children, or the need to restrict ways in which reconciliation may be celebrated.

**The Net**    The third image, the net, climaxes the chapter's judgment motif and closes the discourse on the reign of God. It differs from the story of the wheat and tares in the same chapter, however. In that parable the field is the world. "But the situation in The Net is different. 'It is the righteous as opposed to the evil *within the framework of the church.*' As the interpretation makes explicit, so it will be at the close of the age."[74] As in our age, there will be new wine and old churchskins. Daniel Harrington adds, however, that both parables counsel tolerance and patience with ecclesial warts and old churchskins. In the end, God will set things right.[75]

**The King's Accounting**    (18:21–35—24th Sunday in Ordinary Time, Year A) William Thompson's book on this chapter calls it "Matthew's advice to a divided community."[76] The first verse sets the theme: "Who is the greatest in the kingdom of heaven?" As already noted, Matthew pleads for humility, forgiveness and mercy throughout chapter 18 as a balance to the hard sayings of the Sermon on the Mount. In that context, he tells this story.

Scott claims that Matthew allegorizes the story by identifying the king with God. Jesus has just challenged Peter to unlimited forgiveness. Here, there is no repeated forgiveness, but forgiveness is given then taken back with a lashing out at the first failure.

The original story, according to Scott, is about a Gentile tax farmer involving a large collection. "Ten thousand talents" is folk-tale exaggeration—an impossible amount to repay. The master's command to the farmer to sell the wife and children violates Jewish law and is stereotyped propaganda about Gentile cruelty. Also, no Jew would grovel before a master as this servant does. The original hearers would have understood that the story illustrates Gentile degradation and Jewish superiority. When the servant seizes his fellow servant by the throat and demands payment of his measly debt, the hearer further separates from this Gentile servant. See how these pagans treat one another.

Then the hearer gets trapped. The hearer identifies with the master in expecting the servant's mercy toward the fellow servant. But then this Middle Eastern king goes back on his word and tortures the servant forever, because he can never repay the debt.

> In the Hellenistic world, such an act threatens to destroy the ordered world. With the solidarity of the patron and client violated, the king moves outside the law and all are at risk [including the hearer]. By identifying with the fellow servants in reporting the servant, a hearer bears with them responsibility for unleashing the king's wrath. . . . The fellow servants (and the hearer) have left their own situation in jeopardy. . . . If a king can take back his forgiveness, who is safe?[77]

The superiority of Jew to Gentile is the consistency that held the story together. Now the hearer has entered the Gentile world and forfeited superiority.

Scott suggests three conclusions from the story. First, the fellow servants (and we hearers) call on a higher authority with a logic that failure should lead to punishment. Instead, there is chaos. "Swept into a vortex of chaos, a hearer fails, at least in the story."[78]

Second, the story entraps hearers in a web of evil even though they seek justice. Jesus has just called for unlimited mercy as a counter to justice. The hearer fails to forgive, which leads to an "experience of evil, not intentional evil but implicit, unanticipated, systemic evil. The ability to acknowledge one's entanglement in evil is part of the experience of the kingdom (cf. Romans 3:23 and Romans 7)."[79] All are called on the condition that we recognize that we are sinners.

Third, the hearer must surrender thoughts of moral superiority, reject elitism and see that we all have sinned and need God's mercy. Perhaps this interpretation is too complicated for a homily, but it is appropriate for the catechetical session, especially if catechumens have difficulty with Matthew's equating the harsh judgment of the king with God's judgment and the apparent conflict between this story and Jesus' words about forgiveness to Peter.

***Am I Not Doing You Right?*** (Matthew 20:1–16a—25th Sunday in Ordinary Time, Year A) Even though Matthew's owner of the farm affirms his own generosity, Scott contends that the message of the story is not generosity. A denarius for an hour's work is generous when contrasted with a denarius for a full day's work. In and of itself, however, it is not generous. It is the average peasant's wage for a day's work, which would keep a peasant living in the shadow of poverty. Matthew does create hostility in those who worked all day (and the hearer), because there is the strong impression that they have been cheated.

> In identifying with the complaint of the first-hired, a hearer opts for a world in which justice is defined by a hierarchical relation between individuals. . . . For the parable, value or worth (i.e., a place in the kingdom) is determined not by what is right but by acceptance. The householder's urgent though unexplained need for laborers is the parable's metaphor for grace. It is not wages or hierarchy that counts but the call to go into the vineyard.

One vision of justice in the reign of God in Jesus' time did not make all equal but ensured all their appropriate places. The parable's vision asserts that justice does not organize God's reign into hierarchies based on what we deserve. The owner paid what was just, but the parable's clever strategy makes him seem unjust and outlandishly generous. The generosity lies not in the wage but in the need to invite outcasts into the reign of God, not on what we deserve but by outrageously generous invitation to the undeserving. The reign of God is mercy. "To insist as the parable does, that invitation, not justice, is the way of the kingdom radically subverts the kingdom of God as a reward for a faithful and just life."[80] Once again, the good news is better than we expected.

***Reading of the Will*** (Matthew 21:33–46—27th Sunday in Ordinary Time, Year A) Matthew joins this parable to two others during Jesus' one day of teaching in the Temple. These parables, on the one hand, deprive Judaism of its claim to be the true Israel (this parable) and on the other hand commend the church's claim. The two sendings of servants probably refers to the former and latter prophets, although this causes "a riot of violence that leaves the owner's behavior [in trying a second time] not only foolish but incomprehensible."[81] By mistreating and killing the servant, the tenants refuse Middle Eastern honor, and they shame the owner, who miscalculates and thinks they will honor his son. After the tenants murder the son, the reign of God is taken from them and given to a people (*ethnos*—meaning Gentiles) who bear fruits. The outsiders, then and now, become insiders.[82]

**A Hard-Hearted Man**   (Matthew 25:14–30—33rd Sunday in Ordinary Time, Year A) Once again Matthew allegorizes, this time a parable that stands as the middle panel of the triptych of Jesus' eschatological discourse and exhorts to vigilance until the endtime: Do not only watch for an unknown hour, but as you keep watch, increase in faith or face a tragic judgment.

The talent was one of the largest values of money in the Hellenistic world, so most scholars believe that the original story had *minas*—a lesser sum (the servant has been faithful over "a little") yet still a large sum from a peasant's viewpoint. Giving the one talent to the servant who already had ten restates the common wisdom that "the rich get richer and the poor get poorer," here applied to the spiritual level.

The third servant's description of the master as a hard man establishes sympathy by drawing the hearer to his side. The master's harsh judgment confirms that description, yet he was gracious and generous with the first two servants. At the end the hearer asks: "Whom do I trust?" Scott contends that, in the original parable, the coins were symbols of the Torah, and not personal gifts of economic stewardship. In this reading of the story, the coins mark out a fundamental disagreement between Jesus, who makes all things new and brings the law to fulfillment (e.g. Matthew 5:17–20—6th Sunday in Ordinary Time, Year A), and the Pharisees who, as Matthew sees them, froze the law by merely preserving it. The third servant's image of the master freezes him in fear and thus deprives him of a future. The master never accepts that image but points to his generosity to the other servants. The hearer is asked to choose between the two images—hardness or graciousness. If the hearer chooses the second, the parable becomes "a window onto the kingdom [that] demands that the servant act neither as preserver nor as one afraid; but act boldly he must. . . . This parable, like Jesus' parody of legal sayings in the Sermon on the Mount, forces a hearer to choose a future in which to live."[83]

True disciples, like Jesus, will take new and old things out of the storeroom (Matthew 13:51—17th Sunday in Ordinary Time, Year A). We have often seen how our challenge is not simply to preserve tradition in frozen formulas and precepts that no longer speak to different cultures and people but to be as resilient as Jesus was with the Jewish tradition and as resilient as the early councils were with the Christian tradition through enculturating and connecting God's word to our life and times—new wine into new wineskins.

*The Mustard Seed*    I conclude this journey into Scott's interpretation of the parables with the parable of the mustard seed, which does not appear in the Sunday lectionary but to which Scott gives a fascinating twist (13:31–32). I hope homilies and catechesis on covenant and inclusion might proclaim this parable with its powerful images of the reign of God strangely present in the unclean and lowly on the Sixteenth Sunday of Ordinary Time, Year B, whose readings contain the image of the corrupt leaven (13:33).

Luke probably has this parable right. In the originating parable, the man throws the seed in a garden (Luke 13:18–19). In so doing, he violates diverse kinds of law (Leviticus 19:19 and Deuteronomy 22:9–11): "Not every kind of seed may be sown in a garden-bed; but any kind of vegetable may be sown therein. Mustard and small beans are deemed a kind of seed and large beans a kind of vegetable."[84] These prohibitions maintained the order of creation. Order represented holiness, while disorder meant uncleanliness.

The most common mustard plant in Palestine normally grows to four feet in height. The evangelists changed its meaning to image the growth of the reign of God into a large tree (cf. Daniel 4:12 and Ezekiel 17:23) where birds nest, more properly a cedar of Lebanon. The mustard plant does not grow into any such thing. It is a bothersome weed that spreads rapidly and threatens "proper" plants. The originating parable more likely sees the seed like the leaven, with which it is paired in the parable. Therefore, the original parable creates problems for the hearer. Is the growth of the reign of God blessing or curse, clean or unclean?

Scott suggests three possibilities to make sense of the parable. First, the author knows about the expectation of God's reign as a mighty cedar of Lebanon and offers a light-hearted burlesque of that reign by mocking this noble, apocalyptic cedar tree. Nathan Mitchell's version:

> Instead of being a towering cedar of Lebanon, the kingdom Jesus preached was like a scrawny mustard plant. Instead of being the Chase Manhattan Bank, the kingdom was like a poor woman who lost a dime and swept her house all day until she found it. Instead of being a dramatic "close encounter of the third kind," the kingdom was as hidden and humble as a bit of yeast in a batch of dough.[85]

Second, it is more than burlesque. The cedar stands not only as symbol of strength and protection but also of pride. "All cedars and trees, even Israel, will be brought low. It is the mustard plant that will bear Israel's true destiny."[86]

Third, the parable begins with illegal throwing of the seed into the garden.

> The planting and growth are a scandal—illegitimate, tainted, unclean. . . . The kingdom is associated with uncleanness just as Jesus himself associates with the unclean, the outcast. . . . Many have preferred the mustard tree, this unnatural malformity of mythical botany, to the recognition that God's mighty works are among the unclean and insignificant [in Jesus' community and ours].[87]

Hear then the parable!

## The Ending/Beginning

At the end of Matthew's gospel we have those spectacular apocalyptic events lifted from the prophets' imagery about the end of time and transposed to Jesus' dying and rising. Matthew takes these, perhaps, from the Book of Enoch, written about his time, or from the dead bones of Israel rising in Ezekiel 37:1–14, a passage with special meaning for Judaism in Matthew's era. Not only do doors open. Graves open. At Jesus' death "the curtain of the Temple was torn in two from top to bottom"—all people now have access to the Holy of Holies. "The earth shook and the rocks split. The tombs also were opened, and many bodies of the saints who had fallen asleep were raised." (Matthew 27:51–52—Passion Sunday, Year A) At his resurrection "suddenly there was a great earthquake; for an angel of the Lord descending from heaven, came and rolled back the stone, and sat on it. His appearance was like lightning, and his clothing white as snow"[88] (28:2–3—Easter Vigil, Year A).

Matthew tells stories from his culture about earthquakes and lightning when God snatches life forever from the jaws of death.[89] There has already been a lot of "quaking" going on in Matthew. The term he uses for the storm on the lake is "earthquake" (8:23–26). The earth quakes when Jesus enters Jerusalem (21:10).[90] Now there are quakes at Jesus' death and resurrection. Matthew's community is full of storms and earthquakes that are not death rattles but birth pangs of a new world and a new covenant open to outcasts and outsiders.[91] Those are images and stories, but the meaning of the stories endures. We don't have the facts about the resurrection. We don't have "film at 11." We do have the firm faith of Matthew's community that the Holy One who was crucified and buried now lives, sends them on mission to *all peoples* and promises to "be with you always, to the end of the age" (28:20—Trinity Sunday, Year B).

We live already in that age.[92] The good news is that he is still with us. We have no absentee landlord. He who was from birth Emmanuel, God-with-us (1:23—Vigil of Christmas), who promised his presence to two or three gathered in prayer (18:20—22nd Sunday in Ordinary Time, Year A), now promises his continual presence to his church on the move. During Jesus' lifetime, Matthew restricted discipleship to the Twelve, but now he extends it to the entire community, to all of us.[93] The unsettling, challenging news is that he is still here as he was the first time—in solidarity with the hungry, the thirsty, the stranger, the naked, the sick and the prisoner (25:31–46—Christ the King, Year A). We shall be judged on our solidarity, even our unconscious solidarity ("when did we feed you?), with the outcasts and rejects whom Christ gathers into covenant. That is the final scene on the last Sunday of the liturgical year, toward which all other gospels lead us.[94] Once again we hear that piercing question: Who do you say that I am? Who is Jesus in our life, parish, family, work, community and world? What are we doing to her/him there; because "just as you did it to one of the least of these who are members of my family, you did it to me" (25:40). Might Matthew's story lure us into that drama, that plot, that story of covenant?[95]

## Endnotes

[1] *Fulfilled in Your Hearing* (Washington DC: USCC, 1982), 6.

[2] Thomas Richstatter, "Liturgy of the Eucharist," and Bernard Lee, "Shared Homily: Conversation that Puts Communities at Risk," in *Alternative Futures for Worship, Volume 3: The Eucharist,* ed. Bernard Lee (Collegeville: The Liturgical Press, 1987), 117–74.

[3] Lee, "Liturgy of the Word," 170, 173. That is a very difficult and thin line to walk. Mary Catherine Hilkert may disagree with this approach. She uses Paul Ricoeur's language when describing "the task of the preacher to move from the first naiveté of symbolic language (the language of scripture and liturgy) and the common sense language in which people name their ordinary human experience, through the process of critical reflection on both human experience and the symbols of our faith and the multiple 'conflicts of interpretation' that arise there, to the stage of a 'second naiveté' that returns to symbolic and poetic and evocative language that speaks to all levels of the human personality. . . . The 'second naivete' reflects that he or she has grappled with critical issues, but the preacher does not bring them to the pulpit." "Preaching and Theology: Rethinking the Relationship," *Worship* (September 1991): 406. Cf. Paul Ricoeur, *The Symbolism of Evil* (Boston: Beacon Press, 1967), 347–53. With Lee, I would bring some of that scriptural scholarship to the homily but in narrative form. The contrast is between the didactic language of biblical criticism and the evocative language of image, simple poetry and narrative. Throughout this book I insist that the language of catechesis should never end with the merely didactic; all language in catechesis must evoke faith and conversion. In the homilies in these chapters, I try to stay with the evocative language of scriptural images (sometimes interpreted), contemporary images and stories and, at times common sense "street talk."

[4] Lee, "Liturgy of the Word," 170.

[5] Donald Senior, "Scripture and Homiletics: What the Bible Can Teach the Preacher," *Worship* 65 (September 1991): 387.

[6] All of the Christian scriptures, especially the gospels, are about the reign of God (which is about covenant-union among all peoples), about discipleship (the call to follow Jesus to the cross where he sheds his blood of a new and everlasting covenant), about Jesus (who is now the risen Christ in whom we are in covenant-union with God in the Spirit). I trust that our focus on covenant will include these dimensions of the good news.

[7] J. Massyngbaerde Ford, *Bonded with the Immortal* (Wilmington: Michael Glazier, Inc., 1987), 32.

8 Karl Rahner, "Toward a Fundamental Theological Interpretation of Vatican II," *Theological Studies,* 716–27; *Faith in a Wintry Season* (New York: Crossroad Publishing Co., 1990), 185; and "Perspectives on Pastoral Ministry in the Future," in *Worldchurch: New Dimensions—A Model for the Year 2001,* ed. Walbert Buhlmann (Maryknoll NY: Orbis Books, 1986).

9 Cf. Walbert Buhlmann, *The Coming of the Third Church* (Maryknoll NY: Orbis Books, 1977).

10 Karl Rahner, *The Shape of the Church to Come* (New York: Seabury Press, 1972), 23.

11 Karl Rahner, "Theology and Spirituality of Pastoral Work in the Parish," *Theological Investigations,* vol. 19 (New York: Crossroad Publishing Co., 1983), 96.

12 "Perhaps a lesson of Mark, yet to be learned, is that the community of Christ will come of age when the dignity of woman and her place in his church are acknowledged not only in word but in truth." Wilfred Harrington, *Mark* (Wilmington: Michael Glazier, 1979), xx, 78. Elizabeth Malbon cautions not to idealize the women as an alternative to the faithless Twelve; women also have their times of doubt (3:21, 31–32), violence (6:19–29) and fear (16:8). For Mark there is absolute equality of discipleship (10:41–45) with "disciples, together forming, as it were, a composite portrait of the fallible followers of Jesus." "Fallible Followers: Women and Men in the Gospel of Mark," *Semeia* 28: 31.

13 For a treatment of oppression of women in the Hebrew Scriptures (e.g. Hagar, Tamar and the daughter of Jephthah), see Phyllis Trible, *Texts of Terror: Literary-Feminist Readings of Biblical Narratives* (Philadelphia: Fortress Press, 1984).

14 The last phrase comes from Justin Kelly, "Absence into Presence," Warren Lecture Series, no. 16. Available from the University of Tulsa, Warren Center.

15 Cited in "From the Center," *Church* 7 (Winter 1991): 4.

16 Michael Leach, "The Last Catholics in America," *America* 165 (30 November 1991): 412.

17 Tex Sample, *U.S. Lifestyles and Mainline Churches* (Louisville: Westminster/John Knox Press, 1990), 61.

18 As much as any novelist, Philip Roth portrays the lives of "hard livers": "Not to be rich, not to be famous, not to be mighty, not even to be happy, but to be civilized—that was the dream of his life." *When She Was Good* (New York: Penguin Books, 1967),

3. "Dignity, I was to understand, had nothing to do with one's social station: character, conduct, was everything. . . . A strong character, not a big bankroll, was to them the evidence of one's worth. Good, sensible people." *My Life as a Man* (New York: Penguin Books, 1974), 35. Yet Roth pictures the demonic side of the alienated character without grace: "With unerring fidelity, Roth records the flat surface of provincial American life, the look and feel and sound of it, and then penetrates it to the cesspool of its invisible dynamisms." *Newsweek,* quoted on the back cover of *When She Was Good.*

[19] Cf. Vincent Donovan, *The Church in the Midst of Creation* (Maryknoll NY: Orbis Books, 1989), 20.

[20] In chapter eleven, we shall try to move from a fundamentalist hearing of dogma and law to a pastoral hearing. In this chapter we explore a biblical vision for approaching these issues.

[21] Cf. J. Massyngbaerde Ford, *My Enemy Is My Guest* (Maryknoll NY: Orbis Books, 1984), 72.

[22] Both texts are cited by Kenneth Bailey, *Poet and Peasant and Through Peasant Eyes* (Grand Rapids: Wm. B. Eerdmans, 1980), 90. The full text from Qumran reads: "And let no person smitten with any human impurity whatever enter the Assembly of God. And every person smitten with these impurities, unfit to occupy a place in the midst of the Congregation, and every [person] smitten in the flesh, paralyzed in feet or hands, lame or blind or deaf, or mute or smitten in the flesh with a blemish visible to the eye, or any aged person that totters and is unable to stand firm in the midst of the congregation: let these persons not enter to take their place in the midst of the congregation of [people] renown, for the angels of holiness are in their congregation."

[23] Dialogue about this gospel might also lead to exploration of the assumption of Mary as the resurrection of the feminine, because that feast often occurs around the same time of year as this Sunday's gospel.

[24] Archbishop Roger Mahoney, "The Mission of the Church in Los Angeles," *Origins* 15 (September 9, 1985): 209, 211–13.

[25] Michael Garvey, "Downstairs in the Household of Faith," *America* (November 1, 1986): 261.

[26] Anthony Padovano suggests that another way to approach "the Catholic difference" in general is to say that Catholics faithful to our tradition are more feminine, whereas Protestants are more masculine. Some examples of this include Catholic

silence and nonverbal symbols, Protestant word and preaching; Catholic compromise, and Protestant revolution, change and protest; Catholic compassion and comedy, and Protestant judgment and predestination; Catholic family, a mess but my family, Protestant takes a stand with prophecy; Catholics celebrate community, Protestants the individual; Catholics wary of unformed conscience, Protestants' conscience is their guide; Catholic demon is authoritarianism, Protestant devil is anarchy. Unpublished lecture at Loyola University, Chicago, 1988.

[27] Matthew uses the term "kingdom of heaven" 32 times and "kingdom" 51 times. It is "the single most comprehensive concept in the first gospel. . . . It touches on every major facet of the gospel, whether it be theological, christological, or ecclesiological in nature." Beda Rigaux, *The Testimony of St. Matthew* (Chicago: Franciscan Herald Press, 1968), 137–38. The kingdom is "seen more globally as the sovereign reign of God, realized fully at the end of time, but anticipated in Jesus. Matthew sees the church as the door to the kingdom, not the kingdom itself. Rather, the church draws others to the kingdom." Doohan, *Matthew, Spirituality for the '80s and '90s* (Santa Fe: Bear and Company, 1985) 100.

[28] See Matthew 7:28, 11:1, 13:53, 19:1 and 26:1.

[29] Cf. Meier, *Matthew: An Access Guide for Scripture Study* (New York: Wm. H. Sadlier, Inc., 1983), 16–17; and John Pilch, "The Year of Matthew," *Modern Liturgy* 16 (December 1989): 46.

[30] Cf. Doohan, *Matthew: Spirituality*, 64–65; and Donald Senior, *What Are They Saying about Matthew?* (New York: Paulist Press, 1983), 27.

[31] Some claim that Matthew is written by a "seminar" of Jewish scholars who sought to see what light the Hebrew Scriptures cast on Jesus; cf. Krister Stendahl, *School of Matthew* (Philadelphia: Fortress Press, 1968).

[32] The designations BCE (before the common era) and CE (common era) are used in many disciplines in place of BC (before Christ) and AD (*anno domino*, the year of the Lord).

[33] Cited by Donald Senior, *What Are They Saying*, 7.

[34] Leonard Doohan describes Antioch: "The only major city in the eastern part of the empire, Antioch was a melting pot of pagan, Jewish, Gnostic and Christian religious thought." *Matthew: Spirituality*, 47.

[35] Brown and Meier, *Rome and Antioch*, 1–8.

[36] Meier, *Matthew: An Access Guide,* 11–12.

[37] Only Matthew records Herod's intrigues (2:1–23). This pericope is read on the Feast of the Holy Family in Year A. Catechesis, therefore, might center less on family life and focus rather on "puppet-rulers" who drive the body of Christ into exile in Egypt today.

[38] Daniel Harrington insists that even the antitheses (5:21–48—6th and 7th Sundays of Ordinary Time, Year A) do not abolish the law. "The dynamic of the antitheses is one of sharpening the Torah, getting to the root of what it teaches, moving into the realm of internal dispositions from which evil actions proceed." *Sacra Pagina: The Gospel of Matthew* (Collegeville: The Liturgical Press, 1991), 90–92.

[39] Cf. John Pilch on "the virtue of inconsistency" in Matthew, "Year of Matthew," *Modern Liturgy* 17 (June/July 1990): 32.

[40] Doohan, *Matthew: Spirituality,* 3.

[41] John Meier, *Matthew* (Wilmington: Michael Glazier, Inc., 1980), 38–39; cf. also W. D. Davis, *The Sermon on the Mount* (Cambridge: Cambridge University Press, 1966); and Jan Lambrecht, *The Sermon on the Mount* (Wilmington: Michael Glazier, Inc., 1985).

[42] "The Year of Matthew," *Modern Liturgy* 17 (February 1990).

[43] Giorgio Gonella, "Song of the Beatitudes," *Church* 7 (Winter 1991): 8, 9.

[44] My favorite line on perfectionism comes from *Peanuts.* Charlie Brown asks Lucy, "I wonder what it would be like to be perfect." Lucy responds, "Take it from me, it's a great feeling!"

[45] *The Four Gospels and the Jesus Tradition* (New York: Paulist Press, 1989), 186. Daniel Harrington states, "The idea of God as 'perfect' does not appear in the [Hebrew Scriptures] . . . The background is probably in . . . sayings about God's holiness. . . . The word 'perfect' *(tam)* refers to the 'wholeness' of God who cares for all peoples." *Sacra Pagina: The Gospel of Matthew,* 90. F. W. Beare adds, "The words should not be interpreted as demanding our best human effort to attain the unattainable but rather our 'total engagement,' without half measures or reserves." *The Gospel According to Matthew* (San Francisco: Harper & Row, 1981), 163.

[46] Cf. William Robert Miller, *Nonviolence* (New York: Schocken Books, 1972).

[47] Cf. John Pilch, "The Year of Matthew," *Modern Liturgy* 17 (June/July 1992): 32.

[48] Matthew seems to miss the point of the original story. He and Luke differ on whether it is the coat (Luke 6:29) or the inner shirt (Matthew 5:40) that is being taken. The Jewish practice of giving the outer garment as collateral for a loan argues for Luke's version.

[49] Babylonian Talmud, Baba Kamma 92b.

[50] For elaboration on these interpretations, see Walter Wink, *Violence and Nonviolence in South Africa: Jesus' Third Way* (Philadelphia: New Society Publishers, 1987), 12–22. Wink developed these reflections in South Africa with people committed to militant nonviolence but who rejected Jesus' teaching of what they saw as timid nonviolence. I suggest this is another example of the power of the biblical message when heard with critical pastoral/theological ears and how modern scholarship might remove barriers to faith yet call to a deeper faith. For an alternative interpretation of these texts, cf. Beare, *The Gospel According*, 157–60.

[51] Meier, *Matthew: An Access Guide*, 47–48.

[52] Meier, *Matthew: An Access Guide*, 367; cf. also Doohan, *Matthew: Spirituality*, 126–31; Senior, *What Are They Saying*, 47–55.

[53] Cf. Senior, *What Are They Saying*, 47–55; George Montague, *Companion God: A Cross-Cultural Commentary on the Gospel of Matthew* (New York: Paulist Press, 1989), 70–73. For example, F. W. Beare comments on Matthew's demands regarding no divorce (5:31–32; 19:4–6): "Here again we have an absolute saying, which makes no allowances for the realities of human character ('the hardness of your hearts'). But there is no room to hold that Jesus intended such sayings to be taken as legislation, even for his followers, much less for the state." *The Gospel According*, 155.

[54] Cf. Meier, *Matthew: An Access Guide*, 200–209; Montague, *Companion God*, 194–208.

[55] Meier, *Matthew: An Access Guide*, 205–6.

[56] Unpublished lecture notes. George Montague adds that "this does not mean the community consigns the person as hopelessly lost. If the person is no longer open to the direct invitation to return, as presumably the straying member of v. 12–13 is, there is still hope, and that hope lies in the intercession of the community, as the next verses show ('Where two or three are gathered in my name, there am I among them' [18:20])." *Companion God*, 201. F. W. Beare states, "There is not the least likelihood that Jesus himself ever spoke with such disparagement of Gentiles or tax collectors. These are quite evidently the words of a Jewish Christian group which still thinks of

Gentiles as 'common' (unholy) or 'unclean' (Acts 10:14, 28; 11:8 ff.)." *The Gospel According*, 380.

[57] Beare, *The Gospel*, 163. Beare adds, "The words should not be interpreted as demanding our best human effort to attain the unattainable, but rather our total engagement, without half-measures or reserves."

[58] John Meier comments: "To illustrate this measureless mercy, this forgiveness without frontiers, . . . Jesus speaks parables, . . . the parable of the (forgiving lord and the) unforgiving servant. . . . True (children of God) naturally show their resemblance to their Father by compassion with no question of merit (cf. 5:43– 45) . . . Thus does Matthew place in perspective the disciplinary measures of vv. 15– 20 (on binding and loosing). The final word on church-life and church-order must be forgiveness within the family." *Matthew: An Access Guide*, 208–9; on forgiveness cf. also Doohan, *Matthew: Spirituality*, 110–11.

[59] Ladislas Orsy, "General Absolution: New Law, Old Traditions, Some Questions," *Theological Studies* 45 (December 1984): 681 (emphasis added).

[60] Archbishop Rembert Weakland, "Living the Gospel in an Affluent Society," unpublished reflections on the U.S. Bishops' Economics Pastoral given at the Ninth Annual Chicago Call to Action Conference, November 1, 1986.

[61] Bishop Kenneth Untener, "A Church Remarkable for Tenderness and Mercy," *Origins* 16 (May 7, 1987): 825–26.

[62] Cf. Karl Rahner, *Faith in a Wintry Season* (New York: Crossroad Publishing Co., 1990), 174.

[63] Cf. Senior, *What Are They Saying*, 31–36; and Meier, *Matthew: An Access Guide*, 12–13.

[64] Cf. Montague, *Companion God*, 107–11.

[65] On the miracles cf. Doohan, *Matthew: Spirituality*, 59–60; on Jesus' ministry to rejects and outcasts cf. Doohan, *Matthew: Spirituality*, 151–52.

[66] Paul Bernier suggests that the harsh criticism of the Pharisees, e.g., Matthew 23, probably are not the words of Jesus but reflect a sharpened polemic of evangelists at a time when the Pharisees excluded the Christian sect from the synagogues, "Eucharist: Meal or Sacrifice?" *Emmanuel* 98 (March 1992): 68.

[67] Montague, *Companion God*, 173–75. Beare contends that Jesus' harsh words about not tossing children's bread to dogs "was first coined, and attributed to Jesus, by a prophet who shared these chauvinistic views. . . . But in the handling of the evangelists it is taken up not to establish it as a guideline for the church, but to denature it by diverting attention to the significant outcome—that Jesus actually granted the request of the woman." *The Gospel According*, 344.

[68] Bernard Brandon Scott, *Hear Then the Parable* (Minneapolis: Fortress Press, 1989).

[69] Scott, *Hear*, 361–62.

[70] Scott, *Hear*, 328–29.

[71] John Dominic Crossan, *Finding Is the First Act*, Semeia Supplements (Philadelphia: Fortress Press; Missoula MT: Scholars Press, 1979).

[72] Scott, *Hear*, 402.

[73] Scott, *Hear*, 319.

[74] Scott, *Hear*, 313–14; citing Jack Dean Kingsbury, *The Parables of Jesus in Matthew 13* (Richmond: John Knox Press, 1969), 118 (emphasis added).

[75] *The Gospel of Matthew*, 208–10.

[76] *Matthew's Advice to a Divided Community: Matthew 17:22—18:35* Analecta Biblica 44 (Rome: Biblical Institute Press, 1970).

[77] Scott, *Hear*, 277, 278.

[78] Scott, *Hear*, 279.

[79] Scott, *Hear*, 280.

[80] Scott, *Hear*, 297, 298.

[81] Scott, *Hear*, 247.

[82] Scott claims that the originating parable, preserved in the Gospel of Thomas, does not tie things together at the end. The original story ends with the death of the son. "For a hearer, the story ends with a foolish master, devoid of vineyard, honor and son. The vineyard is in the hands of the shameless. . . . From the vantage point of the

parable, Jesus' resurrection does not overcome death but confirms God's willingness to pay the price." *Hear*, 251, 253. If catechesis explores this story, catechists might refer to the "foolishness of God" in 1 Corinthians 1:18–25.

[83] Scott, *Hear*, 234, 235.

[84] *Mishnah Kilayim* 3.2. *The Mishnah*, trans. Danby, 31.

[85] "Exorcism in the RCIA," in *Christian Initiation Resources Reader III*, ed. James Morgan (New York: Wm. H. Sadlier, Inc., 1984), 53.

[86] Scott, *Hear*, 386.

[87] Scott, *Hear*, 386, 387.

[88] Montague, *Companion*, 315–17.

[89] See endnote 82 in this chapter.

[90] Doohan's translations in *Matthew*, 29.

[91] Cf. Paul Hinnebusch, *St. Matthew's Earthquakes* (Ann Arbor: Servant Books, 1980), ix, 1–12.

[92] Montague, *Companion God*, 317–22, 324–30; Meier, *Matthew*, 366–74.

[93] Cf. Doohan, *Matthew: Spirituality*, 139.

[94] Cf. Montague, *Companion God*, 280–84.

[95] As a summary of Matthew, we listen to Leonard Doohan describe Matthew's world and his response: "People throughout the region struggled with issues of political obedience, redistribution of wealth, mutual tolerance and religious belief. It was a time of searching for some new unity in personal and social life, for answers to the power of a hostile universe, for an explanation of human suffering, for an appreciation of the secrets of life, a revelation of an accessible God: truly a yearning for a savior." Sound familiar? In that world, Doohan describes Matthew's pastoral response: "Matthew was a model pastor, a gifted disciple, a community leader, an insightful theologian, a convert to Christ, a person of the church, a spiritual director, a missionary with a world vision for the church." Might our world have such pastors/homilists/catechists. Doohan, *Matthew: Spirituality*, 34, 161.

# CHAPTER EIGHT

## *Conversing with Mark's Story*

*Jesus went on with his disciples to the villages of Caesarea Philippi; and on the way he asked his disciples, "Who do people say that I am?" And they answered him, "John the Baptist; and others, Elijah; and still others, one of the prophets." He asked them, "But who do you say that I am?" Peter answered him, "You are the Messiah!" Then [Jesus] sternly ordered them not to tell anyone about him.*

*Then he began to teach them that the Son of Man must undergo great suffering and be rejected by the elders, the chief priests and the scribes, and be killed, and after three days rise again. He said all this quite openly. And Peter took him aside and began to rebuke him. But turning and looking at his disciples, he rebuked Peter and said, "Get behind me, Satan! You are setting your mind not on divine things but on human things."*

*He called the crowd with his disciples, and said to them, "If any want to become my followers, let them deny themselves and take up their cross and follow me. For those who want to save their life will lose it, and those who lose their life for my sake and for the sake of the gospel will save it."*

• Mark 8:27–35 — 24th Sunday in Ordinary Time, Year B

A HOMILY ON MARK: Jesus looks us straight in the eye and asks followers then and now, "Who do you say that I am?" No time to blink. No time to check your favorite catechism or theologian. No stammering. Respond! Now! There is no question more important. Our response not only says who we believe Jesus is, it says who we are as the body of Christ. It also calls us to solidarity with everyone else in that body.

Listen to one woman who discovered the cost of that response — Maura Clarke, who wrote these lines one week before she was killed by a death squad in El Salvador: "My fear of death is being challenged as children, lovely young girls, old people are being shot and bodies thrown by the road. One cries out: 'Lord, how long?' I want to stay on now. God is teaching me, and there is real peace in spite of the terror. God is very present in God's seeming absence." Maura Clarke knew that Jesus is still put to death in his new body, and she died in solidarity with him.

Solidarity is Mark's call to Peter and all of us. This passage is at the very center of his gospel as a bridge between the first and second half. We need to situate this bridge to see more clearly the cross at its end.

The first half of Mark is full of storms and eating. The storms are symbols for the storms in Mark's community. Two times his followers cross stormy seas rowing against the winds toward Gentile territory (4:35–41—12th Sunday in Ordinary Time, Year B, and 6:45–52). Mark's church was grappling with the question: Do we let these hated Gentiles in? For Jews "Gentile" was a nasty word. For us it would be spicks, japs, chinks, polacks, niggers, wops, kikes, gooks, faggots, wetbacks—any of the words we use to separate ourselves from those we consider rejects and outcasts.

Back on land in Jewish territory there is the first meal—loaves and fish multiplied for 5,000 people, all Jewish males (6:30–44). Later the disciples finally make it to Gentile territory for the second meal—loaves and fish multiplied for 4,000 people.[1] This time Jews and Gentiles, men and women eat together, just as we are called to eat at one table and heal all divisions of race or sex (8:1–10).[2]

The great images in the second half of Mark are road and cup. Notice in the passage that begins this chapter that Jesus asks his question "on the way." Like Luke, Mark has Jesus on a journey, "on the way" to Jerusalem, to the cross. He tells his disciples that to follow him on that way is to carry the cross.[3] For Mark's church and ours that cross will mean solidarity with all the outcasts and rejects whom Jesus invites to table.

Instead, his wayward followers argue about who is the greatest (9:29–37—25th Sunday in Ordinary Time, Year B), who will sit at Jesus' right hand, what they're going to get out of hitching up with Jesus—who will be "excellency" and "monsignor," who gets the "perks."[4] Jesus answers that what they will get is "the cup of suffering that I must drink. Can you be baptized in the way I must be baptized?" (10:35–45—29th Sunday in Ordinary Time, Year B). They are choosing waters of death, not some comfortable Jacuzzi; the cross of criminals, not the thrones of tyrants or the presidential chairs of prelates. At the end of their journey to Jerusalem, the places at the right and left sides of Jesus' crucified hands have been reserved for two criminals (15:27).

In the midst of storms and meals, road and cup we have today's hinge gospel. In that context we hear Christianity's hinge question:

"Who do you say that I am?" For the Jews to whom Jesus spoke, that language would bring Moses to mind—"Who am I to go to Pharaoh" to set *slaves and outcasts* free? (Exodus 3:11). God answers that "I am" sends you and will be with you. "I have seen and I see today the suffering of my people." Once again "I am" is with Jesus and with us and sends us to set captives free. There are to be no more outcasts and rejects.

Peter thinks he understands. "You are the Messiah!" He is one of the first Christians to mouth a doctrine or creed without the foggiest idea of what it means. "Messiah" for Peter and for Israel meant royal power, the kingdom restored with pomp and circumstance, new hierarchies with power over the people, first places in the kingdom. Jesus rebukes Peter, saying, in so many words, Don't you dare defile and desecrate the word "messiah" until you know that it means the cross.[5] It means navigating stormy seas, eating with rejects, following me down the road that leads to drinking the cup of suffering with our most broken and wounded sisters and brothers. You are like the first Satan who tempted me in the desert to be Jesus the Wonder-worker (1st Sunday of Lent, Year B). Get behind me, Satan! (This phrase can mean not "get out of my sight" but "get back on the road of discipleship and follow me to the cross.") Peter's denial in the garden (14:66–72—Passion Sunday, Year B) begins here with his denial of the cross.

Jesus then teaches about the cross. Only those who take up their cross can be his disciples. Only those who lose their life for Jesus and the gospel will save it. No more "finders, keepers—losers, weepers" It is now "losers, keepers."

What does that cross mean? We spiritualize it and privatize it into any act of self-denial. We trivialize it and hang it around our necks with other bangles and beads. For Mark's community—make no mistake—crucifixion was an act of political terrorism by the ruling Roman power against the lower classes, slaves, violent criminals, other people with no rights. In this gospel, the ruling religious powers fall in with Rome. In taking up the cross, Jesus is choosing solidarity with the most oppressed. He calls us to take up that cross and do the same—with aliens, hostages, minorities, those who don't "produce" (such as the elderly and the unborn), refugees, prisoners, people with no rights, the homeless and jobless, all of us left to pay for mortgage bailouts and savings-and-loan scandals.[6]

The questions keep ringing in our ears. Who do we say that Jesus is? Who do we say that we are? In our lives, our church, our society, are we ready to fight against the stormy seas when we welcome rejects? With whom are we willing to eat at our family table and church table? Shall we get back on the road to the cross in solidarity with all who are crucified today? Shall we drink Jesus' cup? Shall we share baptism into death through which comes resurrection into life? Shall we multiply loaves for all God's people and break our bodies and shed our blood for the life of the world?

During the 1990s, when we celebrate the five-hundredth anniversary of Christianity in North America, we also recall that unlike Maura Clarke's, our solidarity often has not been with those crucified in Jesus' new body in the Americas. An estimated 70 million native people were exterminated by torture, slavery, massacres and disease between 1492 and 1650. Ten million African slaves were transported in that same period to this new world.[7] Yes, we celebrate "liberty and justice," but not for all. We also grieve. Once again Jesus asks, "Who do you say that I am? Do you know better who and where I am in 1992 than you did in 1492?"

> **Conversation Starter:**  In a psychological/personal hearing of this story from Mark, prepare some questions that might lead candidates to enter *personally* into the gospel story on which this homily is based. In a pastoral/theological hearing, prepare some questions that invite the catechumenal and parish *communities* to enter this story.

### Pastorally Hearing Mark's Big Story

"Here begins the gospel of Jesus Christ, the Son of God (1:1–8—2nd Sunday of Advent, Year B). We are so accustomed to the word that we forget that Mark invents "gospel" as a new way of proclaiming Jesus. Not a biography, the gospel is the story of a man with astounding good news about God, proclaimed with and summoning its hearers to faith.[8] Although Hebrew Scriptures refer to the "glad tidings" of Israel's return from exile (Isaiah 52:7–10), in Mark's world "glad tidings" more often meant news of the emperor's victory in battle or of his birth.

[Deification of the emperor] gives *euangelion* its significance and power. . . . Because the emperor is more than a common man, his ordinances are glad messages and his commands are sacred writings. . . . He proclaims *euangelia* through his appearance . . . the first *euangelium* is the news of his birth.[9]

Ched Myers comments: "Mark is taking dead aim at Caesar and his legitimating myths. From the very first line, Mark's literary strategy is revealed as subversive; . . . it is a declaration of war upon the political culture of the empire."[10]

In the original Greek, "here" and "begins" do not appear, yet these words are faithful to Mark's purpose. We can discern four phases in Mark: first, the time of preparation culminating in John the Baptizer; second, Jesus' earthly ministry; third, the postresurrection period; and fourth, the return of Christ in power.

Mark, however, is less interested in a chronology of past and future than in the present. In one sense, Mark writes in a circle, always in the present, always inviting us to hear the story again with the hope that this time we may get it right. Mark uses present-tense verbs frequently—151 times, to be exact. Mark's Jesus is on the move, frequently and hurriedly, from one place to another. He does more acting than talking, and he acts quickly (Mark uses "immediately" 40 times). We are "hurried along with Mark's swift, vivacious style and left awestruck, trembling and doubtful before the empty tomb."[11] Events tumble over each other. We hear the story "here," in this place, in this time, in the present, in our world.

Like Matthew, Mark in his opening verses calls us back to the beginnings of a new creation in our world. He does so again at the end when the young man tells us that Jesus has been raised up "very early on Sunday morning, at sunrise" (16:2—Easter Vigil, Year B)—a symbol of the first day of creation.[12] The story is always beginning.

### Beginning Again

Mark's gospel was meant to be heard—not read—as a whole; the original was written on long scrolls of papyrus without divisions of chapter and verse. When we hear Mark as a whole, the ending sends us back to the beginning. Mark's final story is that of the faithful women at the tomb, hearing of Jesus' rising from a young man dressed in white, and commissioned to tell the disciples to go to Galilee where they will see him, but they "fled from the tomb, for terror and amazement had seized them; and they said nothing to anyone for they were afraid" (16:1–8—Easter Vigil, Year B).

The final words in Mark are not Mark's words. Verses 9 through 20 in chapter 16 are a later addition, many ancient versions of Mark end the gospel with the women fleeing from the tomb in fear. Myers does not deem these added verses worthy of exegesis.

> [These verses] symbolize our unending efforts to domesticate the gospel . . . [with] the eleventh-hour Hollywood rescues, the arrival of the cavalry, the "happily ever after." . . . The "dilemma" of the ending is precisely what Mark refuses to resolve for us; he *means* to leave us to wrestle with whether or not the women at the tomb (that is to say, we ourselves) overcame their fear in order to proclaim the new beginning in Galilee. To provide a "neat closure" to the narrative would allow the reader to finally remain passive; the story would be self-contained, in no need of a response. As it stands, the discipleship narrative can truly resume only if the reader takes up the practice of the messianic vocation, which response is made possible by the fact that Jesus continues to "go before us."[13]

In the original text of Mark, there are no accounts of Jesus appearing to the disciples after the resurrection. Instead Mark questions us: Do we see him in Galilee? Unlike Luke, who rebuilds the community on Jerusalem's hopes, Mark has no time for Jerusalem with its religious and political oppressors.[14] Mark sends us back to Galilee, back to the *outsiders*, to the wilderness, the place of revolt, the place of temptation and suffering where Jesus first called disciples. There he invites us to hear the call again and to see what discipleship means this time. If we do, the one real proof and genuine witness to the risen Jesus is our following him to the cross, in solidarity with all the crucified, as disciples (a word used over 250 times in all the synoptic gospels and over 45 times in Mark). Then we can truly return to Mark's beginning and proclaim, "Here begins the gospel of Jesus Christ, the Son of God."

In that context, *we*, like the disciples, are not allowed to break Mark's "messianic secret"[15] until we see like the two blind men (8:22–26; and 10:46–52—30th Sunday in Ordinary Time, Year B) and see the wedding of discipleship to crucifixion in our "Galilees." In Mark's story, only the demons and political enemies of Jesus name him "Son of God"

(3:11; 5:7; 14:61; 14:1—15:47—Passion Sunday, Year B). Only the Roman centurion at the end of the gospel is allowed to voice faith in Jesus as God's Son, because he has seen what the disciples could not see: that this Son "did not deem equality with God something to be grasped at" but "emptied himself" and "humbled himself, obediently accepting even death, death on a cross" (Philippians 2:6, 7, 8). When Peter calls him "Messiah," not "Son of God," and then even robs that of its cross-bound meaning, Jesus silences him. Aside from Mark's opening line, only the heavenly voice names Jesus as "Son of God." At Jesus' baptism, Mark gives no indication that any bystanders heard anything (1:7–11—Baptism of the Lord, Year B); and at the transfiguration the disciples are told not to say what they had seen or heard, because they really haven't "seen" yet (9:2–10—2nd Sunday of Lent, Year B).

At the end of Mark's gospel, *we* see the cross. *We* see the empty tomb. *We* see and hear a young man dressed in a white robe (like Jesus at the transfiguration and the martyrs of Revelation 7:9, 13). He commands us to go to Galilee (Syracuse, Selma, St. Louis, Seattle), where Jesus goes before us and where *we* shall see him as crucified and risen if we have learned from Mark to see the Son of God and the messiah as he truly is (16:1–8—Easter Vigil, Year B). Then we can begin the story again and proclaim good news about the Son of God by following him and all the crucified to the cross. We can let the secret out if we have heard and seen our way in—to wherever and with whomever the cross leads disciples today.[16]

I keep insisting that all the gospel authors are consumed with a passion to unite and include all people, especially the outcasts, in covenant with the God of Jesus Christ.[17] That is *the* issue for their communities. How does Mark go about telling that story?

## Mark's Plot

Eduard Schweizer says that Mark wrote somewhere in the Roman Empire in the late 60s.[18] Frank Matera adds that Mark is a Greek-speaking Jewish Christian writing for a community that apparently had forgotten the centrality of the cross and was rampant with wild, apocalyptic expectations about Jesus' imminent coming, which would save them from the cross and the horrors of the world.[19] Some scholars believe that Mark wrote in Rome when the Christian community again faced the cross during the brutal persecutions by Nero, who blamed them for burning the city.[20] Others hold that he writes in northern Palestine or in Syria during the turmoil of the Jewish revolt that was accompanied by Roman persecution.[21] Whichever is the case, the setting is the same: a community confronted with the cross.

Eugene LaVerdiere states that part one of the gospel (1:1—8:26) reveals who Jesus is and who we are. There is minimum of dialogue and discourse. The narrator moves fast and throws one story after another at the reader. We are invited into homes and synagogues, to the sea and into fields. Then, according to LaVerdiere, part two of Mark (8:27—16:10) asks: What does all this mean? It means discipleship by following Jesus to the cross.[22]

Unlike Matthew, Mark is not very interested in the ethical teachings of Jesus addressed to the Jewish Christians. Mark gives little discourse material because the good news is not so much "the content of what Jesus says and does, but the power of Jesus himself, present where his story is told."[23] He centers on the life and deeds of Jesus, but in ways that separate Jesus from so-called "divine persons" and "miracle-workers" who worked their magic throughout Greece, Asia Minor and Syria and who worked their way around the cross. Mark's Gentile hearers too often identified Jesus with these wonder-workers and robbed him (and us) of the pain of our human journey.[24] So Mark wants to keep Jesus fully human, flesh of our flesh, bone of our bone. There is nothing magical about Jesus' passion, to which Mark continually gives reference and about which he includes many details. Even his miracle stories are not a magic show of amazing events but disclosures of God's reign and assaults on human and demonic powers of oppression and exclusion. Mark's Jesus does teach, but does not offer miraculous, other-worldly knowledge but obscure parables that those outside his community did not understand.[25]

Mark's is an unrelenting story of invitation and rejection. He announces the invitation in his introduction. In the first half of the gospel (1:14—8:26) there are three acts. Each act begins with an invitation—a summary of Jesus' activity and a call or sending of disciples. Each ends with the invitation rejected (1:14—3:6; 3:7—6:6a; 6:6b—8:26—3rd through 16th, 22nd and 23rd Sundays in Ordinary Time, Year B). He invites—in parables and miracles, in his battle against legalism, in embracing Gentiles, at meals with loaves and fishes. He is rejected—by blind leaders, blind fellow citizens, blind disciples.[26]

Peter's confession and rejection is the hinge of Mark's story (8:27–35—24th Sunday in Ordinary Time, Year B). After that, beginning in the north in Caesarea Philippi, Jesus is on the way, on the road of discipleship through Galilee, on the journey (as in Luke) toward Jerusalem and the cross (9:2—10:52—25th through 30th Sundays in Ordinary Time, Year B). Three times he announces his passion and invites the disciples to follow him. Instead they argue about "perks."[27]

On the mount of the transfiguration, the centerpoint of Mark's story, Mark's Jesus stands in the tradition of Moses whose "work came precisely as the engagement of the *religion of God's freedom* with the *politics of human justice.*"[28] He stands also with the prophet Elijah, who had already come to precede the messiah in the person of John the Baptizer, who denounced kings (6:18) just as Elijah denounced kings (1 Kings 17:1—19:21). Jesus is embroiled in the tradition of the prophets who "bring to public expression the dread of endings, the collapse of our self-madeness, the barriers and pecking orders that secure us at each other's expense, the fearful practice of eating off the table of a hungry brother or sister."[29] In that company of troublemakers, the heavenly voice calls the three disciples to hear and see a Son of God in the Son of Man who "has not come to be served but to serve—to give his life in ransom for many" (10:45).[30] They do not see, so "he strictly enjoined them not to tell anyone what they had seen before the Son of Man had risen from the dead" (9:9—2nd Sunday of Lent, Year B).

In Jerusalem, the storm of rejection increases. Mark intensifies his invitation to God's covenant with Jesus' assaults on legalism and ritualism, and with his welcome of Gentiles (11:17 ff.; 12:9; 13:10; 15:38 ff.). The climax is Jesus' judgment against the Temple (11:15–19 and 13:1–2). Because the God of the new covenant does not live in temples but among those who believe, disciples' prayer even without a temple will still be heard (11:22–26).

In the end, the Jewish leadership aligns itself with the Roman state to do away with this rabble-rouser. The disciples' blindness turns to "sleep" in the garden; they will not "wake up" to Jesus as suffering servant. Later, they turn tail and run; blindness turns to betrayal. Peter's "rebuke" in chapter 8 descends to "denial" in chapter 14. We are left in the tomb with a young martyr-figure clothed in white who calls us to follow Jesus back to Galilee to start again. We are left outside the tomb with a few faithful women—bewildered, fearful and wondering if he really means it.

> Thus the Gospel of Mark is the account of the unprecedented and incomprehensible incarnate love of God. In the person of Jesus, this love seeks and finds [us] despite many kinds of opposition. Because any direct revelation would lead only to a miracle-faith, such as even the demons possess, God has to take the way of death in obscurity, in disgrace and humility. . . . Discipleship is the only form in which faith can exist.[31]

## A Political/Literary Hearing of Mark's Story

I offer you a second summary and invitation into the drama of Mark. This will be a *literary* hearing, which sees a biblical text, as Frank Matera states, "not simply as a window through which the reader views the historical author and his or her contemporaries . . . but as a world in itself apart from the author and the original audience for whom the author wrote. It is a kind of mirror in which the reader sees himself or herself [and the community] reflected in the world of the story."[32] For the categories for this literary criticism—worldview, settings, plot, characters—I turn to Jack Dean Kingsbury, who offers a literary hearing of all three synoptic gospels.[33]

This also will be a *political* literary hearing that will often cite the always stimulating, sometimes maddening commentary by Ched Myers in *Binding the Strong Man* (cf. Mark 3:27), subtitled *A Political Reading of Mark's Story of Jesus* and lauded by Walter Wink as "quite simply, the most important commentary on a book of scripture since Barth's *Romans*."[34] Myers writes in the tradition of Gandhi's militant nonviolence (in which tradition he also sees Mark). Myers is clear about his biases and ideologies. We converse with him with care, with a warning from Walter Brueggemann: "When we embrace ideology uncritically, it is assumed that the Bible squares easily with capitalist ideology, or narcissistic psychology, or revolutionary politics, or conformist morality, or romantic liberalism. There is then no danger, no energy, no possibility, no opening for newness!"[35]

Acknowledging these caveats, I choose to go with Myers' revolutionary ideology precisely because he does call us to energy and newness, far more than Kingsbury's rather prosaic rendering of conflict in Mark. He moves us out of the settled formula of prose into poetry and imagery, which Brueggemann compares to "Bob Gibson's fastball, that jumps at the right moment, that breaks open old worlds with surprise, abrasion and pace."

I caution those who might choose to read Myers to sift out the paragraphs in which he might manipulate scripture to support his pacifist stance as member of the American Friends Service Committee. But although we might not be pacifists, we thank God for their voices, which challenge our ideologies. We need to hear the pacifist voice, for example, in the pain that Myers shares in his poignant final chapter in which he sees the pacifist tradition failing just as Mark's Jesus failed:

> The "gravity" exerted by imperial culture's seductions, deadly mediocrities and deadly codes of conformity pull our aspirations plummeting down. . . . My most astonishing discovery in rereading Mark over and over . . . was this: All of this anguish is anticipated by the gospel. Mark reckoned not only with the moment of the kingdom's dawn, but the moment of failure and disillusionment. Jesus said simply, "You will all desert me" [14:27—Passion Sunday, Year B]. The suggestion is that this desertion is inevitable in any and all discipleship narratives, and that means our own. Failure, in other words, does not lie outside the horizons of the narrative, but at dead center.[36]

**A *Literary Hearing***   In his work of literary criticism, Kingsbury looks for qualities that we find in any work of literature: the broad "world" of the story, the more limited "settings," the "plot" and most important, the "characters."

The *world* of Mark's story for Kingsbury is the story's first-century world. We need to know that Mark's world was the site of cosmic struggles between God and Satan. "God is at work in Jesus to defeat Satan and his minions and to summon Israel . . . to believe in the gospel, and to live in the sphere of his end-time rule."[37] In that world there are no barriers between the realms of the supernatural and the ordinary.

Spatially, Mark's story encompasses earth, Gehenna (hell) and heaven; but there is a distinction between heaven and earth. In heaven,

God rules, and in Jesus, God's rule draws near to earth. Unlike the apocalyptic stories prevalent in Mark's time about other-worldly journeys, however, Jesus takes the earthly journey of all humans, which means journey into death.

Temporally, Mark's world embraces, first, a present age with two phases: the time of *prophecy* from creation to John the Baptist and Jesus, and the time of *fulfillment* (in which we live) from John and Jesus until the final judgment. Second, Mark's world encompasses an age to come in the end-time. Indeed, we need to leave our world of space probes and computers to enter Mark's prescientific world. Kingsbury's limits are that he rarely gives us a mirror on our twentieth-century world that makes pastoral connections.

Clearly, then, it is helpful to see how the biblical authors see their world—with heavens and loving spirits above, hells and evil spirits below, with earthly body/spirits struggling between the two, and marked by defined ages with perhaps an imminent end to this one—so that we can understand why their characters do what they do. Clearly, however, that world has been shattered by our discovery of the life cycles of stars, of earth's place on the edge of its galaxy, of a "big bang," of a universe expanding minute by minute. Does language of "up" and "down," angels and demons, supernatural and natural falter in our new world? How do we speak of "heavenly voices" and "exorcising demons" in our world?[38] I am citing Kingsbury to unveil the problem. Myers (and Wink) may be more helpful in facing the problem. They hint of ways to make biblical and theological worlds more credible.

What Kingsbury calls *settings* are more limited places, times or social circumstances in which the characters act. They are less cosmic, and some lend themselves to images that transcend prescientific and scientific worldviews. The locale in Mark's story is the land of the Jews. He depicts Jesus' ministry as a journey first within and around Galilee, then on the way to and in and about Jerusalem. As we have seen, for Mark this becomes the image of discipleship on the way to the cross and to new beginnings in Galilee. The desert is the place to which John summons Israel to repent and in which Satan is at home and tests Jesus. Galilee is the region of outlaws and outsiders where Jesus begins, ministers and begins again in disciples who see him in all crucified outsiders. Jerusalem is the place of danger and death. The Temple is the house of God's presence but also the seat of the religious authorities' power and the storm center of Jesus' conflict with the status quo.

"The *plot* of a story has to do with the way the events are arranged. Events occur not haphazardly but in a carefully ordered sequence. This sequence is governed by time and causality so as to reach an overall climax and to elicit from the reader some desired response."[39] Mark's plot has a beginning (1:1–13—Baptism of the Lord, Year B), a middle (1:14—8:26—3rd through 23rd Sundays in Ordinary Time, Year B) and an end (8:27—16:8—24th through 33rd Sundays in Ordinary Time and Easter Vigil, Year B).

The force driving the plot forward is *conflict*. At the center of the storm is Jesus. He is clearly in command of the conflict because he has true authority from God, unlike his combatants, who defile the title "religious authorities." He struggles with these authorities to accept him as God's agent in whom God draws near to humankind—insiders and outsiders. Jesus also struggles with the disciples to overcome their incredible ignorance about who he is (his identity), what he is about (identity linked to destiny) and what is true discipleship (their identity and destiny rooted in his). Through these conflicts, the response that Mark seeks from the reader is discipleship—taking up the cross and following Jesus.

John Pilch agrees that conflict marks the plot of all the gospels. He describes Mediterranean culture as "agonistic" or "combative." In general, Mediterranean people are prone to conflict as a natural consequence of their core values: honor and shame. Honor is a public claim to value or worth with public recognition of that claim. The cultural "game" concerned with honor "consists of a *challenge and response*. Individuals challenge the honorable status of their equals in the hope of catching them off guard, of putting them on the spot, so that they are unable to make an appropriate response in defense of their honor. This shames the one challenged and redounds to the honor of the one challenging."[40] Jesus, the religious authorities and the disciples are true to their Mediterranean roots.

Jesus, the religious authorities and the disciples are for Kingsbury the three *characters* in the primary story lines forced by conflict. The secondary story line is with the people in the crowd, who are not his enemies but who also are not his followers. The crowd is open to him at times but without faith. In the end it casts its lot with the authorities. We now follow these characters in Myers's (and others') literary/political hearing of Mark's plot. Mark invites us to enter the conflict. He invites us to choose our authorities, idols, principalities and powers of oppression, or Jesus.

**A Political Hearing**    Myers situates Mark's gospel in northern Palestine in the late 60s, when the Jews had their own conflicts during their revolt against the Roman Empire *before* the destruction of the Temple. Various groups were competing for the allegiance of Mark's community.[41] Mark's Jesus calls them to a different, nonviolent protest. He is a political and religious revolutionary from Nazareth ("Nowheresville"). He begins his ministry in the Galilean wilderness (Galilee was notorious as a place of turmoil and revolt), outside the systems of oppression and in solidarity with outsiders. The titles of Myers's outline reveal his political/literary hearing of Mark's story:

| | |
|---|---|
| 1:1–20 | The "First" Prologue and Call to Discipleship |
| 1:21—3:35 | The First Direct Action Campaign: Jesus' Assault on the Jewish Social Order in Capernaum. |
| 4:1–36 | "Listen!" The First Sermon on Revolutionary Patience. |
| 4:36—8:9 | Jesus' Construction of a New Social Order, I: The Miracle Cycle |
| 6:1–32; 7:1–23; 8:10–21 | The Execution of John and the "First" Epilogue |
| 8:22—9:30 | Midpoint of the Story: The "Second" Prologue and Call to Discipleship |
| 9:30—10:52 | Jesus' Construction of a New Social Order, II: The Teaching Cycle |
| 11:1—13:3 | The Second Direction Action Campaign: Jesus' Showdown with the Powers in Jerusalem |
| 13:4–37 | The Second Sermon on Revolutionary Patience |
| 14:1—15:20 | Jesus' Arrest and Trial by the Powers |
| 15:21—16:8 | The Execution of Jesus and the "Second" Epilogue.[42] |

FIRST HALF OF THE GOSPEL    In the first half of the gospel, Myers sees a "subversive" trajectory and a "constructive" trajectory. The *subversive* trajectory includes the militant aspects of Jesus' conflict with the authorities: exorcism, argument and confrontation (primarily in 1:16–4:35 — 3rd through 11th Sundays in Ordinary Time, Year B).

The *plot crisis* of the subversive trajectory is Jesus' struggle with an imperial Rome (with worship of emperors and oppression of the poor) and an imperious religion (with worship of the law and the elite's exclusion of the poor and all outcasts and outsiders). Myers has powerful and revealing pages on how the elite's legalisms of "ritual impurity became the guiding principle in the division of Jewish society into classes"[43] and how the Temple, which was originally a "central storehouse" from which to share goods with people in need, especially in rural areas, instead became a "central bank" with wealth, trade and jobs for those in the city.[44] "For Mark, the Temple state and its political economy represented the heart of what was wrong with the dominant system. He had no wish for greater access to, or control over, the cultus — only its demise."[45] That is the point of the exorcisms. They assault not so much devilish spirits from hell *below* our world, which bedevil *individuals*. They assault systemic evil, spiritual corruption and political enslavement, which are incarnations of the demonic from *within* our world and which infest and imprison individuals through ecclesial and societal *systems*.[46] John Pilch agrees that Jesus' clear exercise of power over demons (and illness) would be perceived by citizens of that culture as political action, because in the Mediterranean world, power is a value that belongs to the realm of politics.[47] Jesus exercises his power over the demonic principalities and powers that infect religion and politics.[48]

In celebrating and preaching about the scrutinies (see chapter ten, pages 303–307) with their exorcisms, we need to name the demonic evil spirits, principalities and powers in our social and ecclesial systems, what idols we worship, who and what oppress people, what legalisms and elitisms we use to exclude outcasts and outsiders, and who and what keeps people thirsty, blind, entombed and bound in our times (John 4:5–42; 9:1–41; 11:1–45 — 3rd, 4th and 5th Sundays of Lent, Year A).[49]

The *constructive trajectory* is the *redemptive* and *affirmative* dimensions of Jesus' mission in his struggle with disciples: creating and maintaining the discipleship community through the healings, journeys and teachings (primarily in 4:36—8:21—12th through 23rd Sundays in Ordinary Time, Year B). The *plot crisis* is the disciples' ignorance and failure to understand what Jesus and God's reign are about. The irony is that the community seems to come to deepening intimacy with Jesus, but misunderstanding in the first half of Mark becomes antagonism in 8:22—10:45 and finally defection in 14:12—16:8. The disciples flee the cross and betray our crucified brothers and sisters.

Mark knows how outsiders who become insiders can perpetuate exclusion of new outsiders. The disciples do not understand the meaning of the loaves (7:21) with its message of including Gentiles. They eventually seek for themselves a new elitism (9:33–37; 10:35–45—29th Sunday in Ordinary Time, Year B). Outsiders become exclusive insiders in governments, in corporations and in our church communities, where some reformers who worked for Vatican II became a new elite who imposed their own version of that Council or betrayed it.

Mark's community, therefore, needs to hear his stories of blindness and deafness (7:31–37—23rd Sunday in Ordinary Time, Year B; 8:22–26; 10:46–52—30th Sunday in Ordinary Time, Year B). The "enemy" is not just the powers-that-be outside ourselves. The enemy is the blindness and deafness within. We buy into systems and create new divisions and new elites.[50]

In this section, Mark constructs three qualities of a lifestyle of discipleship.[51] First is a voluntary austerity seen in John the Baptizer (1:6) contrasted with his opulent executioners (6:21 ff.); in the call to leave the economic security of the family (1:16 ff.—3rd Sunday in Ordinary Time, Year B); and in the dependence of disciples on hospitality (6:8 ff.—15th Sunday in Ordinary Time, Year B).

Second, there is direct action/protest against social and economic inequities. Jesus offers Sabbath healings, not legalisms with demands that only an elite could follow (2:23–3:6—9th Sunday in Ordinary Time, Year B).

The third and most critical quality is solidarity with the outcast, which is the meaning of the loaves.[52] Mark pictures a world in which crowds prevent the community from eating (3:20; 6:31), and these crowds are hungry (6:36; 8:2). Jesus calls disciples to respond (6:37). They are to multiply through sharing (6:30–43), and all the rejects (Gentiles, outsiders) are reconciled at table (8:1–10). After twice crossing the waters (4:35–41—12th Sunday in Ordinary Time, Year B; 6:45–52), their Red Sea of chaos and flight and the "stormy seas" of conflict over who was welcome to table, they eat this new manna in the desert on a new exodus to freedom.[53] They finally make it to Gentile territory where everyone eats together—Jews and Gentiles, men and women, insiders and outsiders (8:8–9). On their journey, they are now to carry but "one loaf" from which all will eat (8:14), yet they still do not understand. Although fundamentalists see only a miraculous multiplication of "Wonder Bread" and others read eucharistic meanings into these meals, we should see the Last Supper and the eucharist in light of these feedings of the hungry and reconciliation with the outsiders. (For other reflections on the meaning of these meals, see chapter nine, pages 277–291).

SECOND HALF OF THE GOSPEL    In the second half of the gospel, Mark begins with three cycles of revelation/misunderstanding/teaching (8:22–10:52), including three predictions of Jesus' suffering and death (8:31 ff.—24th Sunday in Ordinary Time, Year B; 9:31 ff.—25th Sunday in Ordinary Time, Year B; and 10:33 ff.) and three healings. Myers calls this Mark's catechism.

First, each *revelation/teaching cycle* deepens the meaning of servanthood/nonviolence in the community. There is the political vocation of the cross and solidarity with the crucified —"If any want to become my followers, let them take up their cross . . ." (8:34)—and the social vocation of servanthood—"Whoever wishes to be first among you must be slave of all" (10:43). Therefore, the triple cycle of teaching begins with the pitched battle about the cross between Peter, who tempts Jesus as Satan did in the wilderness (cf. 1:12–15—1st Sunday of Lent, Year B and 8:31–38—24th Sunday in Ordinary Time, Year B). It closes with Jesus' confrontation of James and John about the "first" becoming servants (10:35–45—29th Sunday in Ordinary Time, Year B). Ernest Best insists that for Mark's community (and for ours), the message is that "there can be no suggestion of an inner elite among them; if ever such existed it is now abolished."[54]

In that context, Jesus offers three other teachings about radical discipleship and the fidelity of those who follow him to the cross: the teachings on divorce and on being like little children, and the words to the rich young man to sell all he had. The context is like that of Matthew's Sermon on the Mount—a prophetic vision of life lived in God's Spirit, not a set of laws. Jesus again calls for solidarity with outcasts: women, who had no right to divorce in Jewish society (although a husband could simply divorce his wife by his own written decree if he didn't like her looks or cooking),[55] children and the poor. He calls both wives and husbands, however, to their own unique bearing of the cross, which will always be present when fulfilling our Creator's purpose and dream for marriage—living as two in one flesh. The Pharisees had asked a legal question about rules for divorce. Jesus gave them a prophetic answer about what is possible when living by the Spirit of God (10:2–16—27th Sunday in Ordinary Time, Year B)[56]

Does that mean that we exclude from our communities those who fail in radical discipleship, betray the dream and do not live up to prophetic answers? We don't exclude the rich when they, like the rich young man, reject prophetic answers (10:17–30—28th Sunday in Ordinary Time, Year B).[57] In Mark's community and our own, we do proclaim the prophetic answers.

Second, each *healing* marks the despair of the disciples' obtuse incomprehension and the hope for healing. Mark's "catechism" is framed by the two healings of the blind (8:22–26; 10:46–52—30th Sunday in Ordinary Time, Year B). The disciples simply cannot see and understand the meaning of the loaves—that when all eat of the one loaf (8:14), Jesus simply demolishes all divisions, all boundaries and all hierarchies. No more head tables, segregated lunch counters, awards banquets or special tables from the maître d'. All of this confounds and confronts the cultural and ecclesial demons of pecking orders, cutthroat competition, clerical privileges, survival of the fittest and self-fulfillment.

After Jesus fails as a catechist, he enters into Jerusalem with the disciples. According to Myers,[58] the *historical* background of 11:1—13:37 for Mark's community is the revolt against Rome and the demand of the rebels that others join up with them. Mark is well aware that Jesus' entry into Jerusalem could sound to his hearers like the military procession of a triumphal national hero about to lead the rebellion. So Jesus follows the quite different messianic tradition of Zechariah and comes "meek, riding upon an ass" (Zechariah 9:9 ff.; also cf. Genesis 49:8–12). It is like street theater, antimilitary in tone, a satire on military liberators (11:1–10 — Passion Sunday, Year B, gospel for the procession with palms).

The *theological* background in Mark's time is apocalyptic — it looks toward the end of the world. Mark's Jesus insists that the Jewish rebels' social and religious elites cannot bring down the old order and inaugurate the new. They will only make the suffering worse. They are a barren fig tree (symbol of the Temple state, cf. 11:12–14, 20–21). Only God can bring an end to that oppressive world, and God is doing so through the nonviolent, militant protest of Jesus. Myers insists that unlike some apocalyptic writers who escape conflict because they believe that only God can intervene and inaugurate the new world from outside history, Mark has Jesus actively and directly assault the Temple and all the corruption for which it stands (11:15–19). He foils the traps of his Jewish enemies and refuses to side with Rome or the rebels on the question of the despised poll tax (12:13–17), which sparked a revolt (Acts 5:37).[59] He assaults the Temple establishment for their own "imperial" power plays, for long-winded and empty prayers and for the abuse of widows. In that context, the story of the widow's offering is not a pious example of generous giving but an attack upon the wealthy who rob widows and who should be giving to her and in place of her (12:38–44 — 32nd Sunday in Ordinary Time, Year B).

Then Jesus predicts the destruction of the Temple with graphic symbols of the end of the world. (Recall that if Myers' date for Mark is correct, the Temple was still standing when he was writing.)[60] Mark's community, according to Myers, would have found life unthinkable without their magnificent Temple (cf. 13:2). When the Romans did destroy the Temple, they struck at the heart of Judaism. Mark would say, "It's about time!" It is the messianic time for the demise not of authentic Jewish worship but of the elitism of the Temple state. Mark's Jesus proclaims in frightening, gripping, horrific images the end of that oppressive social and political world (13:1–37 — 1st Sunday of Advent, Year B and 33rd Sunday in Ordinary Time, Year B).

We need not see these images in ways that only conjure up the end of the world and Jesus' final coming.[61] Jesus proclaims the death of the old order of oppression, which was assaulted by his own death when "the curtain in the Temple was torn in two, from top to bottom" (15:38—Passion Sunday, Year B). That symbolizes that all people now have access to the Holy of Holies—God's presence. If Mark's community answers Jesus' call to solidarity with all the outsiders excluded by the Temple state from covenant and access to God, they will be arrested, taken to court, and beaten in synagogues (13:9–13).

Today we still find old worlds of oppression, because disciples then and now betray the call. The results are especially tragic in Latin America and the Philippines where Catholics beat, torture and murder Catholics.[62] In that world, Mark's drama calls us to follow Jesus of Galilee to the cross where God commands the end to all temple states, mighty "Jerusalems" and oppressive worlds. "For Mark the driving force in history is the divine power of the end of time, *operative already* in the history of Jesus, propelling the whole course of history toward its ultimate destiny" in Mark's world and in ours.[63]

## The Ending/Beginning

We conclude this chapter with three interpretations from Myers on Mark 14:1–16:8.[64] First, as I noted earlier, Mark writes in a circle. His story opens with a "voice" crying in the wilderness (1:2), promising a stronger one. That stronger one, in the imagery of Isaiah 49:24–25, later promises to "bind the strong man," symbol of all the powers of oppression (cf. 3:26–34—11th Sunday in Ordinary Time, Year B). The story faces disaster when this stronger one himself is bound and beaten, and his "voice" expires (15:37). At the end, however, the young man tells us that the story begins again in Galilee. Will anyone follow Jesus to the cross this time? The "voices" of both John and Jesus speaking *now* to us promise that some will: "He will baptize you with the Holy Spirit" (1:8—Baptism of the Lord, Year B). "With the baptism with which I am baptized, you will be baptized" (10:39).

Second, in spite of those promises, Mark is unrelenting in his warning to his community (and us) that there is a steady erosion of the solidarity between Jesus and his community. Doohan adds that "while we can presume Jesus' support of his disciples, there is no recorded word of praise for them from Jesus. . . . Mark's is the kind of book that any organization would like to be without!"[65] Mark speaks against the disciples as Jesus' adversaries or enemies not so much in hostility but pastorally for his church and ours, and he calls us to follow Jesus to the cross.[66]

The shared meal during which Jesus invites disciples to stand with him in life and death (14:22–25) is bracketed by predictions of their desertion (14:18–21, 27–31—Passion Sunday, Year B). In this section, the escalation from betrayal to falling away to denial reflects the same escalation in Mark's entire gospel. John is handed over (1:14); Jesus is betrayed 13 times. The falling away of many disciples when threatened by persecution is foreseen in the sower parable (4:17) and warned against in the discipleship catechism (9:42–47—26th Sunday in Ordinary Time, Year B). Disciples hit the bottom with denial in attempts to save their skins; Jesus warned that they would do so (8:34—24th Sunday in Ordinary Time, Year B). They simply will not understand and will not commit.

In our culture of quick fixes, fast food and instant everything, in our culture, which throws away not just styrofoam cups but also marriages and relationships, in a land of shorter and shorter-term commitments, where some people question whether anyone can say forever, we need to hear Mark's warnings of betrayal, falling-away and denial and to hear his call to fidelity. In our church, where we see

> officials who seek to control others and impose their own views on followers from all walks of life, . . . appointments resulting from unquestioning loyalty to other church administrators rather than to the gospel, . . . curial trials similar to those of which sections of the apocalyptic discourse of Mark are clearly descriptive, Mark's blunt rejection of this type of control and his sense of liberty are challenging and full of hope. . . . Mark's evangelical call to respect authorities, challenge them, and imitate the suffering servanthood of Jesus may indicate . . . the main trends of the next decade's ecclesial responsibility.[67]

Third, these final chapters of Mark focus on Jesus' body, anointed at the beginning (14:8) and buried at the end (15:45 ff). In between he gives his body and blood at the meal that seals God's covenant with all people (14:22–25). Jesus replaces the power-grabbing, self-seeking elitism of the Temple cult with meals where powerless, self-giving disciples break their bodies and shed their blood for the life of the world. Jesus' body, which gave life to others, is beaten and spat upon (15:16–20) and in death is juxtaposed with the torn curtain of the sanctuary (15:37 ff.—all these texts are proclaimed on Passion Sunday, Year B). In the aftermath, the body is suddenly absent from the tomb (16:6—Easter Vigil, Year B).

Myers suggests that, on the one hand, Jesus' body replaces the Temple. Disciples who are nourished with that body will replace oppression and exclusion with justice and inclusion. On the other hand, Jesus' body, absent at his death, is replaced by discipleship. Myers identifies and contrasts three "apocalyptic moments" in Mark. In the first two, the baptism and transfiguration, there is speech made from "heaven to earth." In the third, Jesus' death, heaven falls silent. We are to listen to what happens on earth.

> There is no voice from the clouds, only Jesus' voice protesting his abandonment by God; it is not the heavens that are rent, but the veil of the earthly sanctuary; Jesus is not with Moses and Elijah, but between two bandits; it is not the heavenly voice that attests to Jesus as "Son of God," but an enemy, the centurion. When the story is regenerated, it is done so in bodily form: He is risen. The "resurrection" motif is situated not in heaven but in Galilee, the site of earthly practice.[68]

That is precisely where we are. That is where we hear the call to discipleship from him who goes before us. That is where we either respond to Mark's plot with outright rejection like the religious authorities, with ignorance and betrayal like the first disciples, or with the fidelity of those who "see him in Galilee." That is where his new body, the community of his followers, multiplies loaves for all outcasts and outsiders. That is where the story continues; and we begin again "the gospel of Jesus Christ, the Son of God" (Mark 1:1—2nd Sunday of Advent, Year B).

## Endnotes

[1] Cf. Wilfred Harrington, *Mark* (Wilmington: Michael Glazier, Inc., 1979), 89–95, 108–10.

[2] Unfortunately, the lectionary omits both these meals and instead inserts the meal and discourse on the Bread of Life from John's gospel. I suggest that the homilist and catechist have the freedom to refer to Mark's meals with their powerful message of inclusion, even when preaching on John (17th Sunday in Ordinary Time, Year B). For

comments on the parallels and contrasts between the two feedings, see Haarrington, in *Mark*, 88–117.

[3] The word "disciple" is used over 250 times in the synoptic gospels all together and 45 times in Mark alone.

[4] Two thousand years later we still fight for "perks." D. P. Noonan writes, "The thirst for power among priests, monsignors, bishops and cardinals [goes] totally unchecked, simply because there [is] no one to check it . . . Ambition is the ecclesiastical lust!" Cited by Paul Murphy and Rene Arling, *La Popessa* (New York: Warner Books, 1983), 228.

[5] Mark's famous "messianic secret" (better, "Son of God secret," see note #15) is not game playing. No one in Mark (except Jesus' enemies) is allowed to call him messiah until they know that it means the cross. Cf. Frank Matera, *What Are They Saying about Mark?* (New York: Paulist Press, 1987), 18–37.

[6] J. Massyngbaerde Ford, *Bonded with the Immortal* (Wilmington: Michael Glazier, Inc., 1987), 300–303.

[7] Paul McKenna, "1492: Challenging the History," *Scarboro Missions* 72:1, 5.

[8] Throughout Mark, "to see" Jesus means to have faith in him. At the end, Mark says that if the community is to see Jesus, who goes before them to Galilee, it must become involved in the mission to the world that Galilee symbolized. Cf. Harrington, *Mark*, xv.

[9] G. Kittel and G. Friedrich, eds., *Theological Dictionary of the New Testament* (Grand Rapids: Wm. B. Eerdmans, 1985), 2:724.

[10] Ched Myers, *Binding the Strong Man* (Maryknoll NY: Orbis Books, 1989), 124; for widely differing appraisals of this provocative book, see note 34 in this chapter.

[11] Ford, *Bonded*, 208.

[12] Cf. Raymond Apicella, *Journeys into Mark: 16 Lessons of Exploration and Discovery* (Cincinnati: St. Anthony Messenger Press), 3–6.

[13] Myers, *Binding*, 401, 402.

[14] Cf. Leonard Doohan, *Mark: Visionary of Early Christianity* (Santa Fe: Bear and Co.), 63–64.

[15] Frank Matera contends that Mark has not so much a "messianic" secret but a "Son of God" secret. His preferred title is "Son of God." He announces that at the beginning, at Jesus' baptism and transfiguration, and at the cross; but he does not allow the disciples to use it until they see it in the light of a second title, the suffering "Son of Man." *What Are They Saying*, 24, 35–37.

[16] We can exaggerate the extent of this secrecy. Jesus does teach clearly to the disciples and reveals what "messiah" means (e.g., his "catechism" in Mark 8:31—10:52), but they remain blind. Cf. Doohan, *Mark*, 76–80.

[17] Harrington refers to "the little people," the minor characters who are examples of God's reign, as foils to the authorities and disciples and allies of Jesus (cf. 1:29–31, 40–45; 4:18–20, 21–43; 7:24–30, 31–37; 8:22–27; 10:46–52; 14:3–9, 40–41; 16: 1–8); Harrington concludes that "any enlightened reading of Mark's gospel must acknowledge the major contribution of its minor characters." *Mark*, xvii–xviii. Homily/catechesis on the first Sunday when these "little people" appear might introduce us to many others of these "little ones" (in Mark's world and in ours) and to their fidelity in their powerlessness—e.g., the leper in the 6th Sunday of Ordinary Time, Year B.

[18] Eduard Schweitzer, *The Good News According to Mark* (Atlanta: John Knox Press, 1970).

[19] Matera, *What Are They Saying*, 17; Doohan agrees in *Mark: Visionary*, 66–67, 131–32.

[20] Cf. Ford, *Bonded*, 183.

[21] Willi Marxen, *Mark the Evangelist* (Nashville: Abingdon Press, 1969).

[22] LaVerdiere, unpublished notes.

[23] P. J. Achtemeier, *Mark* (Philadelphia: Fortress Press, 1975), 50.

[24] In a wonderful passage, Robert Farrar Capon contends that Americans crave not the Jesus of the cross but a Super-Jesus wonder-worker who is "faster than a speeding bullet. More powerful than a locomotive. . . ." It's true that "he nearly gets done in for good by the Kryptonite Kross, but at the last moment he struggles into the phone booth of the Empty Tomb, changes into his Easter suit and, with a single bound, leaps back up to the planet Heaven," *Hunting the Divine Fox* (New York: Seabury Press, 1974), 90.

[25] More than Matthew and Luke, however, Mark sees Jesus as preeminently a teacher who struggles to heal the blindness of those around him, cf. Doohan, *Mark: Visionary,* 80–82.

[26] Cf. Schweizer, *The Good News,* 384–85.

[27] That clamoring for upward mobility in the early church gathers steam with Clement of Rome and Ignatius of Antioch, who claimed privileges of power; it climaxes in its most blatant form in Gregory XVI (1831–1846): "No one can deny that the church is an unequal society in which God destined some to be governors and others to be servants. The latter are the laity; the former the clergy"; and in Pius X: "Only the college of pastors has the right and authority to lead and govern. The masses have no right or authority except that of being governed, like an obedient flock that follows its shepherd."

[28] Walter Brueggemann, *The Prophetic Imagination* (Philadelphia: Fortress Press, 1978), 17.

[29] Brueggemann, *The Prophetic Imagination,* 50.

[30] Nine uses of "Son of Man" in Mark are in the context of suffering, humiliation and rejection (8:31; 9:9, 12, 31; 10:33, 45; 14:21 [two times], 41) in the tradition of Isaiah's suffering servant (Isaiah 42:1–4; 49:1–6; 50:4–9; 52:13—53:12), cf. Doohan, *Mark,* 89–92.

[31] Schweizer, *The Gospel,* 385–86.

[32] Frank Matera *What Are They Saying,* 86. For example, Donald Senior comments on the "mirror" that the disabled would bring to Mark's story of the paralytic (2:1–12— 7th Sunday in Ordinary Time, Year B) because of their cultural, social and political experience: "It is a bit amusing to see the discussion of this passage in most commentaries. Inevitably, they note that roofs in ancient Palestine were thatch, . . . thereby explaining the action of the paralytic's friends. But this, of course, is not the point of the story, and is certainly not one a disabled reader would catch. Thatch or not, lowering a stretcher through a hole in the roof is not the ordinary way to enter a house! Yet any disabled person who seeks to be active in church or society can supply lots of stories like this one—entering a church through the sacristy, . . . coming into a lecture hall by means of a freight elevator and then through the kitchen or utility room before being able to join the 'normal' people who come in the front door." ". . . with New Eyes," *Stauros Notebook* 9:2, 1. For further reflections on a literary hearing of scripture, see chapter 5, pages 163–67.

[33] Jack Dean Kingsbury, *Conflict in Mark* (Minneapolis: Fortress Press, 1989); *Matthew as Story* (Philadelphia: Fortress Press, second ed., 1988); *Conflict in Luke* (Minneapolis: Fortress Press, 1991); see also his *The Christology of Mark's Gospel* (Philadelphia: Fortress Press, 1983).

[34] Quoted on the jacket cover of *Binding the Strong Man*. In conversation, Frank Matera recommended Kingsbury to me and strongly disagreed with Wink's assessment of Myers. I consulted seven scripture scholars about Myers and found strong negative and positive evaluations. The most negative claimed that Myers embraces a pacifist ideology and a conflict model of society (admitted to by Myers and explained in his book, e.g., pp. 36–38) that renders his commentary hopelessly flawed and, indeed, gives us a mirror of Myers but then distorts Mark like a funhouse mirror (to use Matera's imagery). Others admit Myers's biases but contend that it is solid scholarship within which we can disassociate ourselves from some of his ideology and conclusions. Donald Senior and others at Catholic Theological Union insist that Myers's work is respectable scholarship and that his approach is clearly pastoral/political, with a passion for "so whats." John Pilch agrees, although he states that Myers and all liberation theologians speak to the political situation present in the South and not in the North (I connect Myers more with ecclesial than political oppression). After much hesitation I have decided to survey Myers's book. Walter Brueggeman deems *Binding the Strong Man* "a splendid book."

[35] Walter Brueggeman *Finally Comes the Poet: Daring Speech for Proclamation* (Minneapolis: Fortress Press, 1989), 2.

[36] Myers, *Binding*, 455–56.

[37] Kingsbury, *Conflict in Mark*, 1.

[38] For problems of world gaps and language gaps when we celebrate the Triduum, see Virgil Funk, "Think Big . . . *Real* Big!" *Pastoral Music* 13 (August/September 1989): 22–24. For attempts to move beyond a biblical, prescientific worldview regarding spirits and demons, see the volumes by Walter Wink: *Naming the Powers* and *Unmasking the Powers* (Philadelphia: Fortress Press, 1986).

[39] Kingsbury, *Conflict in Mark*, 27.

[40] John Pilch, *Introducing the Cultural Context of the New Testament* (New York: Paulist Press, 1991), 11–12.

[41] Although many scholars hold that Mark wrote in Rome *after* the destruction of the Temple, Myers claims that this is no longer the dominant school of thought. He is

convinced by James Wilde and others that Mark wrote in 69 CE, and that he wrote in northern Palestine, the place where he situates Jesus' ministry and the place of protest against a still-existing Temple and religious/political elite, cf. *Binding*, 40–42, 328; also see James A. Wilde, "A Social Description of the Community Reflected in the Gospel of Mark," unpublished doctoral dissertation, Drew University, 1974.

[42] Cf. Myers, *Binding*, table of contents, viii-xv.

[43] Myers, *Binding*, 75; cf. pp. 69–80.

[44] Mark's Jesus is very anticity and prorural. Jesus' ministry as an outsider begins and begins again with the disciples in Galilee, outside the city with its caste system perpetrated by the elite. Jerusalem is the place of oppression and of the ultimate rejection of Jesus and the God he preaches.

[45] Myers, *Binding*, 80.

[46] Cf. Myers, *Binding*, 138.

[47] John Pilch, *Introducing the Cultural Context of the New Testament* (New York: Paulist Press, 1991), 210.

[48] This understanding of the demonic is akin to our contemporary understanding of original sin. That was not one sin committed by one set of parents and passed on biologically to all peoples. It is the cumulative evil and sin committed by every family, community, nation and civilization, which is more than the sum of the parts, and into which children are born and infected with racism, violence, greed and all that divides the human family. These are the real evil spirits and demons within us, more than we could produce by our individual acts of selfishness or pride. We shall return to discuss evil spirits and exorcism and Holy Spirit and grace when we treat the scrutinies in chapter ten.

[49] Perhaps it is significant that the Sunday lectionary omits the exorcism stories from Mark. Are we embarrassed by, ignorant of or afraid of evil spirits in our church and society? I suggest that we might sneak these stories in when homilizing/catechizing on Jesus' other miracles (e.g., Mark 1:40–45, 2:1–12, 5:21–43—6th, 7th and 13th Sunday in Ordinary Time, Year B) or stories of Jesus' conflict with the authorities (e.g., Mark 2:18–22, 2:23—3:6, 3:20–35, 6:1–6—8th, 9th, 10th and 13th Sundays in Ordinary Time, Year B).

[50] Cf. Myers, *Binding*, 227–28.

[51] Cf. Myers, *Binding*, 229–31.

[52] Harrington suggests that there are two parallel series in Mark 6:32—8:36, each having five related events, which situate the two feedings with the loaves and the two crossings of the lake with the struggles to see and understand the new covenant with Gentiles, outcasts and outsiders. cf. *Mark*, 88–118.

[53] I suggested already that Mark's version of these stories of table fellowship are so central to the entire Christian gospel that, although the lectionary turns from Mark to John's story of the loaves and his discourse on the Bread of Life, we should also homilize/catechize from these stories in Mark on those Sundays—17th through 21st Sundays in Order Time, Year B.

[54] Ernest Best, "Following Jesus," *Journal of the Studies of the New Testament, Supplement Series, 4* (Sheffield: University of Sheffield, Department of Biblical Studies, 1981), 101. Doohan adds, "Mark consistently confronts authorities that offer themselves as foundations for the kingdom: the Jewish authorities, the city of Jerusalem and its temple cult, the disciples, Peter, James, and John, and the very family of Jesus. . . . The Marcan attack is only explicable in light of problematic leadership in his own church," Doohan, *Mark: Visionary*, 65–66.

[55] In Mark's time, wives could divorce husbands in the Roman world; in that world, Jesus' call to both wives and husbands to absolute fidelity was also counter-cultural; cf. Eugene LaVerdiere, "The Question of Divorce: In the Roman World, Part III" *Emmanuel* 97 (December 1991): 566–69, 582–84.

[56] LaVerdiere, "The Question," 584.

[57] A cartoon, drawn after the U.S. bishops' pastoral letters on race, peace and the economy, pictures a lonely bishop in a field saying to the pope, "The American flock was right behind me, but then we passed a shopping mall." Larry Wright, *The Detroit News*, 12 March 1989.

[58] Cf. Myers, *Binding*, 294–96, 348–53.

[59] Myers comments that Mark's community was under extreme pressure to take sides in the revolt with the Jewish rebels. Instead, Mark's Jesus calls for nonviolent, non-aligned radicalism. Myers compares that to "villagers today in El Salvador or Angola in areas that seesaw back and forth between guerilla and army control. Even if one has clear sympathies (as Mark did), a refusal to publicly align is regarded as apostasy by both sides." *Binding*, 351–52.

[60] Harrington believes, however, that the Temple is already destroyed and that for Mark this is the first sign that Jesus' coming at the end is near. "The evangelist has left

us in no doubt as to his conviction. The parousia will occur in his lifetime," Harrington, *Mark*, 206. Perhaps Myers's literary reading tells us more about what kind of oppressive "worlds" need to end in our lifetime.

[61] For more adequate commentaries on this final end-time, see several articles in *The Bible Today* 30:1. Regarding Mark, John Carroll concludes: "In the healing and teaching mission of Jesus, demonic forces are routed. The liberating power of God's reign is now at work on the human scene through the Messiah, Son of God. . . . Mark's gospel highlights the perils of faithful discipleship, echoing, I think, the time of testing being experienced by the Marcan church. . . . Pictures of end-time deliverance—with the glorious, triumphant return of Jesus as the central image—reassure Mark's readers and thereby enable continuing faithfulness in mission, no matter what the cost." "The End in the Synoptics," 24–25.

[62] Of that world, Guatemalan exile Julia Esquivel writes:
> What keeps us from sleeping
> is that they have threatened us with resurrection!
> Because at each nightfall,
> though exhausted from the endless inventory
> of killings since 1954,
> yet we continue to love life,
> and do not accept their death!

*Threatened by Resurrection* (Elgin IL: Brethren Press, 1982), 59 ff.

[63] James Robinson, *The Problem of History in Mark* (London: SCM Press, 1957), 52 (emphasis added).

[64] Cf. Myers, *Binding*, 404–9.

[65] Doohan, *Mark: Visionary*, 64, 1. Tom Conry adds that Mark doesn't like anyone, especially Paul with all his preaching of resurrection. "Mark retorts, 'The Romans are crucifying my community, and there is nothing of "Pauline beauty" in my neighborhood. We need not escape into risen life but rather choose fidelity when there is no escape.'" Unpublished workshop presentation.

[66] Cf. Matera, *What Are They Saying*, 46–51, 54–55.

[67] Doohan, *Mark: Visionary*, 4, 5.

[68] Myers, *Binding*, 406.

# CHAPTER NINE

## Conversing with Luke's Story

*Jesus, filled with power of the Spirit, returned to Galilee, and a report about him spread through all the surrounding country. He began to teach in their synagogues and was praised by everyone.*

*When he came to Nazareth, where he had been brought up, he went to the synagogue on the sabbath day, as was his custom. He stood up to read, and the scroll of the prophet Isaiah was given to him. He unrolled the scroll and found the place where it was written:*

> *"The Spirit of the Lord is upon me,*
> > *because he has anointed me*
> > > *to bring good news to the poor.*
> 
> *He has sent me to proclaim release*
> > *to the captives*
> 
> *and recovery of sight to the blind,*
> > *to let the oppressed go free,*
> 
> *to proclaim the year of the Lord's favor."*

*And he rolled up the scroll, gave it back to the attendant and sat down. The eyes of all in the synagogue were fixed on him. Then he began to say to them, "Today this scripture has been fulfilled in your hearing."*

• Luke 4:14–19—3rd Sunday in Ordinary Time, Year C

A HOMILY ON LUKE:[1] Decades ago, Brazil's bishops were so enamored of power and prestige that people claimed that the country would surely reject the church and choose Communism. Twenty years ago, the bishops of that same country took a stance for the poor and began to work with poor people. Today, they lead the largest Roman Catholic church in the world, with over 80,000 small Christian communities that are cells not of Communism but of faith wedded to justice.

There is a film of one of these bishops' meetings that hints at how their hypocrisy changed to hope. The bishops are in small groups telling stories of their ministry. One bishop tells of joining a protest demonstration with workers who were seeking a raise from 25 cents an hour to 28 cents. The police turned the bishop's Volkswagen upside down, beat him nearly to death, stripped him, poured a bucket of red paint over his body and dumped him on a street corner. The people took him in, nursed him back to health, and there he is at the bishops' meeting telling what it means to be anointed, like Jesus by his baptism, to bring good news to the poor. At the end the film shows bishops throwing their duffle bags onto an old bus and driving off down a dusty road. The last frame of the film flashes, "These men are dangerous!"

In the gospel reading today, Jesus leaves no doubt that this man is dangerous. Here in his first homily, his inaugural address, his state of the new union with God, his first toast at the banquet called by his Father, Jesus proclaims what his whole life will be about. He cries, "Here's to you—you poor, you blind, you captives, you oppressed prisoners! The Spirit launches me with good news for you!"[2] In Luke, the Spirit drives Jesus like a tornado with this message.[3] The crowds marvel at his eloquence (4:22).

Then he goes too far. He follows these words with the warning that a prophet is never accepted on his own turf and with the promise that, like the prophets Elijah and Elisha, who ministered to a pagan widow and a leper, his God sends him with this good news to the hated Gentiles.[4] He is not acceptable in his own country because his good news is for all countries. In next Sunday's gospel, the crowds turn on him and try to hurl him off a cliff (4:21–30—4th Sunday in Ordinary Time, Year C). This man is dangerous!

There is worse to come. One out of seven verses in Luke is about riches and poverty. Among the poor and oppressed, Luke includes all the rejects of Israel: tax collectors, sinners, the lame, blind and deaf, prostitutes, shepherds, women, children, the sexually mutilated, Samaritan heretics and Gentile foreigners. Luke uses the same Greek word for "release" and "forgiveness" (1:77; 24:47). In Jesus, God forgives all sin. God wipes the slate clean.

Our modern ears also probably miss the astounding meaning of Jesus' promise of "a year of the Lord's favor." That is the Jewish Jubilee year with fields lying fallow, debts cancelled and slaves freed.[5] "You shall hallow the fiftieth year; you shall proclaim liberty throughout the land to all its inhabitants. . . . The land shall not be sold in perpetuity, for the land is mine. . . . If any of your kin fall into difficulty and become dependent on you, you shall support them; they shall live with you as though resident aliens" (Leviticus 25:8–55).

Nearly 2,000 years after Jesus makes his dangerous promise, it becomes a dangerous doctrine at Vatican II: People "are obliged to come to the relief of the poor, and to do so not merely out of their superfluous goods. . . . This sacred Council urges all, both individuals and governments, to remember the saying . . . 'Feed [those] dying of hunger, because if you have not fed [them] you have killed [them].'"[6] Listen to John Paul II echo those words for us: "It is not enough to draw on the surplus goods which in fact our world abundantly produces; it requires above all a change of life-styles."[7] How does that play in a land where the six percent of the world's population who lives there consumes most of the world's goods and where some revel when a former president complains about "welfare queens."

About the promises of Isaiah, Jesus says, "Today this scripture is fulfilled in your hearing." *Today* means not only that Sabbath in the first century. It means our today, all days in the reign of God, every day in the life of those baptized and anointed by the Spirit. Following what our church calls "a preferential option for the poor," the poor and all outcasts are to be queen and king for a day—today. Encountering the homeless, jobless and penniless people born here, the refugees and immigrants who move here and the victims of appalling poverty and oppression in lands outside here, the church calls us as individuals and as a nation to jubilee days and years with the poor in our state of the union. Popes and bishops have no special expertise in finding ways to improve the current mess and mayhem in welfare systems, educational systems, court systems, immigration systems or any social or political system. Some Christians do, and Luke's Jesus issues a clarion call to them to find a way.

The critical question: Will our "today" end as Jesus' did—with crowds trying to hurl him and his message off a cliff? Is our "today" increasingly marked by burning crosses in front of African American homes, by the mocking and complaining on the part of those whose ancestors had an Irish brogue or a German accent against those who speak Asian languages or Spanish, by scrawling swastikas on synagogues, by charlatans running for political office on platforms of not-too-hidden racism,[8] and by the shredding of what Cardinal Bernardin calls the "seamless garment of life"—by capital punishment, by abortion, by abuse of women and children, by sidelining the handicapped and warehousing the aged? Do we hear talk of justice and charity only for the "worthy" poor? Surely there were unworthy poor, even evidence of children in gangs, in Jesus' day. Perhaps they needed "tough love;"[9] but Jesus doesn't say, "Love and save just the good ones." In Matthew's gospel, Jesus says the poor save us because what we do to the least of his brothers and sisters we do to him. On that we are judged (Matthew 25:31–46— Christ the King, Year A). Who is the "least" in our lives?

I close this homily with a story about another dangerous bishop who also toasted the poor and outsiders. Archbishop Raymond Hunthausen suffered vicious criticism and was examined by the Vatican for supposedly letting too many outsiders into the church—divorced and remarried people, resigned priests, gays. He also was dangerous because he abhorred nuclear weapons and withheld his income tax. But I don't believe anyone objected to his care for George.

George was in his 50s, mentally disabled and a "church mouse" at the Seattle cathedral for years. He especially delighted in photo opportunities with himself and the archbishop. After a church dedication and after the usual photo, George asked Archbishop Hunthausen for a ride home and then invited him into his apartment. They walked into some 25 years' worth of garbage. The owner had finally gotten fed up, and George showed the archbishop his eviction notice. The next Saturday the archbishop and his staff began to clean up the garbage. One of the staff found the archbishop in the bathroom scrubbing off the worst of the filth. She told him that others should do that. He replied that archbishops do bathrooms!

That bishop is dangerous. How dangerous are we? If we take Jesus' toast to the poor and outsiders seriously, might the final frame on our movie read, "These Christians were dangerous!"?

> **Conversation Starter:**   In a psychological/personal hearing of this story from Luke, prepare some questions that might invite catechumens *personally* to enter the story. In a pastoral/theological hearing, prepare questions that might invite the catechumenal and parish *communities* to enter the story.

### Luke—A Storm Center

Theories of interpretation abound regarding Luke's gospel. W. C. van Unnick calls Luke "a storm center" in contemporary biblical scholarship.[10] One author says that he is conservative in his use of his sources,[11] and another calls him creative and highly original.[12] There is a growing consensus that Luke was a literary artist and more an innovative author than a conservative editor. Luke challenges us to be as resilient as he was in adapting his sources to his times.

Although some authors contend that a major concern of Luke was the delay of Jesus' second coming,[13] others find evidence of an imminent end-time in Luke.[14] Most agree that Luke's primary focus is not disappointment about Jesus' delay in coming but the laxity during that delay of a church called to mission to the ends of the earth and to living his prophetic message, forever on the edge.[15] Nineteen centuries later, in a church that also loses the freshness of new wineskins and wraps itself in old churchskins, we need to hear Luke's call to live on the edge.[16]

There is disagreement about whether Luke is writing primarily to assure a Gentile community that they are included in the new covenant,[18] or to affirm that, in Jesus, God was faithful to even those rejected by Israel and will be faithful to all people in Jesus' covenant,[19] or to convince a Jewish community that they have inherited God's promises to Israel.[20] There is, however, a growing consensus that Luke probably wrote between 80 and 85 CE for a mixed community of Gentiles and Jews. His is a message of unity in diversity that might speak to our communities.[21] Although Conzelman claims Luke's "today" of salvation belongs to the memories and promises of the past of Jesus' lifetime and will be available again only in the distant future,[22] most scholars hold that Luke sees Jesus' life as the "time of promise" and the church's life in Acts as the "time of fulfillment" and the "time of salvation.[23] That includes our time and our today.

Opinions on Luke's political stance vary. Some say that Luke defends the church as no political threat to the Empire;[24] others say he writes to defend the Empire to the church[25] or to reassure about the possibility of joint allegiance of Roman Christians to both empire and church.[26] Still others envision Luke's Jesus as a nonviolent political revolutionary who uproots power structures and advocates a new society based on service and humility,[27] as a revolutionary who proclaims a Year of Jubilee for the poor in socio-political terms during his lifetime[28] or as a prophet who proclaims the Jubilee year as a reversal of fortunes not just during his lifetime but at the consummation of God's reign in the future for which the church must strive in the present (which is also our present).[29] Finally, although the majority of Lucan scholars affirm that he shows a special concern for women, who were among the oppressed and excluded in society,[30] some claim that Luke limits the role of women.[31]

Confronted with such polarities, catechists and homilists might feel paralyzed and unable to take a stand. We must choose. In what follows, I generally have chosen the majority opinion or I come down on the side of Luke as a creative artist and Luke's Jesus as a prophet[32] and liberator of the outsiders and as nonviolent disturber of the status quo in his past, our present and God's future.

## Pitfalls in Preaching/Catechizing on Luke[33]

Eugene LaVerdiere, while praising Luke for his vivid imagery, captivating stories (in which the reader often has to supply the conclusion, such as how the elder brother of the prodigal son responds) and perhaps the most elegant style of any gospel author, also notes that these qualities cause problems.[34]

First, Luke tells a story to introduce a theme but only fully develops that theme in a later story. He also asks questions twice. This is Luke's "law of two." For example, there is the story of Jesus' family journeying to Jerusalem for Passover where they lose him and find him again on the third day in his Father's house(2:41–52). That story finds its meaning not in panegyrics about Jesus as a precocious youth but in Jesus' great journey to Jerusalem for his final Passover, not just to the cross (as in Mark) but through the cross to the ascension when he reaches his destiny with the Father(9:51–24:53—13th to 34th Sundays in Ordinary Time, Year C, and the Feast of the Ascension). Homilists/catechists must make that connection between the two journeys to reveal God's presence to Jesus and Jesus' intimacy with God throughout his life.

In another example of Luke's "law of two," Satan's tests of Jesus in the desert differ from those in Matthew. Luke's devil taunts Jesus with the words, "If you are the Son of God . . ." (4:1–13—1st Sunday of Lent, Year C). Luke has Jesus respond not just to Israel's temptations in the desert but to Adam's in the garden because his genealogy (different from that in Matthew) already revealed Jesus as "son of Adam, son of God" (3:23–38). Catechesis might connect those texts and explore how pride is the corrosive power at the heart of every temptation of every man and woman "to be like gods" (Genesis 3:5).

A second problem is with the lectionary itself, which, because Luke's story is so long (a quarter of the Christian Scriptures), omits much of it from the Sunday readings. Because Luke is so tightly constructed, one part often builds on or prepares for another. Given the omissions, some building blocks might be missing from the lectionary readings. I have already insisted that homilists and catechists present reflections not just on an individual text but on that text in the light of both the "big story" of the entire gospel and its place in the lectionary. In Luke's case, the "big story" includes all 52 chapters of both Luke and Acts, which Luke sees as a single, two-volume writing.[35]

Therefore, the catechist during the breaking open of the word might also connect a gospel passage with how it develops. LaVerdiere says, "From a literary, historical and pastoral point of view, the Gospel of Luke looks forward to Acts, and Acts presupposes the gospel."[36] He notes that the mission to the Gentiles dramatically announced in Luke 4:16–30 (3rd and 4th Sundays in Ordinary Time, Year C) is not fully told in the gospel but in Acts. The references to Samaritans in the gospel (9:52–55—13th Sunday in Ordinary Time, Year C; 10:25–37—15th Sunday in Ordinary Time, Year C; 17:11–19—28th Sunday in Ordinary Time, Year C) are not clear until Acts' story of the wonderfully successful evangelization of Samaritans (8:4–25—6th Sunday of Easter, Year A).[37]

Third, LaVerdiere notes that the lectionary omits Luke's introductions, which set the scene for his words. For example, Jesus later preaches what he already has done in 6:18–19 and 14:2–6. He first "works the crowd" of foreigners, outcasts, crippled and diseased, and breaks the law by touching the unclean (making himself unclean) and by healing on the Sabbath (6:18–19 and 14:2–6). Then he toasts them in the beatitudes and curses those who will not toast them (6:17, 20–26—6th Sunday in Ordinary Time, Year C) and promises that the cursed will be blessed only if they eat with all these rejects (14:1, 7–14—22nd Sunday in Ordinary

Time, Year C). By setting those scenes with the introductions that tell what Jesus is doing before he speaks, we can connect Luke's church with ours when we put law before healing or insiders before outsiders.

## Pastorally Hearing Luke's Big Story

Eugene LaVerdiere offers the following outline of Luke's gospel.

Preface: A message to Theophilus (1:1–4)
Prologue: The origins and destiny of Jesus (1:5—2:52)
   A. Origins (1:5—2:40)
      1. Annunciations and visitation (1:5–56)
      2. Births and manifestation (1:57—2:40)
   B. Destiny (2:41–52)

The setting and its challenges (3:1—4:13)
   A. Jesus and the mission of John the Baptist (3:1–22)
   B. Jesus and the history of the human race (3:23–38)
   C. Jesus and humanity's most basic challenges (4:1–13)

Jesus in Galilee (4:14—9:50)
   A. Introduction: Jesus at Nazareth and Capernaum (4:14–44)
   B. The origins of the church in the Galilean ministry of Jesus (5:1—9:50)
      1. The church is called: Jesus and the first disciples (5:1—6:11)
      2. The church is constituted as the new Israel: Jesus and the Twelve (6:12—7:50)
      3. The church is formed: the new Israel prepares for the mission (8:1–56)
      4. The church is sent out on mission: Jesus sends the Twelve to proclaim the gospel (9:50)

On the way to Jerusalem (9:51—24:53)
   A. Introduction: the challenges of the missionary journey to God (9:51—10:37)
   B. The destiny of the church in the journey of Jesus (10:38—24:53)
      1. Beginnings in the villages of Galilee (10:38—13:21)

2. The movement from Galilee to the city of the ascension (13:22 — 19:48)
3. In the Temple of Jerusalem (20:1 — 21:38)
4. The climax of Jesus' exodus: passage to the home of the Father (22:1 — 24:53)[38]

## Hearing Luke's Big Story of Meals

A pressing pastoral/theological issue for Luke is the historical absence of Jesus.[39] He promised to return. He has not returned. Apparently in Luke's community the excitement of that promise was waning. Lethargy and the "back-pew syndrome" were setting in. Luke's response is the Emmaus story, which is the climax of all the meal stories in Luke: Jesus is present at meals, where he breaks bread with the broken.

Therefore, one way to explore Luke's big story is to follow Jesus as he eats his way through Israel on the way to Emmaus. Luke is the gospel of the meals. There are nearly as many meals as miracles. This gospel is like one, long progressive dinner. "Jesus is either going to a meal, at a meal, or coming from a meal. . . . The aroma of food issues forth from each and every chapter of Luke's gospel."[40] Luke uses 45 different words to refer to the motif of food. John Navonne claims that at every major transition in Luke, Jesus is at a meal. No wonder that his enemies malign him as that "glutton and drunkard" (7:34) whom the Hebrew Scriptures said should be stoned (cf. Deuteronomy 21:18–21).

Catholics tend to reduce the meal motif to eucharistic references. Demetrius Dumm broadens our vision: "Luke shows a special sensitivity for table fellowship, not only for its own sake but also because it is a sign of a deeper kind of hospitality that entertains the strange and alien elements in life and looks for good everywhere."[41] These meals are enacted parables that also anticipate the feast in the end-time (cf. 13:28 ff. — 21st Sunday in Ordinary Time, Year C).

Donald Senior claims that Luke gives us a hint of who Jesus is and what he is about when he has Mary wrap Jesus in swaddling clothes and lay him in a manger (2:7 — Christmas Mass at Midnight). David and Solomon were also wrapped in swaddling clothes (cf. Wisdom 7:1–6), and a manger is for food. Luke introduces Jesus as king and as food for the world. We have a new king in the line of David, and he will be a king who revels with us at meals.[42] Jesus also begins his public ministry by fasting in the desert: He is one with those who are hungry (4:1–13—1st Sunday of Lent, Year C). If we go to his meals and see those with whom Jesus eats, we shall find the heart of Luke's big story of covenant/inclusion.

More importantly, we shall find a vision of Jesus' God. "The inclusion of sinners in the community of salvation, achieved in table-fellowship, is the most meaningful expression of the message of the redeeming love of God."[43] The God of Luke's Jesus was on the side of those who had been put outside the law—the poor and the lowly, the people of the land—and so were considered outside God's acceptance, with no religious worth or value.

Jesus proclaimed that loyalty to his God meant accepting these rejects, feeding God's hungry creation and healing the wounds that plague it. God is the chief "actor" throughout Luke/Acts; "God" (*theos*) occurs more frequently even than the name "Jesus"—122 times in the gospel and 166 times in Acts. Jesus' message was about a God who rejoiced to sup with sinners.

That is why his eating with outcasts so angered the religious leaders of his time. If "Luke's story of Jesus is primarily a story of conflict between Jesus and Israel, made up of the religious authorities and the people,"[44] then he never stirred up more conflict than he did by the way he ate. We trivialize meals with fast food, convenience food, junk food and meals on the run. But Jesus and his church knew that meals created a holy bond between host and guest. "To take a meal with another was to offer the right hand of fellowship in the deepest sense of the word."[45] It also meant returning to the heart of the covenant and shattering ritualism and legalism. Therefore, Jesus also violated laws that prescribed hand-washing and forbade healing on the Sabbath at these meals. Jesus is a heretic because of how he eats and with whom he eats. "It was almost as if he were using meals as a weapon."[46]

Luke places these meals at the center of his story apparently because some in Luke's church were still trying to kill Jesus' message.

> The whole question of table fellowship, that is, who might dine with whom, was a matter of deep concern and acrimonious conflict in the early Christian

communities. Especially acute was the question of Jews and Jewish-Christians sharing meals with Gentiles and other purportedly unclean persons. The problem affected the heart of the Christian commitment. *If ordinary meals could not be shared, then neither could the eucharist be shared.*[47]

Therefore, Luke insists in Acts that the good news of Jesus is normative for his church. "Those excluded from life—for whatever reason—become central to the church's administration, ministry activity, resources and energy."[48] What if one criterion for ordination as bishop today were that the person had been ostracized by the official church!

Therefore, lest we kill the message in our church, we must look at Jesus' choice of table companions in Luke's story. He begins at his first public meal in the same way that he ends at his last stop before Jerusalem. He eats with tax collectors—Levi at the beginning (5:27–32) and with Zacchaeus at the end (19:1–10—31st Sunday in Ordinary Time, Year C). The abhorred tax collectors were, on the whole, unjust, violent, often murderous, always unscrupulous. What set them apart from other sinners was their continual contact with Gentiles (defiling in itself); therefore, they were also seen as traitors.[49] Here Jesus rubs elbows, breaks bread and shares table-talk with them.

*Levi's Banquet*   At his very first meal in his public ministry, Jesus infuriates his enemies by crossing the tracks, going to the wrong side of town and not only eating with a traitor who is the host (proscribed because this sinful host might not follow Jewish dietary laws) but also calling this host (Levi—probably Matthew) to intimacy in discipleship. Luke embellishes on the other synoptics and makes this a great banquet— a "large crowd of tax collectors and others" (5:29), perhaps a hundred guests or more. Jeremias and Donahue argue that usually the gospels mean not tax collectors (who gathered land and poll taxes) but toll collectors (who gathered "the myriad of minor taxes, sale taxes, customs taxes, taxes on transport"), who were more deeply hated. The "others" probably included sinners, the ritually unclean (such as prostitutes and people with handicaps) and those ostracized because of their trades, such as shopkeepers, physicians, butchers, dung-collectors, copper-smelters and traders.[50] In the eyes of "proper" Jews, Jesus really went "slumming" at his coming out party by dining with the dregs of society.[51]

*At Simon's House*   Then there is that wretched woman, "known in the town to be a sinner," who crashes the party of Simon (7:36–8:3—11th Sunday in Ordinary Time, Year C).[52] She is appalled by Simon's denial to Jesus of the simplest gestures of Jewish hospitality. After traveling the dusty roads of Palestine, guests left their sandals at the door; it was an insult not to wash the feet of guests. In addition, at the beginning of meals both host and guest were to "pile it on" each other with lavish ritual praise. Clearly, Simon did no such thing.

It was the custom for diners to recline for meals, so the woman stands behind Jesus at his feet, ashamed to approach him face to face. Simon did not anoint him with oil (usually cheap olive oil on the hands) and gave him no kiss. Not performing these actions was a marked sign of contempt. The woman anoints Jesus with expensive perfume; she must have prepared this, knowing where he was. Yet it was unthinkable for a sinful woman to anoint a rabbi as Samuel anointed kings. She spontaneously kisses (the verb used here means "to kiss again and again") and washes his feet with all that she had—her tears. She lets down her hair to dry them, something women did only with their husbands and something the rabbis equated with uncovering the bosom. She risks that Jesus will understand.

Then Jesus tells a parable: "Simon, I have something to say to you" means that Simon should prepare himself to hear some blunt speech. The story tells of two debtors, one forgiven (the verb means "to offer grace") a huge debt and the second a smaller one. Who will be more grateful? Of course, Simon falls into the trap and chooses the one forgiven more. At this meal, that, of course, is the woman.

As we noted in chapter six, many texts have botched the punchline and said, "Because she has loved much, she is forgiven much" (as in the *New American Bible* version). That turns the parable on its head. The point is that the debtor and the woman had already been forgiven.[53] The *New Revised Standard Version* has it right: "I tell you, her sins, which were many, have been forgiven; hence she has shown great love." So does the *Jerusalem Bible*: "I tell you that her sins, her many sins, must have been forgiven her, or she would not have shown such great love." She was forgiven before she washed his feet. Her faith, not her works of love, has saved her. Simon loves little, because he does not know that he needs forgiveness. Therefore, we have two great sinners—one who sins outside the law and is forgiven, and one who sins within the law and doesn't ask forgiveness.

Notice that by telling Simon (and the church) the story, Jesus doesn't write him off. He invites him to be forgiven and to forgive. "The mighty are not really put down from their thrones, but offered forgiveness [cf. 23:34—Passion Sunday, Year C] by the Jesus who lives out his teaching on love of enemies . . ."[54] (6:27–28—8th Sunday in Ordinary Time, Year C). If Pharisees grumbled that Jesus ate with tax collectors and sinners, perhaps tax collectors and sinners groused when he ate with Pharisees and the establishment.[55]

*The Feeding of Five Thousand*    The next meal in Luke (9:10–17) is like the first feeding of the 5,000 with loaves and fish in Mark, which we have already discussed. Luke does not have Mark's second feeding of Jews and Gentiles, men and women, which expands the table fellowship. Luke does link the preaching of the reign of God to giving food to a needy creation (9:11). "A hungry creation mocks God's kingly justice. . . . Disciples are to be involved in this justice ministry of feeding the poor."[56]

Parker Palmer offers some insightful comments on that dimension of this story. He suggests that images of hunger and food—both literal and metaphorical—and scarcity and abundance dominate this feeding of the 5,000. The crowd sought a teacher because it was hungry for truth; it felt a scarcity of truth. Jesus reveals truth's abundance. The disciples were sure that food was scarce. They wanted to send the crowd away to buy food. Jesus instead works a "miracle." The world says, "They buy." Jesus says, "You give."

The disciples operated by the illusions of the world, not by the gospel of truth. They say that time is scarce, our energies are scarce, compassion is scarce, food is scarce. Jesus says, "Give what you have. In God's truth you will find abundance." Nowhere does the story say anything about supernatural intervention. No "wonder bread" multiplies in the fields. Might the miracle be that everyone sees Jesus give thanks for what little he has and then gives it away? They become energized by Jesus' example of generosity and give away what they have in their groups. "The pathway from scarcity to abundance is called community. . . . Do we live in a world where what people seek—from food and shelter to a sense of competence and being loved—is available to all? Or is this a world where such goods and feelings are in short supply, available only to those who succeed in beating everyone else to the 'scarce' resources?"[57] Have we heard Jesus' call to turn people away from the illusion of scarcity created by individualism to the reality of abundance created by compassion and community?

*Martha and Mary*   J. Massyngbaerde Ford calls Jesus' meal with Martha and Mary "the meal of feminine discipleship" (10:38–49—16th Sunday in Ordinary Time, Year C). She refuses to reduce this meal story to a pious recommendation of contemplation over action. Contrary to Jewish practice, which saw women as unclean because of menstruation and, therefore, unfit for religious duties and unable even to witness in court, Jesus insists that women not only serve at table like Martha. Like Mary, they are called to hear Jesus' word and to be disciples. Daniel Harrington agrees that "in a culture in which women did not normally share in intellectual discussion, Jesus' insistence that Mary and Martha be allowed to listen to his teaching would have been surprising."[58]

Ford sees this pericope as part of a theme on women in Luke' writings: The woman sinner performed menial tasks of hospitality at Simon's house; the Galilean women served Jesus directly from their own supplies (8:1–3); the woman's role is not always to serve at table but also to hear and announce (as it develops in Acts) the word of God.[59] Our church still struggles with those developments or lack thereof.

*The Midnight Seeker*   There is an oblique reference to eating in the story of the friend who comes asking bread at midnight (11:5–13—17th Sunday in Ordinary Time, Year C).[60] The parable centers not so much on the brashness of the seeker but on the honor of the giver and on avoiding sham. The hearer cannot imagine that a friend or a father will refuse. How much more can we depend on God!

The seeker arrives at night because a journeyer would travel at night to avoid the heat. In the Middle East when a guest arrives, the host must serve the guest; and the guest must eat, hungry or not. Bread is not the meal but the utensil that is dipped into common dishes; so the Middle

Easterner would know that the seeker wants not only bread but an entire meal. The host must provide that, or the entire village will be disgraced. So he starts his rounds, not just of the one house but of many houses, to get enough food plus the finest table setting. As in chapter 15, the entire community is part of the welcome.

The excuses of bolted door and children sleeping are so unthinkable in that culture that they are funny. Many translations say the giver grants the request because of the persistence of the seeker. More likely, it is because of the honor of the giver. If he did not rise, the story would be all over the village. Although Luke speaks of knocking on doors, the seeker would not knock at all. He would call out so as not to frighten the sleeper. Friends call, strangers knock. This is not about our persistent knocking but about God's persistent grace.

*In the Pharisee's House*    In a sixth meal story (11:37–53), unlike the woes in Matthew 23, Luke's Jesus says, "Woe to you!" ("Shame on you!") at table to the Pharisees and lawyers, thus assuring himself of no return invitation to that house. It's not just that he breaks ritual law by not washing hands, and it's not primarily a story of a young renegade blasting his elders. As at all Jesus' meals, he is taking a positive stance for the poor with whom the Pharisees will not eat and whose food they snatch away through the laws of tithing. The very purpose of tithing was to support the Levites and the poor (cf. Deuteronomy 14:22–29). So Pharisees' hands may be washed, but their hearts are soiled with "greed and wickedness." For example, Jesus thunders against the tithing of mint, rue and herbs of all kinds. The biblical precepts required only tithing large crops such as wheat, barley and vines. Jesus (and the pharisaic school of Hillel before him) critiques the tithing of vegetables and herbs, because small landholders could not possibly give a tenth of their gardens. Like God, Jesus honors the powerless and shames these elite ones. After the meal, his enemies begin to contrive challenges to shame him.

*The Humble and the Exalted*    At a seventh meal in Luke's gospel, Jesus teaches the first-place-saving and poor-excluding church how to eat (14:1–14—22nd Sunday in Ordinary Time, Year C and 14:16–30). First, he assaults legalism by healing a man on the Sabbath. Then he castigates religious leaders for grabbing places of honor and turning meals that praise God for food into banquets of self-praise. The Qumran community, for example, had become very disciplinarian and hierarchical. Their rule read: "Let each man sit according to his rank. Let the priests sit in the first [place], and the elders in the second, and then the rest of all the people; let them sit according to their ranks."[61] Jesus attacks such a divisive pecking order.

Then Jesus charges them to change their guest roster from the "good old boys and girls" to outcasts and rejects: "the poor, the crippled, the lame and the blind." This was another assault on the rules of Qumran, which barred such riffraff from their presence.[62] Does that assault our exclusive clubs or the red-lining in our neighborhoods or even the exclusion of women from some sanctuaries?

**The Parable of the Great Banquet**    Next Jesus says, "Let me tell you a story." Crossan includes this story of the great banquet in his "parables of reversal"—the Good Samaritan, the Rich Man and Lazarus, to name two. "When the North Pole becomes the South Pole, a world is reversed and overturned and we find ourselves standing firm on utter uncertainty."[63] In contemporary language, the story is about God

> the eccentric host who, when the country-club crowd all turn out to have other things more important to do than come live it up with him, goes out into the skid rows and soup kitchens and charity wards and brings home a freak show. The man with no legs who sells shoelaces at the corner. The old woman in the moth-eaten fur coat who makes her daily rounds of garbage cans. The old wino with his pint in a brown paper bag. . . . They are seated at the damask-laid table in the great hall. The candles are all lit and the champagne glasses filled. At a sign from the host, the musicians in the gallery strike up "Amazing Grace." If you have to explain it, don't bother.[64]

From a scriptural viewpoint, Kenneth Bailey comments that Mediterranean etiquette demanded that invitations to the banquet would have gone out early and that the last-minute excuses are blatant lies. In that culture, to buy a piece of land without seeing it or to buy oxen without trying them would be like someone in our culture buying the Brooklyn Bridge or buying a Cadillac without test-driving it. Also, no one would have scheduled a wedding (another great social event) after having been invited to this great man's banquet.[65]

Note that the servant goes first goes into the "[large] streets and [narrow] lanes of the city" to bring in precisely those excluded by Qumran—"the poor, the crippled, the blind, and the lame."[66]

The servant then goes beyond the city—that is, "outside the theocracy . . . to those who travel along the world's great highway, or who have fallen down weary, and rest by its hedges; into the busy, or else weary, heathen world."[67] The servant is out there in Gentile and Samaritan territory, out there on Interstate 90. Who knows what kind of rabble will show up at the party—maybe despised Gentiles and heretical Samaritans! Luke uses the word "compel"—"Compel people to come in." In that culture, if people received an invitation to a meal at the last minute, they were to protest their unworthiness for 15 or 20 minutes. Luke uses the same verb when the disciples compel Jesus to eat with them in the Emmaus story. In the gospel of Luke, we have a compelling God who compels outcasts and rejects to come in. Luke's church and our church often choke on such amazing grace.[68]

***Finding the Lost***   Chapter 15 begins with religious leaders grumbling about Jesus "who welcomes sinners and eats with them" (15:1–3; cf. also 5:30 and 7:34–35).[69] That context is key. It sets the stage for three of Jesus' great stories about a lost sheep found, a lost coin found and a lost child found—all of which end with a party and a meal (15:1–32—24th Sunday in Ordinary Time, Year C). These are not stories about private reconciliations—for example, between parents and children. Each story ends with a call to the community to rejoice that the lost are found. Luke's Jesus says, "Church, stop grumbling. Rejoice. Welcome them home. Start partying. Eat as I do. Eat as my God eats." Jesus' God is the real prodigal who breaks all the rules of table fellowship.

First, there is the shepherd searching for the lost sheep. Although the Bible calls Moses and kings "shepherds," in the first century they were considered unclean. Jesus uses a person who is unclean as an image of God. The communal sense of shepherding may be lost on our modern, individualistic ears. Anyone having 100 sheep would either hire a shepherd or else the shepherd would be a member of an extended family, so any loss is a loss to all of them. The community should feel the hurt. The sinner is lost to the community, and the God of Jesus expects not grumbling but a community party when the lost is found.

The shepherd rejoices twice, once when he finds the sheep and again with the community. Sheep are dumb. A lost sheep will lie down and refuse to budge. The shepherd is forced to pick the dumb thing up and carry it over a long distance through the wilderness, yet this shepherd rejoices in the burden of restoration still before him. The God of Jesus Christ rejoices at the burden of restoring and healing sinners. Note also that the sheep does nothing to prompt the shepherd to begin the search except to get lost. The rabbis of Jesus' time and the church of our time demand repentance as a precondition for God's offer of grace. Here there are no conditions. Grace makes repentance possible. The grace *is* life in the community.

Second, there is the woman scurrying around searching for the lost coin. First, the proscribed shepherd and now an inferior, unclean woman are offered as images of God. This is too much to take! Some claim the coin was the woman's dowry, a terrible loss indeed. Bedouin women wear their dowry in the form of coins on their veils, but village women do not. They wear coins on necklaces, and to lose one coin is to destroy the beauty of the necklace as a whole. The whole—the community—suffers over the loss of one. So, when the woman finds the coin, she throws a community party.

Third, there is the father searching the road for the return of his lost son. There is no law or custom among Jews or Arabs entitling sons to share the father's wealth while the father is still alive. The son really is asking for the father's death. The shepherd and the woman did the expected. This father did what had not been done by any father. Any Jew who lost property to Gentiles would be cut off from the entire community, not just from the parent. Property is part of one's identity. The son lost his identity. Also, the polite way to get rid of unwanted moochers is to assign a task they will refuse. By not refusing to herd pigs, the son also became unclean.

The son does not come home because of genuine repentance or conversion.[70] He simply comes to the end of his rope and slinks back hoping for three square meals a day. Most workers were either unfree bondsmen or slaves. He wants to come back as a hired servant who would live free and clean (in all his uncleanness).

To assure the community's acceptance of this traitor, the nobleman father runs down the road. He humiliates himself and runs the gauntlet for the boy in front of everyone. The father's kiss prevents the boy from kissing his hands or feet. A sign of reconciliation was a kiss from the leading men of the town, and here the verb used means "to kiss again and again." Finally the boy accepts sonship, accepts being found—a new relationship, a conversion and not just a ploy for money and food.

The father commands the servants to dress the son as servants do a king. The best robe is the father's. The ring is a signet ring, which means he is trusted. The shoes are a sign of his being a free man in the house. Now he is dressed for the party. Because there were no refrigerators in the first century, the father had to invite the whole community to eat the fatted calf in one sitting, over a hundred people. There is reconciliation with the community. Once again, the message is pure grace and community grace. If a dissolute offspring today signs away the family's life on Visa or MasterCard, most parents would ground the kid for a month, take away the car keys and sell the stereo. This addle-pated old fool is just waiting to run stumbling down the road, embrace the kid, clothe him in finery, ring his finger and throw a party for the whole town with prime rib at Antoine's of Galilee!

Luke's Jesus tells this story because the religious leaders were grumbling and questioning, just like the older brother in the story, about how he ate with outcasts and sinners. Yet the father offers the same acceptance and grace to the older son who humiliates his father by arguing in front of the guests. He should publicly welcome his brother. That reveals that his relationship with the father was already bitter and broken. We have an honorable sinner and a hypocritical saint (like the woman and Simon in 7:36—8:3; 11th Sunday in Ordinary Time, Year C). Jesus presses the Pharisees to see themselves as the older son who is as lost as the younger son had been. We don't know the older son's response. We do know the Pharisees' answer.

In the story, if the older son continues to prove his brother rebellious, the latter could be killed. Instead, Luke tells a story of a prodigal son who wishes his father dead in the beginning of the story, and a father who brings his dead son back to life at the end of the story.

**In the Home of Zacchaeus**  In a twelfth meal story, Luke's Jesus again eats with a tax collector, this time at his last meal before the Last Supper (19:1–10—31st Sunday in Ordinary Time, Year C). The story begins with

Zacchaeus seeking to see Jesus, and it ends with Jesus saying that "the Son of Man came to seek and to save the lost." The seeker doesn't know that he is being sought.

At a meal in Jesus' culture, the one honored is the host when a guest comes to table. Yet this guest defiles himself in this home of the unclean and makes himself ritually impure just before entering Jerusalem, where purity was required to worship in the Temple. Jesus shatters rules about ritual purity to bring unconditional grace and acceptance to this man and his family.

Jesus says, "Today salvation has come to this house." Salvation comes because this wretched tax collector accepts Jesus the prophet with gracious hospitality,[71] and also because he gives half his possessions to the poor. For a chief tax collector that is a tidy sum, and the verb used means "to give often"—a repeated, customary practice. If he makes a profit from a shady practice, he pays it back at the maximum demanded by the Torah. Jesus accepts this despised tax collector as another child of Abraham who, like the indigent, crippled woman (13:16) and the wretched Lazarus (16:19–31—26th Sunday in Ordinary Time, Year C), is an heir of the promise.

Luke Timothy Johnson claims that Luke clearly intends a contrast between Zacchaeus and the rich man in 18:18–23. Both men were powerful, both wealthy. The first kept all the commandments and was considered righteous, but he could not do the "one thing remaining"— to hand over his life to the prophet and to signal that by selling his possessions and giving to the poor. Zacchaeus was considered a sinner, but he eagerly accepted the prophet "with joy" and regularly gave to the poor. Everything about the ruler said piety, but he was closed to the call of the prophet. Everything about the tax agent said corruption, but he is righteous and "a child of Abraham."[72]

Again, the leaders grumble: "He has gone to a sinner's house as a guest." Therefore, they get ready to arrest him after his final meal—his Last Supper, when Judas breaks the most basic rule of conduct by betraying a person with whom one breaks bread.

**The Last Supper**   At that Last Supper in Jerusalem, which should be seen as the last in a sequence of meals (22:14–38—Passion Sunday, Year C), "the center of gravity lies not in the words of institution, but as at earlier tables, in the four key dialogues between Jesus and the disciples."[73] In those dialogues, Jesus commands his followers to eat as he did: "Do this in remembrance of me." What is *this*? *This* is his body broken and the new covenant in his blood shed for the life of the world. But *this* did not begin at the Last Supper. It began at all those other meals.[74] "A meal in memory of Jesus is one which celebrates and prolongs his life-style of justice and of serving the Father's food to all."[75]

Quentin Quesnell and J. Massyngbaerde Ford argue that this last meal was like all those others—shared by not just the Twelve but teeming with great numbers of marginalized men and women, all those outcasts and rejects who were his camp followers. That is why Luke includes teachings about humility and service (22:24–28) recorded earlier in Matthew 20:20–28 and Mark 10:35–45 (29th Sunday in Ordinary Time, Year B). Disciples are to serve at meals as Jesus served. Luke also does not speak about the Twelve sitting on twelve thrones to judge Israel as Matthew does (19:28). "You"—addressing all assembled—will sit on those eschatological thrones. Ford contends that this means discipleship is not confined to the Twelve and not restricted to Jews.[76]

Robert Karris says that when Jesus actually gives his life on the cross for all those with whom he ate, his conversation with the dying criminal (23:40–43—Passion Sunday, Year C)—unique to Luke and which some call the "gospel within the gospel"—is the narrative high point of the gospel. Even here, there is reference to food when Jesus promises, "Today you will be with me in paradise." Paradise conjures up themes of food, New Adam and righteous ones; its gifts are fruits of the tree of life, water and bread of life, banquet of salvation and fellowship with God.[77]

*Emmaus* In Luke there is the story of another meal with another church. It is a long story, "an emotionally satisfying bridge between the shock of absence (the tomb) and the shock of full presence (the appearance to the community in Jerusalem)."[78] The great resurrection story in Luke is not the empty tomb but the story of Jesus who still walks with disciples on the road to Emmaus (and Adelaide, Anaheim, Johannesburg, Pittsburgh, St. Petersburg, São Paulo and San Francisco). He still asks us to remember Moses and all the prophets who proclaim a God who feeds runaway captive Israelites in the desert and all the rejects, strangers and foreigners on holy mountains (cf. Isaiah 25:6–10—28th

Sunday in Ordinary Time, Year A). Jesus calls that church to eat as he did. For eating like that, Jesus and the prophets before him and after him will be killed.

Why Emmaus? "It is typical of Luke that Emmaus, a place which is nowhere in particular, should be lit up with marvelous significance; Nazareth was like that too."[79] This Jesus begins and ends by identifying with all those from "Nowheresville." Who are the two disciples? Some suggest it is Cleopas and his wife. Who is the stranger? Yes, it is the risen Christ; but in Luke's time and in ours, it is the Risen One present through the Spirit in the community. Luke is saying that unless we welcome the stranger, we shall miss the presence of the risen Christ. Like these disciples and like Abraham and Sarah, we enter God's presence and promise when we welcome strangers with hospitality (Genesis 18:1–15).

What is the meaning of "hearts burning within us?" Thomas Rosica says that the Greek text uses a present passive participle, which means a gradual warming of the heart as Jesus spoke to them. Their hearts and ours are at times "veiled, blinded, terrified, heavy, destroyed. . . . The journey motif of this passage is not only a matter of the distance between Jerusalem and Emmaus but also of the painful and gradual journey of words that must descend from the head to the heart; of a coming to faith."[80] After hearing the stories of Moses and all the prophets (on the road and during the liturgy of the word), we come to faith and to an understanding of the whole history of salvation in a totally new way. Then these disciples at table and we disciples—not only at the liturgy of the eucharist but at all our meals and when proclaiming all of Jesus' meals in scripture—might recognize the Lord not just in bread but in broken bread: in our shared brokenness, in our lives broken and given for the life of the world.

Rosica also suggests that we read the Emmaus episode in light of the opening scene of Jesus' ministry in Nazareth (see the homily at the beginning of this chapter). It is a contrast between Jesus the failed evangelist and Jesus the successful evangelist. At Nazareth, the crowd tries to get rid of one of their own. Jesus is defeated, unheeded, unwelcomed. At Emmaus, he is vindicated. Emmaus continues the pursuit of wayward disciples by the shepherd of chapter 15. The theme of the rejected prophet does not trumpet an unredeemable human nature but "the dauntless persistence of the divine will to forgive."[81] Jesus continues to eat with tax collectors and sinners in the persons of these disciples without faith. On the road, they come to experience the meaning of a suffering messiah. They could not have done so without experiencing the meaning of the Hebrew Scriptures and the stories of prophets called and rejected. At table they experience the presence of the risen one in their shared brokenness. The Emmaus story reveals that the resurrection must be first an experience in the heart.

The story tells not only why Jesus had to suffer. It also tells why disciples will suffer, and thus it serves as a bridge between the gospel and Acts. Disciples then and now will suffer, but God in the end will triumph. Luke transforms a traditional recognition story of the risen Lord into a blueprint for Christian mission.[82] Luke's pressing pastoral/theological question (and ours) is Where is Jesus now? Why has he not come as he promised? We are getting tired (and lethargic) waiting. The answer: He is where he always has been—at meals, eating with the broken.[83] For us, he is really present in the scriptures (in the stories) and in the eucharist (in the breaking of the bread).

Luke's final meal story (24:36–49—3rd Sunday of Easter, Year B) has Jesus appearing to and eating with the disciples in Jerusalem just before his ascension. Emmaus stressed the elusiveness of Jesus' presence by his disappearing. This meal stresses the other side: Jesus is not a ghost but a real person. Yet this is resurrection to new life and a new way of being (the Risen One present throughout creation and to all people in all ages), not resuscitation of Jesus as he had been (Jesus of Nazareth in first-century Palestine). In the presence of this Risen One, the disciples are both terrified and joyful. When Jesus speaks, it is not as "when he was with them." He is the commanding, risen Savior, and they worship him. However, as at Emmaus, which showed how Moses and the prophets foretold and interpreted the suffering and resurrection of the messiah, now that same suffering and resurrection give hindsight and interpret both the words of Jesus and the whole of the law, the prophets and the writings. If disciples are to be "ministers of the word" (Luke 1:2), then and now they must experience the dying and rising of Jesus in the word and in the breaking of the bread through the gift of the Spirit, the "power from on high."[84]

## Endnotes

[1] A homiletic suggestion: To involve the assembly in the homily as worship, the homilist might periodically invite the assembly into sung response, in this instance, for example, "The Lord hears the cry of the poor . . . ," by John Foley (Phoenix: North American Liturgy Resources).

[2] For reflections on the beatitudes in Matthew, see chapter 7, page 212. Jacques Dupont: "Christians must hold not that poverty is an ideal but that the poor must be made the object of a completely special love; in this way we share the feelings which God has for them." "The Poor and Poverty in the Gospels and Acts," *Gospel Poverty: Essays in Biblical Theology* (Chicago: Franciscan Herald, 1977), 41.

[3] Luke uses "spirit" (*ruah, pneuma,* the breath of God) 48 times.

[4] Luke 4:27 connects to Acts 10–11. Elisha cleanses Naaman, a Gentile commander; Peter makes clean Cornelius, also a Gentile commander. Luke uses the stories of Elijah and the widow and of Elisha and Naaman as prophecies of God's inclusion of Gentiles. The homily/catechesis might refer back to these stories of covenant with and inclusion of outsiders. Luke's use of the Greek version of the Hebrew scriptures "was dominated by Jewish-Gentile relations, and his attempt to resolve the problem strives toward the view that in spite of the rejection at Nazareth, the destiny of both Jews and Gentiles is bound up with Jesus Christ." Judette Kolasny, "An Example of Rhetorical Criticism: Luke 4:16–30," in *New Views on Luke and Acts*, ed. Earl Richard (Collegeville: The Liturgical Press, 1990), 71; also see Thomas Brodie, "Luke-Acts as an Imitation and Emulation of the Elijah-Elisha Narrative," 78–85 in the same volume.

[5] Here I follow Robert Karris, "The Gospel According to Luke," in *The New Jerome Biblical Commentary* (Englewood Cliffs NJ: Prentice Hall, 1990), 690; J. Massyngbaerde Ford, *My Enemy Is My Guest* (Maryknoll NY: Orbis Books, 1984), 55–56; and Jack Dean Kingsbury, *Conflict in Luke* (Minneapolis: Fortress Press, 1991), 45. Luke Timothy Johnson agrees that this is possible but not supported by the rest of the gospel: "Rather than picturing Jesus' work in terms of a political or economic reform, Luke portrays his liberating work in terms of personal exorcisms, healings, and the teaching of the people." *Sacra Pagina: The Gospel of Luke* (Collegeville: The Liturgical Press, 1991), 81. Later I shall follow those who contend that Luke does have a political dimension.

[6] *Constitution on the Church in the Modern World*, #69. In that same paragraph the Council, citing St. Thomas Aquinas, also states: "If [anyone] is in extreme necessity, [they] have the right to take from the riches of others what [they] need." That should

provide fodder for much discussion during the catechetical session. What if church leaders took that sentence with the same seriousness and urgency that they take Vatican pronouncements on sexuality or artificial contraception?

[7] "On the Hundredth Anniversary of *Rerum Novarum*," #58.

[8] If you think that the threat is from just a few extremists, consider that 52 percent of the Catholic voters in Louisiana voted for "ex-"Klansman David Duke for governor in 1991.

[9] Cf. George Will, "A Sterner Kind of Caring," *Newsweek*, 13 January 1992, 68.

[10] "Luke-Acts, A Storm Center in Contemporary Scholarship," in *Studies in Luke-Acts*, ed. Leander Keck and J. Louis Martyn (Philadelphia: Fortress Press, 1980).

[11] I. H. Marshall, *Luke: Historian and Theologian* (Grand Rapids: Zondervan, 1970).

[12] Robert Tannehill, *The Narrative Unity of Luke-Acts, Foundations and Facets* (Philadelphia: Fortress Press, 1986).

[13] Hans Conzelman, *The Theology of St. Luke* (London: Faber and Faber, 1960).

[14] A. J. Mattill, *Luke and the Last Things* (Dillsboro NC: Western North Carolina Press, 1979).

[15] Mark Allen Powell, *What Are They Saying About Luke?* (New York: Paulist Press, 1987), 44–45; John Carroll, "The End in the Synoptics," *The Bible Today* 30 (January 1992): 27.

[16] "Out on the edge you see all kinds of things you can't see from the center. . . . Big, undreamed of things—the people on the edge see them first." Kurt Vonnegut, *Player Piano* (New York: Delacorte Press, 1952), 73.

[17] J. Jeremias, *The Parables of Jesus* (London: SCM Press, 1963); also see Kenneth Bailey, *Poet and Peasant and Through Peasant Eyes* (Grand Rapids: Wm. B. Eerdmans, combined edition 1983), 22–32.

[18] Robert Maddox, *The Purpose of Luke-Acts* (Edinburgh: T & T Clark, 1985).

[19] Johnson, *Sacra Pagina: The Gospel of Luke*, 16.

[20] Jacob Jervell, *Luke and the People of God* (Minneapolis: Fortress Press, 1972).

[21] Powell, *What Are They Saying*, 59.

[22] Conzelman, *The Theology of St. Luke*.

[23] Powell, *What Are They Saying*, 81.

[24] Conzelman, *The Theology of St. Luke*.

[25] Paul Walaskay, "And So We Came to Rome," *The Political Perspective of St. Luke* (Cambridge: Cambridge University Press, 1983).

[26] Philip Exler, *Community and Gospel in Luke-Acts* (Cambridge: Cambridge University Press, 1987).

[27] Richard J. Cassidy, *Jesus, Politics and Society* (Maryknoll NY: Orbis Books, 1978).

[28] Andre Trocme, *Jesus and the Non-Violent Revolution* (Scottsdale PA: Herald Press, 1973); and John Howard Yoder, *The Politics of Jesus* (Grand Rapids: Wm. B. Eerdmans, 1972).

[29] Robert Sloan, *The Favorable Year of the Lord* (Austin: Schola Press, 1977).

[30] E.g., Jane Kopas, "Jesus and Women: Luke's Gospel," *Theology Today* 42:192–202; and Rosalie Ryan, "The Women from Galilee and Discipleship in Luke," *Biblical Theology Bulletin* 15:56–59.

[31] Elizabeth Tetlow, *Women and Ministry in the New Testament* (New York: Paulist Press, 1980); and Elisabeth Schüssler Fiorenza, *In Memory of Her* (New York: Crossroad Publishing Co., 1987).

[32] "The most distinctive feature in Luke's presentation is his emphasis on Jesus as a prophet, foreshadowed by the Hebrew prophets, fulfilling the prophetic tradition, rejected like prophets before him, murdered in a martyr's death with his life given for the poor and oppressed, but risen to share the prophetic Good News of the God who brings life from death." Daniel Harrington, *Luke: An Access Guide for Scripture Study* (New York: Wm. H. Sadlier, Inc., 1983), 14.

[33] In some of what follows, I am indebted to Leonard Doohan and Tom Conry who offered this unpublished material at Forum workshops.

[34] Eugene LaVerdiere, "Preaching 86: The Gospel of Luke," *Church* 1 (Winter 1985): 3–4.

[35] Cf. Johnson, *Sacra Pagina: The Gospel of Luke*, 1.

[36] LaVerdiere, "Preaching 86," 3.

[37] For other examples, cf. Johnson, *Sacra Pagina: The Gospel of Luke*, 14.

[38] LaVerdiere, "Preaching 86," 5.

[39] Robert Karris adds, "In brief, Luke, the pastoral theologian, is addressing situations of persecution, rich and poor, and continued mission to the Jews." *Luke: Artist and Theologian* (New York: Paulist Press, 1985), 3.

[40] Karris, *Luke*, 47; Karris cites references to food in every chapter of Luke on pages 49–51. Vincent Donovan comments on how far our church distanced itself from Jesus' way of eating: "Modern popes up until John XXIII did not allow anyone to eat with them, an astonishing interpretation of Jesus of Nazareth, who seemed always to be eating with others," *The Church in the Midst of Creation* (Maryknoll NY: Orbis Books, 1989), 91.

[41] "Luke 24:44–49 and Hospitality," in *Sin, Salvation and the Spirit*, ed. Daniel Durken (Collegeville: The Liturgical Press, 1979), 238 (cf. 3rd Sunday of Easter, Year B).

[42] The quotes from Navonne and Senior are from unpublished presentations.

[43] J. Jeremias, *New Testament Theology* (New York: Charles Scribner's Sons, 1971), 115 ff.

[44] Kingsbury, *Conflict in Luke*, 71.

[45] J. Massyngbaerde Ford, *Bonded with the Immortal* (Wilmington: Michael Glazier, Inc., 1987), 280.

[46] Paul Bernier, "Eucharist: Meal or Sacrifice?" *Emmanuel* (March 1992): 69.

[47] Ford, *Bonded*, 281.

[48] Donald Senior, unpublished notes.

[49] Cf. Ford, *My Enemy*, 72.

[50] Cf. John Donahue, "Tax Collectors and Sinners," *Catholic Biblical Quarterly* 33:39–61; J. Jeremias, *Jerusalem in the Time of Jesus* (London: 1969), 307; Ford, *My Enemy*, 65–78.

[51] Later Jesus will praise not the Pharisee but the tax collector in the parable of two men praying, the first "trusted in himself" and the second surrendered to healing grace. The story is less about our humility than about God's unconditional, graceful love. At the end of the journey narrative in Luke, who was found faithful to that love when the Son of Man came? A tax collector! (18:9–14 — 30th Sunday in Ordinary Time, Year C); cf. Ford, *My Enemy*, 74–76.

[52] Most of the following commentary comes from Bailey, *Poet and Peasant and Through Peasant Eyes*, 1–21. I highly recommend this book which treats all the parables of Luke.

[53] There was much argument among the rabbis about whether repentance must precede forgiveness or if forgiveness made repentance possible. Jesus apparently comes down on the side of acceptance and forgiveness. Cf. Bailey, *Poet and Peasant*, 169–87. If in the Catholic tradition grace is mediated in the Spirit-filled community, how could morality and repentance be possible if we excluded people from grace and acceptance in that community?

[54] Karris, *Luke*, 6.

[55] Do we know that this woman "went in peace and sinned no more"? Bishop Kenneth Untener contends that some scholars believe that the adulterous woman hauled before those "perfect gentlemen" to be stoned in John (8:1–11 — 5th Sunday of Lent, Year C) originally was this same woman and that the story was originally in Luke's gospel. Once again, forgiveness was too much good news for the early church, and the story was dropped from Luke in manuscripts in both East and West. Bless her heart! She sneaked her way back into John. "A Church Remarkable for Tenderness and Mercy," *Origins* 16:47.

[56] Karris, *Luke*, 56.

[57] Parker Palmer, "Scarcity, Abundance, and the Gift of the Community," *Occasional Papers* available from Community Renewal Press, 332 Michigan Avenue, Chicago IL 60604.

[58] Harrington, *Luke*, 92. Dennis Sweetland adds that in first-century Israel, where women were among society's marginalized, in Luke-Acts "stories about a man are frequently paralleled by stories about a woman"; the gospel and discipleship are "available to all without regard to gender." "Luke the Christian," in *New Views*, ed. Earl Richard, 60–61.

[59] Ford, *Bonded*, 283.

[60] Cf. Bailey, *Poet and Peasant*, 119–33.

[61] *1 Q S The Rule of the Community* 6:8–9.

[62] *1 Q S The Rule of the Community* 2:3–9.

[63] John Dominic Crossan, *In Parables: The Challenge of the Historical Jesus* (New York: Harper & Row, 1973), 62–66.

[64] Frederick Buechner, *Telling the Truth* (New York: Harper & Row, 1977), 66.

[65] J. Massyngbaerde Ford gives a different interpretation. The Mishnah (*Sotah* 8:1–7) and the *Gospel of Thomas* offer similar excuses for dispensation from service in a war but not for a religious, holy war. She suggests that Jesus is saying, "You waved these dispensations in your holy war but you offer them as excuses when an invitation to the (nonviolent) banquet of the kingdom of God is offered to you." *My Enemy*, 104.

[66] There is also evidence that the Greco-Roman society had a prejudice against the handicapped and that the state took care of only those who were maimed in battle. Cf. W. den Boer, *Private Morality in Greece and Rome* (Leiden: Brill, 1979), 132.

[67] A. Edersheim, *The Life and Times of Jesus the Messiah* (Grand Rapids: Wm. B. Eerdmans, 1947), 440–41.

[68] Bailey, *Poet and Peasant*, 88–113. This story does not appear in the lectionary in Year C, but Matthew's version does in Year A (22:1–14 — 28th Sunday in Ordinary Time, Year A). Preaching and catechesis will attend to some particular concerns of Matthew and also share some of these perspectives from Luke.

[69] Once again, in interpreting these stories I am generally following Bailey, *Poet and Peasant*, 142–206.

[70] Bernard Brandon Scott disagrees with Bailey that Jesus comes down on the side of those who put acceptance before repentance in the sense of moral change. There is "first a motion of sinners toward God, which involves hearing and repentance, and then their reception, signaled by eating." He claims the classic example is this son. *Hear Then the Parable* (Minneapolis: Fortress Press), 308–9.

I find Bailey more convincing, since before the eating, the Father accepts the not-yet repentant son, which makes his genuine repentance possible. In all these meal stories, the God of Jesus loves those who are still outcasts, unclean and sinners. Indeed, 1 John calls us to confess our sins and not to live in sin; but God first loved us as sinners by sending his son to make forgiveness and repentance possible (cf. 1 John 4:9–10).

[71] This unclean tax collector, distanced from Jesus by his trade and also distanced "up a tree," is like the Gentile centurion in Luke 7:10 (9th Sunday in Ordinary Time, Year C) who is distanced by never appearing in the story. He believes that Jesus can heal from afar, not just the physical distance from his servant, but *across the ethnic boundaries maintained by Judaism.* Marion Soards, "The Historical and Cultural Setting of Luke-Acts," in *New Views*, ed. Earl Richard, 40. What boundaries do we need to cross with our new immigrants and refugees?

[72] Johnson, *The Gospel of Luke*, 287.

[73] "Some Glimpses of Luke's Sacramental Theology," *Worship* 44.

[74] Note that John does not have this command to remember. John does have the command to wash feet (13:1–15 — Holy Thursday). He assumes that disciples will do what Jesus did at every meal—humbly serve all those broken people for whom he breaks his body and sheds his blood. Cf. Xavier Leon-Dufour, *Sharing the Eucharistic Bread: The Witness of the New Testament* (New York: Paulist Press, 1987), 281–99.

[75] Karris, *Luke*, 68.

[76] Quentin Quesnell, "The Women at Luke's Supper," in R. J. Cassidy and P. J. Scharper, *Political Issues in Luke-Acts* (Maryknoll NY: Orbis Books, 1983), 59–79; Ford, *Bonded*, 286–87.

[77] Karris, *Luke*, 102; Karris's book is subtitled, *Luke's Passion Account as Literature*, and offers background and commentary on this gospel of Passion Sunday in Year C, especially how Jesus' meals bring him to the cross.

[78] Johnson, *The Gospel*, 398.

[79] Thomas Rosica, "In Search of Jesus: The Emmaus Lesson," *Church* (Spring 1992): 22.

[80] Rosica, "In Search," 24, 25.

[81] Richard Dillon, "Easter Revelation and Mission Program in Luke 24:46–48" (3rd Sunday of Easter, Year B) in *Sin, Salvation*, ed. Daniel Durken, 250.

[82] Luke Timothy Johnson suggests that "the sequence most resembling the present one [Emmaus] is the story of Cornelius' conversion and how that becomes the basis

for a community decision, in Acts 10–15. In those chapters, Luke intertwines experience and narration by several characters, moving progressively and dramatically toward the creation of a community narrative that is the basis for discernment," *The Gospel*, 398–99.

[83] Luke retains some sayings about an imminent judgment but downplays an imminent coming for pastoral concerns. "Luke's shift of emphasis results in the reader focusing more on the presence of Jesus, the risen Lord, and less on his future return, more on Jesus' life and ministry as a guide for Christian conduct and less on the motivating force of an imminent judgment." Sweetland, "Luke," in *New Views*, ed. Earl Richard, 55. Obviously, these are our pastoral concerns.

[84] Cf. Johnson, *The Gospel*, 400–406.

# CHAPTER TEN

## A Brief Conversation with John

*In John's gospel there is no eucharist, no words of institution. In fact, the only dipping of a morsel of any kind is that of Judas, who does it on the way out the door to betray Jesus. At this very point, John reports that Satan entered Judas (13:27). . . . It is not accidental that in place of the eucharist John focuses on the washing of the disciples' feet by Jesus. In those days only two sorts of people washed feet, women and slaves. The point must not be missed that this is the Logos made flesh who has identified himself with slaves and women. The Word made flesh now appears with those who are at the very bottom of society, and this solidarity and this work become the model of discipleship. . . . This event with its graphic portrayal of Judas dipping the morsel and of Christ washing feet could hardly be more stark in contrast; the traitor who consumes the "Lord's Supper" and has Satan enter him and the Word becoming woman and slave.[1]*

• Tex Sample

APOLOGIES TO JOHN. The church gives him no year of his own in the liturgical cycle of readings (although he shows up in all three years), and I give him only a brief chapter because of that. Even in this chapter, I shall focus not primarily on John's gospel but on how John's Jesus continues to eat and serve at table like Jesus, and on the scrutiny liturgies of the Third, Fourth and Fifth Sundays of Lent in Year A, which proclaim John's stories of the Samaritan woman, the blind man and Lazarus. I do so because the scrutinies are perhaps the most misunderstood of the rites of initiation, yet they can be a most powerful echoing of God's Word of forgiveness, healing and liberation.

As I already noted in chapter four, although John's story of Jesus' Last Supper is the longest of the four gospel accounts of that event, John does not narrate Jesus' words over the bread and wine.[2] The synoptics all have Jesus' commands to do eucharist in memory of him and to baptize at the end of their stories. John puts his stories of eucharist and baptism within his gospel. At the end, John places Jesus' command to the disciples to wash feet in the context of a meal (13:1–15 — Holy Thursday).[3]

### Eating and Washing with John

John simply assumes that bread and body broken and wine and blood shed mean that disciples will do what Jesus always did at meals—identify with women, slaves, all the outcasts and outsiders, just as he did at all those meals in Luke's stories. Jesus and his disciples wash feet, that is, we give our lives in humble service and in solidarity with those who usually did the washing. So John tells that story about how we are to eat as Jesus did. He probably tells the story because his church had forgotten how Jesus connected meals to washing the feet of outcasts and multiplying loaves for the hungry.[4] Despite John's "high" Christology, which identifies Jesus with the preexistent divine word through whom all things were made (1:3), John tells us that the word dwells among us (literally, "pitches his tent") and becomes flesh—a human being who washes feet and becomes the flesh of a woman (1:14—Christmas Mass during the Day).

Yet in John's vision, Jesus' dwelling in flesh with us is only fleeting. While with us, he transforms human flesh and human life—he changes water into wine, heals the sick, feeds the crowd, raises Lazarus and walks on water. When he leaves, however, he sends the Spirit into our flesh to transform us and teach us all that Jesus told us (14:26—6th Sunday of Easter, Year C), including how to wash feet and how to eat as Jesus did. That Spirit is already present in every catechumen, community and culture. Our task is to seek out that Spirit—to affirm what God has already been doing to create authentic human life—but it also is to critique and transform a twisted world that keeps women, slaves, outcasts and outsiders in bondage and death.[5]

Some claim that because footwashing is not part of our culture, we should either not do it or we should substitute handwashing. Is there still something about kneeling and washing feet that says more about humble service than washing hands does? Robert Hovda claims,

> We wash each other's feet . . . because of God—blessed be God, whose overwhelming love reduces our silly little human distinctions to trivia. . . . How can we do it better than in kneeling before each other, taking the other's bare foot in our hands, washing it with water, drying it and kissing it, in undiscriminating homage to the mystery of every living person and to the pilgrim path that foot must trod? . . . We are talking about a new creation, a creation finally understood. In this memorial we hear the word together,

whether we are rich or poor, female or male, gay or straight, of one color or another, old or young, sick or well, working or jobless, approved or disapproved by our society.[6]

> **Conversation Starter:** Whose feet get washed and who does the washing on Holy Thursday in your parish? Some parishes invite everyone to participate. Why?

There is in John's gospel a final meal of Jesus with his disciples on the shore of Lake Tiberias (21:1–19 — 3rd Sunday of Easter, Year C). The images and language in that story recall what had happened after the Lord's Supper; they also summon memories of John's entire gospel. Gerald O'Collins claims that these were healing memories for the disciples, especially for Peter, and that they can be healing memories for us.[7] Jesus continues to heal us so that we can be faithful to service, to mission and to washing feet.

Peter says, "I am going fishing" (21:3). He who didn't want his feet washed in the first place goes back to business as usual. None of this hassle of washing feet. O'Collins suggests that at the very least this reveals a return to "normalcy," during which Peter "retreats" to seek the meaning of the empty tomb and of Jesus' appearance when he gives them the Spirit.

Verses 21:1 and 21:14 use the Greek verb meaning "manifest" three times — the same word used at the end of John's story of Jesus' first working of a sign to manifest his glory at Cana (2:1–12 — 2nd Sunday in Ordinary Time, Year C). By saying that one of the seven fishermen, Nathanael, comes from "Cana in Galilee" (21:2), John invites disciples to remember Jesus' first sign in Cana of Galilee and to connect it with this last manifestation in Galilee.

Jesus comes "as day is breaking" (21:4) and darkness slips away, which evokes memories of the cure of the blind man and Jesus' claim that he is light of the world (9:1–39 — 4th Sunday of Lent, Year A). It also recalls the images at the very beginning of the gospel of the light that shines in the darkness to enlighten all (1:4–9 — Christmas Mass during the Day).

The enormous catch of fish recalls the multiplying of loaves and fish (6:1–15 — 17th Sunday in Ordinary Time, Year B). In Jesus' discourse following that story, Jesus tells of people "hauled" or drawn to him (6:44—19th Sunday in Ordinary Time, Year B), a verb that shows up later in the promise, "And I, when I am lifted up from the earth, will draw [literally 'haul'] all people to myself" (12:32). In this last chapter, Peter "hauls" ashore an unbroken net with 153 fish. The moratorium is over. Jesus calls Peter again to be a fisherman with the mission of "hauling" people to God (cf. Mark 1:17—3rd Sunday in Ordinary Time, Year B). When the disciples reach land (John 6:13), Jesus "takes" and "gives" them bread and fish, just as he did when multiplying loaves and fish. "John's text works to summon up a past grace by which we can be touched again."[8]

The charcoal fire (21:9) around which Jesus and the disciples eat recalls the charcoal fire in the high priest's courtyard, the scene of Peter's threefold denial. This remembering especially calls Peter and us to be healed. "A broken past can resurface and be redeemed."[9] This meal also heals the memories of earlier meals of deadly threats (12:1–11), disputes (12:4–8), betrayal (13:21–30) and misunderstanding (2:3–4—2nd Sunday in Ordinary Time, Year C), and the feeding of the 5,000, followed by words about the bread of life, which ends with many disciples leaving Jesus and the first warning about Judas's treachery (6:25–71—18th through 21st Sundays in Ordinary Time, Year B). This story of the meal on the shore also explicitly recalls (21:20) the Last Supper and Jesus' command to wash feet in loving service.

At this meal, Peter is healed of the paralysis of guilt and freed for that service and mission. He renounces his threefold denial (18:15–27—Good Friday) through his threefold profession of love (18:21, 15, 17). However, there are more healing memories in the images of this dialogue than just the threefold profession. At their first meeting Jesus had spoken to Peter as "Simon, son of John" (1:42—2nd Sunday in Ordinary Time, Year B; also the suggested gospel for the rite of acceptance into the order of catechumens). He repeats that address three times in this, their last meeting (21:15–17). In addition, this naming recalls the good shepherd who knows his sheep and calls them by name (10:1–10—4th Sunday of Easter, Year A) but who also dies for the flock (10:11–15, 17–18—4th Sunday of Easter, Year B). Peter is healed; but his mission will bring him, like Jesus, to the cross. He will be carried where he does not wish to go (21:18–19) when he answers this call to faithful discipleship.

Therefore, this final story in John of Jesus eating with disciples depicts Jesus bringing up a buried past and healing old memories for Peter and for us who identify with the characters and communities in the stories. We are invited to recall stories and images into which we have been immersed from the beginning to the end of John to heal our past and present and to send us to follow him into a new future.

With catechumens we ask, How do we, after the splendor of Easter, return to "fishing" and business as usual. How is Jesus still manifest as light of our world in our Spirit-touched community? How are we called to mission and to "haul in fish" for God? How do we experience reconciliation of our paralysis and freedom for service and mission? If we answer the God who calls us (like Peter) by name, where might we go and do we want to go there?

## Scrutinizing with John

In order to remember and to heal, we are called to scrutinize.[10] To scrutinize is to take a long, careful look. John invites us to take that careful look with three of the greatest stories in all of Christian scripture: to see where we thirst with the Samaritan woman (4:5–42—3rd Sunday of Lent, Year A); to see where we are blind like those who surround the man born physically blind (9:1–41—4th Sunday of Lent, Year A); and to see where we are entombed and in bondage like Lazarus (11:1–45—5th Sunday of Lent, Year A).[11] All three stories offer John's vision of baptism with images of moving from thirst to living water, from darkness to light and from death to life. They build on another of John's great stories of baptism—the dialogue with Nicodemus about being born again of water and the Spirit (3:1–21—Trinity Sunday, Year A).[12] I suggest that the scrutiny gospels need little interpretation. They stand on their own. Rather than preach or catechize about them, better to simply proclaim them, perhaps with several persons voicing the words of the characters in the stories with drama and action.

*The Samaritan Woman*    I have recently come to see (literally, to scrutinize), however, that the gospel reading about the Samaritan woman cries for more incisive interpretation, perhaps within the homily, certainly in the catechetical session. In fact, if in the scrutinies we take a long careful look at sin and the demonic, we need to scrutinize what some insist is a "patriarchal, sexist, misogynist misinterpretation," which is itself entrapped in systemic/demonic distortions of what the story of this woman reveals about God.

> The consistent identification of the Samaritan woman in John 4 as a duplicitous whore whom Jesus tricks into self-exposure and then, presumably, converts, both violates the text and allows the woman's role in the evangelization of Samaria to be minimized while the (presumably male) townspeople emerge as virtual self-evangelizers who perspicaciously recognize Jesus while dismissing the woman's testimony. . . . The treatment of the Samaritan woman in the history of interpretation is a textbook case of the trivialization, marginalization, and even sexual demonization of biblical women, which reflects and promotes the parallel treatment of real women in the church.[13]

First, this encounter between Jesus and the woman in Samaria is most likely not an historical event in the life of Jesus. There is nothing in the synoptic tradition to suggest that the earthly Jesus ministered among the Samaritans. The purpose of the story, then, is to legitimate the Samaritan mission in John's community, to establish full equality between Samaritan and Jewish Christians, and to affirm Jewish legitimacy as bearer of covenant faith but with a surprising recognition of the essential validity of Samaritan faith and inclusion in the covenant. Once again, we are back to covenant inclusion (then and now) as the heart of the gospel message.

Second, the story is a "type story," that is, it follows a biblical pattern: that of the meeting of future spouses who then play a key role in salvation history. The pattern emerges in Abraham's servant finding Rebecca, future wife of Isaac, at the well of Nahor (Genesis 24:10–61); Jacob meeting Rachel at the well in Haran (Genesis 29:1–10); and Moses receiving Zipporah as wife after rescuing the seven daughters of Reuel at the well in Midian (Exodus 2:16–22). Jesus, already identified as the Bridegroom who supplies good wine for the wedding at Cana (John 2:9-10—Second Sunday in Ordinary Time, Year C), whom John the Baptist names as the true bridegroom of ancient Israel, comes to the most famous well of all, Jacob's well in Samaria (ancient Israel) to claim Samaria as beloved in the New Israel. "Now, the new Bridegroom who assumes the role of Yahweh, bridegroom of ancient Israel, comes to claim

Samaria as an integral part of the New Israel, namely, the Christian community and specifically the Johannine community."[2]

Third, we hear the story within the "Cana to Cana" journey with its clearly marital motif (chapters 2 to 4). This section begins with the wedding at Cana where Jesus' Jewish disciples come to belief in him through his *signs,* and it ends with the healing of the royal official's son in Cana when a non-Jew and his household come to belief because of the *word* of Jesus (4:46-53). Within this literary unit, John clearly contrasts the Samaritan woman with Nicodemus (3:1-15—Trinity Sunday, Year A). Nicodemus comes to Jesus at *night* and disappears into the shadows confused by Jesus' self-revelation. The woman encounters Jesus at *high noon* (the contrast of darkness with light which often occurs in John),[15] accepts his self-revelation and brings others to him by her witness.

Fourth, this woman, therefore, is a symbolic character[16] who in John's gospel (like the beloved disciple, the royal official, the paralytic at the pool, and the man born blind) is nameless, which bolsters her ability to represent a collectivity. This woman represents not only the Samaritans but the New Israel given to Jesus the bridegroom. This warns readers against sexual literalism regarding the woman's supposedly profligate past.

Fifth, the woman's conversation with Jesus from the first is religious and even theological. She does not bring in theological issues as a smokescreen to fend off Jesus from tracing her shameful sex life. Like a rabbi, she probes Jesus' breaking of Jewish tradition by his speaking in public to a woman and his asking to share utensils with a Samaritan and also by his implying in his offer of living water that he is on a par with Jacob, who gave the well to Israel. Jesus' claim to be equal with the patriarch Jacob would blow a Samaritan's mind.

Also, unlike the Jews who expected a messiah as a descendent of David, the Samaritans expected a prophet like Moses who would restore true worship not in Jerusalem's Temple but in Israel, that is, in the northern kingdom. Jesus vindicates the claim of the Jews to be bearers of the covenant tradition, but goes on to transcend both the Jewish claims for Jerusalem and the Samaritan claims for Mount Gerizim. He insists on worship in spirit and truth, no matter what the territory. The woman suspects that this is the prophetic messiah. Jesus confirms her intuition. He reveals himself not only as prophetic messiah but as *ego eimi,* the very designation that Samaritans preferred for God—the "I am" of Mosaic revelation (Exodus 3:14).

Sixth, into this context of theological scrutiny of Jesus by the woman we situate the dialogue about the five husbands. A historical event of five successive marriages by a woman of that religious culture is totally implausible. "Either [this dialogue] is totally out of place, a trivial bit of moralism or even a shallow display of preternatural knowledge on the part of Jesus, or it is an integral part of this highly theological exchange."[5]

The exchange about the husbands occurs not as prelude to the theological discussion but in the midst of it, after the woman hears Jesus' claim to equality with patriarchs but before she acknowledges him as prophet. So if the scene symbolically incorporates Samaria into the New Israel, bride of the new bridegroom, Jesus first scrutinizes Samaria's adulterous infidelity to the Mosaic covenant symbolized by its worship of the false gods of five foreign tribes (2 Kings 17:13–34) after the return of remnants of the northern tribes from Assyrian captivity. And Samaria in Jesus' day still remains tainted by false worship. Therefore, even the "husband" she now has (her relationship with the God of the covenant) is not really her husband in full integrity (v. 18).

> Jesus' declaration that Samaria "has no husband" is a classic prophetic denunciation of false worship, like Hosea's oracle in which the prophet, expressing God's sentiments toward unfaithful Israel, says, "Plead with your mother, plead—for she is not my wife and I am not her husband—that she put away her harlotry from her face and her adultery from between her breasts" (Hosea 2:2).[18]

The woman (Samaria) is overwhelmed by this interpretation of Samaritan faith and recognizes that Jesus may be the very messiah who would bring true worship of God in spirit. She proclaims that to her fellow townspeople and becomes disciple—the first and only person in the public life of Jesus whose witness brings a group of people to "come and see" and "to believe in Jesus."

> In summary, the entire dialogue between Jesus and the woman is the "wooing" of Samaria to full covenant fidelity in the New Israel by Jesus, the New Bridegroom. It has nothing to do with the woman's private moral life but with the covenant life of the community. Nowhere in the fourth gospel is there a dialogue of such theological depth and intensity.[19]

I shall follow Schneider in naming some homiletic/catechetical possibilities in proclaiming this text. First, the passage invites hearers into a world marked by an astonishing, even shocking, inclusiveness. "Jesus goes to Samaria, the land of the hated 'other,' to confront and to heal the ancient divisions,"[20] to unite into the new covenant not only those ignorant of but those unfaithful to the old covenant. No one is nor may be excluded.

Second, we cannot fail to miss that the recipient of Jesus' invitation to inclusion is a woman, "universal representative of the despised and excluded 'other' not only in ancient Israel but throughout history and all over the world. Not only is she included, but she is engaged with respect. . . ."[21]

Third, hearers, especially women, will also experience the "not yet" quality in this new world. There is the lingering sexism that carries a "God/male/faithful versus human/female/faithless" dynamic. Thus, even in the text freshly interpreted there remains "the world" (in the Johannine sense) that is not yet fully transformed. In John's terms, we are *in* that world but we are called not to be *of* that world.

***The Rites of the Scrutinies***   Having scrutinized interpretations of a Scrutiny gospel to exorcise it of demonic stereotypes, we now scrutinize the rites of the scrutinies, which also need more insightful interpretation.

> **Take a Stand:**   What is your experience of and understanding of the scrutinies?

The rites of the scrutinies, however, do need interpretation. A survey some years ago by the archdiocese of Chicago revealed that the scrutinies were the least celebrated of all the liturgies of initiation. Perhaps parishes interpret the scrutiny as an examination of just the catechumens. Perhaps our modern age is just a bit uncomfortable with and embarrassed by talk of demons and exorcism because we identify devils with Flip Wilson's "the devil made me do it" or the horrific, spectacular, but rare (thank God!) machinations of devils in *The Exorcist* and other popular books and movies.[22] The demonic is far worse and far more subtle than that.

> **Take a Stand:** Do you believe that every baby is born into a state of original sin and into a community infected by evil spirits? What is your understanding of original sin and of the demonic?

### Sin and Demons—Worse than We Thought!

Morris West contends, "With all the evil that we are able to devise for ourselves, a personal Prince of Darkness seems a redundancy."[23] Like original sin, the demonic often refers to people's experience of evil, which they know is much more than their own production. This evil is more than the sum of the parts. With that perspective, we speak of the spirit of a people, a mob spirit or the spirit of Nazism.

The demonic that we scrutinize on these Sundays, then, is more akin to what we call original sin, seen not just as the pride of our first parents but the collective evil into which families and communities in all times immerse their children— racism, sexism, consumerism, privatism, the social sin of all the "isms" that cause thirst, that put cataracts over eyes so that we do not see (nor want to see) pain or possibility, and that entomb us, enslave us and keep us bound and addicted. Walter Wink admits that demons "are the drunk uncle of the twentieth century; we keep them out of sight." Yet he identifies the demonic with "the psychic or spiritual power emanated by societies or institutions or individuals . . . whose energies are bent on overpowering others."[24] On the scrutiny Sundays, we scrutinize not just the sins of the catechumens but the places where our political, economic, social and ecclesial communities and systems cause thirst, blindness and death, and also the places where we might be a community that offers Christ's living water, light and life. Nathan Mitchell claims,

> Jesus is presented in the gospels as one who is unalterably opposed to whatever keeps people from being free: sin, disease, illness, possession by evil spirits. Jesus' work as exorcist is a work of passionate liberation, a manifesto for human freedom. He strikes out against anything that makes human beings helpless, hostile and impotent [thirsty, blind or entombed]. His ultimate act of exorcism was the cross. . . . Nailed to a tree, Jesus was forced to face everything that is demonic about human life: despair, hopelessness, rebellion, hostility, pain, loss, suffering. But by becoming death's 'slave' on the cross, Jesus rose as liberator of a new humanity. Jesus 'exorcised' death by allowing himself to become its captive.[25]

Unlike Morris West, the gospels personify these death-dealing principalities and powers with names: "Satan," "the father of lies," "the prince of darkness." Whether we personify them or not, we still experience them not through direct encounter[26] but through what St. Paul calls "the flesh." "'Flesh' does not mean our physical skin and bones; . . . it refers to an attitude of life that is either willfully or unconsciously blind to the power and action of God in the world. . . . To submit . . . causes us to live lives of futility, helplessness, greed, impotence and despair."[27]

Therefore, we scrutinize the community of which the catechumens are a part for all that keeps us unfree, powerless and desperate. We ask not just privatistic questions about sin and evil—Why don't I accept living water? How am I blind? How am I enslaved and entombed?—we also ask What forces keep people from the well that belongs to all?[28] What powers in church and society blind us or refuse to recognize our new sight? Who owns and controls the gnawing, consuming powers that subtly but surely keep people bound and enslaved?

With this understanding of these rites, I have little difficulty with the word "scrutiny" but great difficulty with the scrutiny prayers as they appear in the rite, especially the petitions. They are weak. To exorcise is to name the evil ones, powerfully and courageously, so that living in the presence and promise of the Holy One in community we can have power over them. Exorcism does not mean that we rid the world of communities or systems infested with evil spirits. Exorcism liberates by freeing us from thirsting for their subtle glamour, by opening our eyes to their cunning deceits and by freeing us from bondage to their corrosive power and freeing us for life in a community which lives by the Holy Spirit.

Therefore, we use the "greatest freedom" given in #35 of the *Rite of Christian Initiation of Adults* to invite people, during Lenten sessions before the scrutiny liturgies, to prepare for these rites by naming the evil spirits from which we need forgiveness, healing and freedom. We name these principalities and powers in a powerful sung litany during the scrutinies. The evils that people name vary from somewhat general "powers that be," such as materialism and cutthroat competition, to very concrete assaults on life issues, such as abortion, capital punishment, abuse in families, sidelining the handicapped, warehousing the elderly and polluting the environment, to very particular examples such as the riots in Los Angeles—blind spirits in Simi Valley and mob spirit in

South Central L.A., supermarkets and industries that abandon neighborhoods, gun shops that infest neighborhoods, brutal police and brutal gangs. As a community we are afflicted by and participate in those evils.

> **Take a Stand:**   Do you believe that every baby is born in a state of original grace and into a community touched by the Holy Spirit? What is your understanding of grace?

### Grace—Better than We Thought!

When the community lifts its voice to exorcise and name the powers of evil, we proclaim to the candidates and to each other that we are not only together in thirst, blindness and death, but that in the Spirit we are also healing water, light and life for each other. We need not confront the demons alone. We live not by the tyranny of "flesh" but by the freedom of the Spirit in a community that proclaims that God is at work in our world. Morris West notes, "This is how the battle of good against evil always begins: . . . [a] voice raised in the crowd, proclaiming that the king has no clothes, that the new gods are hollow plaster, that the new masters in the land are crooks and charlatans. Once it is heard, courage, like crime, proves contagious and the tattered banners are raised once more against the ancient adversary."[29]

The scrutinies are not just petition but promise—the promise of the community to live together in the power of the Spirit. They are promise to the candidates and to each other that we need not confront the evil spirits alone. "The scrutinies are meant . . . to bring out, then strengthen all that is upright, strong and good" in the candidates and the community (RCIA, #141). No Christian liturgy should end without hope. The last words are not sin, thirst, blindness and death, but living water, light and life.

Grace is not some ethereal thing but the life of the Holy Spirit incarnate in persons and communities. In the scrutinies, we celebrate grace—the Spirit-touched life of the community that exorcises evil spirits of division, violence, vengeance, domination, fear and slavery by giving us poverty of spirit, humility, purity of heart and peacemaking (Matthew 5:1–12a—4th Sunday in Ordinary Time, Year A). We need to craft prayers that better invite us to celebrate that gift and make that promise.

In the introduction to this book, I shared my first scrutiny, my first long look at the hideous horror and terror of the appalling, demonic evil of apartheid in South Africa. The monstrous violence of apartheid reveals once again that evil is a mystery that we shall never fully comprehend. Still, South African theologian Albert Nolan claims that what finally resounds in South Africa is not the violence but the singing. With John, these oppressed people continue to sing that the light shines in the darkness, and the darkness will never put it out (1:5—Christmas Mass during the Day) just as they sang *"Nkosi sikeli-Afrika"* ("God Bless Africa") at that eucharist that I celebrated with them in Johannesburg. Grace, present in Christ and in the people baptized in the Spirit, is also a mystery that we shall never understand. The scrutinies invite us to take a long, careful look at both evil and grace. They invite us to celebrate and be part of the ultimate triumph of the mystery of grace in Christ who is living water, light of the world, and the resurrection and the life.

> **Conversation Starter:** Do you have answers to the problem of evil—why do bad things happen to good people?[30] Or do you agree that both sin and grace are mysteries, not in the sense that we can know nothing about them but that they forever elude our total grasp and ultimately are rooted in what is beyond our experience—the demonic and the divine? If so, share some examples of both.

### Endnotes

[1] Tex Sample, *U.S. Lifestyles and Mainline Churches* (Louisville: Westminster/John Knox Press, 1990), 152, 153.

[2] Cf. Leon Xavier-Dufour, *The Eucharistic Bread* (New York: Paulist Press, 1987), 283–85.

[3] The command to do what Jesus did is so clear that for many centuries, many areas of the church saw the washing of feet as a sacrament, although the meaning of "sacrament" was not as precise as it is today. In parts of the church, footwashing was part of the rites of initiation. Monastic communities washed the feet of guests,

especially the poor, and there was a weekly footwashing of the members of the community. This was in addition to the washing on Holy Thursday. Cf. Peter Jeffery, "*Mandatum Novum Do Vobis:* Toward a Renewal of the Holy Thursday Footwashing Rite," *Worship* (March 1990), 107–41.

[4] "The Eucharistic bread is an empty symbol if the hungry are not fed. . . . The action of feeding the hungry is eucharistic ministry, whether it is done on a private level or a government level. Soup kitchens, Meals on Wheels for the elderly, and aid for the starving children of Africa is eucharistic ministry." Vincent Donovan, *The Church in the Midst of Creation* (Maryknoll NY: Orbis Books, 1990), 79. In light of that, we would commission as eucharistic ministers in church those who are icons and sacraments to us of feeding the hungry outside church.

[5] Cf. Sample, *U.S. Lifestyles,* 149–54. Richard McBrien adds: "The whole world 'needs' the church, for the human community cannot long survive without fidelity to what is essentially human and criticism of what is fundamentally inhuman or antihuman. Without criticism, freedom yields to totalitarianism, justice gives way to exploitation, charity recedes into ruthlessness, peace dissolves into rivalry and hostility. The church must offer itself as one of the principal agents whereby the human community is made to stand under the judgment of the enduring values of the Gospel of Jesus Christ: freedom, justice, peace, charity, compassion, reconciliation." *Do We Need the Church?* (New York: Harper & Row, 1965), 228–29.

[6] "Eating, Drinking and Washing Each Other's Feet," *Summit & Fount,* newsletter of the diocese of Galveston-Houston (Winter 1992), 6.

[7] O'Collins, "An Easter Healing of Memories," *America* 166:13, 322–23.

[8] O'Collins, "An Easter," 323.

[9] Ibid.

[10] Cf. James Dunning, "Scrutinizing Sin and Grace," in a special issue on "Lent and Conversion" of *Modern Liturgy* 19:2, 13–15.

[11] Those who compiled the Scrutinies did so with a focus on personal sin with the Samaritan woman, social sin with the blind man, and community and cosmic sin with the tomb of Lazarus. I suggest that this approach is too analytical for good liturgy. It also obscures the interrelationships between personal and communal sin.

[12] A Jew becomes a member of the people of God and a child of Abraham by birth in the flesh through a Jewish mother. According to John, with Christ, God gives a new birth through water and the Spirit, so there is no human or earthly barrier to being a

member. All can be disciples. Cf. Raymond Brown, "The Church's Three Favorite Stories from John's Gospel," audiocassette (Simi Valley CA: Convention Seminar Cassettes, 1991), Los Angeles Religious Education Congress; and Raymond Brown, *The Community of the Beloved Disciples* (New York: Paulist Press, 1979), 48, 56.

[13] Sandra Schneiders, *The Revelatory Text.* (San Francisco: Harper San Francisco, 1991), 186, 188. I am following Schneiders's insightful interpretation in the following paragraphs.

[14] Schneiders, *The Revelatory Text,* 187.

[15] Contrast this symbol with the woman-as-whore interpretation which has the woman come at high noon to avoid being ostracized by the other women who normally come to the well in the early hours of the morning.

[16] Raymond Collins, "The Representative Figures in the Fourth Gospel," *Downside Review* 94:26–46 and 118–32.

[17] Schneiders, *The Revelatory Text,* 190.

[18] Schneiders, *The Revelatory Text,* 191. Schneiders still rightly objects that this prophetic imagery still "always casts God as the faithful and forgiving husband and Israel as the faithless and adulterous wife, thus consolidating the entrenched tendency to divinize men and demonize women. . . . The fact that the evangelist uses the metaphor continues its legitimation in the Christian community" (p. 195).

[19] Schneiders, *The Revelatory Text,* 191. In the dialogue among the disciples who return with food, which Jesus says he does not need, Schneiders submits that his discussion with the woman has satisfied his hunger to do God's will and the thirst that mediated their encounter. The Samaritan mission, clearly in the hands of the woman, is one in which the male disciples will participate as "reapers." They do not initiate it. They do not control it. "It seems not unlikely that whoever wrote the fourth gospel had some experience of women Christians as theologians and as apostles, was aware of the tension this aroused in the community, and wanted to present Jesus as legitimating female participation in male-appropriated roles. Again, one cannot help wondering about the identity of the evangelist [a woman?]" (p. 191).

[20] Schneiders, *The Revelatory Text,* 196.

[21] Ibid.

[22] Nathan Mitchell comments, "The evil celebrated by *The Exorcist* was not the subtly corrosive power that seeps into our lives unawares, but the dramatic, repulsive

'evil' everyone finds disgusting and ugly. Unfortunately, Blatty's novel did little to sharpen our awareness of the hidden evil that robs human beings of their dignity and freedom; it merely shocked our glands into revolt against a situation that was uncanny and detestable." "Exorcism in the RCIA," in *Christian Initiation Resources Reader, Volume III* (New York: Wm. H. Sadlier, Inc., 1984), 49.

[23] Morris West, "A Perception of Evil," *America* (December 1990), 469. West adds about demons: "The plural word expresses aggregation, collective action, collective strength. It is precisely thus that we have seen the most monstrous evils of our time brought to pass: Europe tyrannized and tumbled to ruins by collectivist philosophies: Fascism, Nazism, Stalinism (20 million killed); the Holocausts committed in a collective conspiracy of silence; the South American dictatorships buttressed by U.S. presidential policies; the drug barons creating their new empires with the new currency of narcotics—so much more stable than paper and gold, so much more valuable than human lives; the Middle East turned into a battleground over oil and God," 469.

[24] Walter Wink, *Unmasking the Powers* (Philadelphia: Fortress Press, 1986), 41, 68.

[25] Mitchell, "Exorcism," 54.

[26] Philosophers and theologians agree that all experience of the spirit world, divine and demonic, is mediated through creation and our humanity; for Christians, that climaxed in our experience of the humanity of Jesus of Nazareth; e.g., Karl Rahner, *Hominization* (New York: Herder and Herder, 1965); and John E. Smith, *Experience and God* (New York: Oxford University Press, 1968).

[27] Mitchell, "Exorcism," 58.

[28] Although this question is usually metaphorical, I know one case where sin did indeed keep people from the well that belongs to all. When I was in South Africa, one black township was staging a nonviolent protest by withholding their rent because the "demonic" officials were stealing their money, which was meant to provide them with water. The gospel for the Sunday I was there was Jesus' command to render to Caesar what is Caesar's (Matthew 22:1–14—29th Sunday in Ordinary Time, Year A). The people with whom I talked were quick to point out that Jesus did not say *when* they had to give money to the state.

[29] West, "A Perception," 469.

[30] Harold Kushner surveys all the answers people give to the problem of evil and rejects all of them in *When Bad Things Happen to Good People* (New York: Schocken Books, 1981).

# CHAPTER ELEVEN

# Conversing with Dogmas and Precepts

*[In the beginning] God called the embryos before Him[1] and saw that they were good. . . . God said, "Now, you embryos, here you are, all looking exactly the same, and We are going to give you the choice of what you want to be. . . . You may alter any parts of yourselves into anything which you think would be useful to you in later life. . . ."*

*Some chose to use their arms as flying machines and their mouths as weapons, or crackers, or drillers, or spoons, while others chose to use their bodies as boats and their hands as oars. . . . At the very end of the sixth day, . . . they had got through all the little embryos except one. This embryo was Man.*

*"Well, Our little Man," said God. . . . "What can We do for you?"*

*"Please, God, I think that You made me in the shape which I now have for reasons best known to Yourselves, and that it would be rude to change. . . . I will stay a defenseless embryo all my life, doing my best to make myself a few feeble implements out of the wood, iron, and the other materials which You have seen fit to put before me. . . ."*

*"Well done," exclaimed the Creator. "Here, all you embryos, come here with your beaks and whatnots to look upon Our first Man. He is the only one who has guessed Our riddle. . . . We have great pleasure in conferring upon him the Order of Dominion over the Fowls of the Air, and the Beasts of the Earth, and the Fishes of the Sea. . . . As for you, Man, you will be a naked tool all your life, though a user of tools. . . . Eternally undeveloped, you will always remain potential in Our image, able to see some of Our sorrows and to feel some of Our joys. We are partly sorry for you, but partly hopeful. Run along then, and do your best."[2]*

• T. H. White

# WHAT WHITE PROCLAIMS in the language of story, John Shea says in the language of theology:

The symbol of God the Creator, when it is functioning symbolically, initially directs attention to contingency. This symbol establishes [us] within an imaginative setting where the limits of life are consciously brought to attention. It focuses on the wonder and giveness of [our] own birth and all birth. Even more attention is drawn to the sense of rebirth in those heightened moments of mystery and awe and joy when [we] sense that through [us] pulses more than [we] are. . . . So the symbol of God the Creator awakens consciousness to the events of birth and death that are continually active within life and to an ultimacy that contacts [us] through these limits.[3]

This chapter will not survey all postbiblical, Catholic Christian tradition, teaching, dogmas and doctrines, or precepts and laws. But I will suggest ways to converse with and hear that tradition.

First, just as with scripture, we need to hear postbiblical tradition not with fundamentalist or historicist ears; we give the tradition a pastoral/theological hearing. As with scripture, we interpret not texts, primarily, but our lives. White, in popular language, and Shea, in more complicated words, both see the doctrine of God the Creator not as a historical text about the first days but as a lens through which to see all our days. Karl Rahner calls this theological anthropology—all reflection about God (*theos*) is reflection on the meaning of human life (*anthropos*).[4] Talk about God should reveal something about the truly good life for humans, or it isn't much of a theology.

Second, just as fundamentalism and historicism separate scripture and doctrine from their meanings for our lives today, so also legalism separates precepts and laws from the human values present in concrete situations today. Therefore, we shall explore a pastoral/theological hearing of law that goes beyond legalism and looks to human values.

Third, I shall suggest (as in chapter four) that the particular experiential and doctrinal lens through which Catholics and members of other sacramental traditions see our lives is the sacramentality of all creation— all creation can be a visible sign of invisible grace. It is the principle of the incarnation—God's enfleshment in the world, especially in humans, who are images of God (Genesis 1:26) and in Jesus, who is *the* image of the invisible God (Colossians 1:15). Put another way, sacramentality is the analogical imagination that sees the things of this world more like God than unlike God.[5] As I suggested in chapter three, this lens will lead to the catechetical language of image and story (like T. H. White), not to the somewhat arid language of official dogmas and precepts, nor of systematic theologians (such as John Shea, who, while quoted earlier above using theological language, also writes stories and poetry).

### A Pastoral/Theological Hearing of Dogmas and Doctrines

What John Baldovin and Elisabeth Schüssler Fiorenza say of biblical texts is true also of postbiblical tradition: "Texts are given their due as documents that respond to pastoral problems in a theological way. . . . The biblical critic tries to understand the original context for this or that portion of scripture and then to apply it to appropriate parallels in contemporary life."[6] We hear postbiblical texts not as fundamentalists or literalists (for example, the doctrine of creation is not about the pseudo-science of creationism), nor as historicists (the historical fact of evolution, if proven, would not negate faith in a creator God), nor as with doctrinalists (mouthing the first line of the creed *about* God the Creator without experience *of* a God who created us as "defenseless embryos, eternally undeveloped, but able to see some of [God's] pains and feel some of [God's] joys"). Nor do we hear just with psychological/privatistic ears, which would, for example, reduce belief in a creating God in my life to "the force within you" leading to self-actualization and self-fulfillment.

We hear this tradition as *pastors* (those charged with the care of the community) and as *theologians* (those who are able to discern the vision of God and creation that earlier communities brought to their problems and who are able to connect that vision with issues in our contemporary communities). We also apply a literary criticism to postbiblical texts: We look for the story out of which these texts emerged and, because of our contemporary stories, we may hear more in these texts than their authors intended.

The emphasis in this chapter is on *pastoral* theology. The research of biblical scholars and systematic theologians frees us not to construct massive systems and structures in our pastoral care with people. Rather, their scholarly work sends us back to human experience as the place of God's presence, and we tell of that experience in the language of story just as Jesus did. Vincent Donovan contends that Jesus apparently gave short shrift to, and even railed against the massive legal system of the religious establishment (Matthew 23). That system went to great lengths with prescriptions for marriage and divorce. Jesus simply preached against all divorce. The Bible is filled with laws to deal with disputes. Jesus' answer when someone appealed to him for a just judgment about an inheritance was, "Who has made me judge over you?" (Luke 12:13–15 — 18th Sunday in Ordinary Time, Year C).[7] Jesus insists that his message is hidden from the learned and the wise.[8]

I stress this because, in my experience, some of the people most wedded to inquiry classes and most resistant to the spiritual journey and faith-sharing of the catechumenate are those who can spew forth theologies because of their degrees in religious education. Sometimes they even equate theological constructs, such as transubstantiation or infallibility, with basic faith. Karl Rahner, however, insists that some Christians might say,

> "Yes, but to be honest, I have the feeling that I don't know or understand amany important teachings of the church. I no longer know, for example, how many sacraments there are. And, to be honest, I also don't really know what the First Vatican Council said about the pope's authority in the church. I don't mean to imply in any way that I reject it, but basically I just don't comprehend it. I really can't begin to deal with all that mass of data. I have the feeling that it's not very important for my life and death. To such Christians I can say only that they are completely normal, good and lively Christians."[9]

When catechizing "normal, good and lively Christians," and especially when initiating new Christians, we stick to the basics discussed in chapter four. They eventually may choose to study systematic theology.

> **Conversation Starter:** Name some church teachings that you do not understand or that you do not consider important for your life.

*Hearing Defined Dogma*   With defined church dogma (there is relatively little of it in the total body of church teaching), perhaps even more than with biblical texts, we interpret with a hermeneutic of suspicion. As noted in chapter five, this enables us to critique in a positive way both distortions within texts and false (though perhaps dominant) interpretations of texts. Because much dogma, especially that about God and Christ, was defined in the first six centuries of Christianity, it is described in the language of Greek philosophy (e.g., "person" and "nature," "substance" and "accidents"), which is not well understood by people today.[10] Dogma is also a response to particular pastoral problems that sometimes do not exist today.

With a hermeneutic of creative commitment to the text, however, we may be able to connect the tradition with the issues of our times—if we can penetrate to the story out of which dogma emerged. We can tell about the plots, settings, characters and conflicts, and we can construct the story of doctrinal texts just as we can with biblical texts. Although the history of dogma is less important than biblical history, a bit of history, especially for catechumens who are history buffs, can bring dogma alive.

A BIT OF HISTORY    "The times, they were a-changin'" when the Council of Chalcedon met in the year 453 and defined the incarnation: Jesus is truly divine and truly human. Immutability, changelessness was the greatest of gifts for the Greeks. But the barbarians were at the gates. Greek wisdom was under assault, as was Roman law and order. In those times of cultural collapse and change, gnostic heresies throve.

The gnostics hated the world and the human. For them, human history was fractured and shattered everywhere, and humanity was at a dead end. The gnostics had, they claimed, special knowledge (*gnosis*) and revelations from above that saved them from this vale of tears. Another group of gnositcs, the Monophysites (*mono*, one; *physis*, nature) denied Jesus' humanity. They said he was obviously God, and God would not defile God's self by becoming human. Yet another gnostic group, the Arians (followers of Arius), denied Jesus' divinity. They said that he was obviously human and that God would not get messed up with the human. For the same reason, hatred of the human, these two opposite gnostic heresies denied the incarnation.

In the midst of this turmoil, the Council of Chalcedon, demonstrating the resiliency of orthodoxy, proclaimed that Jesus is truly divine and truly human,[11] "like us in all things but sin."[12] We see God's love precisely in the turmoil and anguish of a human story of death and crucifixion. Can we also discover God's love in our own sufferings and death? This pastoral/theological hearing of dogma about Christ moves beyond a text about him to dogma as revelation about God and us. But does it have meaning for our lives and the times we live in? Does a pastoral/ theological hearing of the resilient faith of our ancestors have relevance for our stories, our vision of ourselves, our hopes for the human, our giving lives for our friends? Does it speak to the search for God in these tumultuous times? How does it do this when so many religious folk see turmoil as a revelation about the end of the world, not as the birthpangs of new creation?[13]

> **Take a Stand:**   What do you understand the meaning of Mary's assumption to be for our life today?

*A Pastoral/Theological/Literary Hearing of the Assumption*   One of the defined dogmas that many Catholics find remote from our lives is that of Mary's assumption. How could we possibly view that through the lens of a theological anthropology as a statement about us? Many Catholics limit the doctrine to a fundamentalist/literalist meaning as a fact about Mary: Her entire being, body and spirit, is caught up into the resurrection of her Son. That's great for Mary, but it doesn't say much about us. Yet in the early church, John Chrysostom, from within our tradition, asserted that all doctrines about Mary are also doctrines about us. Psychoanalyst Carl Jung thought the assumption said a lot about us. In a world racked by the appalling violence of the Second World War and the Holocaust, Jung found the so-called "masculine" traits of power and control running wild and dominating the lives of many of his patients. Jung called for a rediscovery and resurrection of the "feminine" traits in both males and females: receptivity, acceptance, warmth, gentleness, compassion, caring. More than a doctrine, Mary as risen woman is an image, story and symbol of the resurrection of the feminine in all of us, a meaning that most certainly goes beyond the intention of Pius XII, but one that gives meaning to the story of our times. That is a pastoral/ theological/literary hearing of Mary's assumption.

Our challenge, like that of the Greeks, is to move beyond scripture and the time-bound language of defined dogma. We must, instead, connect the stories and plots that gave them birth to the stories and plots and pastoral issues of our times. And we must do this in language that speaks to our cultures.

*A Theological/Anthropological Hearing*   The general approach to Catholic Christian teaching and doctrine (both defined and undefined) taken by most theologians today is that of Rahner's theological anthropology, i.e., all talk of God is also talk about the human and life's meaning.

DOCTRINE   Taking doctrine as an example, Gregory Baum writes, using the language of systematic theology:

> "God is Father" means that human life is oriented toward a gracious future, and "God is Word and Spirit" means that a summons revealing sin and the gift to freedom to move beyond it into newness are offered to [us] in [our] life, constituting the orientation towards [our] gracious future. "God is person" means that [we] are related to the deepest dimension of [our] life in a personal way, that [we] listen to the summons addressed to [us] and respond to the gifts offered. "God is creator" means that [we] are unfinished and open to the irreducibly new. . . . "God is redeemer" means that this selfsame mystery which saves [us] from the ambiguity into which [we are] born and which [we confirm] by [our lives], again and again, beyond expectation and desert, offers the possibility of escaping the destructive past and entering into new life, into an ever-recreated new way of being, beyond all death.[14]

Andrew Greeley submits, in more popularized catechetical language, that all the great doctrines are responses to questions about the meaning of human life. Doctrine about the mystery of God responds to the human question, Is there any purpose in my life? Teachings about the mystery of Jesus of Nazareth addresses the need to ask, Are there grounds for hope? The mystery of the Spirit considers the question, Is it safe to trust? The mystery of the cross and resurrection: Why is there evil in the world? The mystery of salvation: Is human nature totally depraved? The mystery of grace: Can our guilt be wiped away? The mystery of the eucharist: Is it possible to have friends? The mystery of the church: Can there be unity among humankind? The mystery of baptism: Can we live in harmony with nature? The mystery of Mary the mother of Jesus: Can we find our sexual identity? The mystery of heaven: Why is life not fair? The mystery of the return of Jesus: Can we ever find peace?[15]

> **Conversation Starter:**   How would you connect the doctrines Greeley mentions with the questions he asks so that they cast light on our lives today?

With this perspective on creeds and doctrines, some have adapted the presentation of the Creed in the order of initiation. During a catechetical session (preferably during the catechumenate period, when catechumens are learning the Catholic creedal heritage) the presider proclaims the Creed's words about God—Father, Creator—and then asks the baptized who are present to share their experience of that God in their lives today. The presider does the same for Jesus, the Spirit and the church. Clearly the community is handing on not a text but their lived faith and experience of God. Then the baptized proclaim the entire Creed and continue with the prayers from the ritual text. This also gives new meaning to the Creed for baptized candidates for full communion, even though they may think they've heard it all before.

SACRAMENTS    About sacraments, George McCauley says,

> Sacraments are secular gestures; they deal with secular reality; they promote a greater secularity than we are accustomed to associate with human existence; in themselves they embody secular experience; in one sense, an enriched secular experience *is* the grace of the sacraments.[16]

> **Take a Stand:**  How might the eucharist connect with care for our earth and environment? Take a stand, then read endnote #16.

PRAYER    About prayer, Grace Marie Schutte writes,

> Rather than an "elevation of the mind and heart to God" in a kind of closed circuit, or telephone-type conversation with God, prayer is a penetration through the world about us, through our fellow [humans] to the very ground and root of our existence, to "[God] in whom we live and move and have our being" (Acts 17:28). It is holding one's self wide open to the cosmic influence of God's magnetic creation and by [other humans]—a "being rooted and grounded in love" (Ephesians 3:17) in God who is love (1 John 4:8).[17]

> **Take a Stand:**  Which language do you prefer: "All work is prayer," or "We can do all work prayerfully, with a spirit of contemplation of God's presence in our work and world"? Take a stand, then read endnote #17.

What we said about the presentation of the Creed can also apply to the presentation of the Lord's Prayer. The Lord's Prayer is not primarily a text for a prayer; it is primarily a way of praying. When the disciples ask Jesus how to pray (cf. Luke 11:1–13—17th Sunday in Ordinary Time, Year C), he responds that all prayer is marked by praise of God ("hallowed be thy name"), commitment to the reign of God ("thy kingdom come") and absolute dependence on God ("give us this day our daily bread . . . deliver us from evil").

Therefore, at a catechetical session during the catechumenate period, the presider proclaims the words about praise and then invites the baptized to tell why and for what they praise and thank God. Then the words about God's reign and our dependence on God in the prayer can invite the baptized to share their commitments and their dependence and God's loving care for them. After that, the baptized hand on the entire Lord's Prayer and conclude with the prayers in the ritual text.

> **Conversation Starter:** Does humanism always mean atheistic humanism to you? What else might it mean?

ETHICS    John Giles Milhaven writes on the subject of ethics,

> Christian faith reveals a radically new dimension of human life, but as I presented it, it alters in no way the secular, humanistic dimensions. The Christian dimension reinforces the value and importance of being a fully secular [human being].[18]

I would qualify Milhaven by saying that our experience of the God of Jesus Christ brings us to a radically deepened vision of the world in its deepest mystery: a world that is the place of God's presence, as well as the place of human beings who are called to love as God would love—by being willing to give up our lives for our friends. That is why we invite catechumens "not only to an appropriate acquaintance with dogmas and precepts but also to a profound sense of the mystery of salvation in which they desire to participate" (#75.1). For the Christian believer, sainthood (living in the presence and mystery of God) is the ultimate fulfillment of personhood.

## A Pastoral/Theological Hearing of Precepts and Law

The remarks by Milhaven offer a transition from an emphasis on hearing dogma and doctrine to a pastoral/theological hearing of precepts and law. Such a hearing moves us beyond legalism to a vision of law and ethics that leads to the good life. That vision flows from our faith in Jesus, in whom we see God and what the good life can be. If not rooted in faith,

> the simplicity and splendor of a moral theology—and pastoral catechesis—anchored in and dominated by charity gets hopelessly blurred. Enamored of the parts, we grow blind to the whole. That is why it is still timely—and indeed urgent—to dream of a moral theology in the year 2000 that can recover and reproduce the glorious and demanding simplicity of Christianity's founder.[19]

Canon lawyer Ladislas Orsy seeks that simplicity with a one-liner. It states that just as theology is faith seeking understanding, so law is faith seeking action.[20]

> **Take a Stand:**   How do you understand legalism? Was there a time when you were a legalist? What helped you change?

*From Legalism to Conscience*    I describe legalism as the separation of law from the faith, values and human goods that gave birth to law. For example, if we phrase the Ten Commandments positively, we might name those values: You shall reverence life (fifth commandment). You shall honor fidelity (sixth commandment). You shall commit yourselves to truth, honesty and integrity (eighth commandment).

Perhaps a classic example of legalism is the approach of some people to the Sunday Mass obligation. The dialogue might go as follows:

> "I missed Mass," the penitent confesses.
> "Why did you miss Mass?" the priest asks.
> "I was sick."
> "So you couldn't participate in the Mass?"
> "No."
> "Then, that's not a sin. Why did you confess it?"
> "I broke the law."
> "That's still not a sin. But did you pray at home?" (the value behind the law)
> "I never thought of that."

Our challenge is to help catechumens move beyond legalism to the values that gave birth to laws and commandments so that the catechumens might not feel moved to say, with the irrepressibly caustic H. L. Mencken, "Say what you will about the Ten Commandments, you always come back to the pleasant fact that there are only ten of them."[21]

To frame the commandments in a positive way is to acknowledge that an "appropriate acquaintance with precepts" (#75.1) allows us to move beyond legalism and form a Christian conscience. One helpful booklet catches that task in its title—*Adults Making Responsible Moral Decisions.*[22] Every word in that title is important. We treat a catechumen as an *adult*—"a self-directing person who makes informed decisions and accepts the consequences of them."[23] Adults are *responsible*, "able to respond" to the human possibilities for life and love and the values in a given context.[24] Adults respond *morally*: For Christians, to act in light of Jesus' message is to grow in the life of the Spirit; to refuse to do so is a sin. Adults make *decisions* by actively forming their consciences and deciding to act—faith seeking action.

> **Take a Stand:** When is conscience most active—before we act or after we act? How do you understand conscience?

At Forum workshops I often ask catechumenate team members to tell me when they believe conscience is most active. Usually the group divides into thirds—one third saying that conscience is most active before we act, one third saying after we act, and a third with no opinion. The common view—that conscience is most active after we act—is a description of superego and guilt feelings, not of conscience. Superego is that Freudian parent figure who, like Santa Claus, "sees us when we're sleeping and knows when we're awake, he knows if we've been bad or good, so be good for goodness' sake!" Superego is like the horse's eyes in the play *Equus*, constantly watching until we are driven to tear them out. Conscience, however, surveys the scene, gets the facts, discerns the possibilities for acting in light of Christian values, decides on the best action and takes responsibility for that action. For contrasts between superego and conscience, see figure 6.[25]

## Figure 6

| SUPEREGO | CONSCIENCE |
| --- | --- |
| 1. *Commands* us to act for the sake of gaining approval, or out of fear of losing love. | 1. *Responds to an invitation* to love; in the very act of responding to others, one becomes a certain sort of person and co-creates self-value. |
| 2. *Turned in toward self* in order to secure one's sense of being of value, of being lovable. | 2. *Fundamental openness* that is oriented toward the other and toward the value which calls for action. |
| 3. Tends to be *static* by merely repeating a prior command. Unable to learn or function creatively in a new situation. | 3. Tends to be *dynamic* by a sensitivity to the demand of values which call for new ways of responding. |
| 4. Oriented primarily *toward authority:* not a matter of responding to value, but of obeying the command of authority "blindly." | 4. Oriented primarily *toward value:* responds to the value that deserves preference regardless of whether authority recognizes it or not. |
| 5. Primary attention is given to *individual acts* as being important in themselves apart from the larger context or pattern of actions. | 5. Primary attention is given to the *larger process* or *pattern.* Individual acts become important within this larger context. |
| 6. Oriented toward the *past:* "The way we were." | 6. Oriented toward the *future:* "The sort of person one ought to become." |
| 7. *Punishment* is the sure guarantee of reconciliation. The more severe the punishment, the more certain one is of being reconciled. | 7. Reparation comes through *structuring the future* orientation toward the value in question. Creating a new future is also the way to make good the past. |
| 8. The transition from *guilt to self-renewal* comes fairly easily and rapidly by means of confessing to the authority. | 8. *Self-renewal* is a gradual process of growth which characterizes all dimensions of personal development. |
| 9. Often finds a *great disproportion* between feelings of guilt experienced and the value at stake, for extent of guilt depends more on the significance of authority figure "disobeyed" than the weight of the value at stake. | 9. Experience of *guilt is proportionate* to the degree of knowledge and freedom as well as the weight of the value at stake, even though the authority may never have addressed the specific value. |

*The Dimensions of Conscience*   Timothy O'Connell names three dimensions of conscience, which he calls conscience/1, conscience/2 and conscience/3.[26] Conscience/1 is who we are and how we image ourselves as response-able *persons*.[27] Conscience/2 is the *process* of forming our conscience. Conscience/3 is the *decision* and judgment for action that we make as a result of that process.

CONSCIENCE/1: THE PERSON[28]   Too often we limit conscience to our analytical reason, but conscience/1 includes the entire accountable person that one has become through personal, social, ecclesial and cultural experience. That person includes the mind and heart, the fears, hopes and dreams, the more-than-rational passion that we bring to the analysis by conscience/2. For example, in Flannery O'Connor's short story "A Good Man Is Hard to Find," a superficially religious, elderly woman is confronted at gunpoint by a murderer. Her words with the killer jolt her out of her settled assumptions, and she sees both her complicity in the messy world in which she lives and her connectedness to the gunman. She reaches out to him in a spontaneous gesture of solidarity and claims him as a son, only to have him recoil and shoot her. She moves beyond dry religiosity and becomes a person with feelings and passion, but it took confrontation with terror to do it. The murderer comments, "She would have been a good woman . . . if there had been somebody there to shoot her every minute of her life."[29] More than analysis, we bring our person and passion to the critical times of decision in our lives.

The bedrock of conscience is the self whom one has become—one who is accountable for his or her actions (conscience/1). Once again, images are more important than ideas—how we imagine ourselves, other people, the church,[30] the world and God. These images contribute more to our eventual decisions and judgments (conscience/3) than all the processes and methods of analysis (conscience/2). Who we are and how we imagine ourselves as persons is the source of our responsibility.

There is no self without a cause. Every cause emerges from the hopes, dreams and values of a community. For the Christian community, that cause and identity is the cause of Jesus—the cause of grace, gathering people into covenant-union with God and each other in the reign of God. Jesus, in the Spirit who is present at the very center of every person, gave himself to that cause and promised good news, liberty, sight and a year of jubilee (Luke 4:16–21—3rd Sunday in Ordinary Time, Year C). He ate with whom he ate because he imaged God as an outrageous, rollicking giver of parties for the oppressed and for sinners, a God who would have him break human laws if they got in the way. Because that brought him into conflict with the religious and civil authorities, which led him to the cross, crucifixion and dying to self are part of who Jesus is and part of who we are called to be. By centering our ethics on images of God and Jesus as self-giving love (cf. 1 John 4:16–17), we move ethics beyond "morality" as the rightness or wrongness of certain actions. According to Richard McCormick,

> A Christian theological ethic is founded on the fact that something *has been done* to and for us, and that something is Jesus. There is a prior action of God at once revelatory and response-engendering. . . . In and through Jesus we know what [our] God relationship is—total self-gift. For that is what God is, and we are created in [God's] image. To miss this is, I believe, to leave the realm of Christian ethics.[31]

Conscience/1 (the response-able person), therefore, is formed in us by the presence of the Holy Spirit in our family lives and stories, in the lives and stories of our church and social communities and by hearing and experiencing people telling and living the stories of Jesus from womb to tomb.[32] A purpose of this book is to help preachers and catechists tap more deeply into those stories so that, week after week, children and adults are formed by the stories and images of Jesus and the Jewish-Christian tradition. That tradition imagines humans as being created in God's image and likeness, capable of wondrous self-giving love, able "to see some of [God's] pains and feel some of [God's] joys." Yet the tradition also imagines humans as "eternally undeveloped," and more than that, mired in sin and the demonic, capable of monstrous evil.[33] How sweet it is, then, that this same tradition imagines God as the giver of parties for sinners!

The key is images. For example, is it not true that people on both sides of the abortion issue come to different decisions and talk past each other because of the different ways that they imagine human life, women, the unborn, God? There is a growing consensus among moral theologians that our images are the first critical entry point into forming conscience. For example, Philip Keane writes,

> I believe that it may well be more possible to stimulate adult moral growth through fresh images than through new logical patterns. If we can open adults to a new vision, to new symbolisms, to a new sense of the human dream and the human story, such adults might very well be able to move to new levels of moral awareness. . . ."[34]

Andrew Greeley offers an example of the way positive images of God and human life influence morality. His research on young people under the age of 20 reveals that "they are much more likely than Catholics only a few years older to have warm, tender and affectionate images of God. . . . This new sensibility correlates positively with social generosity, religious devotion, marital fulfillment and even chastity."[35]

CONSCIENCE/2: CONSCIENCE FORMATION    Because we are touched by both grace and sin, the process of conscience formation (conscience/2) is flawed and fragile. We can have blind spots, not only because of bad will, but because of our history. The German people during World War II are an example, as are many North Americans today in areas of human life and sexuality. Conscience/2 admits disagreement and error. Therefore, conscience/2 demands the hard work of analyzing the context that we are in, our tradition of values, and the possible options. It is an honest search for truth.

> Be honest in weighing the values at stake so as not to proceed in a spirit of selfishness and self-interest. While we are to love and take care of self, we are not to make of "self" a god. The troubling paradox of the cross must be allowed to challenge us: It is in dying to self that we come to life; it is in giving of self that we receive.[36]

The formation of conscience is also a humble search for truth. "Conscience/2 is not an arrogant thing, not proud. Rather we might say that it kneels before the truth. In the realm of conscience/2, truth is supreme; truth is the object which is sought. And conscience/2 sincerely and docilely undertakes the task of finding and respecting that truth." The church, guided by the Spirit, journeys with us toward truth by handing on our tradition of moral values. "But note that conscience/2 is not directly accountable to the church. No, it is accountable to the truth and nothing else. In its search for truth, conscience/2 makes use of sources of wisdom wherever they may be found. And major among those sources is the church, the religious community."[37] Later in this chapter we shall explore one process for the formation of conscience/2.

CONSCIENCE/3: DECISION AND ACTION   After we have honestly and humbly engaged in the process of forming conscience, we have no choice but to decide and act (conscience/3). "It has been the wise insight of philosophy in our century that our highest achievement is not contemplation (as Aristotle said) but rather intelligent action. . . . At some point we must finally declare: 'It is theoretically possible that I may be wrong, but it seems to me that I ought to do *this.*'"[38] It is possible that what we do is objectively wrong. That does not mean that we have been morally wrong, that we sinned. We must do what we *believe* to be right.[39]

O'Connell suggests that a clear distinction between conscience/2 and conscience/3 might ease the fuss and furor about the maxim that we must always follow our conscience. We do not follow conscience/2. Conscience/2 honestly and humbly seeks and follows the truth, not always very well. We must follow conscience/3, for in the end that is the only reliable and possible guide for an intelligent and free human being. According to Bernard Häring, "Everyone, of course, must ultimately follow [their] conscience; this means that [they] must do right as [they] see the right [conscience/3] with desire and effort to find and do what is right [conscience/2]."[40]

**The Place of Conscience**   All this talk of following conscience raises the question: In these "wintry times" surveyed in chapter one, what is the place of conscience in our church? Do we want adults making their own responsible moral decisions? Some seem to hold that if people truly form their consciences, they can always follow church law.[41]

Indeed, this is not the first wintry time for conscience in our church. Pope Gregory XVI (1831–1846), in the encyclicals *Mirari Vos* and *Singulari Nos*, flatly condemned liberalism, including "this false and absurd maxim, or better this madness, that everyone should have and practice freedom of conscience." Closer to our times, Cardinal Pericle Fellici, a leading reactionary at Vatican II, proclaimed, "Canon law must not be subverted by theology and pastoral concerns."

We have had more springlike times. St. Thomas Aquinas stated that he would rather choose conscience and be excommunicated than violate conscience.[42] Cardinal John Henry Newman wrote, "I shall toast conscience first and the pope second."[43]

On the level of official teaching, we get the spiritual bends moving from the words of Gregory XVI to those of Paul VI and the bishops of Vatican II:

> A sense of the dignity of the human person has been impressing itself more and more deeply on the consciousness of contemporary people. And the demand is increasingly made that people should act on their own judgment, enjoying and making use of a responsible freedom, not driven by coercion but motivated by a sense of duty. . . . This sacred Synod likewise professes its belief that it is upon the human conscience that these obligations fall and exert their binding force. The truth cannot impose itself except by virtue of its own truth.[44]

The Canadian bishops affirm, "In all . . . activity, a [person] is bound to follow his [or her] conscience faithfully." They add, "The confessor or counselor must show sympathetic understanding and reverence for the sincere good faith of those who fail in their effort to accept some point of the encyclical."[45] Although the focus for their comments is Paul VI's encyclical *Humanae Vitae* with its ban on artificial contraception, their stance on conscience in general applies to other moral issues. They counsel Catholics to form their "conscience according to truly Christian values."

Again, what Cardinal Joseph Bernardin says of *in vitro* fertilization using the sperm and ovum of a husband and wife, also banned by a Vatican document,[46] gives an approach to other moral issues.

> I have heard the pain of loving couples, Catholic and non-Catholic, who desperately want the gift of a child. My heart reaches out to them. Theirs is a difficult burden, and I share their pain. We must offer them love, support and understanding. And in the end, after prayerful and conscientious reflection on this teaching, they must make their own decision.[47]

Before he was bishop or pope, Karol Wojtyla wrote, "Conscience is the ultimate judge of the authenticity of human attitudes. . . . Communal life is actually enriched by conflict that is expressed dialogically, bringing to light what is right and true in these differences. . . . If solidarity and opposition are 'authentic attitudes,' a 'sterile' conformism is 'unauthentic.'"[48] More recently, in 1992, John Paul II cites Catherine of Siena's critique of papal policies that "demonstrate the possibility and the usefulness of freedom of speech in the church: freedom that can also be manifested in the form of constructive criticism . . . [which] cannot be done with bitterness. . . ."[49] The blizzards of a wintry time may batter and buffet conscience in some quarters of the church, but she still has some husky friends to pull her through the storms.

*Values in Conflict*   Are there times when a person's conscience decides that he or she *cannot* follow church law? Regarding that question, I offer a conservative approach that I hope is both faithful to our tradition on conscience and also helps us to offer pastoral care for catechumens and others. Developed by Peter Chirico, the theological consultant for the archdiocese of Seattle, this approach originally responded to the ban on artificial contraception in *Humanae Vitae* in 1968, but it also applies to other moral issues.[50] It came about when more than 30 priests in the archdiocese of Washington, D.C., dissented from the teaching on artificial birth control. Following their protest, their archbishop suspended their faculties to offer the sacrament of penance. More than 100 theologians signed a statement of dissent. But Chirico refused to sign that statement. He suggested a route other than dissent and counseled the archbishop (a canon lawyer and hardly a radical) and clergy of the archdiocese of Seattle to take a pastoral approach that both avoided suspension and helped resolve the tensions and conflicts that married couples had with this teaching. The key words in this approach are "tensions" and "conflicts."

When confronting the complexities of life in modern times in concrete contexts,[51] we find multiple values affirmed by Christian Catholic teaching and law that are in tension and even in conflict with each other. This is not to sell out to the observation of Jonathan Swift that "The scripture, in time of disputes, is like an open town in time of war, which serves indifferently the occasions of both parties," or to that of George Bernard Shaw: "No [one] in these islands ever believes that the Bible means what it says; [they are] always convinced that it means what [they say]."[52] Rather, we recognize that because of changing needs and contexts, the scriptures and postbiblical teaching may opt for seemingly competing values.

Some of these conflicts have been around for awhile, and there are religious teachings and laws supporting conflicting values. The resolution of these conflicts is relatively simple although sometimes painful.[53] In the example about Sunday Mass given earlier, if we move beyond legalism, we choose between the value of communal worship and the value of caring for our health. If we're sick, we don't go to Mass. To cite another example, if we harm or kill a person in self-defense or to protect another, we choose the value of self-preservation or of saving a beloved, even if we fail to preserve the value of reverencing every human life. Similarly, when we withhold the truth to save a life, we choose the values of the fifth commandment over the values of the eighth commandment.[54]

Earlier generations did not face the conflict of choosing between the value of prolonging life through machines and the value of compassion for the spiritual, emotional and financial agony of the patient and family. Earlier times did not have the option of choosing between the value of caring in the home for elderly, perhaps ill or senile parents who may disrupt family life, and the value of peace and stability of the family by turning to a nursing home. Birth-control pills, *in vitro* fertilization, surrogate mothers, nuclear reactors, "smart bombs," welfare and workfare, automation, awareness of global interdependence regarding rain forests and ozone layers,[55] nutrition and hydration for comatose patients, new career opportunities for women, the liberation of women and minorities— these are the options for our generation. Even if we do not choose them, they are there for the choosing. What values in our faith would lead to deciding for or against these options or for making other choices?

**Conversation Starter:** What is your experience of these or other new options?

There are times when we *cannot* do everything. To think that we can is to miss the awesome vision of God's grace and our possibilities enfleshed, especially in the Sermon on the Mount (see chapter seven of this book). These possibilities are captured in the great commandments— to love God with all our heart, all our soul and all our mind, and to love our neighbor as ourself (Matthew 22:37–40—30th Sunday in Ordinary Time, Year A). How can we achieve racial balance *and* preserve neighborhood identity? How can we humanize the judicial and penal systems *and* protect citizens from crime and violence? How do mothers and fathers provide for children's education and for the family's economic security *and* maintain their personal identities and careers, *and* give enough time and love to their family? How can we avoid nuclear holocaust (for our generation perhaps not by a superpower but by a smaller nation or terrorist group) *and* deter such action with our own nuclear stockpile? How do we protect our environment *and* create jobs? Of course, all of this will never happen on this side of the future reign of God; but we do believe that what we do in this world should give hints of that coming world of fulsome love of God and neighbor.

If we cannot do everything, ethicists say that after forming our conscience and naming all the values that the options present, we use the virtue of prudence—we choose the option which allows the values and goods that are most humanly possible. In some cases that evil may be especially tragic, such as in killing in self-defense. In these cases we shall not act on some value, law or church teaching. We do not dissent, however, from that law or teaching. We do not deny that usually "honesty is the best policy" and that killing is always tragic. We may break a law (as in the simple case of missing Sunday Mass because of illness), but we do not sin—we do not deny the value enfleshed in the law. Therefore, we need to be careful about our language. We might withhold the truth, but we do not necessarily say that we lie, which has moral overtones of sin. We may have killed a person, but we may not have committed murder.

Regarding the ban on artificial contraception, Chirico's approach suggests that not acting on the teaching of *Humanae Vitae*, affirmed repeatedly by John Paul II, need not be a matter of dissent. Cardinal Carter of Toronto agrees. Before the 1989 Vatican synod on the family, when there was some talk of a change in the ban on contraception, he said,

> The Synod . . . won't recommend a change. People will have to realize there is a difference between saying, "I know this is what the church says but I can't practice it for practical reasons," and saying, "The church has no right to tell me this, so I quit." If a person studies the ruling and can't obey it, then he or she

will have to say that for them it is a matter of conscience. A good Roman Catholic should want to obey, but if they can't, they have to resolve it as best they can. This is not dissent from the church in my view.[56]

I am thinking of a couple with an RH problem. They were told by medical experts that their next child would be born deformed or dead. With some counseling they looked at all the values present: responsible parenthood, which would honor the spiritual, emotional and physical life of the family and the possible newborn; the call to grow in love for each other in all the ways that wife and husband can give themselves to each other, including sacrifice and self-denial but also including sexual intercourse; the call of Paul VI in *Humanae Vitae* always to unite love-giving and life-giving in sexual intercourse by giving birth or using only natural means to limit the family. They chose the values of responsible parenthood and mutual love over the values of giving birth to a child and of natural means of family limitation. But in doing so they did not see themselves as dissenting from the teaching against artificial contraception. They agreed that spiritually, symbolically and emotionally, sexual intercourse has the most meaning when responsible parents, in love, consciously try to create new life. They decided they could not act on that last value by risking the birth of a dead or deformed baby. Further, they did act on the value enfleshed in that official teaching by adopting a child.

For Chirico that last choice is key. When we frail and fragile humans in a twisted, flawed and imperfect world cannot do everything we are still called to do what we can to enflesh all possible values. In this case the couple did so by adopting a child. We are also called to commit ourselves to building a better world in which these values are more possible; through research, it has now become possible to correct or prevent such an RH problem. If people refuse to act on the church teaching that rejects capital punishment, they still must do what they can to heal the causes of violence. Yet I have the impression that most people have little sense of this obligation.[57]

There is wonderful Hasidic story about a king confronting values in conflict. His courtiers brought news that all who ate the current year's grain crop went insane. Yet there was not enough grain from the previous year to feed all the people. The king reflected and pondered. Then he decreed, "We shall feed the people with this year's crop. We shall go insane. But we must feed a few people on last year's crop, so they can remind us that we are insane!" If, in conflict, we must ever choose against life for anyone in any way, we must remind ourselves that this is insane and that we are called to build a saner, more life-giving world.

> **Conversation Starter:**  Tell of some times when you experienced values in conflict, when you *could not* act on all church teaching and laws. What values did you choose and why?

While this approach acknowledges human limits, it goes beyond minimalism and calls us to stretch our humanity with hopes, visions and dreams that commit us to a better future. Richard McCormick calls these the "3 AM questions,"

> the types of concerns we have as we hover between sleep and wakefulness. . . . We see this in medicine as physicians grow bored and restive with the commercialization of their profession. . . . We see it in business people who are sick and tired of a climate that makes profit not only a requirement but an obsession, that forgets there are stakeholders other than stockholders. We see it in educators, attorneys and even ministers who feel that a merely functional or sacramental description of their challenges diminishes them. . . . [This calls for an ethics not of minimal duty but an] ethics of aspiration that is demanding, positive, aesthetic, centered on who we might become. It deals with questions of guilt, personal integrity, of what my life is becoming, of God in my life, of genuine love, of mortality. . . . [These questions] are much more invitational than obligational.[58]

The ethics of aspiration (from the Latin *aspirare*, "from the spirit"), which focus on Jesus and who we can become in the Spirit, also need contemporary images and stories of people who soar beyond minimalism. For example, Jean Vanier, the founder of L'Arche communities, where the mentally handicapped live with a diverse community, was born into a life of prestige and power. He tells how he learned from the powerless:

> The poor are prophetic, they *disturb*, they cry out their anger, their pain and their depression. [Yet] the fundamental mystery of L'Arche is that of belonging and of communion. It is to enter into communion with the poor. The heart of the mystery of the church is that she is essentially a place of communion. Little by little we are being called to that gift.[59]

Such contemporary stories and images will shape our values more than theologies.

**A PROCESS FOR CATHOLIC-CHRISTIAN CONSCIENCE FORMATION**

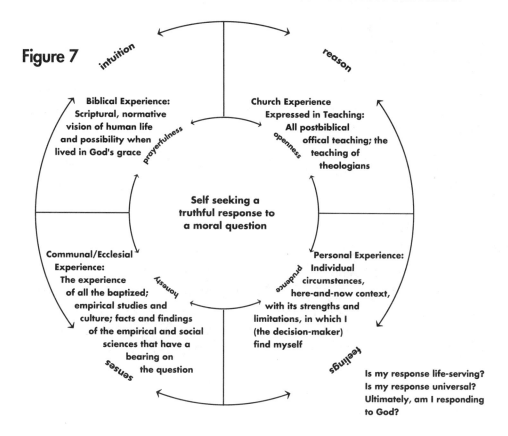

Figure 7

In Figure 7, I offer one process for forming the Christian/Catholic conscience.[60] In the paragraphs that follow, I shall make special application of this conscience circle to moral issues concerning marriage and divorce, issues of particular concern to many people.

At the center of the circle is the whole person (intuition, reason, feelings, senses)[61] the self that seeks a truthful response to a moral question with prayerfulness, openness, prudence and honesty. The goal is a response that honors the question: Is my response life-serving, universal and a response to God (conscience/3)? This kind of truthful response, especially concerning important moral questions, assumes that we consult other resources so that we are truth-serving and not just self-serving. In the circle of conscience formation those resources include: scripture, church experience and teaching, culture and empirical studies, and personal experience. Some comments and cautions regarding these resources:

SCRIPTURE   Some Christians insist that the Bible spells out God's will for us and our moral behavior. That generally has not been true of Roman Catholic tradition, although too often scripture has been used (and abused) as proof texts for or against certain acts. Today we look more for the big story of covenant/inclusion (see chapters seven through ten of this book), for the interaction between God and God's people,

> with greater attention given to the possible moral themes which characterize the way one who loves acts toward the beloved. . . . The moralist studies the scriptures . . . and finds that a lover (God/Christ) is merciful, always faithful, compassionate, just, challenging, etc. These become moral themes which help to specify appropriate moral response between every lover and the beloved.[62]

As we have seen, contemporary biblical study calls us to move beyond fundamentalism, historicism and psychologism (chapter five). In areas of sexual and marital ethics, for example, we know that the text about Onan spilling his semen on the ground should not be used as the basis for the church's prohibition of masturbation and contraception (as Pius XI does in *Casti Connubii*). That text is about the Levirate law, which directed that a man marry the wife of his brother if the brother died without a male child to carry on the family name. Although you might spark some lively discussion with catechumens, beware of applying some of the prohibitions of Leviticus to our culture, e.g., "Do not charge interest, but obey God and let your fellow Israelite live near you" (Leviticus 26:36). We also have seen that in the Sermon on the Mount (balanced by the teaching on forgiveness in chapter 18), Jesus clearly prohibits all divorce (Matthew 5:31–32) but proclaims this not as a new law "but a proclamation of the gospel . . . [and] a lived faith which is actually experienced, at least sometimes in life. We are not concerned with a perfectionist demand."[63]

CHURCH EXPERIENCE AND OFFICIAL CHURCH TEACHING   The second resource in our conscience circle is the past and present postbiblical faith experience of the community of the baptized, especially that which is expressed in official teaching. In the spirit of Vatican II, I do not intend to separate scripture and postbiblical tradition into two sources of revelation.[64] For the sake of convenience, I separate out the following paragraphs on the ongoing faith experience of the church since biblical times.

Also, I emphasize papal and episcopal teaching not because faith begins there but because faith is officially expressed there. Avery Dulles cites Vatican II in insisting that the gift of truth is given primarily to the whole church:

> "The body of the faithful as a whole, anointed as it is by the Holy One (see 1 John 2:20, 27), cannot err in matters of belief." . . . The hierarchy are themselves part of the believing church, so the distinction [between the faithful and the hierarchy] is an inadequate one. . . . [The hierarchy] cannot teach anything except the revelation committed to the whole church.[65]

If large numbers of apparently faithful people agree in past or present on a doctrinal or moral issue, at least that must be considered, especially in questions about of sexuality and marriage.

> There is no area of faith and morals where the faithful have a greater right to be heard than in the area of sex and marriage. A life involving sexual activity is the faithful's normal state for salvation. . . . So teachings about sexuality vitally concern them in a very practical way because, as Patrick Granfield reminds us, "Christian truth is not an abstraction, but exists only in the living faith of the people." Or as Virgil Michel used to say, "Any theology that is not a lived theology is no theology at all."[66]

Although it is nonsense to say that we determine doctrine by putting it to a vote of the baptized, we do have new methods of sociological research that can make available the experience of the faithful.[67] For example, every survey that I have seen reveals that a large majority of Catholics would welcome divorced and remarried Catholics to the sacraments. A recent study concludes that 75 percent of Catholic women in the United States even believe that divorced people should be allowed to remarry in the church.[68] Even those who contest such opinions are served by this research, because it reveals that we have a problem, and they are challenged to make more credible the official teaching prohibiting such practices.

> **Conversation Starter:** What is your understanding of infallible church teaching and of the extraordinary and ordinary magisterium (teaching authority)?

Regarding official teaching, some Catholics grow up with a case of "creeping infallibility," the notion that in every papal document and even every statement from the Vatican, the church "cannot err when it teaches or believes a doctrine of faith and morals."[69] But infallible statements are limited to the pope or to the pope with the bishops, and only when they clearly intend in each instance to exercise that authority. Strange as it may seem, "There have been no teachings on morals or morality explicitly *defined* as infallible Catholic teachings."[70]

This does not mean that other papal and episcopal teachings do not carry special weight (much more weight than this author or this book!). Infallible teaching is called the extraordinary magisterium because it is rarely used. But the ordinary magisterium of declarations, exhortations and pronouncements, especially conciliar documents and papal encyclicals, is vast and compelling of our attention.

Because many of these documents include theological and philosophical reasoning (e.g., natural law theory regarding morals), they certainly are not written in the "poetic simple" language recommended for most catechesis. They may be less compelling for catechumens than for catechists, who need to tap these resources and make them accessible. If candidates raise questions about or seem to disagree with official teachings, catechists are obligated to present these teachings as clearly and as convincingly as possible.

Regarding noninfallible church teachings, the new code of canon law states that "no assent of faith but religious respect of mind and will is due" (canon 752). Might we give that respect and also help catechumens wrestle with the values in conflict provoked by such teachings as this from Vatican II: "If anyone is in extreme necessity, they have the right to take from the riches of others what they themselves need."[71]

In privatistic North America, which attempts to restrict religion to church sanctuaries, the pastoral letters of the United States bishops on peace and economic justice written in the 1980s might also provoke much agreement and disagreement among candidates.[72] The bishops themselves say in "The Challenge of Peace" that people should take seriously their applications of principles, but they are "not binding in conscience." Many candidates will also have to wrestle with issues of morality and church teaching and canon law regarding past marriages.[73]

> **Conversation Starter:** What is your experience of candidates for initiation who, in the eyes of the church, are in invalid marriages?

First, in approaching marriage in general, we need to do much more as a community before and during marriages to support married people and call them to the sacrifice, suffering, dying/rising and self-giving love of the followers of Jesus. It is not an accident that in Latin, love (*amore*) has roots in death (*morte*).

Second, regarding past marital unions, in an estimated 90 percent of cases submitted in the United States, marriage tribunals either declare that there was no sacramental marriage in the first place (an annulment)[74] or dissolve a marriage according to Pauline or Petrine privilege. I take no position here on whether or not this truly honors Jesus' call to self-giving love and his prohibition of divorce and remarriage. Nor will I speculate on whether in the popular mind this constitutes "Catholic divorce." On the positive side, the paper work for a marriage case can be a form of story telling that heals wounds and renews commitments to spouses and families and to God.

> **Conversation Starter:** What is your experience, personal or with catechumens, of the ministry of your local marriage tribunal? Is it healing or hurtful?

Third, in some cases people are convinced in conscience of the health of and hope for their present marriage and of the invalidity of a former union. If, however, this invalidity cannot be substantiated on paper because of insufficient testimony, the annulment is denied. For such people, Cardinal Seper, then prefect of the Congregation for the Doctrine of the Faith, in 1973 counseled pastors of souls "on the one hand, to stress observance of current discipline [regarding indissolubility of sacramental marriage] and, on the other hand, to . . . exercise special care to seek out those who are living in an irregular union" and not to remarry them but to explore their celebration of reconciliation and eucharist.[75] Subsequently, this "approved practice of the church" was followed by two Cincinnati archbishops—first Archbishop Bernardin and later Archbishop Pilarczyk—in publishing conditions which, if present, would allow such persons to "to be reconciled and to receive the sacraments for spiritual and not merely social reasons."[76]

Finally, we come to the most difficult marriage situation of all: when a valid prior marriage has failed and the spouses in a second marriage are torn between honoring the value of the permanence of that first marriage and the values of family unity through participation in the sacraments. Some papal teaching insists that such participation in the eucharist is at the heart of the Christian life. John Paul II envisions the eucharist as "the necessary condition for the development of the evangelical life."[77] Paul VI states that "a fully Christian life is unthinkable without participation in the celebration of the eucharist."[78]

However, after the synod on the family, John Paul II reiterated the official teaching, which bans such people from the sacraments: "The church insists on the custom, rooted in the very sacred scriptures, not to admit to the eucharistic communion those who after divorce entered a new marriage." Nevertheless, he immediately calls them to live the full evangelical life for which he has said the eucharist is the necessary condition:

> They should be exhorted to hear the word of God, to be present at the sacrifice of the Mass, to persevere in prayer, to help the charitable works and the undertakings of the community for justice, to instruct their children in the Christian faith, to cultivate the spirit and works of penance, to implore thus the grace of God.[79]

There seem to be values in conflict in these papal teachings. Ladislas Orsy comments,

> It would be difficult to find a precedent for a group of faithful to be invited to participate in the devotional, charitable, even apostolic life of the church and at the same time to be barred from the reception of the eucharist because they are public sinners. Further, ordinarily we assume that the gift of life received at baptism must be nourished by the eucharist; now this group of persons is called to lead a full Christian life in every way, but without the strength that normally is given through the eucharist.

Thus at present, papal teaching clearly upholds this prohibition from participation in the eucharist, but Orsy suggests that in light of this call of the pope to live the full Christian life, "We are in the midst of a development that has not reached its final goal."[80] In the future there may be more possibilities.

For over two decades, some bishops have made tentative explorations of ecclesially approved possibilities. Cardinal Joseph Ratzinger, presently head of the Vatican Congregation for the Doctrine on the Faith, wrote in 1972,

> Marriage is a sacrament; it consists of an unbreakable structure, created by a firm decision. But this should not exclude the grant of ecclesial communion to those persons who acknowledge this teaching as a principle of life but find themselves in an emergency situation of a specific kind, in which they have a particular need to be in communion with the body of the Lord.[81]

Walter Kaspar, the pope's theologian at the 1987 extraordinary synod of bishops and now Bishop of Rottenburg-Stuttgart, Germany, takes a similar stance:

> A broken marriage is not simply canceled out. It continues to exist, even though it can be compared with a ruin. It is therefore not possible to replace it with a second marriage equal to the first. What is possible, however, and in many cases necessary for survival, is some kind of emergency accommodation. This image would seem in accordance with the way in which God acts in the history of human salvation. [God] often writes straight with crooked lines.[82]

At the Vatican synod on family life, 15 bishops asked for greater inclusion in sacramental life for couples in irregular marriages. One of these, Archbishop Karl Berg of Salzburg, suggested, "Perhaps after a period of penance they might be readmitted to the sacraments." Archbishop Peter Shiragyanagi of Tokyo observed that exclusion from the sacraments "seemed an especially cruel measure." He asked for a way to be found "so that these people can fully participate in the life of the church." Archbishop Derek Worlock of Liverpool asked, "Is this spirit of repentance and desire for sacramental strength to be forever frustrated?"[83] After this same synod, Cardinal Ratzinger wrote a letter that encouraged a consideration of the Eastern Church's practice of allowing remarriage in some cases.[84]

CULTURE AND EMPIRICAL STUDIES    The third resource in our conscience circle, culture and empirical studies, refers to the past and present experience of society in general. In chapter three we explored cultural angels and demons that might influence us in many areas of our life. Here I shall limit consideration to marriage and sexuality.

Cultural attitudes, past and present, toward marriage and sexuality undeniably have an impact on church teaching and on our own moral decisions.[85] In a brief history of our postbiblical tradition on sexuality and celibacy, Anthony Padovano claims that by the end of the second century, culture, politics and Plato influenced church life and teaching more than the gospel and Jesus. "Jesus was not primarily a celibate; he was a prophet whose celibacy made sense only in the context of prophecy. . . . Jesus makes no reference to his celibacy, and expects it of none of his disciples."[86] At the end of the second century, however, celibacy becomes more important than prophecy. Eventually, it becomes *the* prophetic witness. After surveying this history, given over to what he calls at times "a pitch of pathological hysteria," Padovano concludes: "The second to the fourth centuries psychologically destroyed the respect for marriage, sex and women. The eleventh and twelfth centuries destroyed the married priesthood and moved to create an imperial church."[87]

In the second to the fourth centuries, influenced by Greek asceticism as the fashionable way to redeem or develop our humanity, spirituality begins to value martyrdom over life, the desert over the community, virginity over family, men over women. The words of the philosopher Seneca, for example, may lie behind attitudes toward sexuality and women: "When a woman thinks alone, she thinks evil. . . . They are feebler both in mind and body . . . and it is a natural vice in them not to be disciplined."[88]

Origen yearned to die a martyr's death as his father did. Since he could not, he had himself castrated at age 20 to redeem himself in the blood of that mutilation. Later, Ambrose declares that all that is best in Jesus' teaching is in Plato, and further, that celibacy is the one experience that distinguishes us from beasts.

Still later, in reaction to a profligate sexual life, Augustine became a Manichean for nine years and learned that the body was "blood and bile and flatulence and excrement . . . a mold of defilement." Because sexual intercourse is a bodily function, it was not, therefore, an act of love and grace but of lust (with woman as co-conspirator), tolerated by God only because it conceives children. Augustine writes of his son Adeodatus, "I had no part in that boy except the sin." He writes of women, "How sordid, filthy and horrible a woman's embraces."[89]

In the eleventh century, Peter Damian was saved by the pleading of the wife of a priest when his impoverished mother tried to starve him. Even so, he became a vicious adversary of sexuality and married priests. He warns priests and their wives (whom he refers to as whores): "The hands that touch the body and blood of Christ must not touch the genitals of a whore."[90] Women are called "flesh of the devil," "cause of our ruin," "the very stuff of sin," "pigs."[91]

Obviously, not all church teaching and law on marriage emerged from the pathology of these early centuries; but some theology and, more importantly, popular Puritan and Jansenist attitudes, which separate sex from love (as does the resulting "Playboy philosophy"), clearly arose from an emaciated Platonic view of the body as prison of the soul.

Ironically, the controversy over artificial contraception raised by Paul VI in *Humanae Vitae* caused many to miss the intimate connection between love-making and life-giving so beautifully expressed by the pope. That document undid the separation made by previous popes of primary (procreation) and secondary (mutual love) ends of marriage, a dichotomy that almost certainly emerged in part from the skewed experience and theology of Augustine. A Catholic sacramental understanding of sexuality confronts the attitudes that separate sex from relationship and commitment, and instead envisions sexual intercourse as deepening communion with God through each other.[92] John Paul II elaborated on that vision, especially in the many conferences he gave early in his ministry as pope.

> **Conversation Starter:** Are you and the people you know familiar with this dramatic shift by Paul VI or have you heard only of the prohibition of artificial contraception? Might you consider reading the entire encyclical?

Some empirical studies indicate that in the eighteenth century, first marriages that did not end in divorce lasted an average of seven years; in the nineteenth century, twelve years; in the twentieth century, forty-two years.[93] In earlier times, many women died in childbirth; it was not uncommon for men to marry three times due to the deaths of their wives. Again, sociological data do not determine church teaching; but at least we should consider that we ask for a much longer commitment in marriage in our times.

> **Take a Stand:** How in this century have societal attitudes changed with regard to the experience of marriage and sexuality?

In the present century, attitudes toward marriage clearly have changed. The bad news is that in a throw-away, mobile, fast-food and fast-relationship culture, there is an assault on the permanence of and fidelity in marriage. The good news is that our culture has moved away from marriages arranged by parents for their children. But as our culture has moved toward the critical importance of personal choice and romantic love between spouses, that same culture has also raised the expectations of married couples. And those with the highest expectations may have the highest divorce rate if hopes are dashed. Yet, if people fulfill their hopes and dreams in a second marriage, the current papal teaching bars them from reconciliation and communion.

PERSONAL EXPERIENCE   On the one hand, personal experience will be the source for vast disagreements concerning values and decisions. On the other hand, and more positively, because of our precious and unique histories we come to deeper commitments to certain values (perhaps not shared by others) and to give ourselves more vigorously and zestfully to a cause. For example, because of their experience, Mohandas Gandhi, Dorothy Day and Martin Luther King gave their lives to the cause of change through nonviolence. We might not choose nonviolence as an absolute value, but we thank God for those who offer a vision of who we can be and how things will be in the reign of God.[94]

> **Conversation Starter:** Who are your heroines and heroes, from the past and in the present, who by their vision and dreams most challenge you?

This resource of personal experience is especially important in moral issues regarding sexuality and marriage. The experience of spouses with their families must enter the conversation. For example, our church values the call to grow in mutual love in marriage more clearly and more deeply today than it has in the past (as do Paul VI in *Humanae Vitae* and John Paul II in many papal addresses). But if a couple finds that without sexual intimacy their Christian love for each other is threatened, or their fidelity to each other threatened, they must bring that experience to their decision. The church acknowledges that experience. Although the bishops at Vatican II, before *Humanae Vitae*, counseled against "methods of regulating procreation which are found blameworthy by the teaching authority of the church" (most notably Pius XI and Pius XII), they add, "Where the intimacy of married life is broken off, it is not rare for its faithfulness to be imperiled and its quality of fruitfulness ruined."[95]

Within personal experience we also include people's faith experience of the sacraments. For example, some Catholics have a very shallow faith concerning the eucharist; not participating might not move them deeply. However, we hope that we have formed candidates for initiation with a deep understanding and love for the eucharist, the repeatable sacrament of initiation. We hope that they envision the eucharist not just as receiving communion but as entering more deeply into God's life and God's people in Christ's covenant/inclusion explored throughout this book. We hope that they would see the marriage covenant as their life in the "domestic church," which they bring to eucharist. Celebrating in eucharist that covenant would then be the great joy of their faith experience; exclusion would be their great pain.

When discussing official church teaching, I noted that although some bishops have called for a change, papal teaching clearly excludes some divorced and remarried Catholics from the sacraments. However, if persons have tried to form their conscience and believe that for them participation in the sacraments would not be sinful, church teaching does affirm their subjective experience. Cardinal John Wright cites the United States bishops' pastoral letter on human life: "Particular circumstances surrounding an objectively evil human act, while they cannot make it objectively virtuous, can make it 'inculpable, diminished in guilt or subjectively defensible.'"[96]

Robert Friday constructs a conversation between a priest and a woman who cannot legally remarry in the church. With him she has tried to form her conscience, but she believes that

I'd fail God utterly if I did not marry. I truly regret any failure on my part in the first marriage; I also deeply regret . . . going against the Church's teaching, and breaking the law, but I do believe it's responsible and not sinful.

The priest responds,

The church cannot say that your decision is a good one or the right one . . . The church, too, regrets your decision to go contrary to its teaching in this matter. But Sarah, it does not call it sin, nor does it call you a sinner. That judgment is known to you and to God. It is sin that keeps us from the sacraments. Prudent sensitivity to the question of scandal should direct how you act upon this.[97]

This concludes our journey around the "conscience circle" as a process for conscience formation, with its special focus on marriage. I close this section with words from David O'Rourke about accepting into covenant/inclusion the "least" ones among us whose lives have known failure (including marital failure). He tells of an Easter Vigil in his parish in California during which a dozen people were baptized: English and Arab, Japanese and Mexican and a young gypsy. I mentioned in chapter one that for some people, belonging to a community and meeting lifestyle needs is more important than religious heritage and ritual. O'Rourke says that for these people, many of whom are immigrants, migrants, spiritual wanderers and outsiders to his suburban community, it was the opposite. They "were brought ritually into the Catholic Church more than socially into a parish community." Many don't speak either the cultural language or churchy language well. They have known suffering and failure.

Only the wrenching experiences of failure—of not making it—bring the mercy of a suffering God into human focus. When such experiences are consciously connected to the life of the church in the public liturgy, they prove especially helpful and powerful. Liturgy, however, can ill make the connection if . . . it is primarily a celebration for those who are successful, articulate and devout. But if the people who run the liturgy . . . admit the religiously unlettered, the nondevout, the failed and all those who cannot, for their lack of churchy chatter, talk their way through the usual checkpoints, then the gathered people may, in their very diversity, be a sign of God's mercy.[98]

**Conversation Starter:** How diverse are the catechumens in your parish?

### The Catholic Experience of Sacramentality

I want to conclude this chapter on conversing with our postbiblical Catholic tradition by focusing, if only briefly, on the heart of that tradition—sacramentality.

Even a casual observer such as humorist Garrison Keillor is fascinated by this Catholic difference (see chapter four), which he remembers from his childhood and which he now tells in stories about the church of Our Lady of Perpetual Responsibility in Lake Wobegon:

> [I was] tainted with a sneaking admiration of Catholics—Catholic Christmas, Easter, the Living Rosary, and the Blessing of the Animals, all magnificent . . . especially the Feast Day of St. Francis, which they did right out in the open, a feast for the eyes. Cows, horses, some pigs, right on the church lawn. The turmoil, animals bellowing and barking and clucking . . . and the ocarina band of third-graders playing Catholic dirges, and the great calm of the sisters, and the flags, and the Knights of Columbus decked out in their handsome black suits—I stared at it until my eyes almost fell out. . . . I wasn't allowed inside the church, of course, but if the Blessing of the Animals on the Feast Day of St. Francis was any indication, Lord, I didn't know but what they had elephants in there and acrobats.[99]

*Incarnation and Creation*[100]   This sacramental experience of God in all creation brings us to give thanks for and bless everything from cows to elephants. And in one sense it rests on how seriously we take the incarnation (*in carnis*—"enfleshment") of God in Jesus as *the* image of the invisible God (Colossians 1:15). We let the words of 1 John 1: 1–3 resound:

> We declare to you what was from the beginning, what we have heard, what we have seen with our eyes, what we have looked at and touched with our hands, concerning the word of life—this life was revealed, and we have seen it and testify to it, and declare to you the eternal life that was with the Father and was revealed to us—we declare to you what we have seen and heard so that you also may have fellowship with us.

Christian faith proclaims that God has never been more fully present than in the flesh of a human being—Jesus of Nazareth. But he is no longer Jesus of Nazareth—Jewish male of the first century. He is the Risen Christ who has cast his Spirit broadside to unite all creation and all peoples, so that "there is no longer Jew or Greek, there is no longer slave or free, there is no longer male and female; for all of you are one in Christ Jesus" (Galatians 3:28).

Yet our vision of sacramentality also rests on how seriously we take creation as the incarnation of God, not just in Jesus but in all created things. John proclaims in his gospel that "in the beginning was the Word. . . . All things came into being through him" (John 1:1, 3). The Word became flesh from the very beginning. We were simply too dense to see it. Like Jesus, humans were created in God's image from the very beginning (Genesis 1:26), able "to feel God's pain and joy" yet "eternally undeveloped."

We might draw an analogy between what William Lynch says of human imagination and God's "imagination." Lynch states that we humans pour our whole selves—our whole history, life and heritage, our experience, concepts, judgments, decisions, wishes, hopes, disappointments, loves and hates—into our images. "This is true of the image we have of a man, a woman, a child, birth, life, death, morning, night, food, friend, the enemy, the self, the human, the world as world. . . . *Thus one cannot get closer to [people], nor can [people] get closer to [themselves], than through [their] images.*"[101]

> **Conversation Starter:** What is your image of your self: clown, explorer, prophet, "worm, not a human," competitor, martyr, dreamer, wounded healer, other images? What key experiences and relationships formed that image?

Let's apply that to God. God has poured God's self into images—into Jesus, into us, into all creation. We found that *we could not get closer to God than through God's image in Jesus.* Now that we know that we are one in and with Christ Jesus through the Spirit, we know that *we cannot get closer to God than through God's images* in us and in a sacramental world. Jesus opens our eyes to God's presence in humankind as God's images, and he calls us to be who we are—icons and sacraments of the Holy One.[102]

*The Analogical Imagination*  If we open those eyes, we shall recover what David Tracy calls the analogical imagination, an idea popularized by Andrew Greeley and Mary Greeley Durkin. The Catholic religious imagination, which includes the other sacramental churches,

> tend[s] to emphasize the similarity between God and objects, events, experiences and persons in the natural world. . . . The Protestant [dialectical] imagination stresses opposition between God and World; God is totally Other, radically, drastically, and absolutely different from [God's] creation. The Catholic imagination responds by saying that God is similar to the world and has revealed Himself/Herself in the world, especially through the human dimension of Jesus.[103]

Catholics assert that if creatures exist at all, they must be at least a little bit like God.

Catholic, analogical imagination is not better than the Protestant, dialectical imagination, just different. Both have their pluses and minuses.[104] The Catholic danger is idolatry—to forget that analogy means both similar and dissimilar, partly like and partly unlike, and to identify the human (e.g., authoritarian popes or "automatic" sacraments) with the divine. That is precisely why the Protestant imagination emerged—in protest to what the reformers saw as idolatry. In that tradition, Karl Barth will denounce Thomas Aquinas's analogy of being[105] as the work of the devil because it can lead us to forget that we are not God and that we shall never capture the mystery of God. But Aquinas never forgot. He writes, "[We] reach the highest point of [our] knowledge about God when [we] know that [we] do not know [God]."[106] Before Aquinas died, he was unable to speak, unable to say anymore, proclaiming that all that he had written was straw, because he was overwhelmed by the mystery of God.

> **Conversation Starter:** Complete the sentence, "She is . . ." or "He is . . ." as many times as you can about someone you love. Have you begun to capture or define the mystery of that person? Mystery is not something about which we can know nothing. Rather, is something about which we know much and yet there is so much more to know that we cannot ever know it all (see Ephesians 3:1–13).

The Catholic plus is that because creation is shot through with God's presence, it is chock-full of hints of what God is like. God is like creation: rock, light, fortress, wind, river, vine. God is like humans: mother, father, lover, judge, friend, liberator, reconciler. God is like what is best in us: peace, compassion, mercy, forgiveness, justice, freedom, love.

Religion happens, first of all, when these "things that God is like," these analogies, emerge as dreams, poems, stories, myths, art and symbols. Religion emerges first in the activity of the right hemisphere of the brain, where imagination resides. That is why throughout this book I have shown a bias for reawakening what is asleep in many of us—our capacity to wonder and imagine. After this happens, then we can name and critique the meaning of the stories with propositions, theologies, dogmas, and precepts constructed in the left hemisphere. My purpose is Greeley and Durkin's:

> The purpose of this book is not to sweep away propositional religion but to encourage the church to develop policies that will integrate more decisively imaginative religion and propositional religion. . . . [There] is no opposition between intellect and imagination, between prose and poetry, between symbol and doctrine, between reflection and imagination. In any religious experience the whole human personality is affected.[107]

Nonetheless, because of our predominately analogical imagination, Catholics tend to play and cavort in the rituals of sacraments and sacramentals, in smells and bells, gesture and vesture, especially in the great images of Christmas and the initiation rites of the Easter Vigil. Both of these feasts take their dates and images from pagan festivals with their earthy symbols of darkness and light, death and life expressed in earth, air, fire and water. In fact "pagan" means "person of the earth"—peasants and farmers—just as "heathen" means "person on the heath." Some claim that our liturgies need to be more pagan for the citified people of our times who no longer have roots in images of earth.

Sacramental images also show up in thoroughly Catholic poets and writers. Gerard Manley Hopkins sees "the dearest freshness deep-down things"[108] and celebrates Christ playing "in ten thousand places: Lovely in limbs and lovely in eyes not his, To the Father through the features of [our] faces."[109]

Flannery O'Connor says that she writes as she does because she is Catholic down to her fingertips:

One of the awful things about writing when you are a Christian is that for you the ultimate reality is the Incarnation, the present reality is the Incarnation, the whole reality is the Incarnation. . . . I feel that if I were not a Catholic, I would have no reason to write, no reason to *see*, no reason ever to feel horrified or even to enjoy anything. . . . I feel myself that being a Catholic has saved a couple thousand years in learning to write.[110]

Walker Percy speaks of being a human "in a predicament and on the move in a real world of real things, a world which is a sacrament and a mystery. . . . The sacraments, whatever else they do, confer the highest significance upon the ordinary things of this world, bread, wine, water, touch, breath, words, talking, listening."[111]

Although she is not a Catholic, Annie Dillard wrote the following during a time when she was worshiping at a Catholic eucharist:

On the whole, I do not find Christians, outside of the catacombs, sufficiently sensible of conditions. Does anyone have the foggiest idea what sort of power we so blithely invoke? Or, as I suspect, does no one believe a word of it? The churches are children playing on the floor with their chemistry sets, mixing up a batch of TNT to kill a Sunday morning. It is madness to wear ladies' straw hats to church; we should be wearing crash helmets. . . . For the sleeping god may wake someday and take offense, or the waking god may draw us out to where we can never return.[112]

> **Conversation Starter:** Who are your favorite religious poets, novelists, artists, musicians? What do you mean by "religious?"

Because their critical intelligence is not yet developed, little children also cavort in a sacramental world of images and wonder lost to many adults. Here are a few samples of things children have written to God. John, when coming in from the playground: "I've heard lots of silence out there." Eugene: "Dear God: I didn't think orange went with purple until I saw the sunset you made on Tuesday. That was *cool*." Glenn: "Dear God: I like the story about Chanuka the best of all of them. You really made up some good ones."[113] At the first session of a children's precatechumenate, two inquirers asked, "If God is so smart, how come he didn't create all of us as grownups so we could do everything right away?" and "Jesus was God's first son. What about the next man God made? Wasn't he God's son too?"

> **Conversation Starter:** Do you have any "wonder stories" about children?

> **Take a Stand:** If we are filled with wonder at all creation, how might that affect our approach to sexuality? To ecumenism toward all religions? To social, political, and economic justice? To limiting sacraments to seven church rituals?

*The Catholic Difference*   If we can recapture the wonder of poets and children, nothing will be the same again. We enter a world brimming with sacraments, icons and images of God. Sexuality and bodily love cease to be Manichean "blood and bile and excrement, a mold of defilement." Sexual intercourse becomes "a body language in which the erotic becomes the channel of communication for personal love"[114] and a sacrament of God's love. "God not only reveals himself/herself to us through each other in sexual love; she is somehow present in the body of the lover in the act of sexual love."[115]

We would move other Christians and people of other world religions from "outside the church where there is no salvation" to being sacraments of God's presence whenever they live their truth in love. I am Catholic in part because I believe God is universal, catholic, in all peoples. That is precisely where I part company with some Christians who believe that God is present only in those "baptized by water and the Holy Spirit."

We would move religion from sacramental rituals only in sanctuaries to freedom and justice in the streets where the hungry, thirsty, stranger, naked, sick and imprisoned (Matthew 25:31–46 — 34th Sunday in Ordinary Time, Year A) are sacraments of the crucified Christ today.

We would see not just the water in fonts and the bread and wine on altars as communicating the presence of God in Christ. All waters, meals, forests and fields, flora and fauna; all creeping, crawling, swimming, slithering, prancing, dancing creatures and all those that hum and chirp and go bump in the night; all people who live in love, live in God and God in them; in all farms, villages, shantytowns, barrios, towns and cities;

all "brother suns and sister moons," stars and galaxies, black holes, earth, air, fire and water throughout all creation—all these become sacraments of God's presence. As Greeley and Durkin say,

> A sacrament is a created reality that discloses to us Uncreated Reality. It is a sign of goodness, a hint of an explanation, an experience of otherness, a promise of life, a touch of grace, a rumor of angels. . . . Those realities that are especially likely to do so (water, fire, food, drink, sex) are the sacraments par excellence.[116]

For example, if they are well-formed biblically, catechumens will see water as sacrament of all the mighty things God has done in our Hebrew and Christian stories:

- a story of a watery chaos pushed back by God when earth was formed from the void

- a story of seas burst forth by God's anger with humankind, wiping out every living thing in the flood in days of Noah, the first sailor; but also a story of a God who hangs up a bow in the skies and promises never to make war on us again

- a story of a people led from slavery through waters to a Promised Land as imperial chariots foundered

- a story of Jonah sloshing about in the waters of a fish's belly until he is spit up on land to save a people

- a story of a Jewish virgin visited by God in the waters of her womb in a way that confounded her fiance but caused her to sing

- a story of a crazy man out in the desert proclaiming a new reign of God coming in water and fire

- a story of disciples crying out in terror to the proclaimer of that reign of God in the storms on the sea

- a story of that same man who saved us by an issue of water and blood from his side

- a story of the stormy life of the baptized disciple Paul, a prisoner on his way to Rome, pounded with captors for fourteen days by the seas, then taking bread, giving thanks, breaking and eating bread, surely an image of the eucharist nourishing us through baptismal storms.[117]

That is what catechumens might experience in the sacramental waters of baptism. "Baptism is the initiation of the entire person into the story of Israel and Jesus. . . . We can imagine how long it would take simply to read the biblical story from creation to consummation. Yet baptism . . . leaves none of the story out."[118]

Catechumens also might experience this Catholic sacramental difference in each of the four dimensions of catechesis surveyed in chapter four. First, *scripture* and our postbiblical tradition of *dogmas and precepts* (#75.1) Don't simply drop down from heaven. They are not dictated by God to the minds of the evangelists and popes. They emerge from the very human stories and events that are sacraments of God's presence to communities of past and present. They are also enfleshed, incarnate in the cultures, images and languages of their time.[119]

Second, the Christian *community* (#75.2) is not just a support to conversion and faith. The community is *the* sacrament[120] of Christ's presence through the Spirit enfleshed in people who are not just a support but the very place where the Spirit brings us to conversion, faith and being "born again and again."

Third, *liturgical rites* (#75.3) are not just remembering what happened in the past, nor are they empty rituals or performances by the presiding minister. They are actions of the community expressing who we are: sacrament of Christ's dying and rising in our world—journeying with people into that death and resurrection by initiating into that community, eating, reconciling, healing, leading, marrying, and in a final meal, preparing for death. The order of initiation, more clearly than any other sacramental action of this community, invites the faithful and the catechumens into Christ's presence through the myriad of actions that reveal who we are as God's covenant community. These actions are welcoming, processing, proclaiming the word, signing with the cross, sponsoring, anointing, laying on hands in exorcising, presenting our life of faith and prayer, calling names, signing books and scrutinizing, all brought to a climax at the Easter Vigil by gathering round the fire, proclaiming the word, bathing, anointing, eating and drinking. Perhaps these times more than any other reveal whether catechumens are experiencing and celebrating the Catholic difference.

Fourth, *apostolic witness* in the world (#75.4) is not just our witness to the Sermon on the Mount or to Matthew 25 by our commitments to justice, liberation, healing, compassion and peace. In Matthew 25 we are judged on whether or not we reverence, even unconsciously, the least of Christ's sisters and brothers as sacraments of his presence in the world.

## Conclusion

I conclude this chapter on Catholic Christian dogmas and precepts with a creed born from the cultural experience of the Masai tribe in Africa.[121]

### *The Creed of the Masai*

We believe in the one High God . . .
God promised in the book of his word, the Bible,
  that [God] would save the world
  and all nations and tribes.
We believe that God made good [that] promise
  by sending [the] Son Jesus Christ:
  A man in the flesh,
  A Jew by tribe,
  Born poor in a little village,
  Who left his home and was always on safari doing good. . . .
He was rejected by his people,
  tortured, and nailed hands and feet to a cross,
  and died.
He was buried in the grave,
  but the hyenas did not touch Him,
  and on the third day He rose from the grave. . . .
We are waiting for Him.
He is alive. He lives.
This we believe. Amen!

## Endnotes

[1] I have not changed to inclusive language in this quotation; White was writing in 1939, before such consciousness arose.

[2] T. H. White, *The Once and Future King* (New York: Berkley Publishing Corporation, 1939), 191–93.

[3] "Human Experience and Religious Symbolization," *The Ecumenist* IX:4, 51.

[4] Karl Rahner, "Theology and Anthropology," in *The Word in History*, ed. T. Patrick Burke (New York: Sheed and Ward, 1966), 1–23. Elsewhere Rahner writes, "For the theologian there is a God-man: Jesus the Christ. Only those who are able to find themselves can find God. The alternative 'theology or anthropology' is false" (*Faith in a Wintry Season* [New York: Crossroad Publishing Co., 1990], 158).

[5] Cf. David Tracy, *The Analogical Imagination* (New York: Crossroad Publishing Co., 1981). For a more popularized treatment, see Andrew Greeley and Mary Greeley Durkin, *How to Save the Catholic Church* (New York: Viking Press, 1984), chapter four.

[6] John Baldovin, "The Bible and the Liturgy, Part One: The Status of the Bible Today," *Catechumenate* 11 (September 1989): 18.

[7] Kenneth Bailey comments that the brother seeking his rightful inheritance demands a justice that would have meant total alienation from his brother, but "Jesus insists that he has not come as a 'divider.' The obvious alternative is 'reconciler.' . . . Indeed, it takes a special brand of courage to tell antagonists that their naked cry for justice is not enough, that they must begin with a new understanding of themselves." *Poet and Peasant and Through Peasant Eyes* (Grand Rapids: Wm. B. Eerdmans, 1976), 60, 61.

[8] Vincent Donovan, *The Church in the Midst of Creation* (Maryknoll NY: Orbis Books, 1990), 22–24. As a missionary, Donovan also adds that because Jesus was free of most Jewish cultural systems, the message he proclaimed is not wedded to Jewish culture and can be adapted to all cultures.

[9] Karl Rahner, *Faith in a Wintry Season*, 178. Rahner adds that these Christians "will not vaunt and declare from on high their own infallibility, or that they know with absolute assuredness, . . . that the pope is not infallible. Such a thing they cannot know absolutely. If, therefore, in what is ultimately a secondary question, they cannot decide something with absolute assuredness, then they would be well advised, knowing their limits and in all modesty, to leave that question aside and to focus instead on the really substantial matters of Christian life in the church" (pp. 178–79).

[10] When Cardinal Ratzinger announced the "universal" catechism, he said that it would apply everywhere because the doctrine of the church is the same everywhere. He explained, "The Trinity is the Trinity in the North as well as in the South" ("The New Catechism? Here It Is!" *The Wanderer* 119:2, 1). Missionary Vincent Donovan comments that "Trinity" may have meaning for that part of humankind that understands personhood, nature, substance and being. "Perhaps the nonbiblical word 'Trinity,' conveying the concept of three distinct Persons in one divine nature, is not the only way to express the truth we hold when we profess, in that same Apostles'

Creed, belief in 'the Father, Son and Holy Spirit'—one God . . . in the context of the cultures of Hinduism, Buddhism and other non-Christian religions or in terms of modern science. If 'the Trinity is the Trinity in the North as well as in the South,' then other concepts must be the same . . . such as hypostatic union, transubstantiation, sanctifying grace. . . . Culture blindness is alive and well in the church" (*The Church in the Midst of Creation*, 96).

[11] However, as Cardinal John Henry Newman discovered, most bishops signed the creedal document about Jesus as God and human and went on teaching as they always had, usually some version of Arianism. It was the laity who passed on the fullness of faith in Jesus as divine and human. See Newman's essay "On Consulting the Faithful in Matters of Doctrine": "In that time of immense confusion, the divine dogma of our Lord's divinity was proclaimed, enforced, maintained, and (humanly speaking) preserved, far more by the [laity] than by the [hierarchy]; that the body of the episcopate was unfaithful to its baptism." Cited by Bob Maxwell, "On Consulting the Laity: 1859," *Gathering* (February 1987): 8.

[12] In an unpublished talk at Theological College in Washington, D.C., in 1963, John Courtney Murray contended that the great ecumenical question is not "What think ye of Christ?" nor "What think ye of the church?" but "What think ye of the *homo-ousion*?" Chalcedon proclaimed that Jesus is *homo-ousion* (of one nature) with the Father and *homo-ousion* with us, fully divine and fully human. By using the language of Greek culture, the church made the momentous decision that we could move beyond fundamentalism and use the language of contemporary culture to speak of God (over the objections of Emperor Constantine's son who, like literalists today, insisted on using only scriptural language). With that decision, however, the church called all generations to be as resilient as the Greeks and speak of God and Christ with the language and idioms of all cultures.

[13] Cf. John McIntyre, *The Shape of Christology* (Philadelphia: Westminster Press, 1966); Hans Jonas, *The Gnostic Religion* (Boston: Beacon Press, 1963); Jaroslav Pelikan, *The Christian Tradition, A History of the Development of Doctrine, Volume 1, The Emergence of the Catholic Tradition (100–600)* (Chicago: University of Chicago Press, 1971); Piet Schoonenberg, *The Christ* (New York: Herder and Herder, 1971).

[14] Gregory Baum, *Man Becoming* (New York: Herder and Herder, 1970), 217.

[15] Andrew Greeley, *The Great Mysteries: An Essential Catechism* (New York: Seabury Press, 1976).

[16] George McAuley, *Sacraments for Secular Man* (New York: Herder and Herder, 1969), 15–16. Vincent Donovan depicts the breadth of a worldly vision of sacrament:

"Sincere and compassionate efforts at preserving our planet from nuclear or poisonous destruction are eucharistic ministry at its most basic and obvious level. The words of Christ concerning the eucharist take on a poignant and urgent meaning for the people of our age, a meaning that perhaps would have been incomprehensible to men and women of another age: 'The bread of God is that which comes down from heaven and gives life to the world . . . and the bread that I shall give is my flesh, for the life of the world'" (John 6:27, 51—18th and 19th Sundays in Ordinary Time, Year B) (*The Church in the Midst of Creation*, 82).

[17] "Reflections on Prayer and Worldly Holiness," *Worship* 41 (March 1967): 108; also see Douglas Rhymes, *Prayer in the Secular City* (Philadelphia: Westminster Press, 1967). Dolores Leckey connects contemplative prayer to work and suggests that we sometimes recognize only "church work" as valuable because we do not honor a theology of creation that enlivens work in the world: "Church leadership may not really believe the theological argument: that the world is good, shot through with grace; that God is available to us in our daily work; that our work can and should be a means of growing in the knowledge of God. . . . But at a much deeper level I wonder if a reluctance to place these questions at the center of the church agenda is not related to unfamiliarity with contemplative prayer. A contemplative mood allows us to see the intimacy between the individual acts of work and the ongoing creative work of God." *Laity Stirring the Church* (Philadelphia: Fortress Press, 1987), 37.

[18] "The Behavioral Sciences and Christian Ethics," in *Projections: Shaping an American Theology for the Future*, ed. Thomas O'Meara and Donald Weisser (Garden City NJ: Doubleday, 1970), 147. A fascinating dialogue between Catholics and humanists took place in May, 1972. It indicated how unaware humanists are of Catholic reflection on ethics and secularity; cf. John Haughey, "Humanists Encounter a 'Pilgrim' Church," *America* 126: 564–67. Humanists would do well to reflect on the official teaching of the church in the magnificent opening words of the *Pastoral Constitution on the Church in the Modern World*: "The joys and the hopes, the griefs and the anxieties of the [people] of this age, especially those who are poor or in any way afflicted, these too are the joys and hopes, the griefs and anxieties of the followers of Christ. Indeed, nothing genuinely human fails to raise an echo in their hearts."

[19] In this fine article, which I shall cite often in this section, Richard McCormick offers a dream of "Moral Theology in the Year 2000," *America* 166 (April 18, 1992): 314. At the end he summarizes his dream: "I dream of a moral theology that is: 1. Christocentric and anchored in charity (vs. one that is one-sidedly philosophical). 2. Universalizing in its appeal (vs. one narrowly sectarian). 3. With appropriate subsidiarity (vs. over-centralization). 4. Personalistic (vs. excessively biologistic). 5. Modest and tentative (vs. "infallibilistic"). 6. Ecumenical (vs. exclusively parochial and Roman). 7. Inductive (vs. abstractly deductive in method). 8. Pluralistic

(vs. a universal conformism). 9. Aspirational (vs. minimalistic). 10. Specialist (vs. omnicompetent)," p. 318.

[20] Ladislas Orsy, *Theology and Canon Law* (Collegeville: The Liturgical Press, 1992). For a comprehensive treatment of the history and developments in Roman Catholic moral theology, see John Mahoney, *The Making of Moral Theology* (Oxford: Clarendon Paperbacks, 1987).

[21] Cited by Geoffrey Wigoder, gen. ed., *Almanac of the Bible* (New York: Prentice-Hall, 1991), 435.

[22] Robert Friday, *Adults Making Responsible Moral Decisions* (Washington DC: National Conference of Diocesan Directors of Religious Education [NCDD], 1979), revised in 1986 after Vatican documents on sexual ethics.

[23] James DeBoy, *Getting Started in Adult Religious Education* (New York: Paulist Press, 1979), 22.

[24] A key theme in reflection on ethics today is responsibility; cf. Albert Jonsen, *Responsibility in Modern Religious Ethics* (Washington DC: Corpus Books, 1968).

[25] Richard Gula, *Reason Informed by Faith* (New York: Paulist Press, 1989); Gula develops these contrasts from insights originally offered by John Galser, "Conscience and Superego: A Key Distinction," in *Conscience: Theological and Psychological Perspectives,* ed. C. Ellis Nelson (New York: Paulist Press, 1973). See also Timothy O'Connell, *Principles for a Catholic Morality* (San Francisco: Harper & Row, 1978), 83–85.

[26] O'Connell, *Principles,* 88–93. For reflections on conscience, also see Gula, *Reason Informed by Faith,* chapters 9–10; and Friday, *Adults Making Responsible Moral Decisions,* 47–73.

[27] Although much of the recent exciting theological reflection on character and the virtues is too complicated for this volume, these theologians, I believe, are turning to who we are as persons in conscience/1 as critical and key to our ability to do the process of forming conscience/2 and to make the judgments of conscience/3: Alasdair MacIntyre's masterful *After Virtue* (Notre Dame: University of Notre Dame Press, 1981); L. Gregory Jones, *Transformed Judgment* (Notre Dame: University of Notre Dame Press, 1991); Romanus Cessario, *The Moral Virtues and Theological Ethics* (Notre Dame: University of Notre Dame Press, 1991).

[28] It should be abundantly clear that the following understanding of conscience differs radically from the relativist, individualistic view critiqued by Cardinal Joseph

Ratzinger: "No longer is conscience understood as that knowledge which derives from a higher form of knowing. It is instead the individual's self-determination which may not be directed by someone else, a determination by which each person decides for himself [herself] what is moral in a given situation." Address to European Doctrinal Commission, at Laxemburg (Vienna), May 1989, in *Christian Order* 31 (February 1990): 108. Indeed persons must decide; but in commenting on Ratzinger, Joseph Schall more clearly identifies the "someone else" as the God the Creator of nature and grace: "The relativist, self-actualizing notion of religious liberty immediately assumes an understanding of conscience that separates itself from any norms in nature or grace. This separation leaves conscience, not as a judge of what is moral on the basis of the order of things, but as itself the creator of what is right;" "American Spirituality," *The Living Light* 29 (Fall 1992): 11.

[29] In *The Complete Stories of Flannery O'Connor* (New York: Farrar, Straus and Giroux, 1953), 133.

[30] Archbishop Weakland connects our image of the church to our moral values: "We are living at a time when we must re-imagine the Catholic Church. We must examine our own moral convictions, work through them in the light of the gospel so that we hold them deeply for ourselves." Cited by McCormick, "Moral Theology in the Year 2000," *America* 166 (April 18, 1992): 312.

[31] McCormick, "Moral Theology in the Year 2000," *America* 166 (April 18, 1992): 313.

[32] It is especially through our personal experience of the moral values lived in a community (#75.2) that we prevent moral precepts and laws (#75.1) from being legalisms.

[33] Reflecting on this good news and bad news, John Shea images humans as creatures who stand tall but never so tall that we can't be brought to our rears by a banana peel.

[34] Philip Keane, *Christian Ethics and Imagination* (New York: Paulist Press, 1984).

[35] Andrew Greeley, *How to Save The Catholic Church*, 16–17. For the results of his research on the critical importance of warm, gracious images, see Andrew Greeley, *The Religious Imagination* (New York: Wm. H. Sadlier, 1981).

[36] Friday, *Adults Making Responsible Moral Decisions*, 71–72.

[37] O'Connell, *Principles*, 91. Also see Gula, *Reason Informed*, chapter 11; and Friday, *Adults Making Responsible Moral Decisions*, 11–16.

[38] O'Connell, *Principles for a Catholic Morality*, 92.

[39] The bishops at Vatican II stated, "Conscience frequently errs from invincible ignorance without losing its dignity. The same cannot be said of [one] who cares but little for truth and goodness, or of a conscience which by degrees grows practically sightless as a result of habitual sin" (*Pastoral Constitution on the Church in the Modern World*, #16).

[40] *The Law of Christ*, volume I (Westminster MD: Newman, 1961), 151.

[41] Bernard Häring notes that even the giant of moral theology, St. Alphonsus Liguori, was assailed by church authorities for asserting the rights of conscience. "According to the conviction of Alphonsus, the first duty that pastors, and particularly confessors, owe to the faithful is the highest possible respect for their consciences. . . . Indeed, he never begins with law. He always gives primacy to conscience." "Moral Theologian under Attack: Saint Alphonsus Liguori," *America* 156:17, 364.

[42] "Anyone upon whom the ecclesiastical authority, in ignorance of the true facts, imposes a demand that offends against [a] clear conscience, should perish in excommunication rather than violate conscience." *IV Sent.*, dist. 38, art. 4.

[43] Cited by Timothy O'Connell at Loyola University, Chicago, in unpublished notes. In mellower tones, Newman counsels respect for the pope, but he still opts for the priority of conscience: "When I speak of conscience, I mean conscience truly so-called. . . . If in a particular case it is to be taken as a sacred and sovereign monitor, its dictates, in order to prevail against the voice of the pope, must follow upon serious thought, prayer and all available means of arriving at a right judgment on the matter in question." Cited by the U. S. bishops' pastoral letter *Human Life in Our Day* (Washington DC: USCC, 1968), 14.

[44] *Declaration on Religious Freedom*, #1.

[45] "Canadian Bishops' Statement on the Encyclical *Humanae Vitae*" (August 1, 1971), #8, 9, 24.

[46] "Instruction on Respect for Human Life in Its Origins and on the Dignity of Procreation" (March 1987). In approaching Vatican documents, some Catholics might think them infallible teaching. Such documents are noninfallible, but they are official church teaching to which we give a special hearing and respect.
      A friend of mine, after observing what he considered a response of panic to one Vatican document on sexuality, researched how many ways that the pope and Vatican congregations can speak. He found 33! The document cited in this footnote is not at the top of the scale of authoritative teaching.

[47] "Dignity of Procreation: Science and the Creation of Life," *Origins* 17 (May 28, 1987): 25.

[48] *Sources of Renewal,* cited by Richard McBrien, "He Won't Go Far with Ideas Like That," *The Progress* (March 19, 1991): 7.

[49] "Constructive criticism useful for church," *The Progress* (July 30, 1992): 9.

[50] "Tension Morality and Birth Control," *Theological Studies* 28: 659–82; I also popularized this approach in *Values in Conflict* (Cincinnati: Pflaum, 1976), sponsored by the National Center of Religious Education—CCD. For a stimulating and provocative application of this approach to many moral issues, see Richard McCormick, *The Critical Calling* (Washington DC: Georgetown University Press, 1989); Richard McCormick and Paul Ramsey, eds., *Doing Evil to Achieve Good: Moral Choice in Conflict Situations* (Chicago: Loyola University Press, 1978); and Sydney Callahan, *In Good Conscience* (San Francisco: Harper & Row, 1992).

[51] Chirico used the term "context" rather than "situation" to separate himself from some situation ethicists who assert that some situations are so unique that we cannot and need not look to universal principles of value for guidance.

[52] Both cited by Wigoder, *Almanac of the Bible,* 435, 436.

[53] Other conflicts have long been present, but we have chosen to see only one set of values. As I write these lines, for example, people in the Northwest are torn between the values of jobs in lumbering and of preserving the habitat for the spotted owl. If we had honored the habitat long ago, we might not be facing this dilemma today.

[54] Moral theologians often have offered ways to deal with conflicts. For example, there are the principles of just war in issues of defense against an unjust aggressor; ethicists said that we could withhold the truth if a person had no right to the truth or through mental reservation—we simply did not say all that we knew. The approach offered here suggests that in all such examples it was a matter of values-in-conflict.

[55] This awareness emerges in a pastoral statement of the U. S. bishops that probably would not have been addressed as a moral issue in previous times. Cf. "Renewing the Earth" (Washington DC: USCC, 1991).

[56] Cited by Gula, *Reason Informed by Faith,* 160. Indeed, in a culture permeated by a "contraceptive mentality," some couples will practice birth control in ways that deny Christian values. Carter and the story in the next paragraph speak about couples grappling with conflicts and trying to do their best.

[57] "The Catholic Church and most other major religious denominations oppose the death penalty, but the American public overwhelmingly supports it. . . . In a 1980 statement, the U. S. Catholic Conference noted that the common justifications for capital punishment—retribution and deterrence—are inadequate. . . . 'I suspect that the vast majority of Americans do not have a clear idea of what the bishops have taught,' said Jesuit Father Richard Roach" ("The Death Penalty," *The Progress* [March 19, 1991]: 3).

[58] McCormick "Moral Theology in the Year 2000," *America* 166 (April 18, 1992): 318.

[59] Martin O'Malley, "An Interview with Jean Vanier," *America* 166 (April 18, 1992): 319, 321.

[60] Adapted from Suzanne DeBenneditus, *Teaching Faith and Morals* (Minneapolis: Winston Press, 1981).

[61] Those familiar with the Myers/Briggs personality profiles will recognize the S (sensate) and N (intuitive) and the T (thinking) and F (feeling) types.

[62] Friday, *Adults Making Responsible Moral Decisions*, 25–26.

[63] John O'Grady, *The Four Gospels and the Jesus Tradition* (New York: Paulist Press, 1989), 186.

[64] The bishops both connect and separate scripture and tradition in *Dei Verbum*, #9–10.

[65] Avery Dulles, "Sensus Fidelium," *America* (November 1, 1986): 240, 242, 263; Dulles is citing the *Constitution on the Church*, #12.

[66] Richard Sipe, "The Future of the Priesthood: Celibacy, Sex, and the Place of Women," in "Shaping the Future Priesthood," p. 13, available from Corpus, PO Box 2247, Mill Valley CA 94941. The citation of Granfield is from *The Limits of the Papacy* (New York: Crossroad Publishing Co., 1987), 148.

[67] Avery Dulles contends that even with defined doctrine, "In no significant case do we find a truly universal consensus. Whenever this criterion has been invoked, there has actually been a clash of opinions. In some cases the vast majority of the faithful have spontaneously rallied to defend the true faith against a heretical sect; but in other cases the authentic doctrine had been maintained . . . by a 'faithful remnant' or a privileged vanguard." "Sensus Fidelium," *America* (November 1, 1986): 241.

[68] Taken by *Time*/CNN, June 3–4, 1992. Cited in *Time* (June 22, 1992): 65.

[69] Francis J. Connell, *The New Confraternity Edition Revised Baltimore Catechism, no. 3* (New York: Benziger Brothers, 1949), 92.

[70] Friday, *Adults Making Responsible Moral Decisions*, 13.

[71] *Constitution on the Church in the Modern World*, #69.

[72] National Conference of Catholic Bishops, "The Challenge of Peace" (Washington DC: USCC, 1983); "Economic Justice for All" (Washington DC: USCC, 1986). Vatican II limits the competence of the church to apply revelation to concrete social or moral questions: "The church, as guardian of the deposit of God's word, draws religious and moral principles from it, but it does not always have a ready answer to particular questions, wishing to combine the light of revelation with universal experiences so that illumination can be forthcoming on the direction which humanity has recently begun to take," *Gaudium et Spes*, #33.

[73] For an extended treatment of this issue, see Theodore Mackin, *Divorce and Remarriage* (New York: Paulist Press, 1984).

[74] Cf. Joseph Zwack, *Annulment: Your Chance to Remarry within the Catholic Church* (San Francisco: Harper & Row, 1983). Many of those annulments are granted due to "lack of consent." In a culture of weak and flabby commitments, where some people rarely say "forever" to anything, especially some young people, their "I do" to "until death do us part" is about as permanent as that of the characters on the soaps on which they have been raised.

[75] Letter to bishops, "Indissolubility of Marriage: Administration of Sacraments to those in Irregular Unions," April 11, 1973.

[76] The Tribunal of the Archdiocese of Cincinnati, *Handbook for Marriage Cases* (Cincinnati: Tribunal Office, 1989): 82. Robert Garafalo calls for renewed scriptural and pastoral links between reconciliation and celebration: "Grace is the divine love that can flood the human heart and transform it by its own dynamic power. The church exists to create, by word and witness and sacrament, that expectation of release that will allow God's saving word a proper hearing. . . . In an effort to ensure that sinners are not painlessly brought back into the fold, the church has established conditions for receiving divine mercy: conditions that do not appear grounded in the earthly ministry of Jesus, but in a desire to protect the sacrament from trivialization. In the gospels, however, it is the return of a single sinner that is deserving celebration, not a guarantee that all are properly disposed. . . . The church must duplicate the ministry of Jesus in a freely given, spontaneous gesture of forgiveness that restores the

scriptural link between reconciliation and celebration" ("Reconciliation and Celebration," *Worship* [September 1989]: 454–56).

[77] Cited in a pastoral letter by Archbishop Raymond Hunthausen.

[78] *Directory for Masses with Children*. It should be clear by now that my vision of celebrating the eucharist is not just "receiving communion" but coming to covenant-union with Christ in a community of saints and sinners.

[79] *Familiaris Consortio*, #84.

[80] Ladislas Orsy, *Marriage in Canon Law* (Wilmington DE: Michael Glazier, 1986), 290–93.

[81] Cited by Ladislas Orsy, *Marriage in Canon Law*, 293. Ratzinger was asked in the late 1980s if he still held that position. He replied, "At least for the innocent party."

[82] *Ibid*. Kaspar may sound vague, but clearly the context is pastoral care regarding the eucharist for the remarried. Ladislas Orsy states that what these theologians "propose in no way conflicts with the doctrine of indissolubility. On that point they stand firm. Rather, they all make an appeal to a radical power in the church that can go beyond the ordinary rules and can provide forgiveness and healing when most needed" (293).

[83] All cited by McCormick, *The Critical*, 232.

[84] Cited by Norbert Greinacher, "The Problem of Divorce and Remarriage," *Theology Digest* 35:3, 222.

[85] Cf. Peter Brown, *Augustine of Hyppo: A Biography* (Berkeley: University of California Press, 1967), and *The Body and Society* (New York: Columbia University Press, 1990); Vern Bullough and James Brundage, *Sexual Practices and the Medieval Church* (Buffalo: Prometheus Books, 1982); Ute Ranke-Heinemann, *Eunuchs for the Kingdom of Heaven* (Garden City NJ: Doubleday, 1990).

[86] Anthony Padovano "Redeeming Humanity," 1. Available from Corpus, PO Box 2247, Mill Valley CA 94941.

[87] Anthony Padovano "Redeeming Humanity," 3, 5. Similarly, Greeley and Durkin conclude: "The less sex a husband and wife had with one another, the more a sacrament their marriage was—the equivalent of saying that the more passionless a

relationship is, the more effective it is as a sign of God's love, hardly what Saint Paul had in mind" (*How to Save the Catholic Church*, 66).

[88] Heinrich Kramer and James Sprenger, *The Malleus Maleficarum* (New York: Dover, 1971), 44, 45. After surveying Cicero, Seneca, St. Jerome and John Chrysostom, these authors conclude that woman "is more carnal than a man, as is clear from her many carnal abominations" and that carnal lust "in women is insatiable" (p. 44).

[89] All quotations cited in Padovano, "Redeeming Humanity," 2.

[90] A woman once told me that she could never receive communion from a married priest who might have "had sex" the night before.

[91] *Christianity, Social Tolerance and Homosexuality*, cited by Padovano, "Redeeming Humanity," 4.

[92] "Intercourse is a body language in which the erotic becomes the channel of communication for personal love." Jack Dominian, "The Use of Sex," *London Tablet* (February 11, 1984).

[93] Timothy O'Connell, unpublished notes.

[94] I write these lines on the day when Los Angeles burns and other cities erupt in rage and violence after the acquittal of the police in the Rodney King trial. Martin Luther King's dream today is a nightmare.

[95] *Constitution on the Church in the Modern World*, #51.

[96] Letter to clergy in Washington, DC; and *Human Life In Our Day, a Collective Pastoral of the American Hierarchy*, #15 (Washington DC: USCC, 1968), 12.

[97] Friday, *Adults Making Responsible Moral Decisions*, 65.

[98] "Many Mansions," *Church* 8:1, 6, 7.

[99] Garrison Keillor, *Lake Wobegon Days* (New York: Penguin Books, 1986), 127–28.

[100] Lucien Richard adopts a similar stance to that in paragraphs that follow on the unity of incarnation and creation: "*The evangelization of the American culture, and its healing, is ultimately linked to a re-emphasis of the sacramental holiness of creation. Central here is a retrieval of a doctrine of the Incarnation as the intensification of creation. . . .* By virtue of the creation, and still more the Incarnation, nothing here

below is profane for those who know how to see." "On Evangelization, Culture, and Spirituality," *The Catholic World* 234:1400, 65.

[101] William Lynch, *Christ and Prometheus* (Notre Dame: University of Notre Dame Press, 1970), 23.

[102] In *Ministries: Sharing God's Gifts* (Winona MN: St. Mary's Press, 1980), I ground our call to mission and ministries on this experience of ourselves as images of God's presence. We need to remember, however, that we are fallen, flawed images and that we *scrutinize* ourselves for both sin and grace.

[103] Greeley, *How to Save the Catholic Church*, 52.

[104] Greeley and Durkin summarize the risks: "If [Catholics] wish to rejoice in the Mariological genius of Gerard Manley Hopkins and in the dazzling stained glass of Notre Dame de Paris, they have to run the risk of the multiplication of indulgences and medals and inane private revelations and devotions and the ever-present possibility of pagan contamination. Protestants on the other hand must also be clear about their risks: If they throw out statues and stained-glass windows and images of all kinds, if they strip their churches . . . of everything but cross and candle and book and the proclaimed Word, they may also strip the churches bare of people" (*How to Save the Catholic Church*, 58).

[105] Lesser beings participate in the Being who is Being-in-itself, so we can find hints of what God is like by exploring what creation and humans are like.

[106] Thomas Aquinas, *De Potentia*, 7, 5, ad 14.

[107] Greeley, *How to Save the Catholic Church*, 27. William O'Malley, a high school teacher, complains that many young people's faith is "fluff and nonsense." He calls this "The Creed in Brand X Religion": "I (sort of) believe in God, who started the whole thing and lives way out there somewhere, a lot farther than Voyager is ever going to get. But, therefore, (1) it's impossible to communicate across such an enormous gap, and (2) [God's] far too busy with more important things [than to be concerned] over my trivial misdeeds. It's consoling, though to remember that somebody is 'there for' me, sort of like by Fairy Godperson." O'Malley also complains that teachers do not stretch the minds of young people with ultimate questions and theologies precisely when those minds are capable of more left-hemisphere thinking. He attempts to offer credible theology in *Converting the Baptized* (Allen TX: Tabor Publishing, 1990).

[108] Gerard Manley Hopkins, "God's Grandeur."

[109] Gerard Manley Hopkins, "As kingfishers catch fire."

[110] Flannery O'Connor, *The Habit of Being* (New York: Farrar, Straus & Giroux Inc., 1979), 92, 114. She adds, "For me a dogma is only a gateway to contemplation and is an instrument of freedom and not of restriction" (92).

[111] *Boston College Magazine*, cited by George Hunt, "Of Many Things," *America* (May 26, 1990): 1.

[112] Annie Dillard, *Teaching a Stone to Talk* (New York: Harper & Row, 1982), 40.

[113] Stuart Hample and Eric Marshall, *Children's Letters to God*, cited by George Hunt, "Of Many Things," *America* (May 25, 1991): 1.

[114] Jack Dominian, "The Use of Sex," *London Tablet* (February 11, 1984).

[115] Greeley, *How to Save the Catholic Church*, 43. Greeley's sociological research with young married people also concludes that "there is empirical evidence to sustain the position: The more frequently a husband and wife pray, the more satisfactory their sex life. And the correlation runs the other way: The more satisfactory their sex life, the more frequently they pray" (48).

[116] Greeley, *How to Save the Catholic Church*, 20, 33.

[117] I am adapting and adding to language used by William Willimon, *Peculiar Speech* (Grand Rapids: Wm. B. Eerdmans, 1992), 5.

[118] Robert Weber and Rodney Clapp, *People of the Truth* (San Francisco: Harper & Row, 1988), 74.

[119] In chapter three I expressed the preference of some theologians for the language of "incarnation" rather than "inculturation": We don't bring God to a culture; God's Spirit is already present.

[120] *Constitution on the Church*, #1.

[121] Cited by Vincent Donovan, *Christianity Rediscovered* (Maryknoll NY: Orbis Books, 1982).

# Epilogue:
## A Final Homily on Luke

*When the days drew near for Jesus to be taken up, he set his face to go to Jerusalem. And he sent messengers ahead of him. On their way they entered a village of the Samaritans to make ready for him, but they did not receive him because his face was set toward Jerusalem. When his disciples James and John saw it, they said, "Lord, do you want us to command fire to come down from heaven and consume them?" But he turned and rebuked them. Then they went on to another village.*

*As they were going along the road, someone said to him, "I will follow you wherever you go." And Jesus said to him, "The foxes have holes, and birds of the air have nests, but the Son of Man has nowhere to lay his head." To another he said, "Follow me." But he said, "Lord, first let me go and bury my father." But Jesus said to him, "Let the dead bury their own dead; but as for you, go and proclaim the kingdom of God." Another said to him, "I will follow you, Lord; but first let me say farewell to those at my home." Jesus said to him, "No one who puts a hand to the plow and looks back is fit for the kingdom of God."[1]*

• (Luke 9:51–62—Thirteenth Sunday of Ordinary Time, Year C)

Praise to you, Lord Jesus Christ. Really? "Praise to you, Lord Jesus Christ," for that?!? Nowhere to lay our head if we follow this man Jesus? Let the dead bury our parents? No looking back? No procrastination? Discipleship now! "I want a few good men and women now!" Do you really praise the Lord Jesus Christ for that? What is going on here?

Like us, the first man hears Jesus' call to follow him and glibly chirps, "I will follow you wherever you go." He knows not the cost. In Luke, one out of seven verses of Jesus' message is about riches and poverty. That means one out of seven "verses" of disciples' lives will be given to a "preferential option for the poor." We are consumed with justice, not with commodities.

Therefore, to his glib protestation Jesus responds, "The enemies of Israel—the Ammonites (symbolized by foxes) and the Gentiles (symbolized by birds of the air)—have a home but not the true Israel, those faithful to God's covenant with the outcasts and the poor."

Translated to our times: The bureaucrats, the legalists, the ecclesiastical climbers, the clerical and professional clubs, the educational and liturgical establishments, even those who can afford this book and who come to institutes of the North American Forum on the Catechumenate have cozy homes in chanceries, pastoral centers and rectories, but not those struggling for a gospel of inclusion, reconciliation and justice. Jesus warns this first disciple and us: Follow me and you will be homeless *in the church*, in the ecclesiastical establishments, and in your community, in the political and economic establishments, if you let too many "tax collectors and sinners" into covenant.[2] The enemies of the gospel, like James and John, still would "call down fire from heaven" on all "Samaritans" (heretics, outcasts, rejects)—fire and brimstone for those who cross the boundaries of church law and the fires of Los Angeles on those who set up boundaries of economic class and racist "laws."

Still Jesus thunders, "I want you *now*! No delays! Decide! Now!"

The next prospective disciple wants to delay and bury his father. Lie! In that culture, *if* the father really had died, the son would have been at home keeping vigil. He really wants to go home and wait until his father dies and postpone discipleship. Jesus knows that and insists, "Decide! Now!"

What keeps us comfortable in our ecclesiastical homes, waiting for nothing to happen, unwilling to get out there and make things happen? In this ministry of initiation, what keeps us fearful of confronting (lovingly) those perpetuating old "churchskins" and church ministry and business as usual? What paradigm shifts do we need to confront in our personal, family, work, civic and ecclesial lives?

The third inductee to discipleship pleads, "Let me take leave of my people at home." Lie! That is a Middle Eastern custom of seeking permission to leave of those who stay at home, especially the father. In that culture to become a disciple of a sage was not like taking a summer school course or attending a Forum institute. It meant cementing a lifelong relationship. Jesus demands not just decision now but decision forever. No young man in his thirties like Jesus would claim precedence over a father. This son knows it. He knows that his father will not let him leave. He can come back and cry crocodile tears about not being able to leave, but he really contrived his excuse. Jesus commands, "Decide! Now! Forever!"

He also commands absolute concentration. "Keep your hand at the plow! No looking back!" Listen to this description of Palestinian plowing:

> The very light Palestinian plough is guided with one hand. This one hand, generally the left, must at the same time keep the plough upright, regulate its depth by pressure, and lift it over the rocks and stones in its path. The ploughman uses the other hand to drive the unruly oxen with a goad about two yards long, fitted with an iron spike. At the same time he must continually look between the hindquarters of the oxen, keeping the furrow in sight. This primitive kind of plough needs dexterity and concentrated attention. If the ploughman looks round, the new furrow becomes crooked. Thus, whoever wishes to follow Jesus must be resolved to break every link with the past and fix eyes only on the coming (reign of God).[3]

So—not only decide now and decide forever, but decide with absolute commitment, fixation, concentration on plowing for the reign of God.

I described Palestinian plowing during a homily in Arizona, and a young Mexican American priest said that his father taught him to plow precisely in this way. However, he was not goading oxen but a donkey, with a rope tied round his neck and to the plow. One day he got frustrated because the donkey wouldn't move, so he threw a rock at its rear end. The donkey took off and dragged him flailing the air and kicking and screaming behind. Isn't that a grand image—dragged kicking and screaming into the reign of God!

Will this be one more book on a dusty bookshelf? Or in a modest way will it echo God's word and God's call to you, perhaps kicking and screaming, to plow for the reign of God: to exchange old churchskins for new wineskins (chapter one), to a vision of catechesis as a ministry of the word that is a "red-hot iron" (chapter two), to constructing a new "map" of catechesis (chapter three), with catechesis in community and the grand vision of echoing God's Word enfleshed in #75 (chapter four), to hearing God's word especially with "pastoral/theological ears" (chapter five), with catechists and homilists conversing together round God's Word (chapter six), in genuine conversation with the big stories of Matthew, Mark, Luke and John (chapters seven through ten), and our postbiblical tradition (chapter eleven)? Are we ready to keep our eyes on our plowing for the reign of God and support each other when those still wearing old churchskins try to throw us over the cliff (cf. Luke 4) because we unearth throngs of rejects and outcasts presently homeless in our church and world but welcomed to table by the Jesus of Luke who calls us to set that table—now, forever, with total concentration on plowing for God's covenant and God's reign?

I end this book with a prayer by Archbishop Oscar Romero, a disciple who knew the cost of that kind of plowing:[4]

> It helps, now and then, to step back and take the long view.
>     The Kingdom is not only beyond our efforts,
>     it is even beyond our vision.
> We accomplish in our lifetime only a tiny fraction of
>     the magnificent enterprise that is God's work.
> Nothing we do is complete,
>     which is another way of saying that
>     the Kingdom always lies beyond us.
>
> No statement says all that should be said.
> No prayer fully expresses our faith.
> No confession brings perfection,
>     no pastoral visit brings wholeness.
> No program accomplishes the church's mission.
> No set of goals and objectives includes everything.
>
> This is what we are about.
> We plant the seeds that one day will grow.
> We water seeds already planted,
>     knowing that they hold future promise.
> We lay foundations that will need further development.
> We provide yeast that produces effects far beyond our capabilities.
>
> We cannot do everything,
>     and there is a sense of liberation in realizing that.
> This enables us to do something,
>     and to do it very well.
> It may be incomplete,
>     but it is a beginning,
>     a step along the way,
>     an opportunity for the Lord's grace to enter
>     and do the rest.
>
> We may never see the end results,
>     but that is the difference
>     between the master builder and the worker.

We are workers, not master builders,
   ministers, not messiahs.
We are prophets of a future that is not our own.
Amen.


## Endnotes

[1] We have used this gospel when celebrating the rite of acceptance into the order of catechumens at institutes sponsored by the North American Forum on the Catechumenate.

[2] Cf. commentaries on Luke's meals and especially on Luke 15 in chapter nine of this book.

[3] Joachim Jeremias, *The Parables of Jesus*, 195; cited by Kenneth Bailey, *Poet and Peasant and Through Peasant Eyes* (Grand Rapids: William B. Eerdmans, 1980), 29–30.

[4] This prayer is a much more compelling expression of the Forum aphorism that I cited in chapter one: "If we fail, at least we fail trying the right thing."

# APPENDIX I

*References to the Gospels for Sundays and Solemnities*

## The Gospel of Matthew

## The Gospel of Mark

## The Gospel of Luke

## The Gospel of John

# APPENDIX II
## *Church as Initiating Community: An Evaluation Tool*

What if we were to "echo God's word" for the baptized with the same dimensions of catechesis that we implement with catechumens? What if this vision of initiation/conversion were to become a model for ongoing conversion? Many have spoken of the order of Christian initiation as a model for all parish life. That is an abuse if it means calling any catechetical program (such as preparation for couples planning to marry) a catechumenate, or if various rites are simply transferred over to liturgies with baptized children or adults.

*Liturgically*, "model" does mean that with adapted prayers, the ritual actions of adult initiation (such as signing the senses, anointing, blessing, laying on hands) might be celebrated to renew our initiation and vocation. And the rites with catechumens, especially during every Lent and Easter, do summon the entire community to renew its own conversion (cf. #4). And it is true that every eucharist is a repeatable sacrament of initiation.

*Catechetically*, "model" means that adult initiation offers a vision of conversion and catechesis distinct from schooling and religious studies, which might be aimed at information, not transformation.

*Strategically*, "model" means that the best catechesis happens within a community of the faithful called to ongoing conversion.

We have seen that this vision is best captured in #75 of the order. In fact, the catechetical directory for the United States, *Sharing the Light of Faith*, #213, does commend for all the baptized that same holistic vision of church and catechesis (ministry of the word, community, worship and witness). The following pages reflect my interpretation of what might happen if the vision of #75 were enfleshed in a church community. With (1) low and (5) high, you might evaluate your parish with this vision of church as initiating community. If you don't know, evaluate your own ministry or leave it blank.

#75.1:    Catechesis, accommodated to liturgical year, supported by celebrations of the word, leading to appropriate acquaintance with dogmas and precepts and profound sense of mystery—ministry of the word.

_____1. We carefully accommodate all catechesis to the liturgical year.

_____2. A separate liturgy of the word for children on Sunday is prime catechetical time for young children.

_____3. We say "scripture, scripture and more scripture."

_____4. Homilies are biblical homilies.

_____5. Other catechetical sessions are more like homilies than like theology classes.

_____6. Youth and adults are moving beyond scriptural literalism.

_____7. Youth and adults are moving beyond doctrinal literalism.

_____8. Youth and adults know the basic doctrines and precepts.

_____9. We consciously and constantly invite all ages into a sense of the mystery of God's presence in their lives.

#75.2:   Catechumens learn Christian life through sponsors and community, to pray, to witness to faith, hope, love, to journey with a progressive change of conduct manifest in social consequences—ministry of community.

_____1. In all evangelization/catechesis we offer permanent parish sponsors.

_____2. Our community is remarkable for its hospitality.

_____3. All catechesis offers a small community; and all sacramental formation follows Aidan Kavanagh's dictum that the new catechists are old people who know how to pray, sick people who know how to suffer, married people who know fidelity, parents who know how to be parents, and not just people with degrees in religious education.

_____4. We pray a lot, in lots of different ways, including our catechesis itself, which is prayerful and leads to prayer.

_____5. People witness to their faith with increasing confidence.

_____6. We call people to progressive, ongoing conversion.

_____7. We communicate a clear message of reconciliation when people fail or falter in that journey of ongoing conversion.

_____8. We support people in living their vocation and mission in their families, neighborhood, work, and civic community.

_____9. We are good at conscience formation for both personal and social issues.

**#75.3:** Catechumens are helped by liturgical rites, which purify and bless, including celebrations of the word and the Sunday liturgy of the Word after which they are invited to leave and break open the word.

_____1. We see and practice the close relationship between liturgy and catechesis, e.g., word and rite are part of every liturgy and catechetical session.

_____2. All sacramental formation offers liturgies to celebrate the journey of ongoing conversion.

_____3. Our liturgical rituals and symbols are strong and robust. They catechize through powerful images.

_____4. The assembly is becoming the prime actor in liturgy — more action happens in the assembly in movement, procession, ritual action, gesture, word, song and active participation.

_____5. For catechumens, breaking open the word after the homily is the prime catechetical time, and all the baptized have similar opportunities weekly at other times.

_____6. All liturgies reflect the many ministries of adult initiation.

_____7. Lent and Eastertime is our great yearly time of renewal.

_____8. The Easter Vigil is our great celebration, and no leader or minister would miss the Vigil.

_____9. We are exploring the order of penitents for reconciliation with returning Catholics as a parallel journey to initiation.

**#75.4:** Catechumens work actively to spread the gospel and to build up the church by apostolic witness.

_____1. During the catechumenate period, candidates witness, especially through ministries of social concern.

_____2. Both apprentice members (catechumens) and the baptized receive formation for, recognition and celebration of their primary mission in the world.

_____3. Our catechesis assumes people meet Christ where he said he would be—in the hungry, thirsty, prisoner, sick and stranger, as it says in Matthew 25.

_____4. People are invited to ecclesial ministries after they have given witness by their lives in family, work and world.

_____5. After initiation, the new members have a support group for their baptismal mission for at least one year.

_____6. Our sacramental formation is not a terminal program. It supports mission after the celebration of sacraments—infant baptism or marriage.

_____7. Our sacramental formation is not made up of classes. It is but a spiritual journey adapted to individuals, as the catechumenate is.

_____8. Many of our people are active in service organizations in the civic community.

_____9. Our vision and practice reveal that "our purpose . . . is not to pass on religion but to create a new world" (George Coe).

# BIBLIOGRAPHY

*Select Bibliography for Homilies and Catechesis Based on the Liturgy of the Word*

This very select bibliography includes the resources that I found most helpful in writing this book. Please also consult the many footnotes for other material. For an annotated bibliography, see the book by Philip McBrien listed below.

## On Preaching

"Fulfilled in Your Hearing." Washington DC: USCC Publications, 1979.

Hilkert, Mary Catherine. "Preaching and Theology: Rethinking the Relationship." *Worship* (September 1991).

Senior, Donald. "Scripture and Homiletics: What the Bible Can Teach the Preacher." *Worship* (September 1991).

Sloyan, Gerard. "Is Church Teaching Neglected When the Lectionary Is Preached?" *Worship* 61:2, 133.

## On Method and Ways of Hearing Scripture

Baldovin, John. "The Bible and Liturgy, Part One: The Status of the Bible Today." *Catechumenate* (September 1989): 12.

Lee, Bernard. "Liturgy of the Word—Shared Homily: Conversation that Puts Communities at Risk." In Lee, Bernard, ed., *Alternative Futures for Worship, Volume 3: The Eucharist.* Collegeville: The Liturgical Press, 1987.

McBrien, Philip. *How to Teach with the Lectionary.* Mystic CT: Twenty-third Publications, 1992.

Wink, Walter. *Transforming Bible Study.* Nashville: Abingdon Press, 1980.

## General Commentaries

Bergant, Diane, and Robert Karris, gen. eds. *The Collegeville Bible Commentary*. Collegeville: The Liturgical Press, 1989.

Black, Matthew, ed. *Peake's Commentary on the Bible*. Nashville: Thomas Nelson, 1962.

Mays, James, ed. *Harper's Bible Commentary*. New York: Harper & Row, 1988.

Pilch, John. *The Cultural World of Jesus Sunday by Sunday*. Quarterly. Available from *Initiatives* Publications, PO Box 218332, Columbus OH 43221; 1-800-745-8018.

Scott, Bernard Brandon. *Hear Then the Parable*. Minneapolis: Fortress Press, 1989.

"Readings" and "Eucharistic Celebrations." Commentaries and homilies mailed monthly from Pastoral Service, PO Box 1323, 1099 Manila, Philippines.

## Lectionary Commentaries

Fuller, Reginald. *Preaching the Lectionary*. Collegeville: The Liturgical Press, 1984.

Sloyan, Gerard. *A Commentary on the New Lectionary*. New York: Paulist Press, 1975.

## Popular Resources for Catechesis on the Liturgy of the Word

Episcopal Diocese of Colorado. *Living the Good News*. Materials available for pre-schoolers through adults. Phone: 1-800-824-1813. Both *Catechumenate* and *Modern Liturgy* magazines, after reviewing all popular resources, evaluated this publication as the best; they now offer a Roman Catholic edition.

## On Matthew

Harrington, Daniel. *Sacra Pagina: The Gospel of Matthew*. Collegeville: The Liturgical Press, 1991.

Meir, John. *Matthew*. Wilmington: Michael Glazier, 1980.

Senior, Donald. *What Are They Saying about Matthew?* New York: Paulist Press, 1989.

## On Mark

Harrington, Wilfred. *Mark*. Wilmington: Michael Glazier, 1979.

Humphrey, Hugh. *He Is Risen*. New York: Paulist Press, 1992.

Matera, Frank. *What Are They Saying about Mark?* New York: Paulist Press, 1987.

Myers, Ched. *Binding the Strong Man*. Maryknoll NY: Orbis Books, 1988.

### On Luke

Bailey, Kenneth. *Poet and Peasant and Through Peasant Eyes*. Grand Rapids: Wm. B. Eerdmans, 1976 (just on Luke's parables).

Johnson, Luke Timothy. *Sacra Pagina: The Gospel of Luke*. Collegeville: The Liturgical Press, 1991.

Powell, Mark Allen. *What Are They Saying about Luke?* New York: Paulist, 1990.

### On John

Brown, Raymond. Everything!